Color categories in thought and language

	1-10	11-20	21-30	31-40	
A	1 2 3 4 5 6 7 8 9 0	1 2 3 4 5 6 7 8 9 0	1 2 3 4 5 6 7 8 9 0	1 2 3 4 5 6 7 8 9 0	9.5
B	2 2 2 2 2 2 2 2 4 6	6 6 6 2 2 2 2 2 2 2	2 2 2 2 2 2 2 2 2 2	2 2 2 2 2 2 2 2 2 2	9.0
C	6 6 6 6 6 6 6 8 14 16	14 12 12 12 4 10 8 8 6 6	6 6 4 4 4 4 4 4 6 6	4 4 4 4 6 6 6 6 6 6	8.0
D	8 8 10 10 10 14 14 14 12 12	12 12 12 6 10 10 10 8 8 8	8 8 6 6 6 6 6 8 8 8	6 6 6 6 8 8 10 10 8 8	7.0
E	12 12 12 14 16 12 12 12 10 10	10 10 10 8 12 12 10 10 10 10	8 8 8 8 8 8 10 10 10 8	8 8 8 10 10 10 10 12 12 12	6.0
F	14 14 14 16 14 12 10 10 8 8	8 8 8 8 10 10 12 12 10 10	10 10 8 8 8 8 8 8 10 12	12 10 10 10 10 12 12 12 14 14	5.0
G	14 14 14 14 10 8 8 6 6 6	6 6 6 12 8 8 10 10 10 10	8 8 8 6 6 8 10 10 12 12	10 10 10 10 12 12 12 12 14	4.0
H	10 10 12 10 8 6 6 6 6 4	4 4 4 4 10 6 6 8 8 10	8 6 6 6 6 6 6 8 10 10	12 10 10 10 10 10 10 10 10 10	3.0
I	8 8 8 6 4 4 4 4 2 2	2 2 2 2 4 4 4 4 6 6	6 4 4 4 4 4 4 6 6 6	8 10 8 8 8 6 6 8 8 8	2.0
K	2.5 5 7.5 10 / 5 10	5 10 / 5 10	5 10 / 5 10	5 10 / 5 10	0.5

R YR Y GY G BG B BP P RP

On the cover is a printed representation of the Munsell color array used in the World Color Survey. This representation is only an approximation to that array. It is designed to give the reader an intuitive feeling for the stimuli used in the field and to assist in reading several of the figures in this book. Because of the inherent inaccuracies of commercial color printing, it is not suitable for use as a research tool.

The figure above gives the specifications of the Munsell color chips that were used in the array and in the original color-naming stimuli. On the left and at the top are the designations that are printed on the field array and on the figures in this book. The corresponding Munsell specifications for Hue are given at the bottom, and the specifications for Value appear on the right. The numbers within each cell specify the Munsell Chroma. Heavy lines distinguish Chroma at /6 and below from Chroma at /8 and above. The left column represents the achromatic Value scale, all of whose chips have a Munsell Chroma of /0. *Representation of Munsell color array courtesy of Nick Hale; frontispiece courtesy of Robert MacLaury.*

Color categories in thought and language

edited by **C. L. Hardin**
Syracuse University

Luisa Maffi
University of California at Berkeley

CAMBRIDGE
UNIVERSITY PRESS

Published by the Press Syndicate of the University of Cambridge

The Pitt Building, Trumpington Street, Cambridge CB2 1RP

40 West 20th Street, New York, NY 10011-4211, USA

10 Stamford Road, Oakleigh, Melbourne 3166, Australia

First published 1997

Designed in Quark XPress, FF Thesis and Swift

A catalogue record for this book is available from the British Library

Library of Congress cataloguing in publication data
Color categories in thought and language / edited by C. L. Hardin and
Luisa Maffi

    p.   cm.

Based on papers presented at a conference, Asilomar Conference Center,
California in 1992.
Includes index
ISBN 0 521 49693 4 (hardback) – ISBN 0 521 49800 7 (paperback)
1. Color–Psychological aspects.   2. Color vision–Cross-cultural
studies.   3. Psycholinguistics.   I. Hardin, C. L., 1932–
II. Maffi, Luisa.
BF789.C7C585   1997
152.14'5–dc20   96-7898 CIP

ISBN 0 521 49693 4 hardback
ISBN 0 521 49800 7 paperback

Transferred to digital printing 2002

Contents

Notes on contributors

In addition to the authors featured in the present volume, the list below includes the other participants in the Color Categories conference, held in Asilomar, California, October 25–28, 1992, on which the volume is based. All authors have greatly benefited from the commentaries provided by the other conference participants, whose valuable contributions are gratefully acknowledged here as well as mentioned in the text wherever they have been incorporated.

Israel Abramov is Professor of Psychology at Brooklyn College and Rockefeller University in New York. He has worked in both the psychophysics and electrophysiology of the color-vision system, and has written, with James Gordon, the ten-year review of the physiology of color vision for the *Annual Review of Psychology*.

Giovanni Bennardo is a graduate student in linguistics and anthropology at the University of Illinois, where he is working on the relationships between vision, cognition, and language.

Brent Berlin is Professor of Anthropology at the University of Georgia at Athens and Emeritus Professor of Anthropology at the University of California at Berkeley. He is co-author with Paul Kay of *Basic Color Terms: Their Universality and Evolution* and co-Principal Investigator with Kay and William Merrifield on the World Color Survey project, a cross-linguistic investigation of color categorization and naming.

Robert M. Boynton is Professor Emeritus of Psychology at the University of California, San Diego. He is author of the classic text, *Human Color Vision* (Optical Society of America), which is appearing in a revised edition in collaboration with Peter Kaiser.

Ronald W. Casson is Professor of Anthropology at Oberlin College. He has recently been studying the evolution of color categories in Old and Middle English.

Greville G. Corbett is Professor of Linguistics and Russian Language at the University of Surrey. His research interests are in linguistic typology and in color terms in Russian.

Roy G. D'Andrade is Chair of the Department of Anthropology at the University of California, San Diego. A Fellow of the American Academy of Arts and Sciences, he has recently returned to his earlier study of color language and culture.

Jules Davidoff is a neuropsychologist and Head of the Psychology Department at the University of Essex. His *Cognition Through Color* was recently published by MIT Press.

Ian R. L. Davies is a psychologist at the University of Surrey who specializes in cognitive psychology and visual perception. He has been collaborating with Greville Corbett on cross-cultural studies of color categorization.

Clyde L. Hardin, Professor of Philosophy Emeritus at Syracuse University, is the author of *Color for Philosophers: Unweaving the Rainbow* (Hackett Publishing Company).

Kimberly Jameson is at the University of California, San Diego. Trained in cognitive psychology, she is collaborating with anthropologist Roy D'Andrade on the cognitive dynamics of color naming.

Paul Kay is Professor of Linguistics Emeritus at the University of California, Berkeley. He is co-author of *Basic Color Terms: Their Universality and Evolution* (University of California Press), and Principal Investigator on the World Color Survey project.

Willett Kempton is an anthropologist currently working on problems of public policy at the University of Delaware. He has studied Amerindian color terminology and linguistic effects on color perception.

John A. Lucy is Professor of Anthropology at the University of Pennsylvania. He is the author of *Grammatical Categories and Cognitive Processes: A Case Study of the Linguistic Relativity Hypothesis* (Cambridge University Press).

Robert E. MacLaury is Visiting Professor of Anthropology at George Washington University. His *Color in Mesoamerica: Viewpoint and Category Change* is being published by the University of Texas Press.

Luisa Maffi is a postdoctoral researcher at the University of California at Berkeley, currently involved with Brent Berlin, Paul Kay, and William Merrifield in the preparation of the volume The World Color Survey.

William Merrifield is a member of the Summer Institute of Linguistics, Adjunct Professor of Linguistics at the University of Texas at Arlington, and Executive Director of the International Museum of Cultures in Dallas, Texas.

He is involved with Berlin and Kay in the World Color Survey.

David L. Miller teaches at Brown University. His dissertation is about a suite of experimental studies of color categorization, some of which challenge prevailing views of categorical perception.

Stephen E. Palmer is the Director of the Institute of Cognitive Studies at the University of California, Berkeley. He is concerned with issues of perceptual representation.

Lars Sivik, Professor of Psychology at the University of Göteborg, is a codeveloper of the Natural Color System, the Swedish standard. For the past twenty years he has been studying human response to color.

James Stanlaw is Assistant Professor of Anthropology at Illinois State University. His current research project is a study of color terminology and culture contact among Japanese living in the Midwest.

Bill Wooten is Professor of Psychology at Brown University. A specialist in the psychophysics of color, he has published papers on color naming and color categories.

Stephen L. Zegura is Professor of Physical Anthropology at the University of Arizona. An evolutionary biologist, he has begun to study the relationships between genetic variation and linguistic variation in collaboration with Robert MacLaury.

1 Introduction

C. L. Hardin and Luisa Maffi

Do visual science and anthropological linguistics have anything to say to each other? Does the makeup of the human color-vision system constrain the linguistic expression of color categories in any interesting ways? Does the way we use color language suggest anything about the biological organization of color vision? In the early 1950s, an open-minded reading of the relevant scientific literature would have offered scant reason to answer such questions affirmatively. Color scientists concerned themselves with color matching and discrimination, adaptation, and the measurement of thresholds, but said little about the categorical structure of color appearance. For their part, anthropological linguists had long since put behind them earlier attempts to arrange systems of color naming in evolutionary schemes from "primitive" to "developed," or to relate the paucity of color words in some languages to color-vision deficiencies in the peoples who spoke them. Indeed, the supposed arbitrariness with which various languages divided color space came to be taken as paradigmatic not only of cultural relativity, but of the capacity of language to shape the perceptions of its speakers.

Hering's opponent-process theory

A pronounced sea-change in the thinking of visual scientists began in 1955 with a series of papers in which Leo M. Hurvich and Dorothea Jameson advanced a quantitative opponent-process theory. A qualitative version of the theory had earlier been propounded by Ewald Hering, who claimed on introspective grounds that there are two perceptually elementary achromatic colors, black and white, and four perceptually elementary chromatic colors, red, yellow, green, and blue, all other colors being seen as perceptual blends of those six. Furthermore, said Hering, our failure to see red-greens or yellow-blues tells us that the color-vision system, like many other bodily systems, must be set up in antagonistic fashion, with red opposed to green and yellow opposed to blue. (The achromatic colors are a bit different. Although black is inversely related to white, it is not fully incompatible with it: a particular gray can always be described in terms of its percentage of either whiteness or blackness.) The framework of opponency enables one to make ready sense of many details of a variety of visual processes, including simultaneous and successive contrast, chromatic adaptation, and color deficiency.

Hering's theory was rejected by most visual scientists for three reasons. (a) A qualitative theory does not lend itself well either to elaboration or to test, whereas the existing Young–Helmholtz trichromatic theory could be quantitatively formulated, and this led to many useful experimental results. Furthermore, Hering's account rested on introspective data, and introspective methods had long since proved themselves to be not only controversial but also fruitless. (b) Hering called for four elementary chromatic processes, and this was understood as an assertion that there are four types of color receptors. However, abundant behavioral and physiological data made it clear that there could be but three. (c) The Hering opponent processes called for antagonistic responses on either side of a neutral point, so that when the red and green responses, for example, were equally excited, the net result would be a null response, experienced as achromatic. However, the then-known responses of sensory neurons were of the all-or-none variety, and it was difficult to see how a configuration of such neurons could support a system requiring bipolar graded responses.

The advent of the microelectrode made it possible to record the responses of individual neurons *in vivo*. Svaetichin discovered visual neurons in fish that displayed graded responses, and shortly thereafter it was shown that ganglion cells in primate retinas vary their firing rates as a function of wavelength. Direct recordings from primate lateral geniculate nucleus cells suggested that they have some of the response properties required by the four elementary Hering processes. Taken together, these discoveries undercut not only the third objection, but the second as well. This objection, Hurvich and Jameson pointed out, was based on a misreading of Hering, who had never claimed that the four elementary chromatic *processes* required four types of *receptors*. What Hurvich and Jameson proposed was a two-stage configuration, with a first stage consisting of short-, middle-, and long-wave receptors that were cross-connected to yield a second, opponent stage, consisting of red–green, yellow–blue, and white–black channels. Hurvich and Jameson's theory, like Hering's, was psychophysical in character, with opponent channels defined functionally rather than anatomically. However, by making the theory quantitative, Hurvich and Jameson could begin to impose constraints that any putative set of neural mechanisms subserving color vision would have to satisfy.

As Wooten explains in greater detail later in this volume, by asking a subject to cancel the chromatic appearance of one monochromatic beam of light by adding another beam to it, Hurvich and Jameson were able to establish the relative strengths and null points of the subject's chromatic responses, and thus to derive a chromatic response function for that subject. From this they could calculate with fair accuracy other psychophysical responses, such as the subject's wavelength discrimination and saturation functions. The procedure was replicable, reliable, and made minimal appeal to introspection (the instructions were sophisticated variants of the form: "Turn this knob back and forth until what you see looks neither yellowish nor bluish," or "Turn the knob until all the redness disappears."). The first objection to the Hering scheme was thus met as well, and opponent-process theory became a cornerstone of color-vision research.

Berlin and Kay's *Basic Color Terms*

The sea-change in anthropological linguistics came in 1969 with the publication of Brent Berlin and Paul Kay's *Basic Color Terms*. Berlin and Kay were struck by the ease with which common color terms could be translated between languages from locales as diverse as Tahiti and Mesoamerica. If, however, as the then-prevailing wisdom held, languages divide color space arbitrarily, and moreover shape the way that their speakers perceive colored objects, how was this possible? To investigate the question, Berlin and Kay proposed criteria to separate the basic from the non-basic color terms of a language. Basic terms were to be those that were *general* and *salient*. A term is general if it applies to diverse classes of objects and its meaning is not subsumable under the meaning of another term. A term is salient if it is readily elicitable, occurs in the idiolects of most speakers, and is used consistently by individuals and with a high degree of consensus among individuals. To determine the reference of the basic color terms of a language, Berlin and Kay employed a rectangular array of Munsell color chips of maximum available relative saturation (Chroma), vertically ordered in ten equal lightness (Value) steps, and horizontally ordered by hue (Hue), each column differing from its neighbors by a nominal 2.5 Hue steps. (The array, a representation of which appears on the cover of this book, is essentially a Mercator projection of the outer skin of the Munsell solid – cf. the frontispiece.) The test array was covered by transparent acetate, and each participant was asked, for each basic color term, to mark with a grease pencil (a) the best example of the color, and (b) the region of chips that could be called by the color term.

The investigation on which *Basic Color Terms* was based used native speakers of twenty languages who resided in the San Francisco Bay Area, supplementing this limited field study with a literature search on seventy-eight additional languages. The *synchronic* results were that languages varied in numbers of basic color terms, from a minimum of two terms (Papuan Dani) to a (probable) maximum of eleven, Russian and Hungarian being possible exceptions; but no matter how many basic color terms languages might have, their foci reliably tended to cluster in relatively narrow regions of the array, whereas boundaries were drawn unreliably, with low consistency and consensus for any language.

The *diachronic* conclusion was that if languages were ordered according to numbers of basic color terms, the sequence of encoding of foci was tightly constrained. (Berlin and Kay subsequently abandoned their conception of successive *encoding* of foci in favor of the idea that the steps represented the progressive *division* of the color space, yielding three types of basic categories: composite, fundamental, and derived; cf. Kay, Berlin, Maffi, and Merrifield, this volume.) For example, if a language has two basic color terms (a "Stage I" language), those terms will encode black and white. If it has three ("Stage II"), those terms will encode black, white, and red. If it has four ("Stage III"), the terms will be for black, white, red, and either yellow or green. The entire sequence, as originally conceived, comprised seven stages and eleven basic color terms.

Berlin and Kay interpreted this as an evolutionary sequence. Their claim was controversial for two reasons. First, because, if it were correct, this would be one of the few instances in which linguistic development proceeds unidirectionally from simplicity to complexity. Second, because it readily suggested to some the now-taboo late-nineteenth-century picture of an evolutionary culture chain, with Papua New Guineans at the bottom, scarcely a step above the beasts, and sophisticated Europeans situated comfortably and properly at the top. This second reading, however much it may have affected the subsequent reception of the Berlin–Kay theses in certain quarters, was no part of the authors' perspective, and will be given no further attention on these pages.

Linkages

The connection between the findings of *Basic Color Terms* and Hering's opponent-process theory did not escape Berlin and Kay. Hering's elementary red is of *unique* or *unitary* hue, i.e., it is a red that is neither yellowish nor bluish. Unique green is likewise neither yellowish nor bluish, and unique yellow and blue are neither reddish nor greenish. Unique red (or unique green) appears whenever the red–green process is positive (or negative) and the yellow–blue process is at a null point. Similarly, unique yellow (or unique blue) is seen whenever the yellow–blue process is positive (or negative), and the red–green process is at a null point. All other hues, such as orange or purple, are seen when both processes are active. Orange is thus perceived as a red–yellow and purple as a red–blue blend (or *binary*). The Berlin–Kay focal reds, yellows, greens, and blues have hues that are close to the average unique hue points, as casual inspection of the Munsell chips suggests and as Chad McDaniel established experimentally. Moreover, since red, yellow, green, and blue are perceptual ingredients in every chromatic color, one would expect them to be more salient than any of the blends. Lightness and darkness are of course the most salient visual experiences, and so we would anticipate that they would be encoded first in the Berlin–Kay developmental sequence. Red, yellow, green, and blue follow in more or less that order. That they as a group should be labeled before the colors of binary hue comes as no surprise, but Hering's theory offers us no explanation for the particular order of their appearance. Nor does opponent-process theory help us to understand many other features of the Berlin–Kay evolutionary sequence, or, for that matter, several of the synchronic results. Why, for example, are red–yellow and red–blue binaries represented (orange and purple), but not yellow–green (chartreuse) or green–blue (turquoise)? Examples could be multiplied. Opponent processes are far from being all there is to the study of color vision, and one might hope to gain further insight into such aspects of the linguistic domain of color by further investigations into the phenomenology and mechanisms of seeing.

In an important study published in the *Journal of the Optical Society of America* in 1966, DeValois, Abramov, and Jacobs flashed colored lights before the eyes of macaque monkeys while simultaneously recording the responses of individual lateral geniculate nucleus cells. The LGN, part of the thalamus, is an intermediate point on the optic pathway that leads from the retina to the primary visual cortex in the brain. LGN cells are closely similar in response to ganglion cells, which are the last cells in the retinal processing chain (the photoreceptors are the first). The DeValois team sampled the spectral responses of 147 cells, grouping them into four classes according to the spectral wavelength that caused them to cross over from excitation to inhibition, and labeled these groups as the $+R-G$, $-R+G$, $+Y-B$, and $-Y+B$ cells respectively. At the time, these seemed to be promising candidates for the neural substrates of Hering's processes. Berlin and Kay took this to heart, and, frequently citing the DeValois *et al.* paper, called red, yellow, green, and blue categories the "neural primaries." As Abramov shows in his contribution to the present volume, this is now understood to be in error: the LGN cells cannot be the sites of the Hering elementary processes, although they mark a very important stage in opponent processing. Those sites must be found further upstream, in the cortex; the matter is being actively investigated.

In the two decades since the original publication of *Basic Color Terms*, much has happened in the study of color vision and in the elaboration, criticism, and modification of the Berlin–Kay theses. More is now known about the neurophysiology of color vision, and there is a new appreciation of its puzzles and complexities. Color-naming techniques have been developed and shown to track closely the subjects' chromatic response functions. Color categorization has been more systematically explored using alternative color-order systems, such as the Optical Society of America–Uniform Color Space and the Swedish Natural Color System, and much wider samplings of color space. These have in turn been suggesting constraints on the physiological mechanisms of color perception. The cross-cultural data base for color-term use has been vastly expanded, with Robert MacLaury's Mesoamerican Color Survey as well as the Berlin–Kay–Merrifield World Color Survey. Berlin, Kay, McDaniel, and others have contributed to revised theoretical accounts, while MacLaury has devised a theory of the dynamics of color-term development. The fundamental assumptions and methods of the Berlin–Kay tradition have been questioned by several critics, and the nature and limits of the enterprise are being clarified as a result. Finally, new ideas and techniques are being introduced by a generation of younger scholars, as are new extensions of the Berlin–Kay approach.

The chapters in this volume

In 1992, the National Science Foundation and Syracuse University sponsored a working conference on color categories in thought and language at the Asilomar Conference Center in California. Its purpose was to bring together both junior and senior visual scientists, anthropologists, and linguists to inform one another about the state of the art and to formulate agendas for new research. The essays in the present volume are based on talks and discussions from the Asilomar conference, revised and updated. They begin with a sneak preview of the World Color Survey and its analysis. The next section is devoted to the questions that the Berlin–Kay findings have raised for visual science, as well as the efforts that visual scientists have made to deepen our understanding of cross-linguistic color naming. In the third section linguists and anthropologists present some recent empirical and theoretical work in the Berlin–Kay tradition. The fourth section presents two dissenting views, one questioning the application of opponent-process theory to color-term research, the other challenging the Berlin–Kay research program. In the concluding chapter, the editors reflect upon some of the themes and issues in the present volume, and point out some directions for future research.

In the first essay, **Kay, Berlin, Maffi, and Merrifield** present the most recent results of the ongoing analysis of cross-linguistic data on color categorization and naming that have issued from the World Color Survey (WCS), and discuss the WCS data within the context of some new theoretical proposals concerning the classification and evolutionary trajectory of basic color-term systems. These proposals include a reconceptualization and simplification of the notion of "basic (color) stage" of a language, now understood as the developmental status of a language vis-à-vis its composite and fundamental color categories. Two distinct, although interacting, processes are proposed as providing the main mechanisms of color term evolution: the dissolution of the white/warm "channel" and the dissolution of the black/cool "channel." Based on this new conceptual framework, a more perspicuous notation for color system types is presented. Analyses of WCS languages are offered to illustrate the stages of the new evolutionary scheme.

The links between the findings of the WCS and visual science must be sought at several levels. We begin our examination of color vision at its foundations, in psychophysics, the systematic, quantitative study of human perceptual response. **Wooten and Miller** give us a brief history of psychophysical investigations into color vision that touches on the contributions of Newton, Young and Helmholtz, and finally Hering. Special attention is paid to Hering's distinction between the light–dark and black–white systems, and to the differences between both of these achromatic systems and the chromatic system. Wooten and Miller describe the Hurvich–Jameson cancellation technique for measuring the relative responses of the opponent systems, and exhibits representative measurements. The red–green system proves to be a linear fit to the appropriate photopigment responses, but the blue–yellow system is not. When people are asked to name the percentages of red, yellow, green, or blue that they see in a spot of light, they are able to do so reliably, and the color-naming data closely track the chromatic response curves obtained by the cancellation technique. Sternheim and Boynton developed a procedure that has been used to show that red, yellow, green, and blue are both necessary and sufficient to name all of the spectral hues; they are in this sense more elemental than orange, say, or purple. An extension of the procedure to simulated surface colors shows that brown is not elemental either, despite its *prima facie* dissimilarity to its parent, yellow (browns are *blackened* yellows). An anomalous outcome of the Sternheim–Boynton procedure is that for a few people, green seems not to be elemental, but a new procedure by Miller (see below) indicates that this is subject bias rather than a genuine perceptual effect. The link between the psychophysical results and the Berlin–Kay sequence seems clear for the Hering elementary colors, but not for the particular Berlin–Kay pattern for derived colors. Why, for instance, is orange basic whereas chartreuse is not?

What do we know about the neural mechanisms that underlie the perceptual phenomena that are described by psychophysics? **Abramov** first sketches the overall functional physiology of the color-vision system, leading from the cones through the lateral geniculate nucleus to the visual cortex, and tells us that much of what was previously believed about the neural basis of color requires revision. For example, it had been supposed that it is the existence of three distinct kinds of photopigment that establishes the trichromacy of human color vision, but it is now known that there is a wide variety of human photopigments, so trichromacy must be established at a later stage – the LGN cells – where cone outputs are compared. The spectral responses of the LGN cells fall into four general classes, and, according to earlier thinking, these correspond to the four unique hue sensations. Although their responses do in many ways parallel color naming in human subjects and are centrally involved in color vision, the LGN cells cannot be identified with the ultimate hue mechanisms, since they do not explain the perception of redness at the short-wave end of the spectrum. More importantly, they respond well to white light and therefore cannot disambiguate hue from luminance, and their crosspoints are widely scattered and much too labile. Nevertheless, LGN and cone responses do strongly constrain the characteristics of neural hue mechanisms, as do the psychophysical responses at the other end. Very recent models require four rather than two opponent mechanisms to yield the hue channels. Some of the possible brain sites for these mechanisms are discussed, along with the response criteria that any putative site would have to satisfy.

Rather than looking at the behavior of small groups of neurons, one can examine underlying mechanisms of color perception and categorization by studying the changes of perception and behavior that occur with brain-damaged people, and correlating these deficits with brain function. **Davidoff** asks whether our brains have distinct mechanisms for color perception, color categorization, and color naming, or whether all of these are handled by the same basic processes. He suggests that we can gain a foothold on such questions by examining disorders of color perception consequent on injury to specific areas of the brain, particularly in cases of acquired central achromatopsia. In the clearest cases of this disorder, brightness perception is good, boundaries are readily detected, thresholds indicate that retinal opponent processes are operative, but there is a total loss of the ability to discriminate hue, and patients report that they are unable to see color. What is damaged is an area in the lingual and fusiform gyri of the temporal lobe. Some patients suffering from such damage remember and imagine colors and are able to name them. However, there are patients with different conditions who are able to see colors and categorize them but cannot name them. Others see colors and remember color names but are unable to apply the names correctly or to sort objects by color. Yet others can identify the colors of objects but are otherwise unable to identify those objects. Taken together, these cases suggest a functional and modular arrangement involving a pictorial register in which colors and shapes are brought together, an internal color space which serves as a memory store, and a color-naming center. Infant studies give us some reason for supposing that the default organization of the internal color space is based upon the Hering elemental hues, but it is much less clear that opponency is hard-wired as well; this may be a function of experience and the properties of the neural inputs to central mechanisms. What other constraints the default neural organization of the internal color space might place on the formation of linguistic categories for color is at the moment unclear, though clinical cases suggest that the internal color space is unlikely to include other surface attributes such as pattern.

Boynton is interested in what psychological significance attaches to Berlin and Kay's distinction between basic and non-basic color terms. He describes a series of investigations of color categories in which he used a variation of color-naming applied to an extensive sampling of color space rather than just to spectral colors, as in the Sternheim–Boynton procedure, or just to the outer skin of the space, as with the Berlin–Kay stimulus materials. For this purpose, he used the Optical Society of America–Uniform Color Space. The OSA color space contains 424 samples that, unlike the Munsell set, are equally spaced across all three dimensions. Boynton and his collaborators asked native English (and subsequently Japanese) subjects to name each member of the randomly presented set twice, with any monolexemic names they chose to use. Responses were compared with respect to consistency, consensus among subjects, and time between presentation and first response. On all of these measures, basic color terms are clearly differentiated from non-basic terms, but there is no clear differentiation between terms for the Hering elemental colors and the derived basic colors. Weighted averages ("centroids") of color chip choices were calculated for each basic term. The centroids of chromatic terms (save brown and pink) are typically highly saturated, and for those whose memberships overlap, are never separated from one another by more than 7.5 OSA units. Red and yellow never overlap, but both frequently overlap with chips called "orange." Orange thus serves as a bridge between red and yellow, and yellow bridges orange and green. This is surprising, given the composite nature of the one and the elemental nature of the other. A large region, called "tan" or "peach," is unnamed by any basic color term. Consensus samples for red and yellow are found at relatively narrow lightness levels, whereas consensus samples for green and blue extend over virtually all lightness levels. No chromatic plane at any lightness level includes all of the basic chromatic colors. Boynton concludes, "I feel it reasonable to suppose that there may be eleven categorically separate varieties of [brain] activity, corresponding to each of eleven kinds of color sensations that are identified by the eleven basic color terms. It might be productive, I think, to consider these as the pan-human perceptual fundamentals."

By the standards of the Sternheim–Boynton computed-hue technique, for some people green is not an elemental color. To explore the suspicion that these people are "paint-biased," i.e., influenced in their performance of the task by early experience with pigment mixing, **Miller** employed a new technique in which people were asked to estimate the percentage of a *single* hue in their perception. The results of the technique agree well with applications of the Sternheim–Boynton method in other cases, and by using it one can counteract the effects of paint bias in people's responses: green is indeed elemental. In a second application of single-hue naming, a fast-response forced-choice technique shows that "chartreuse" is a redundant term, whereas "orange" is not. The first procedure distinguishes elemental from non-elemental basic hues, the second distinguishes basic from non-basic binary hues. Both techniques were designed to minimize high-level cognitive factors. The experiment with orange and chartreuse provides the beginnings of an answer to one of the questions we posed earlier: why some binaries but not others are encoded as basic color terms. As Miller concludes, "Our findings suggest that the distinctions between elemental hues, basic, and nonbasic colors are useful and measurable."

So far, two systems of ordering perceived colors, the Munsell and the OSA, have been mentioned. **Sivik** introduces us to a third, the Swedish Natural Color System (NCS), which is based on the principles of opponent-process theory. The Munsell system, widely used in the US, is based on a lightness dimension (Value), a saturation dimension (Chroma), and a Hue dimension. Its design aim was to achieve equal perceptual distance within each dimension. Munsell divided the hue circuit into five sectors of twenty steps each, the resulting principal hue divisions being purple, red, yellow, green, and blue. Subsequent adjustments to the system to improve the spacing have put Munsell 5R, 5Y, and 5G – but not 5B – close to their respective unique hue points. The NCS is scaled by estimating the degree of resemblance that a color sample bears to ideal red, yellow, green, blue, black, and white. A sample is specified by estimating its chromaticness, hue, and blackness in percentage terms, the total of the three adding to 100. There are several important differences between Munsell and NCS. NCS is based on direct estimation rather than by comparison with samples, so use of the NCS (but not the NCS atlas) is independent of lighting conditions. Munsell is open on the saturation dimension, whereas NCS is closed (thus NCS chromaticness can be estimated and Munsell Chroma cannot). Munsell space is based on just-noticeable differences between neighboring colors, NCS on degree of resemblance to elementary colors. Munsell takes lightness to be fundamental, NCS uses blackness instead, regarding lightness as a derived dimension. Which, if either, of the two systems better represents the psychological space by which people categorize colors is a matter of dispute. In any case, Berlin and Kay's selection of samples from just the "outer skin" of the Munsell solid leaves color categorization in the interior portion unexplored. Sivik then describes how he and his associates have been using the NCS atlas and semantic differential techniques to study the references of pairs of terms frequently applied to color such as "warm–cold," "weak–strong," "beautiful–ugly," "active–passive," etc. The whole color space has been sampled, and the work has been extended to cross-cultural comparisons. In later studies other connotations of colors have been studied, using a descriptive model of color combinations based on dimensions such as interval/contrast, chord/color content, and balance/tuning. Strong relationships have been shown to exist between these stimulus-describing variables and the semantic connotative dimensions.

Linguistic and anthropological work on color categorization and naming in the Berlin and Kay tradition has spanned all levels of research, from methodology to theory to specific points of analysis. The essays included in this volume present some of the most recent advances at these various levels, addressing such key issues as the concept of basicness and its measurement; basic and non-basic terms; the nature and factors of color category evolution; universality and relativity in color classification; new methods of data collection; previously unreported types of color categories and cognitive mechanisms of category formation; and the possible genetic and evolutionary underpinnings of human color classificatory behavior.

The notion of basicness is taken up by **Corbett and Davies**. Assuming Berlin and Kay's original criteria for basicness, these authors propose to test the validity of various behavioral and linguistic measures of basicness against languages such as English, Russian, Japanese, French, Hebrew, and Spanish, whose inventories of basic color terms are well established. They assess the performance of each test in predicting the basic color term inventory of each language sampled (or separating basics from non-basics); in discriminating, within basic terms, among primary basics (the Hering fundamentals) and secondary basics (the derived categories); and in revealing regularities in the ordering of the basic terms in a given language, to be compared to the Berlin and Kay evolutionary sequence. The results, while providing overall support for Berlin and Kay's theory, indicate that different measures do better at different tasks, in a way that is consistent across languages. Elicited lists of color terms perform best in distinguishing between basic and non-basic terms; they can constitute a reliable, easy-to-use field tool for data collection on basic color terms. Frequency of occurrence in a text corpus discriminates between primary and secondary basics and is the best predictor of correlation with the Berlin and Kay sequence. A complementarity between these two measures is suggested.

Issues of color-category evolution are taken up by **Casson**, in the context of the development of English color terminology. Casson's study of basic and secondary color terminology from Old English to Modern English, from the seventh century to the present, reveals patterns that are similar to those observed in other languages of the world. Old English color terminology was mostly focused on brightness (lightness as well as shininess). Even those terms that would later become the basic color terms of English originally had prevalent brightness rather than hue senses. Hue senses became prevalent in Middle English (c. 1150–1500). This shift was paralleled, in the same period, by the emergence of secondary color terms that were exclusively hue terms and were derived by metonymic extension from words for physical entities. Casson relates this shift in English color terminology to the development of dyeing and textile manufacture as one factor that tended to bring about an increased complexity of the color world and a greater need for effective communication at this level.

Questions of color category evolution are also addressed by **Stanlaw** in his study of Japanese color terminology. He examines the role of language and culture contact in promoting change in this domain, along with the possible implications of the phenomena observed for the issue of universality vs. relativity in color classification. Stanlaw focuses on two aspects of Japanese color vocabulary. The first one is the use of English loanwords for derived color categories. Both color-name listings and word-frequency counts show a high correlation for Japanese with Berlin and Kay's evolutionary sequence. However, they also show color loanwords to be more salient than their Japanese counterparts. Such loanwords appear to be replacing the corresponding Japanese terms in an order approximately inverse to that of the Berlin and Kay sequence. The second aspect of Japanese color nomenclature considered in this chapter relates to the use of the term *ao*, currently meaning "blue," but previously naming a green–blue category, to refer to the color of the green ("go") traffic light. This choice seems to be due to the specific connotations carried by *ao*. Native Japanese people residing in the US for extended periods of time tend to remember the color of the "go" light in Japan as being bluer than those who have come from Japan more recently, suggesting a mild "Whorfian effect" (influence on thought by language).

MacLaury, in his chapter, introduces the reader to the methodology and some of the results of his Mesoamerican Color Survey (MCS), and presents a theoretical framework, "vantage theory," that he has elaborated to account for his findings. A data collection procedure, partially modified from that of the WCS by the addition of a category range mapping task, reveals a peculiar pattern of color categorization in some of the Mesoamerican languages studied by MacLaury: the range of the black category encompasses that of the Cool (green–blue) category, although the term for the Cool category is amply used in color naming. This and related observations, such as that of "coextensive" ranges in the Warm category, discussed elsewhere by MacLaury, have led him to propose that color (and possibly other) categories are constructed in a way analogous to the construction of a physical point of view, with variable coordinates. According to MacLaury, the organization of a category results from the interplay of neurally grounded perception and a cognitive mechanism he refers to as "selective emphasis" on, or attendance to, similarity vs. difference. The implications of the "vantage theory" model are discussed here with special reference to the finding that first, when the focus of the Cool category in MCS languages is in blue, this focus appears to be skewed, or polarized, and second, when green and blue are categorized separately, their respective foci tend to darken, although more in blue than in green. MacLaury asserts that his model provides the active cognitive principle that propels category change, as distinctiveness gets progressively emphasized over similarity.

The body of research on cross-linguistic color categorization and naming is examined by Zegura from a human evolutionary perspective and in relation to recent findings on the genetics of color vision. The prevalent assumption in color classification studies has been that of an essential sameness of human color vision, presumably based on close genetic similarities. The existence of cross-linguistic universals in the domain of color has generally been traced to this assumed common biological basis. However, Zegura points to the discovery by Nathans and his associates that individuals with normal phenotypic function present greater polymorphism than was previously thought in the genes for the so-called "blue," "green," and "red" photopigments (opsins). This applies both within and across various primate species, including *Homo sapiens*. Psychophysical correlates have been suggested for this genetic polymorphism, in the form of color-matching differences in human populations. Zegura raises the question of whether such genetic differences may also underlie intra- and interpopulational differences in color term systems. Since humans display ongoing genetic evolution in the opsin system, Zegura also considers the possibility that this may provide the underlying mechanism for the continued development of basic color terminologies – perhaps correlating with a cognitive mechanism, such as that proposed by MacLaury, of shifting attendance to difference vs. similarity.

The prevailing tenor of the essays in the present volume is that the opponent-process theory of color perception is the fundamental starting-point for forging the links between color vision and color categorization. The Natural Color System is explicitly organized in accordance with the opponent scheme, and Sivik and others have for that reason urged that it be more widely used in studies of color categorization. **Jameson and D'Andrade** argue instead that opponent theory and the NCS are problematic foundations for the understanding of color categorization. They maintain that studies of the similarities that colors bear to each other generally do not yield opponent color space, but correspond more nearly to a Munsell space, with a five-hue rather than a four-hue organization. Neither additive mixture nor successive contrast yields an opponent structure, especially where red and green are concerned, but both sorts of complementation are well approximated by the oppositions in Munsell space. The electrophysiological studies of LGN cells also fail to speak unambiguously in favor of the fourfold-hue scheme of opponent theory. Furthermore, the scaling of large-scale perceptual color differences is not precise enough to determine what pairs of colors are psychologically furthest apart. Rather than appealing to the psychophysiological importance of the Hering primaries, the authors suggest that it might be fruitful to explain the Berlin–Kay evolutionary sequence in terms of those successive partitions of color space that are most informative: if one has only two color terms, the most informative system is one that would split the color solid most nearly in two. A dark/cool versus light/warm division accomplishes this. The next area of the space most distant from these two is red, since it is the most saturated color most distant from the focus of dark/cool (a dark blue or green) and the focus of light/warm (a light yellow). Once these divisions are in place, the next most distant region is green, followed by yellow, then blue, then orange, purple, pink, and brown, as in the Berlin and Kay most frequent ordering.

Another dissenting voice is that of **Lucy**. He takes issue with the linguistic assumptions of the Berlin and Kay research program. His critique centers around the notion of meaning that underlies most color categorization research. Lucy charges that the notion commonly used in this tradition is confined to denotational, decontextualized meaning (a term's ability to label a specific referent – in this case a color chip), and ignores the contextual, structural aspects of meaning, such as a term's characteristic referential range (its typical uses in a variety of different contexts) and its formal distributional potential (its contrastive and combinatorial position within the categories available in a language). He contends that this restriction to denotation, along with the choice of the Munsell array for data collection, predetermines the universalistic findings by limiting the possible meanings of a word to its hue and lightness dimensions, excluding other possible non-color components, such as luster, texture, or degree of succulence. Lucy sees this approach as stemming directly from a folk understanding of how meaning works in English, and therefore finds the whole cross-linguistic color research program to be an exercise in determining if and to what extent a given language's "color" vocabulary matches the model of English. In his opinion, such an approach precludes even establishing whether a "color system" actually exists in a given language as a well-defined and salient domain. It also prevents resolution of the long-standing universalism vs. relativism debate about the relation of language and thought: do observable cross-linguistic differences have an impact on the way people think? The way out of the impasse, says Lucy, is to avoid the conflation of cognitive and linguistic categories. This conflation arises as a consequence of assuming the existence of some innate physical or functional system for every lexical item in a language, or, vice versa, assuming that the existence of a category of some sort implies its incorporation in the structure of the language in question. In his view, the in-depth formal–functional study of a language is a prerequisite for any kind of generalization.

The discussions at Asilomar were lively and wide-ranging. In a concluding essay, **Maffi and Hardin** examine their chief threads, to which they add some reflections of their own, in order to assess the present state of knowledge in the field. They first look at the concept of "basic color term" as well as the semantic validity of the Berlin–Kay investigations. They next consider how well visual science can account for primary color categories and their structure, what insights have been gained about derived and composite categories, and whether the number of basic categories might exceed eleven. Several hypotheses about the dynamics of color category change were proposed at the conference, as well as some evidence supporting the existence of a posited brightness sequence. They are discussed here, along with some recent insights into the warm–cool division of colors that may pertain to the formation of composite categories. Throughout, Maffi and Hardin touch on the many open questions that require further investigation, and point to new collaborations between linguistic anthropologists and visual scientists and psychologists that promise to keep this interdisciplinary field of investigation active and fruitful in years to come.

I | THE WORLD COLOR SURVEY

2 Color naming across languages

Paul Kay, Brent Berlin, Luisa Maffi, and William Merrifield

Introduction: prior cross-linguistic research on color naming

This chapter summarizes some of the research on cross-linguistic color categorization and naming that has addressed issues raised in *Basic Color Terms: Their Universality and Evolution* (Berlin and Kay 1969, hereafter B&K). It then advances some speculations regarding future developments – especially regarding the analysis, now in progress, of the data of the World Color Survey (hereafter WCS). In the latter respect the chapter serves as something of a progress report on the current state of analysis of the WCS data, as well as a promissory note on the full analysis to come.

B&K proposed two general hypotheses about basic color terms and the categories they name: (a) there is a restricted universal inventory of such categories; (b) a language adds basic color terms in a constrained order, interpreted as an evolutionary sequence. These two hypotheses have been substantially confirmed by subsequent research.[1]

There have been changes in the more detailed formulation of the hypotheses, as well as additional empirical findings and theoretical interpretations since 1969. Rosch's experimental work on Dani color (Heider 1972a, 1972b), supplemented by personal communications from anthropologists and linguists, showed that two-term systems contain, not terms for dark and light shades regardless of hue – as B&K had inferred – but rather one term covering white, red, and yellow and one term covering black, green and blue, that is, a category of white plus "warm" colors versus one of black plus "cool" colors. Rosch reported further that these "composite" categories, as they were later christened by Kay and McDaniel (1978, hereafter K&McD), tend to be focused not only in white and black, but sometimes at the foci of red or yellow, on the one hand, and of green or blue on the other. B&K had conceived basic color categories in terms of foci and extensions and had expressed the evolutionary sequence of hypothesis (b) as a sequence of constraints on the successive encoding of foci. Rosch's finding that composite categories may have multiple foci was a major reason for the reconception of the evolutionary sequence in terms of successive divisions of the color space (see e.g. Kay 1975: 258–262).[2]

K&McD modeled these successive divisions of the color space as fuzzy partitions. They interpreted individual color categories as fuzzy sets (Zadeh 1965),[3] and defined the notion of fuzzy partition in terms of a (standard) set of fuzzy sets (K&McD: 641–644). Accordingly, basic color categories were divided into three types. The first type consists of the six fundamental categories, corresponding to Hering's primaries (Hering 1964): black, white, red, yellow, green, blue.[4] The second type, the composites, consists of fuzzy unions of the fundamentals. These include the "white/warm" and "black/cool" categories of two-term systems, as well as several categories comprised by unions of pairs of the six fundamentals (about which more presently). The third type were called "derived" categories and were defined in terms of the fuzzy intersections of the fundamentals. Examples of this type are colors that are seen as mixtures of fundamentals: for example, orange is seen as a mixture of red and yellow (Sternheim and Boynton 1966).[5]

The WCS was begun in 1976.[6] It was designed for two major purposes. The first was to assess the general hypotheses advanced by B&K against a broader empirical basis. Methodological objections had been raised to the empirical generalizations of B&K. The most important of these were that: (a) the twenty languages studied experimentally were not *prima facie* sufficiently numerous to justify universal conclusions; (b) the data were obtained in Berkeley rather than in native communities; (c) most of the speakers interviewed spoke English as well as their native language; (d) the number of speakers interviewed for most of the languages was three or fewer; and (e) the interviewers were not, for the most part, skilled speakers of the languages studied.[7] The second major purpose of the WCS was to deepen our knowledge regarding universals, variation, and historical development in basic color-term systems.

The methods and some initial results of the WCS are reported in Kay, Berlin, and Merrifield (1991, hereafter KBM). With the help of field linguists of the Summer Institute of Linguistics and using a stimulus array substantially the same as that of B&K, comparable data on naming ranges and focal choices for basic color terms were collected on 110 languages *in situ*. In most cases 25 speakers were interviewed per language. Monolingual speakers were sought insofar as possible. A methodological departure of the WCS from the method of B&K was that chip-naming judgments were obtained on individual chip presentations, rather than the full array of stimuli. Judgments of best example (focal judgments) were obtained in the same way as in the original study, by requesting selection of the chip or chips that best represent each basic color word of the native language from an array of 330 color patches, representing 40 equally spaced Munsell hues at 8 levels of lightness (at maximum saturation) plus 10 levels of lightness of neutral (black, grey, white) shade.

The preliminary results of the WCS, as reported in KBM, were as follows. (a) B&K had defined evolutionary stages on the assumption that all composite categories are eliminated in favor of the six fundamentals before any derived categories appear. Kay (1975) and K&McD had taken over this assumption in their reformulations of the evolutionary sequence, except for the latter's making formal provision for the optional early appearance of grey.[8] KBM report further cases of early grey and point out, more importantly, that either brown or purple or both not infrequently appear before the green/blue composite is dissolved. (b) Kay (1975: 260–261) had noted evidence from several sources that there might be languages with composite categories comprising yellow and green. MacLaury (1986, 1987a) was the first to document such categories with controlled stimuli. Several more have been found in the WCS languages and were reported in KBM. (c) Prior to the WCS, there had been no rationale offered in the literature for the restricted inventory of composite categories actually reported, distinctly fewer than the sixty-three logically possible combinations of the six fundamentals. KBM both extended the inventory of composite categories empirically attested and provided a partial explanation, in terms of generally acknowledged properties of the visual system, for the restricted membership of this inventory (KBM: 15ff.).

The current state of analysis of the WCS data

The initial stage of processing of the WCS data converted the hand-collected data for each collaborating speaker into two arrays, one for naming choices and one for focal choices. The data for the first five

speakers of Buglere are displayed in part 2 of Figure 2.1, naming
choices to the left and focal choices to the right. Each symbol in these
arrays corresponds to a Buglere color term, as indicated in part 1 of
Figure 2.1.[9] The columns represent the forty equally spaced Munsell
hues mentioned earlier[10] and the rows, levels of lightness.[11]

Numerous recombinations of the data in the individual speaker
arrays were performed, two of which merit particular mention here.
First, the reader will note in the middle of part 1 of Figure 2.1 four
Aggregate Naming arrays of the same general shape as those in part 2
of Figure 2.1. These also refer to Buglere but they characterize the data
for the language sample as a whole, rather than for each speaker individually. They are labeled Modal Agreement level, 30% agreement
level, 70% agreement level, and 100% agreement level. The Modal
Agreement array displays for each stimulus chip the symbol corresponding to the term most often applied to that chip, regardless of
how often that was. The 30% agreement array displays for each stimulus chip the symbol corresponding to the term most often applied to
that chip only if that term was used for that chip by at least 30% of the
respondents; otherwise no symbol is recorded for the chip. The 70%
agreement and the 100% agreement arrays are constructed
correspondingly, according to the obvious substitutions. These displays are called "naming arrays" because they record a mapping from
stimulus colors to the terms assigned to them in the naming task.

Arrays of the other type to be considered here are called "term
maps." The term maps are illustrated for Candoshi in Figure 2.2, part
2. There is a separate map for each term. In the map for a given term,
each chip c receives a typographical symbol (including blank) of visual
"density" intuitively commensurate with the frequency with which
speakers named c with that term, this frequency expressed as a proportion of the number of speakers naming any stimulus with that
term.[12] Term maps give a graphic portrayal of the meaning of each
term. High-agreement symbols tend to occur in the interior of categories and lower-agreement symbols at the edges. Term maps also give
a quick but accurate insight into the degree of consensus of speakers
regarding the reference of a term. Compare the very high agreement
("#") throughout the blue region in the application of the traditional
Candoshi green/blue term and the lower consensus on the emergent
green term and the purple term. Note finally that the two phonolog-

Figure 2.1,
part 1 Buglere

Language	Country	Family	Tot. interviewees	Fieldworker(s)	Date
Buglere	Panama	Unclassified	25 (15 F; 10 M)	K. Fisher and J. Gunn	1978

Terms Appearing In Aggregate Naming Arrays

Symbol	Term	Users	Symbol	Term	Users
/	jere/jerere	25	*	moloin/ moloinre	25
-	jutre/jusa	25	@	lere/lerere	25
+	dabe/dabere	25	#	leren	24

Aggregate Naming Arrays

```
        Modal Agreement Level                          30% Agreement Level, 8 of 25 speakers
          1         2         3         4                       1         2         3         4
  01234567890123456789012345678901234567890     01234567890123456789012345678901234567890
A ----------------------------------------- A   A ----------------------------------------- A
B ----------****--------------------------- B   B ----------****--------------------------- B
C -*************@@@@@@@@@-----#------*** C       C -*************@@@@@@@@@-----#------*** C
D -*************@@@@@@@@@@@#@#----*+**** D       D -*************@@@@@@@@@@@#@#----*+**** D
E -+++++*******@*@@@@@@@@@@@@@@####*#*++** E     E -+++++*******@*@@@@@@@@@@@@@@####*#*++** E
F /++++*******@@@@@@@@@@@@@@@@##########++++ F   F /++++*******@@@@@@@@@@@@@@@@##########++++ F
G /+++++*////@@@@@@@@@@@@@#@#@@######*+++++ G    G /+++++*////@@@@@@@@@@@@@#@#@@######*+++++ G
H /++++//////////@@@@@@@@@@#@##########++++ H    H /++++//////////@@@@@@@@@@#@##########++++ H
I /+++/////////////@@@@@@@/@#/############+ I    I /+++ /////////////@@@@@@@/@#/############+ I
J ///////////////////////////////////////// J   J ///////////////////////////////////////// J


      70% Agreement Level, 18 of 25 speakers          100% Agreement Level, 25 of 25 speakers
          1         2         3         4                       1         2         3         4
  01234567890123456789012345678901234567890     01234567890123456789012345678901234567890
A ----------------------------------------- A   A                                           A
B --- ----- **  ---- - ------------------- B    B                                           B
C -*   ******            ----              C    C                                           C
D -    ******   @@@@@@@                    D    D                                           D
E  + +  ****    @@@@@@@                    E    E                                           E
F +++    *   @@@ @@@@       ##       + F        F                                           F
G /+++        @ @@ @        ###      ++ G        G                                           G
H /++++   // /  @@           ##        H         H                                           H
I /   ////////          #             I         I                                           I
J ///////////////////////////////////////// J   J                                           J
```

Terms Not Appearing In Aggregate Naming Arrays

Symbol	Term	Users	Symbol	Term	Users
o	lejre	10	>	mnule	2
=	kwajusa	7	x	dagikwale	2

Speakers (By I.D. Number, Age And Sex)

1 21 F	6 30 F	11 40 F	16 18 M	21 26 M
2 22 F	7 35 F	12 40 F	17 18 M	22 35 M
3 22 F	8 35 F	13 40 F	18 18 M	23 45 M
4 23 F	9 35 F	14 45 F	19 20 M	24 45 M
5 30 F	10 38 F	15 50 F	20 23 M	25 45 M

Figure 2.1,
part 2 Buglere

Individual Naming Arrays

```
                        *** Speaker  1  ***
          1         2         3         4                    1         2         3         4
  0123456789012345678901234567890123456789          0123456789012345678901234567890123456789
A ----------------------------------------  A     A ----------------------------------------  A
B ---------*****-------#-----------------  B     B                                          B
C -**--*-********@@@#@@-#@@--##-#------****  C     C    +++        *                          C
D -*-***********@@@@@@@##@####/---**+**+-  D     D                                          D
E /*+********@*@@@@@@@@@#######/#*@++**  E     E                                          E
F -+++***-****@@@@@@@@@@#####@####**+++  F     F *F              #        #                 F
G /+++*+*////@/@@@@@@@#@@#########*+#+++  G     G              @                            G
H /++++/////////@@@@@##@#########+++  H     H                                          H
I ///+////////////@@@o@@@@@@//##/#####/###/  I     I                                          I
J ////////////////////////////////////////  J     J                                          J

                        *** Speaker  2  ***
          1         2         3         4                    1         2         3         4
  0123456789012345678901234567890123456789          0123456789012345678901234567890123456789
A ----------------------------------------  A     A ----------------------------------------  A
B ---------*-***@-----o@*---------------  B     B                                          B
C -*************@@o@ooo@@@-@@@###-#----****  C     C                                          C
D /+**********oo@@o@o@@@@oo######@o#+****-  D     D        *                                 D
E /+++*-*******@*@o@o@@@@@oo#########***  E     E                                          E
F /+++********@@@o@@@oo@@o#####o#####++++  F     F                 @                        F
G /++++++****@o@oooooo@o#########+#-*+  G     G +                                          G
H /++++++++/o/oo@/ooooo@o@#/######o####++#+  H     H                        #               H
I /++++///////////@ooo@oooo/o/##o/#####++o++  I     I                                          I
J ////////////////////////////////////////  J     J ////////////////////////////////////////  J

                        *** Speaker  3  ***
          1         2         3         4                    1         2         3         4
  0123456789012345678901234567890123456789          0123456789012345678901234567890123456789
A ----------------------------------------  A     A ----------------------------------------  A
B ---*>>-->-****-*---@-@------>>--->--->--->-+  B     B                                          B
C -++*+-*********o@@@@@@@>->------>->-*--+  C     C        *                                 C
D >*++++********@@@@@@@@@-@-@-@#-#--##--*+  D     D                                          D
E >++++++***@@@@@@@@@@@@@@@@>*-##++++  E     E              @                            E
F /++++++++*@@@@@@@@@@@@@@#@######-++++  F     F    +              #                       F
G -+++++/+++@@@@@@@@@@@@###########+++  G     G                                          G
H /+++++///////@/@@@@@@@@@@#####@###-##++++  H     H                                          H
I /++++////////////@@@@@@#//#########-###+  I     I                                          I
J ////////////////////////////////////////  J     J                                          J

                        *** Speaker  4  ***
          1         2         3         4                    1         2         3         4
  0123456789012345678901234567890123456789          0123456789012345678901234567890123456789
A ----------------------------------------  A     A ----------------------------------------  A
B ---**-*--****@--####@----------------  B     B                                          B
C +*--***********@@@@@@@#####--#=#----+-**++  C     C        *                                 C
D -+-*+++******@@@@@@@@@#@#@@@####-#@#+#**+  D     D                                          D
E /++-+++*+**#@@@@@@@@@@@#####-###**++  E     E                                          E
F /++++**+@*@@#@@@@@@@@#@@@########**+  F     F                 @                        F
G /+++++*+@@@@+@#@@@@@#@@@#####@#####@####*+  G     G +                        #               G
H /#+++///+@//@/@#@@@@@@/@#@#######*#@+  H     H                                          H
I /+++-@//////////@##@@@/@#/@###########/+  I     I                                          I
J ////////////////////////////////////////  J     J ////////////////////////////////////////  J

                        *** Speaker  5  ***
          1         2         3         4                    1         2         3         4
  0123456789012345678901234567890123456789          0123456789012345678901234567890123456789
A ----------------------------------------  A     A ----------------------------------------  A
B -*+*+--*-*+*++o-----o-o@o--------------**  B     B                                          B
C -*+**+*******o*o@o#oo#o@oooooooo----+*+++*  C     C                                          C
D -+*+*****+**@ooo#ooo@#oo#oo-**#*++**  D     D                                          D
E /****++*++**ooooooooooooo##oooooooo****++++*  E     E *****                                    E
F /*+*+****/**@#oo#oooooooooo##@ooo*++*++*  F     F                                          F
G /**+*++/+///o/o#oo#oooooooooo##o##o#oo**+*+  G     G +++              @        #             G
H /+++++/**//////ooo#o@oooooooooo#o#oo*****  H     H                                          H
I /*******//////////#ooooo#/##oo##oooo#+****  I     I                                          I
J ////////////////////////////////////////  J     J ////////////////////////////////////////  J
```

Figure 2.2,
part 1 Candoshi
(Peru: Jivaroan;
map: x[13]; B. Hinson[14])

Basic stage	IV. $G/Bu \to V$
Derived categories	purple (weak)
Heterogeneous categories	desaturated (weak)

Basic Color Terms

Term	Gloss	Symbol
kantsirpi	'black'	•
borshi	'white'	o
chobiapi	'red'	+
ptsiyaro(mashi)	'yellow'	|
kavabana	'green/blue (blue-focused)' → 'blue'	=
kamachpa	'(emergent) green'	*
tarika	'purple'	P
pozani	'desaturated'	x

Aggregate Naming Arrays

```
       Modal Agreement Level                      30% Agreement Level, 4 of 11 speakers
     1         2         3         4                    1         2         3         4
   01234567890123456789012345678901234567890        01234567890123456789012345678901234567890
A  ooooooooooooooooooooooooooooooooooooooooo A     A  ooooooooooooooooooooooooooooooooooooooooo A
B  oooooooooo|||||oooo=o=ooo==ooooooooooooooo B     B  oooooooooo|||||oooo=o=ooo==ooooooooooooooo B
C  o++++++|||||||||**===*==*=======oooo++++++ C     C  o++++++|||||||||**===*==*=======oooo++++++ C
D  o+++++|||||||||**===*============xx++++++ D      D  o+++++|||||||||**===*============xx++++++ D
E  x++++++|||||*******============================++++ E  E  x+++++|||||*******========================++++ E
F  •+++++++|||||*****===============================+++++ F  F  •+++++++|||||  ****===============================+++++ F
G  ++++++x++x*x*****===========================+++++++ G  G  ++++++x+   x*****=========================+++++++ G
H  ++++++++x•••••***=***===========================+++++ H  H  ++++++++  •••••***=***===========================+++++ H
I  •+++++++++••**=**==*============================P++++ I  I  •+++++++++••**=**==*============================P++++ I
J  •••••••••••••••••••••••••••••••••••••••••• J     J  •••••••••••••••••••••••••••••••••••••••••• J

      70% Agreement Level, 8 of 11 speakers           100% Agreement Level, 11 of 11 speakers
     1         2         3         4                    1         2         3         4
   01234567890123456789012345678901234567890        01234567890123456789012345678901234567890
A  ooooooooooooooooooooooooooooooooooooooooo A     A  ooooooooooooooooooooooooooooooooooooooooo A
B  oo oooooo |     ooo      o    ooooo ooooo o B    B  o                         o   ooo o  oo o  B
C  o  +        |       =  = = = o            C     C  o                                          C
D  o+ +             *        ==========        +    D                               =  =          D
E  +++++      |     **        ==========        +++  E  E  ++++               = ====         E
F  +++++                      ==========        +++  F  F  +++                = =====         F
G  •+++++         *    *  =  =  ==========        ++++ G  G  + ++             === ==          + G
H  +++++             **   *    ==========        ++ H  H  •  +               = =====          H
I  •         •••••••••*          =======          I  I  •      •• •••          ====           I
J  •••••••••••••••••••••••••••••••••••••••••• J     J  •••••••••••••••••••••••••••••••••••••••••• J
```

Figure 2.2,
part 2 Candoshi

Term Maps
(# = 81-100% agreement, + = 61-80 % agreement, - = 41-60% agreement, . = 21-40% agreement)

•: *kantsirpi* 'black'

o: *borshi* 'white'

+: *chobiapi* 'red'

I: *ptsiyaro* 'yellow 1'

I: *ptsiyaromashi* 'yellow 2'

=: *kavabana* 'green/blue'

*: *kamachpa* '(emergent) green'

P: *tarika* 'purple'

x: *pozani* 'desaturated'

11 of 11 speakers searched; 11 used term

11 of 11 speakers searched; 11 used term

11 of 11 speakers searched; 11 used term

11 of 11 speakers searched; 5 used term: 1..3,5,11

11 of 11 speakers searched; 8 used term: 1,4..10

11 of 11 speakers searched; 11 used term

11 of 11 speakers searched; 11 used term

11 of 11 speakers searched; 6 used term: 1,3,4,6,8,9

11 of 11 speakers searched; 10 used term: 1..4,6..11

ically similar–and doubtless morphologically related–Candoshi words for yellow have similar term maps. Term maps provide important information, beyond that given in the naming arrays, for characterizing an internally variable speech community with respect to its degree of basic color-term development.

Candoshi is transitional between stages IV and V. An original green/blue composite category (*kavabana* [=]) appears to have recently split and a new term for green (*kamachpa* [*]) has emerged. *Kavabana* extends at 30% agreement to unique green and the green term is almost exclusively confined to yellowish and brownish greens. Nonetheless, all eleven speakers used *kamachpa* "green." These facts suggest that *kavabana* was originally focused in blue and denoted all of blue or green and that this term is currently retracting from green. Two similar expressions are found for "yellow" (*ptsiyaro* and *ptsiyaro-mashi*), the second of which is treated here as a morphological variant of the first.[15]

A weak term for purple (*tarika* "P") has begun to emerge: four speakers have a well-established word for this category and two show incipient purple.

Finally, a desaturated term (*pozani* "x") occurs with a discontinuous distribution. It is also weak and displays low consensus in the term map.

Recent conceptual developments

Analysis of the WCS data is currently being conducted within the following conceptual framework, based on our provisional examination of the data (and therefore subject to revision as the analysis proceeds).

(a) Ever since B&K (41–45) discussed the "premature" appearance of gray, evidence has accumulated suggesting that the temporal development of basic color-term systems should be seen, not as a single process, but as two partially independent processes: (i) the division of composite categories into the six fundamentals, and (ii) the combination of fundamental categories into derived categories.[16] (Recall KBM's report that purple or brown or both frequently appear before green and blue separate.) Consequently, the developmental status of a system is now expressed in terms of a "basic stage," which characterizes the system with respect to its composite and fundamental categories, plus a list (often very short) of the derived and heterogeneous[17] categories which correspond to basic color terms in this system. For example, we might have a system characterized as "Stage V; purple, pink", which would be a system containing basic color terms corresponding to black, white, red, yellow, green, blue, purple, and pink. There are just five basic stages, corresponding to systems containing two to six composite or fundamental categories. This conceptual simplification leads to a more perspicuous notation for the sequence of stages, which will be described presently.

(b) The categories spanning yellow and green remain a problem, as discussed in KBM. They are few in number, but they unquestionably exist and cannot be dismissed as ethnographic or experimental error. A special study of systems containing categories of this kind is planned. For the moment, systems with a category spanning yellow and green are set aside. (They are taken up again in connection with Figure 2.4.)

(c) Composite category reduction is itself profitably viewed as consisting of two partially independent processes: dissolution of the white/warm channel (w) and dissolution of the black/cool channel (c).[18] From this perspective, composite category reduction is the same thing as basic stage evolution, that is, the progressive division of the two original composite categories into their six constituent funda-mentals, representing the sequence of basic stages I through V. Progress from Stage I (two composite categories comprising three fundamentals each) to Stage V (six fundamental categories) requires two divisions in each of the w and c channels.

(d) Although w-division and c-division are partially independent processes, they interact. In our model, the first of the four divisions is always in the w channel, with the result that Stage II systems retain the 3-fundamental c-composite category (Bk/G/Bu). Also, the fourth and final division is always in the c channel, entailing that Stage IV systems always retain a c-composite (and, of course, no w-composite). (See Figure 2.3 below.)

(e) In addition to such constraints on the interaction between the w and c channels, our model also sets constraints on the process of division within each channel. The w channel is more tightly constrained than the c channel. These intra-channel constraints are presented in Table 2.1 in both words and symbols.

Table 2.1

w(arm)1:	$\begin{bmatrix} \dots \\ W/R/Y \\ \dots \end{bmatrix} \rightarrow$	$\begin{bmatrix} W \\ R/Y \\ \dots \end{bmatrix}$	A W/R/Y category (always) divides into a W category and a R/Y category.
w(arm)2:	$\begin{bmatrix} \dots \\ W \\ R/Y \\ \dots \end{bmatrix} \rightarrow$	$\begin{bmatrix} W \\ R \\ Y \\ \dots \end{bmatrix}$	A R/Y category divides into a R category and a Y category.
c(ool)1:	$\begin{bmatrix} \dots \\ Bk/G/Bu \\ \dots \end{bmatrix} \rightarrow$	$\left\{ \begin{bmatrix} G/Bu \\ Bk \\ \dots \end{bmatrix} \text{ or } \begin{bmatrix} G \\ Bk/Bu \\ \dots \end{bmatrix} \right\}$	A Bk/G/Bu category divides either into a G/Bu category and a Bk category or into a G category and a Bk/Bu category.
c(ool)2:	$\left\{ \begin{bmatrix} G/Bu \\ Bk \\ \dots \end{bmatrix} \text{ or } \begin{bmatrix} G \\ Bk/Bu \\ \dots \end{bmatrix} \right\} \rightarrow$	$\begin{bmatrix} G \\ Bu \\ Bk \\ \dots \end{bmatrix}$	A two-component cool category (either G/Bu or Bk/Bu) divides into its components.

(f) The between-channel and intra-channel constraints introduced by our model restrict basic stage evolution to the system types and developmental trajectories portrayed in Figure 2.3. Within this framework, there are just eight basic system types possible, with three possibilities at Stage III and two possibilities at Stage IV.[19]

(g) The limitation to basic stages and to just the types shown in Figure 2.3 allows a more transparent notation for types than was previously available. Each of the five types constituting Stages III and IV is unambiguously represented by subscripting to the roman numeral denoting the stage an indication of the composite category representing the c channel, as shown in boldface in Figure 2.3.

(h) Our initial screening of the data indicates that the vast majority of the languages in the WCS sample fit the model set out in Table 2.1 and Figure 2.3 and thus correspond to one of the eight basic system types shown in Figure 2.3. One important aspect of the ongoing analysis of the WCS materials is to evaluate this claim on a careful language-by-language basis and to establish the extent to which every

Figure 2.3

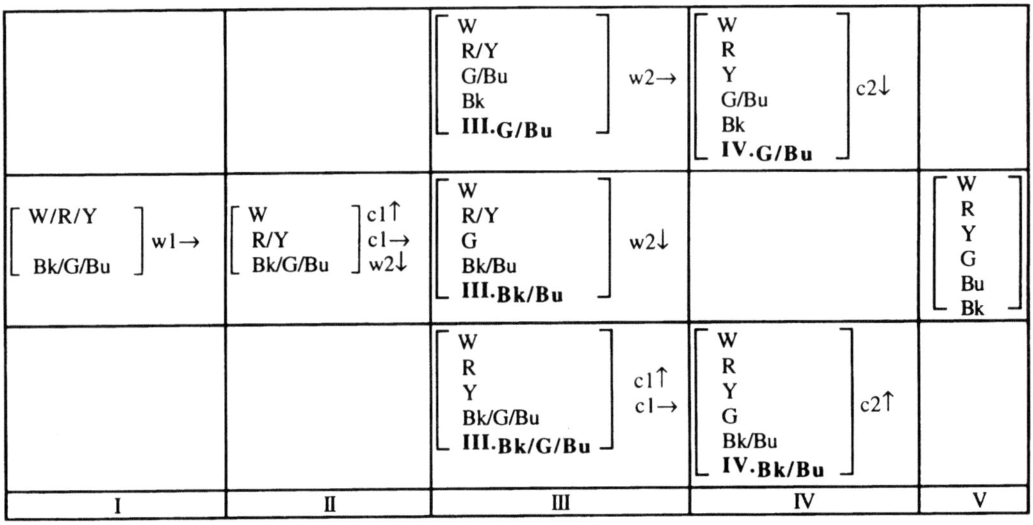

		$\begin{bmatrix} W \\ R/Y \\ G/Bu \\ Bk \\ \textbf{III.G/Bu} \end{bmatrix}$ w2→	$\begin{bmatrix} W \\ R \\ Y \\ G/Bu \\ Bk \\ \textbf{IV.G/Bu} \end{bmatrix}$ c2↓	
$\begin{bmatrix} W/R/Y \\ Bk/G/Bu \end{bmatrix}$ w1→	$\begin{bmatrix} W \\ R/Y \\ Bk/G/Bu \end{bmatrix}$ c1↑ c1→ w2↓	$\begin{bmatrix} W \\ R/Y \\ G \\ Bk/Bu \\ \textbf{III.Bk/Bu} \end{bmatrix}$ w2↓		$\begin{bmatrix} W \\ R \\ Y \\ G \\ Bu \\ Bk \end{bmatrix}$
		$\begin{bmatrix} W \\ R \\ Y \\ Bk/G/Bu \\ \textbf{III.Bk/G/Bu} \end{bmatrix}$ c1↑ c1→	$\begin{bmatrix} W \\ R \\ Y \\ G \\ Bk/Bu \\ \textbf{IV.Bk/Bu} \end{bmatrix}$ c2↑	
I	II	III	IV	V

language in the sample can be revealingly characterized in terms of this model. It should be noted that, according to the model, a given stage subtype may be reached by more than a single route. Type IV.$_{G/Bu}$ can develop either from III.$_{G/Bu}$ via w2 or from III.$_{Bk/G/Bu}$ via c1. Type IV.$_{Bk/Bu}$ may develop either from III.$_{Bk/Bu}$ via w2 or from III.$_{Bk/G/Bu}$ via c1. Type V may develop, via c2, from either IV.$_{G/Bu}$ or IV.$_{Bk/Bu}$. It is clear from our preliminary analysis that some languages are better characterized as transitional between subtypes (according to a specific transition; see Table 2.1) than as belonging to a single stage or type. Also, while some languages seem to be best characterized as recently emerged instances of their type, others appear to be on the verge of evolving into a new type. Related to the goal of discovering whether the data of every language are naturally organized by the model is the converse goal of checking the extent to which every subtype and transition generated by the model is realized in attested languages (cf. note 20).

(i) When applied to the data from individual speakers, it appears that the specific inter-category transitions proposed in Table 2.1 and displayed for full systems in Figure 2.3, will go a long way toward ordering language-internal variation as well. Evaluating this preliminary generalization constitutes another current research activity.

(j) Systems containing yellow/green composites can now be added

Figure 2.4

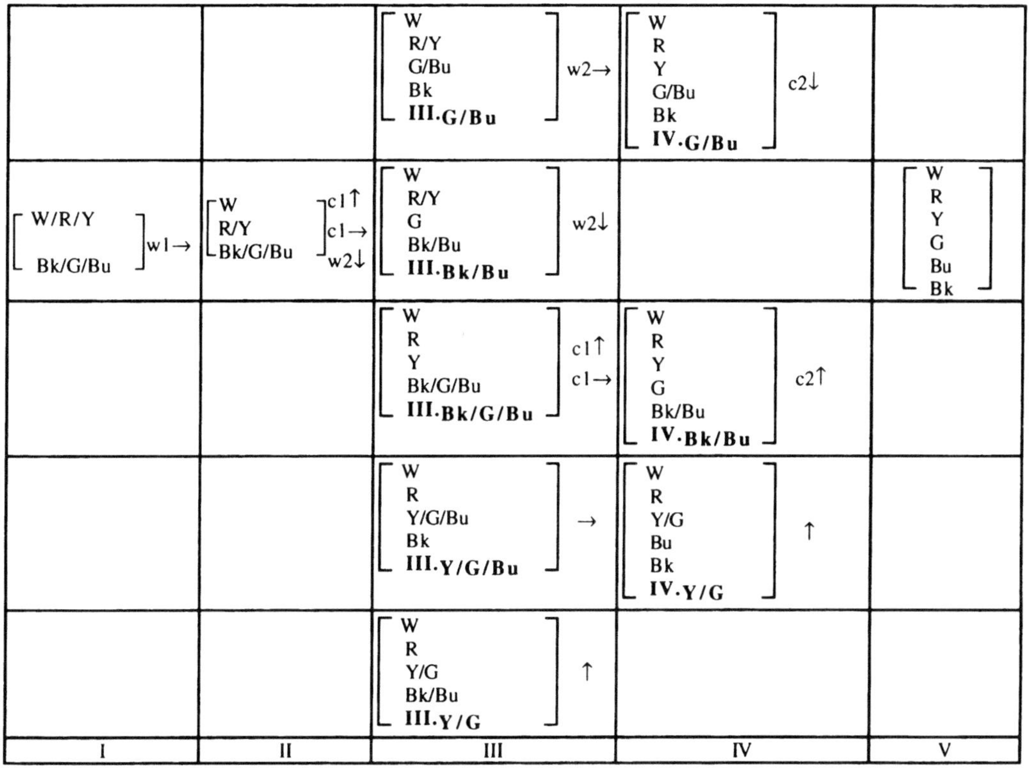

I	II	III	IV	V
		W R/Y G/Bu Bk III.**G/Bu** w2→	W R Y G/Bu Bk IV.**G/Bu** c2↓	
W/R/Y Bk/G/Bu w1→	W R/Y Bk/G/Bu c1↑ c1→ w2↓	W R/Y G Bk/Bu III.**Bk/Bu** w2↓		W R Y G Bu Bk
		W R Y Bk/G/Bu III.**Bk/G/Bu** c1↑ c1→	W R Y G Bk/Bu IV.**Bk/Bu** c2↑	
		W R Y/G/Bu Bk III.**Y/G/Bu** →	W R Y/G Bu Bk IV.**Y/G** ↑	
		W R Y/G Bk/Bu III.**Y/G** ↑		

to the picture, as shown in Figure 2.4. Extension of the model to yellow/green systems requires us to add significant complexity of an *ad hoc* kind[20] to cover a small amount of data. Yellow/green systems remain an area that needs careful additional work.

(k) Two categories have turned up in the preliminary analysis that do not fit any of the generalizations mentioned so far (see also Greenfield 1987). One is a category of desaturated, non-vivid, or "bad" color. Usually this category contains grey and a diverse collection of hues that never attain high saturation. An example is Candoshi *pozani*. Note in the aggregate naming arrays (Figure 2.2) that at modal and 30% agreement *pozani* ([x]) has a scattered distribution and that this term does not occur at all in the 70% agreement array. The term map for this term (Figure 2.2) shows a wide range, with no chip attaining a high level of consensus. Compare the lack of [#] and [+]

here to the maps for the other terms (emergent purple being a partial exception). Lack of focus appears to be characteristic of desaturated terms, and probably of heterogeneous terms generally. Since the WCS data contain only hues at maximum available saturation, careful study will be required to decide if and when a 'desaturated' term may name an unbroken volume of the color solid. Another problematical category for which there appears to be some evidence is a category one is tempted to gloss 'peripheral red.' Several languages have a term that includes colors on the long wavelength border of red, such as parts of pink, orange, maroon, or brown, and also colors on the other, purple, side of red, including a variety of red-purples and lavenders of different lightness levels. We characterize categories which do not name a continuous area of the surface of the color solid as *heterogeneous*.[21]

Current and future activities of the WCS

The research activities currently underway are conveniently described within the framework of a planned publication.[22] This is to be a two-volume monograph of which the first volume is devoted to analysis and the second to presentation of the WCS data in a format that will make them readily available to all scholars.

It is convenient to describe the second volume first. This volume will present the full WCS data for each speaker of each language along with some summary information for that language. A prototype Volume II entry for one language, Buglere, is given in Figure 2.1.

In Figure 2.1, the initial table gives language name, country, language family (if known), number of interviewees, name(s) of fieldworker(s), and date of data collection.

The second table lists the terms that occur in the aggregate naming arrays, each term preceded by the typographical symbol representing it in the arrays which follow. This list contains every term which was the most popular name given to any chip. It will always include all the basic terms, and sometimes include one or two non-basic terms as well.

The four aggregate naming arrays at modal, 30%, 70%, and 100% agreement appear as the third item of Figure 2.1. These have already been discussed.

Following the aggregate naming arrays are a table listing the remaining terms for the language (those not appearing in the aggregate arrays), and a table representing each native collaborator by an identifying number, followed by corresponding age and sex information.[23]

In the second part of Figure 2.1, the individual naming arrays for each collaborator are given, with naming data on the left and focus data on the right. Figure 2.1 shows only the first five of the twenty-five Buglere speakers participating in the study. The full volume II entries will of course include the data from all participating speakers of the languages in question. Thus, each volume II entry presents the full WCS data on chip naming and focus identification, arranged in such a way as to maximize their utility to other researchers.

Volume I of the proposed monograph will present the analysis of the WCS data. There will be chapters on a number of theoretical topics, several of which were touched on above. Chief among these are the accuracy and generality of the hypotheses embodied in Table 2.1 and Figures 2.3 and 2.4. Also, the nature and extent of heterogeneous categories, the prevalence in the data (or lack thereof) of the phenomenon of coextension (MacLaury 1986, 1987b,1991,1992), and the special problems posed by yellow/green categories must be considered.[24] A number of other general issues have not been mentioned. Notable among these is the treatment of purple in languages which lack a basic term for purple. This question is important because of the apparently privileged position purple holds perceptually in "closing the hue circle," that is, shading into short-wavelength blue on one side and long-wavelength red on the other, just as green and yellow each shades into the adjacent shorter- and longer-wavelength colors (see, e.g. J&D: 311). Preliminary screening of the 110 WCS languages reveals 16 with a basic term for purple and at least one undivided composite. No other non-fundamental hue comes close to this number, suggesting independently a special status for purple.

In addition to chapters, or sections, devoted to the topics sketched in the preceding paragraph, a significant portion of volume I will be devoted to an analysis of each language in the sample on the model of the prototype entry for Candoshi given in Figure 2.2.

In Figure 2.2, the title line gives the country in which the data were gathered, the genetic affiliation, and an indication of which map the language is marked on, there being a section with maps indicating the location of each language elsewhere in the volume.

The table just below the title line gives the evolutionary stage coordinates of the language in terms of (a) basic stage, (b) derived categories, and (c) heterogeneous categories. The notation "IV.$_{\cdot G/Bu} \rightarrow$ V" in Figure 2.2 indicates that Candoshi is classified as transitional between stages IV.$_{\cdot G/Bu}$ and V. The full range of possibilities envisaged for basic stage characterizations is as follows.

X → Y	in transition from X to Y
X	stable X
→ X	entering ("early") X
X →	exiting ("late") X

Below the table characterizing the evolutionary stage, there is a portion of text which reports the analysis, based on the aggregate naming arrays and the term maps (both shown further on in the Figure), which underlies the classification assigned.[25] Candoshi represents an interesting example partly because it demonstrates how the distinctions established in connection with Table 2.1 and Figure 2.3 can order what might otherwise be confusing data. It is projected that the set of analytical distinctions proposed here will permit stage characterizations and brief analyses which capture the main features of internal variation of each color-term system while simultaneously placing it in the developmental sequence with some finesse. Analysis of the stage status of the language concludes with a discussion of the derived and heterogeneous categories, if any.

The table in the middle of the first part of Figure 2.2 presents the basic color terms of Candoshi. As mentioned, this set of terms will normally coincide with the set of terms represented in the aggregate naming arrays, although additional criteria are used to determine the basic color terms. These include all the criteria of B&K: 5–7, especially as these have been evaluated by the field linguist (in response to instructions accompanying the field kit).

The list of basic color terms is followed by the four aggregate naming arrays.[26]

The second part of Figure 2.2 presents the term maps for Candoshi.

To summarize, volume I will consist of a number of chapters dealing with theoretical topics as indicated above, plus a long section containing an analysis of each language in the WCS sample in the format of the analysis of Candoshi constituting Figure 2.2.

Examples of individual color naming systems

In this section, we apply the conceptual framework developed above. Here we present analyses of WCS languages that are representative of the basic stage types predicted by the theoretical scheme embodied in Table 2.1 and Figure 2.3, following the format envisaged for volume I entries.

Stage I

$$\begin{bmatrix} \text{W/R/Y} \\ \text{Bk/G/Bu} \end{bmatrix}$$

As indicated in footnote 20, the World Color Survey sample includes no languages exhibiting a Stage I color system, although earlier field research by Rosch on the Dani shows that such systems do exist and that they conform to the typology suggested here. Furthermore, while the WCS files contain no single language whose basic stage could be classified as Stage I, numerous individual speakers in several languages, e.g. Martu-Wangka of Australia, show Stage I systems of color naming.

Stage II

$$\begin{bmatrix} \text{W} \\ \text{R/Y} \\ \text{Bk/G/Bu} \end{bmatrix}$$

Ejagham (Nigeria, Cameroon; Niger-Congo [J. Watters])

Basic stage	II
Derived categories	none
Heterogeneous categories	none

Basic Color Terms

Term	Gloss	Symbol
ényàgà	'black/green/blue'	•
ébáré	'white'	○
ébí	'red/yellow'	+

Aggregate Naming Arrays

```
           Modal Agreement Level                        30% Agreement Level,   8 of 25 speakers
               1         2         3         4              1         2         3         4
      0123456789012345678901234567890123456789 0     0123456789012345678901234567890123456789 0
A  oooooooooooooooooooooooooooooooooooooooooo  A   A  oooooooooooooooooooooooooooooooooooooooooo  A
B  oooooooooooooooooooooooooooooooooooooooooo  B   B  oooooooooooooooooooooooooooooooooooooooooo  B
C  o++++++++++++++.....•oooooooooooooooooo+o++++ C  C  o++++++++++++++.....•oooooooooooooooooo,o++++ C
D  o++++++++++++++.....•.......oooo+++++  D        D  o++++++++++++++.....•.......oooo+++++  D
E  •++++++++++++....•...............+++++++  E     E  •++++++++++++....•...............+++++++  E
F  •+++++++++++....•................+++++++  F     F  •+++++++++++....•................+++++++  F
G  •+++++++++....•..................++++++  G      G  •+++++++++....•..................++++++  G
H  •++++++++•...•...................+++++++  H     H  •++++++++•...•...................+++++++  H
I  •++++++....•.....................+++++  I       I  •++++++....•.....................+++++  I
J  •••••••....•....................•••••  J        J  •••••••....•....................•••••  J

           70% Agreement Level,  18 of 25 speakers       100% Agreement Level,  25 of 25 speakers
               1         2         3         4              1         2         3         4
      0123456789012345678901234567890123456789 0     0123456789012345678901234567890123456789 0
A  oooooooooooooooooooooooooooooooooooooooooo  A   A  oooooooooooooooooooooooooooooooooooooooooo  A
B  ooooooooooooo          oooooooooooooooooooo B   B  oo  oo  o          ooo o oo oo oooo o oooooo B
C  o+++ + +++++             ooooooooooo  ++++ C    C  o                                    o       C
D  o++++++++++       •••••• • •  •    ++++++  D    D    +  +++                            ++   D
E  ++++++++++  • •••••••• •••••••• •  ++++++  E    E  ++++++                            ++++  E
F  ++++++++  •••••••••••••••••••••••  +++++++  F   F  +++++        ••  •        •      +++  F
G  •+++++++  •••••••••••••••••••••••  ++++++  G    G  •++      • ••• •••• • •••         +  G
H  ++++++  ••••••••••••••••••••••••  +++++  H      H  +++++•  • •••••••••••••••  H
I  • +  ••••••••••••••••••••••••••••  +  I         I  •   • •••••••••• •••••••••  I
J  •••••••••••••••••••••••••••••••••  J            J  •••••••••••••••••••••••••••••••  J
```

Term Maps

(# = 81-100% agreement, + = 61-80 % agreement, - = 41-60% agreement, . = 21-40% agreement)

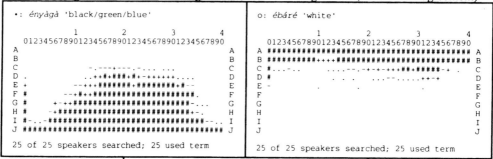

```
•: ényàgà 'black/green/blue'
          1         2         3         4
 0123456789012345678901234567890123456789
A                                           A
B                                           B
C          -.---+---.-...  ..               C
D  .         ..++#.###.#-.++++++....        D
E  +          --++.######+.########+#--     E
F  #          --+.#.+#########♯######..     F
G  #       +-.+.#############♯#######-...    G
H  #      -.+#########♯#########♯#####+-.    H
I  #-..-.#########♯##############♯####---.. I
J  #############♯###############♯#######♯## J
25 of 25 speakers searched; 25 used term

o: ébáré 'white'
          1         2         3         4
 0123456789012345678901234567890123456789
A  ############♯####################♯######## A
B  ##########♯##+++.###################♯## B
C  #.....-.        ...--.-+-+++##+#####-+ . C
D  #           . .   ...--....++-+        D
E  -          .    .     ..         .        E
F                                           F
G                                           G
H                                           H
I                                           I
J                                           J
25 of 25 speakers searched; 25 used term

+: ébí 'red/yellow'
          1         2         3         4
 0123456789012345678901234567890123456789
A                                           A
B        ....                               B
C  +##-#-#####+..                --####     C
D  ##########♯++-.             . #####      D
E  #########..-..              .-+#####     E
F  #######-..                  .+#####      F
G  #####.-..                  -+#####       G
H  ####-.                     --#####       H
I  -+#-                        .  --++      I
J                                           J
25 of 25 speakers searched; 25 used term
```

Ejagham is a Niger-Congo language spoken by 80,000 people in
Nigeria (45,000) and Cameroon (35,000).[27] Its color classification illustrates a typical Stage II system, with terms for Bk/G/Bu (*ényàgà*), W
(*ébáré*), and R/Y (*ébí*). These categories are strongly established at high
levels of consensus (80–100% agreement in the term maps). In the
WCS sample, Stage II systems are found predominantly in Africa.

Stage III.$_{G/Bu}$

$$\begin{bmatrix} W \\ R/Y \\ G/Bu \\ Bk \end{bmatrix}$$

Múra-Pirahã (Brazil; Unclassified [S. Sheldon])

Basic stage	III.$_{G/Bu}$
Derived categories	none
Heterogeneous categories	none

Múra-Pirahã is an unclassified language spoken by a small group
of foragers residing in four villages along the Maici River in west-
central Brazil. The language exemplifies a Stage III.$_{G/Bu}$ system, with
color terms for four basic color categories (W, R/Y, G/Bu, Bk). All four
are well established at the 70% level of agreement in the aggregate
naming arrays. Múra-Pirahã naming responses suggest that the focus
of the composite R/Y category is in red while that of G/Bu is in green.

Basic Color Terms*

Term	Gloss	Symbol	Term	Gloss	Symbol
bio³pai²ai³	'black'	•	*bi³i¹sai³*	'red/yellow'	+
ko³biai³	'white'	○	*a³hoa³saa³ga¹*	'green/blue'	=

* Raised numerals represent phonemic tones.

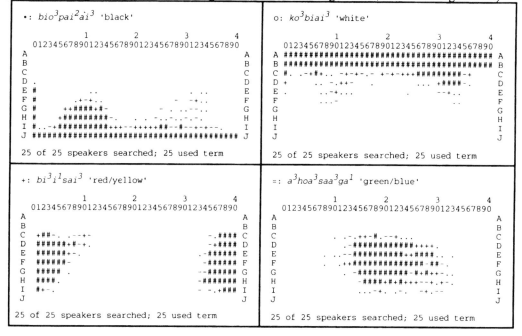

Aggregate Naming Arrays

```
            Modal Agreement Level
                 1         2         3         4
       0123456789012345678901234567890123456789 0
A  oooooooooooooooooooooooooooooooooooooooo  A
B  oooooooooooooooooooooooooooooooooooooooo  B
C  o+++ooo+++oo=o==o=o=o=ooooooooooooo++++  C
D  o+++++++o+o+ooo===============ooooo+++++  D
E  •+++++++oo===================oooo++++++  E
F  •++++++o•o•===================•••+++++  F
G  •++++•••••••===========•=====•+++++++  G
H  •++++••••••••===========•==•==•++++++++  H
I  •+++•••••••••=•••••••=••=••=•++++++++  I
J  •••••••••••••••••••••••••••••••••••••  J
```

```
        30% Agreement Level,  8 of 25 speakers
                 1         2         3         4
       0123456789012345678901234567890123456789 0
A  oooooooooooooooooooooooooooooooooooooooo  A
B  oooooooooooooooooooooooooooooooooooooooo  B
C  o+++ooo+++oo=o==o=o=o=ooooooooooooo++++  C
D  o+++++++o+o+ooo===============ooooo+++++  D
E  •+++++++oo===================oooo++++++  E
F  •++++++o•o•===================•••+++++  F
G  •++++•••••••===========•=====•+++++++  G
H  •++++••••••••===========•==•==•++++++++  H
I  •+++•••••••••=•••••••=••=••=•++++++++  I
J  •••••••••••••••••••••••••••••••••••••  J
```

```
        70% Agreement Level, 18 of 25 speakers
                 1         2         3         4
       0123456789012345678901234567890123456789 0
A  oooooooooooooooooooooooooooooooooooooooo  A
B  oooooooooooooooooooooooooooooooooooooooo  B
C  o+++ oo        o   =o       ooooooooo  ++++  C
D  o++++++++      ============= = oooo +++++  D
E  •+++++++       ===============     +++++  E
F  •+++++++       ===============  ==   +++++  F
G  •+++++•  •••••  ==========  = ==    +++++  G
H  •++++ •••••••••  ========   =      +++++++  H
I  •++  •••••••••••   ••  •••   •  • •    +++  I
J  ••••••••••••••••••••••••   •••••••••  J
```

```
       100% Agreement Level, 25 of 25 speakers
                 1         2         3         4
       0123456789012345678901234567890123456789 0
A  oooooooooooooooooooooooooooooooooooooooo  A
B  o oooooooo    o oo o     o o oooooooo oooooo  B
C                       =            o       C
D  + +                             +       D
E  +++        = == =      =        ++++  E
F  ++           ====            +++++  F
G  •++            ===              +++  G
H   +++      •                    ++++  H
I    •••                             I
J                                       J
```

Term Maps
(# = 81-100% agreement, + = 61-80 % agreement, - = 41-60% agreement, . = 21-40% agreement)

```
•: bio³pai²ai³ 'black'

                 1         2         3         4
       0123456789012345678901234567890123456789 0
A                                       A
B                                       B
C                                       C
D  .                                    D
E  #              ..              ...    E
F  #        .+-+..            -   -+..   F
G  #       ++####+#-         - . ..-.   G
H  #      +#########-.    . . -..-..-.-.  H
I  #..-+############+++--+++++##--#--+-+--.  I
J  ########################################  J

25 of 25 speakers searched; 25 used term
```

```
o: ko³biai³ 'white'

                 1         2         3         4
       0123456789012345678901234567890123456789 0
A  ######################################## A
B  ######################################## B
C  #.. .-+#..  -+-+--.- +-+-+++#########-+  C
D  +      .. -.++-     ... +####--.       D
E  .      ..-+...        .   --+..        E
F         . ..-                  ..       F
G                                         G
H                                         H
I                                         I
J                                         J

25 of 25 speakers searched; 25 used term
```

```
+: bi³i¹sai³ 'red/yellow'

                 1         2         3         4
       0123456789012345678901234567890123456789 0
A                                       A
B                                       B
C  +##-.  .--+-              -.####  C
D  ######+#-+.              -+####  D
E  ######+-.               .-######  E
F  ######-                -######  F
G  ##### .                --######  G
H  ####.                  -#######  H
I  #+-.                  - -.+###  I
J                                   J

25 of 25 speakers searched; 25 used term
```

```
=: a³hoa³saa³ga¹ 'green/blue'

                 1         2         3         4
       0123456789012345678901234567890123456789 0
A                                       A
B                                       B
C        . .-.++-#.--+...           C
D         .-#############++++.       D
E        . .-############++####...     E
F        . .++################--##-.     F
G        . -##########-#+#++-.-      G
H         -####+#+#+++--+.+-.       H
I         ...-+. .-. -+.--        I
J                                   J

25 of 25 speakers searched; 25 used term
```

Stage III.$_{Bk/Bu}$

$$\begin{bmatrix} W \\ R/Y \\ G \\ Bk/Bu \end{bmatrix}$$

As previously mentioned (cf. note 19), no unequivocal Stage III.$_{Bk/Bu}$ language has yet been attested in the preliminary analysis of the WCS data sets. However, the presence at Stage IV of four languages with W, R, Y, G, and Bk/Bu, and at Stage III of three yellow/green languages with W, R, Y/G, and Bk/Bu, indicates that Stage III.$_{Bk/Bu}$ systems are likely to be discovered. Furthermore, Konkomba shows several Stage III.$_{Bk/Bu}$ features and is worthy of discussion here.

Konkomba (Ghana, Togo; Niger-Congo [M.A. Langdon])

Basic stage	II→ ?III.$_{Bk/Bu}$→?IV.$_{Bk/Bu}$
Derived categories	none
Heterogeneous categories	none

Konkomba is a Niger-Congo language spoken in northeastern Ghana (220,000 speakers) and Togo (50,000 speakers). The aggregate naming arrays for this language suggest that, like many other African languages, it originally exhibited a Stage II color system but is moving toward a Stage III.$_{Bk/Bu}$ system (developing a term for G), or, alternatively, may be in rapid transition toward IV.$_{Bk/Bu}$ (developing in addition a term for Y). The data suggest that the terms *bɔmbɔn*, *pipi(i)n*, and *maman* at one time marked the categories Bk/G/Bu, W, and R/Y, respectively. These terms are used by all 25 speakers in the sample.[28] A new term, *ŋaankal*, used by 19 speakers, is emerging at 30% agreement level as the name of the category G (primarily in the light greens, while its full range appears to be that of a G or G/Bu term), leaving *bɔmbɔn* to cover the category Bk/Bu. Finally, the term *diyun*, used by a small number of speakers (9) and emerging at modal agreement level, appears to be developing as a term for Y. While *maman* remains the most popular term for the yellow area of the spectrum, including focal yellow, *diyun* is a well-established Y for a majority of its users, as seen in its term map. Its full range indicates that some users extend it to other light colors in the warm area.

Basic Color Terms

Term	Gloss	Symbol	Term	Gloss	Symbol
bɔmbɔn	'black/blue'	•	*ŋaankal*	'green'	*
pipi(i)n	'white'	o	*diyun*	'yellow'	ǀ
maman	'red/?yellow'	+			

Aggregate Naming Arrays

```
         Modal Agreement Level                          30% Agreement Level, 8 of 25 Speakers
       1         2         3         4                    1         2         3         4
  012345678901234567890123456789012345678         012345678901234567890123456789012345678
A oooooooooooooooooooooooooooooooooooooooo A     A oooooooooooooooooooooooooooooooooooooooo A
B oooooooooooooooooooooooooooooooooooooooo B     B oooooooooo ooooooooooooooooooooooooooooo B
C o+++++++++|ǀ*******o*ooooooooooooooo+o++++ C   C o+++++++++  * *  *o oooooooooooooo+o++++ C
D o+++++++++|*****•*•*•o*ooooo•oooo+++++ D         D o+++++++++  *****•*•* *oooo •oo o+++++ D
E •++++++++++•**•***•••*••••••o+++++++ E          E •++++++++++ • **•***•••*••••••  ++++++ E
F •+++++++++•••••••••**•••••••••++++++++ F        F •++++++++++ ••••••*•••••••••••++++++ F
G •+++++++++•••••••••*•••••••••++++++++ G         G •++++++++++•••••••••••••••••••++++++ G
H •+++++++++•••••••••••••••••++++++++ H           H •++++++++++••••••••••••••••••++++++ H
I •++++++••••••••••••••••••••++++++ I             I •+++++••••••••••••••••••••••++++++ I
J •••••••••••••••••••••••••••••• J                 J •••••••••••••••••••••••••••••• J

         70% Agreement Level, 18 of 25 Speakers         100% Agreement Level, 25 of 25 Speakers
       1         2         3         4                    1         2         3         4
  012345678901234567890123456789012345678         012345678901234567890123456789012345678
A                                        A       A                                        A
B              o              o          B       B                                        B
C   +                                    C       C                                        C
D ++++++++              ++++ D                    D                                        D
E ++++++                •    +++++ E             E +++++                              E
F ++++++                •  ++++++ F              F ++++                          +++ F
G ++++++          •  •• •     +++++ G            G ++                            ++ G
H •++++   ••••••• •• ••••••••    +++++ H         H  ++                       + H
I •+   •••••••••••••••••••••• I                   I              • •            I
J •••••••••••••••••••••••••••• J                  J                                        J
```

Term Maps

(# = 81-100% agreement, + = 61-80 % agreement, - = 41-60% agreement, . = 21-40% agreement)

```
•: bombɔn 'black/blue'                        o: pipin 'white'
         1         2         3         4                1         2         3         4
   01234567890123456789012345678901234567890      01234567890123456789012345678901234567890
A                                          A   A  +++++++++++++++++++++++++++++++++++++++++  A
B                                          B   B  +++-----+-....++#####--+++++++++++++++---+  B
C                                          C   C  +                 ..  -..-...++-.++-+.....  C
D                .  .....  .                D   D  +                    . ......-....-...      D
E  -             .  .-.. .-...-.--+-..      E   E  .                       . .....      ..     E
F          .........--.-.--++-+---.--       F   F                                             F
G  #       -.--+-.-----.+++-#++-++--.       G   G                                             G
H  #       ...-+#+#++++-++-+#++#######+--.  H   H                                             H
I  #....++-##+.#######+#+++##########-+--.... I   I                                             I
J  ######################################### J   J                                             J

   25 of 25 speakers searched; 25 used term       25 of 25 speakers searched; 23 used term:
                                                  2,4..25

o: pipiin 'white'                             +: maman 'red/?yellow'
         1         2         3         4                1         2         3         4
   01234567890123456789012345678901234567890      01234567890123456789012345678901234567890
A  ----------------------------------------- A   A                                          A
B  --.--.......  ..  ....  ...-...-.--- B   B                                          B
C  .                        ...  ..-.-.   C   C  -+++--.---  .                . ----     C
D  .                          .. .-.  . D   D  #+#++##+.-.                  +-+#++     D
E                                   .  . E   E  ######-+-.                  ..+#####    E
F                                       F   F  ######+-.  .                 . +#####    F
G                                       G   G  #####--.                    .-+#####    G
H                                       H   H  ####---.                    +++#####    H
I                                       I   I  +++-..                      .....----   I
J                                       J   J                                          J

   25 of 25 speakers searched; 21 used term:      25 of 25 speakers searched; 25 used term
   1..3,6..10,12,14..25

*: ŋaankal 'green'                            |: diyun 'yellow'
         1         2         3         4                1         2         3         4
   01234567890123456789012345678901234567890      01234567890123456789012345678901234567890
A                                          A   A                                          A
B                                          B   B                 ..-                     .  B
C             -.-..+..  .                   C   C  . .     -.++-+-.. ..          .....-.    C
D          ..++-#---.-..-.                  D   D          .--+..                   ..     D
E          ....-+--+++--.+... ...           E   E          . ...-                       .   E
F          --.---------...--.               F   F                                          F
G          .  ---.--+....  ...              G   G                                          G
H              .......  .                   H   H                                          H
I                                          I   I                                          I
J                                          J   J                                          J

   25 of 25 speakers searched; 19 used term:      25 of 25 speakers searched; 9 used term:
   2..10,12..15,17,20..24                        5..8,10,11,19,21,24
```

Stage III.Bk/G/Bu

$$\begin{bmatrix} W \\ R \\ Y \\ Bk/G/Bu \end{bmatrix}$$

Kwerba (Irian Jaya, Indonesia; Trans-New Guinea [J. and S. De Vries])

Basic stage	→ III.Bk/G/Bu
Derived categories	none
Heterogeneous categories	none

Kwerba, a Trans-New-Guinea language, is spoken by some 1,500 people in the Upper Tor River area of Irian Jaya, Indonesia (western half of the island of New Guinea). It typifies an early Stage III.$_{Bk/G/Bu}$ system. In this language, an expression is attested for the composite category Bk/G/Bu, words for W and R are well established, and a term for Y, *kainanesɛnum,* has begun to emerge. Sixteen of the twenty-five speakers interviewed use this term, and the category appears to be well on its way to becoming fully established for the language as a whole.

Basic Color Terms

Term	Gloss	Symbol	Term	Gloss	Symbol
icɛm	'black/green/blue'	•	*nokonim*	'red'	+
əsiram (*əhɛrɛm, ərɛm*)*	'white'	o	*kainanesɛnum*	'yellow'	|

* Terms in parentheses are synonyms for *əsiram* .

Aggregate Naming Arrays

```
        Modal Agreement Level              30% Agreement Level,  8 of 25 speakers
          1         2         3         4            1         2         3         4
  0123456789012345678901234567890         0123456789012345678901234567890
A ooooooooooooooooooooooooooooooooooooooo A    A ooooooooooooooooooooooooooooooooooooooo A
B oooooooooooooooooooooooooooooooooooooooo B   B ooooooooooooooooooooooooooooooooooooooo B
C o++o+oo||||lo|ooooooooooooooooooo++++ C       C o++o+o |||||  lo oooooooooooooooooo++++ C
D o++++++++||||lol••••••••ooo•••ooooooo+++++ D  D o+++++++||||lol •• •• oo••ooooooo+++++ D
E •++++++++l•||•loo••∘••••••••o••••∘oooo++++++ E E •+++++++  ||•lo •••o•••• •• ••••ooo++++++ E
F •++++++++••••••••∘•••••••••••••••••••++++++ F  F •+++++++••••••••∘•••••••••••••••••••++++++ F
G •+++++••••••••••••••••••••••••••••••+++++++ G   G •+++++••••••••••••••••••••••••••••••+++++++ G
H •+++++••••••••••••••••••••••••••••••+++++++ H   H •+++++••••••••••••••••••••••••••••••+++++++ H
I •++++••••••••••••••••••••••••••••••+++++ I      I •++++••••••••••••••••••••••••••••••+++++ I
J •••••••••••••••••••••••••••••••••••••••• J      J •••••••••••••••••••••••••••••••••••••• J
```

```
      70% Agreement Level, 18 of 25 speakers        100% Agreement Level, 25 of 25 speakers
        1         2         3         4               1         2         3         4
  0123456789012345678901234567890                 0123456789012345678901234567890
A                                        A      A                                        A
B   o  o  o        oo oooooo o  ooo o oooo B     B                                        B
C o                      o              C        C                                        C
D  +++++                      +++++ D            D    +                              D
E  ++++++                     ++++++ E           E  +                          + +  E
F •++++++            • •       ++++++ F           F + ++                         +  F
G •++++++        ••       •• ••• ••• ++++++ G     G  ++                       + +  G
H •++++++  •••••••••••  •••••••••••• +++++++ H    H +++                        +  H
I •+++ •••••• ••••••• •••••••••••• ++++ I         I                                        I
J •••••••••••••••••••••••••••••••••• J            J                                        J
```

Term Maps

(# = 81-100% agreement, + = 61-80 % agreement, - = 41-60% agreement, . = 21-40% agreement)

```
•: icɛm 'black/green/blue'                  o: ɔsiram 'white'
           1         2         3         4             1         2         3         4
    0123456789012345678901234567890123456789012     0123456789012345678901234567890123456789012
A                                             A     A  +++++++++++++++++++++++++++++++++++++++  A
B                                             B     B  +++++++++++-----+++++++++#+++++++++#+++++  B
C                . . . .                      C     C  +.....-.  ..... -.-.--+--+++++--+++++-+....  C
D   .               ..-.-.........   .        D     D  - .          .. ...  ..............-.---+.   D
E   -           . . .-.---.,--.---+...         E     E        .........  .  ....  .  ...-...       E
F   +         .+.-+---.-+-++++-+-+++#+---      F     F                                             F
G   #          --+++#++-++---+++++#++++#++     G     G        . .   .                              G
H   #         .+++#+####+#+++#+++##+##++-      H     H        .                                    H
I   #        -#####+##++#++#-#+##+##+##+---  . I     I             .                               I
J   #############################################  J  J                                            J
                                                   I
25 of 25 speakers searched; 25 used term           25 of 25 speakers searched; 24 used term:
                                                   1..9,11..25
```

```
+: nokonim 'red'                            I: kainanesɛnum 'yellow'
           1         2         3         4             1         2         3         4
    0123456789012345678901234567890123456789012     0123456789012345678901234567890123456789012
A                                             A     A                                             A
B                                             B     B                  ....                       B
C   -++.-.  . .                    . ---+  C        C         . ..+++#+--.                         C
D   ++##++-                        -####+  D        D         . --++++-..                          D
E   ######-.                      .-+#####  E       E            --.+-.+.                          E
F   #####+-                      .-#####  F         F             .- ..                            F
G   #####  .                    .+######  G         G                                             G
H   ####+                       .+######  H         H                                             H
I   ###-                        ..- #+##  I         I                                             I
J                                           J       J                                             J

25 of 25 speakers searched; 25 used term           25 of 25 speakers searched;16 used term:
                                                   1,2,4..6,8..13,15,17,18,23,24
```

Stage IV.G/Bu

$$\begin{bmatrix} W \\ R \\ Y \\ G/Bu \\ Bk \end{bmatrix}$$

Sirionó (Bolivia; Tupí [P. and A. Priest])

Basic stage	IV.G/Bu
Derived categories	none
Heterogeneous categories	none

Sirionó is a Tupian language spoken by approximately 500 individuals in the eastern Beni and northwestern Santa Cruz departments of the Bolivian lowlands. It is classified as Stage IV.G/Bu. The language shows well-established terms for W, R, Y, G/Bu, Bk. The G/Bu composite category is focused in blue.

Basic Color Terms

Term	Gloss	Symbol	Term	Gloss	Symbol
erondei	'black'	•	*echo*	'yellow'	|
eshĩ	'white'	o	*eruba*	'green/blue'	=
eirẽi	'red'	+			

Aggregate Naming Arrays

```
        Modal Agreement Level                      30% Agreement Level,  8 of 24 speakers
        1         2         3         4            1         2         3         4
  01234567890123456789012345678901234567890        01234567890123456789012345678901234567890
A ooooooooooooooooooooooooooooooooooooooooo A    A ooooooooooooooooooooooooooooooooooooooooo A
B ooooooooooo|||||ooooooooooooooooooooooooo B    B ooooooooooo|||||ooooooooooooooooooooooooo B
C o|++++||||||||||||o=o==o=o=oo=oooooo|o++|+ C    C o|++++||||||||||| =o= o o=oo=oooooo|o++|+ C
D o++++||||||||||||||===============oooo+++++ D    D o++++|||||||||||||===============oooo +++++ D
E •+++++|||||||||||===================+++++++ E    E •+++++|||||||||||===================+++++++ E
F •++++++|||||||||===================++++++ F    F •++++++||||| |||===================++++++ F
G •+++++•••••••||===================+++++ G    G •+++++ ••••••||===================+++++ G
H •+++•••••••••===================+++++++ H    H •+++•••••••••===================+++++++ H
I •+++•••••••••=•••••••••====•=•••••••+ I    I •+++•••••••••===•••••••••====• • +++ I
J •••••••••••••••••••••••••••••••••••••••• J    J •••••••••••••••••••••••••••••••••••••••• J


        70% Agreement Level, 17 of 24 speakers           100% Agreement Level, 24 of 24 informants
        1         2         3         4            1         2         3         4
  01234567890123456789012345678901234567890        01234567890123456789012345678901234567890
A ooooooooooooooooooooooooooooooooooooooooo A    A ooooooooooooooooooooooooooooooooooooooooo A
B oooooooo      oooo o ooooooooooooooooooo B    B o                           o           B
C o         |||||||||         ooo          C    C                                         C
D o+ +   |||||||||     == = =      + +    D    D                                         D
E ++++++  |||| ||    ==== ====     +++++   E    E                                         E
F •++++++            =  ====        ++++  F    F    +                          ++       F
G •++++          =  = == ===       +++++  G    G ++                            ++      G
H •++++  • •••••               ++++   H    H  +                            +       H
I •++  •••••••••                    +   I    I                                         I
J ••••••••••••••••••••••••••••••••••••••••• J    J                                         J
```

Term Maps

(# = 81-100% agreement, + = 61-80 % agreement, - = 41-60% agreement, . = 21-40% agreement)

```
•: erondei 'black'                          o: eshi 'white'
              1         2         3         4              1         2         3         4
    0123456789012345678901234567890123456789    0123456789012345678901234567890123456789
A                                         A    A ########################################## A
B                                         B    B ##+##+####+... .+#++++-#+##+#############  B
C                                         C    C #               . . .- ---+-+-###+ .      C
D                                         D    D +                     . .. --..          D
E -              .                  .     E    E ..                                        E
F +          .. ...                       F    F  .                                        F
G #        .++----.          . .     .    G    G                                           G
H #      .++-#####+-.       ...... .. .   H    H                                           H
I #   ..-+###+#####+-- -.+-++-+-+-- .. ... I   I                                           I
J ########################################## J   J                                           J

24 of 24 speakers searched; 24 used term        24 of 24 speakers searched; 24 used term

+: eirei 'red'                              l: echo 'yellow'
              1         2         3         4              1         2         3         4
    0123456789012345678901234567890123456789    0123456789012345678901234567890123456789
A                                         A    A                                           A
B                                         B    B       . .+-++-                            B
C  .--.-                       ..--.-  C    C  .. ..-#######+--.. ..  .        ....  C
D ++#-.                       .+++-  D    D    .-+#####+++--..           .  .  D
E +####.                   ..-+####  E    E      .+++#-.++...              E
F ####+-.                   -+####  F    F       .------...              F
G ####-                     .++####  G    G      .  . --.-                 G
H ####.                     ---#### H    H                                 H
I +-+.                       . .--+. I    I                                 I
J                                         J    J                                           J

24 of 24 speakers searched; 24 used term        24 of 24 speakers searched; 24 used term

                    =: eruba 'green/blue'
                              1         2         3         4
                    0123456789012345678901234567890123456789
                  A                                         A
                  B                  ..                     B
                  C              ...-.-....-.. .            C
                  D           ..-.+-++--#-+++--...          D
                  E         ..  ----+++#-++##+--.           E
                  F         .....-+---+++#+#+#+--..         F
                  G         .----+---+++++##+++..          G
                  H         ..---+--.++-+-++++--...         H
                  I      ..        ..-... ....--+-..... . . I
                  J                                         J

                    24 of 24 speakers searched; 24 used term
```

Stage IV.Bk/Bu

$$\begin{bmatrix} W \\ R \\ Y \\ G \\ Bk/Bu \end{bmatrix}$$

Martu-Wangka (Australia; Pama-Nyungan [J. and M. Marsh])

Basic stage	IV.Bk/Bu
Derived categories	none
Heterogeneous categories	peripheral red?

Martu-Wangka is an Australian (Pama-Nyungan) language spoken
by about 820 people in the Jigalong area of Western Australia. It is classified in the WCS as Stage IV.$_{Bk/Bu}$, with terms for W, R, Y, G, and a composite color category encompassing black and blue. At the 30% level
of agreement, *parnaly-parnaly*, a term restricted in its distribution to
brownish reds, is used by fifteen speakers. According to the field linguists for Martu-Wangka, *parna* is the word for "earth, ground, sand"
and "probably does not qualify as a 'basic' color term, as it would
appear to mean 'earth-like'." The term map for *parnaly-parnaly*, however, suggests a possible meaning of 'peripheral red.' Although the
judgment of the field linguists that *parnaly-parnaly* should not be considered a basic color term is probably deserving of acceptance, we have
included the discussion of this term for completeness and to illustrate
the kind of borderline cases that can arise in analyzing the WCS data.

Martu-Wangka color terms commonly exhibit reduplication and
appear to be derived from verbs or nouns, e.g. *maru-maru* "black, blue"
< *maru* "to darken or become black"; *miji-miji* "red" < *miji* "blood";
yukuri-yukuri "green" < *yukuri* "grass." The unreduplicated term
karntawarra is the word for "yellow ochre."

Basic Color Terms

Term	Gloss	Symbol	Term	Gloss	Symbol
maru-maru	'black/blue'	•	*karntawarra*	'yellow'	|
piila-piila/piily-piily/ pily-pily/pilya-pilya/ pira-pira/piirl-piirl/ piily/pilya/pirilypa/ pirilyi/pirly	'white'	○	*yukuri-yukuri, yakuripiti*	'green'	*
miji-miji	'red'	+	*parnaly-parnaly, pama*	'peripheral red'?	~

Aggregate Naming Arrays

```
            Modal Agreement Level                           30% Agreement Level,  8 of 25 speakers
           1         2         3         4                          1         2         3         4
      01234567890123456789012345678901234567890         01234567890123456789012345678901234567890
  A oooooooooooooooooooooooooooooooooooooooooo A     A oooooooooooooooooooooooooooooooooooooooooo A
  B ooooooooooo||**ooooooooooooooooooooooooooo B     B ooooooooooo|| *ooooooooooooooooooooooooooo B
  C o+++++++|||||***********oooooooooo+++++++ C      C o+++ + |||||***********  ooooooooo   +++++ C
  D o+++++|||||***********...*.......ooo+++++++ D    D o+++++|||||***********..  .... oo+++++++ D
  E •++++++||||***********...........+++++++++ E     E •++++++ |  |***********........ +++++++ E
  F •+++++~~~•~•***********.........+++++++++ F      F •+++++~~  ***********...........+++++++ F
  G •+++++~+~••••***********......++++++++++ G       G •+++++~ ~••••*...••••*............ +++++++ G
  H •++++~•••••••••••••••••**•••••••••++++++++ H     H •++++~•••••••••••••••***•••••••••••++++++ H
  I •+++++••••••••••••••••••••••••••••••+++++ I      I •+++++••••••••••••••••••••••••••••••+++++ I
  J ••••••••••••••••••••••••••••••••••••••••• J      J ••••••••••••••••••••••••••••••••••••••••• J
```

```
            70% Agreement Level, 18 of 25 speakers            100% Agreement Level, 25 of 25 speakers
           1         2         3         4                          1         2         3         4
      01234567890123456789012345678901234567890         01234567890123456789012345678901234567890
  A                                          A       A                                          A
  B                                          B       B                                          B
  C               * ****                     C       C                                          C
  D               **********          ++     D       D                                          D
  E  +++          *********       +  +++      E       E                                          E
  F  ++++         *********      ..  +++++    F       F                                          F
  G •++++          ******      . .   ++++++   G       G  +                                       G
  H •+ ++        ••••••      •••••••• •  ++++  H       H                                          H
  I •     •••••••••••••••••••••••••••          I      I                                          I
  J ••••••••••••••••••••••••••••••••••••••••• J       J                                          J
```

Term Maps*

(# = 81-100% agreement, + = 61-80 % agreement, - = 41-60% agreement, . = 21-40% agreement)

* A single linguistic variant for each basic category is shown in the arrays

```
•: maru-maru 'black/blue'                            o: piila-piila 'white'
           1         2         3         4                      1         2         3         4
  0123456789012345678901234567890123456789              0123456789012345678901234567890123456789
A                                            A       A ######################################### A
B                                            B       B +++++-++-+ .. -+-+-++-+-++-+++++++-++-+++ B
C                      . ...    ..           C       C -. ..#.....       .- .------+-+...    . C
D                     ..-.-.-.               D       D -.                .     ..... ...      . D
E +                 ...--.--++-              E       E                      . ..... ..          E
F -           . ...   .--.-+++++++-.          F       F .                         .             F
G +          ...--.-.--  ......-++++++++++.   G       G                                         G
H #          .--#+###+-+-.,--+++##++#+++-.    H       H                                         H
I #      .-+################+####+-+.-.. ... I       I                                         I
J ######################################## J       J                                         J

25 of 25 speakers searched; 25 used term             25 of 25 speakers searched; 21 used term:
                                                     1..5,7..9,11..18,20..23,25
```

```
+: miji-miji 'red'                                   l: karntawarra 'yellow'
           1         2         3         4                      1         2         3         4
  0123456789012345678901234567890123456789              0123456789012345678901234567890123456789
A                                            A       A                                         A
B                                            B       B                                         B
C  -.....              ...---- C       C            ---.                                       C
D +----.             ..--+++- D       D            -+#--.                                      D
E #+++++-             .+-+++#+-+ E       E          -#+++-                                      E
F ####-  .            ---++#### F       F           ----                                       F
G ###+- .             .-++#+### G       G          ..                                          G
H #+#+.               .--+++##+ H       H                                                      H
I ----.               . -......-. I     I                                                      I
J                                            J       J                                         J

25 of 25 speakers searched; 25 used term             25 of 25 speakers searched; 17 used term:
                                                     1,3..5,7..9,12,13,15,16,18..20,22,24,25
```

```
*: yukuri-yukuri 'green'                             ~: parnaly-parnaly 'peripheral red'?
           1         2         3         4                      1         2         3         4
  0123456789012345678901234567890123456789              0123456789012345678901234567890123456789
A                                            A       A                                         A
B        ..-.                                 B       B                                         B
C      ..-+#+####++-.-                        C       C . .-.-.                   ...           C
D      .+##########.                          D       D .....                            .     D
E      .-+#########++-.                       E       E  . .-..                          .     E
F      --+######+#-..                         F       F   .#+--.                              F
G      ....-###++++.                          G       G  .-#.+-...                            G
H         -.++-.,.                            H       H  .. ---+..  .                         H
I                                             I       I  ...                                  I
J                                             J       J                                         J

25 of 25 speakers searched; 23 used term:            25 of 25 speakers searched; 15 used term:
1..5,7..13,15..25                                    1..3,5,7,9,11..13,15,16,21,23..25
```

Stage V

$$\begin{bmatrix} W \\ R \\ Y \\ G \\ Bu \\ Bk \end{bmatrix}$$

Kalam (Papua New Guinea; Trans-New Guinea [L. Scholz])

Basic stage	V
Derived categories	none
Heterogeneous categories	none

Kalam is a Trans-New-Guinea language spoken by 15,000 people in the Hagen district of the Western New Guinea Highlands. It is classified as a Stage V system, with distinct terms for each of the six fundamental categories, W, R, Y, G, Bu, and Bk. At the modal level of agreement, a single purple chip is given the name *anje ŋ-ay*. Eight of the twenty-five Kalam collaborators use this term; in all cases it has an uneven, roughly 'peripheral red' distribution. *Anje ŋ-ay* is probably best not considered a basic color term of Kalam.

Basic Color Terms

Term	Gloss	Symbol	Term	Gloss	Symbol
mosimb	'black'	•	*walin*	'yellow'	l
tund	'white'	o	*minj-kimemb*	'green'	*
likañ	'red'	+	*muk*	'blue'	-

Aggregate Naming Arrays

```
       Modal Agreement Level                          30% Agreement Level,  8 of 25 speakers
        1         2         3         4                 1         2         3         4
   0123456789012345678901234567890                 0123456789012345678901234567890
A  ooooooooooooooooooooooooooooooo  A           A  ooooooooooooooooooooooooooooooo  A
B  ooooooooooollllloooooooooooooooooooooo  B     B  ooooooooooollllloooooooooooooooooooooo  B
C  ollllllllllllllllll*********ooooooooooo+oo+  C C  ol   llllllllllll*********ooooooooooo       C
D  o+l+llllllllllll********-**-*--ooooo*+++++  D D  o+ +lllllllllllll********-**-*--ooooo   +++  D
E  •+++++llllllllll**********---------o-++++++  E E  +++++llllllll**********--------   ++++++  E
F  o+++++llllllll**********-----------++++++  F  F  o+++++ llllll**********--------- -++++++  F
G  •+++++llll••ll•**********-----------*++++++  G G  •+++++ l •l *********----------  ++++++  G
H  •++++•••••••••*********-----------+++++++  H  H  •++++••• •••*********----------  +++++++  H
I  •+++++•••••••••*****•*-----------++G++++  I   I  +++++ •••••••••*** * *-----------  + ++++  I
J  •••••••••••••••••••••••••••••••••••••  J      J  •••••••••••••••••••••••••••••••••••••  J


       70% Agreement Level, 18 of 25 speakers             100% Agreement Level, 25 of 25 speakers
        1         2         3         4                 1         2         3         4
   0123456789012345678901234567890                 0123456789012345678901234567890
A  ooooooooooooooooooooooooooooooo  A           A                                         A
B  ooooooooooollllll ooo oo ooooooooooooooo  B  B                                         B
C  o        lllllll       *    o  oooooo o  C   C  o                                      C
D  o        lllllll      **          o      D   D                                         D
E  ++ +    llllll     *              ++  E      E                                         E
F  +++             *         - ----      +++ F  F                                         F
G  + ++             ** *      -----      +++ G  G                                         G
H  ++++                       - ----    +++++ H  H                                         H
I  +++                         ----      ++ I   I                                         I
J                                          J      J                                         J
```

Term Maps
(# = 81-100% agreement, + = 61-80 % agreement, - = 41-60% agreement, . = 21-40% agreement)

```
•: mosimb 'black'                              o: tund 'white'

          1         2         3         4                 1         2         3         4
  0123456789012345678901234567890123456789       0123456789012345678901234567890123456789
A                                         A    A ######################################### A
B                                         B    B #####+##++    -+##++++################### B
C                                         C    C #.   ...         . .-#++#+####-+ ..       C
D                          .              D    D +                        -+-#+             D
E .                                       E    E .                          . .            E
F .            .. .                       F    F -                                         F
G +          ...-...                      G    G                                           G
H -        ---.-.----.                    H    H                                           H
I -      .--+--+-+--.- ... .-.. .         I    I                                           I
J ######################################### J  J                                           J

25 of 25 speakers searched; 18 used term:      25 of 25 speakers searched; 25 used term
1..6,8..11,14,16..19,21,23,24
```

```
+: likañ 'red'                                 |: walin 'yellow'

          1         2         3         4                 1         2         3         4
  0123456789012345678901234567890123456789       0123456789012345678901234567890123456789
A                                         A    A                                           A
B                                         B    B        ..####-.                           B
C   ..                          . . C           C   ....--+#####++- .                  .. C
D - -.                         .-.-. D          D   . .-#######+-                           D
E #++#+.                      -.+++# E          E       .#####+-.                          E
F ###++.                      -++##+ F          F       .---+-..                          F
G #+##+                      ..+++#+# G         G       . ... .                           G
H ####.                      --+###+ H          H                                          H
I #+#-                       .. ++## I          I                                          I
J                                         J    J                                           J

25 of 25 speakers searched; 23 used term:      25 of 25 speakers searched; 24 used term:
1..18,20..23,25                                 1..6,8..25
```

```
*: minj-kimemb 'green'                         -: muk 'blue'

          1         2         3         4                 1         2         3         4
  0123456789012345678901234567890123456789       0123456789012345678901234567890123456789
A                                         A    A                                           A
B                                         B    B                                           B
C            ---++---+.                   C    C                    .                      C
D          ..-++++----.-..                D    D                ..-.-+.+-.                  D
E        .-+++-++.--....      .           E    E              .......---+#++...             E
F      ...++#++-+-+-. .                   F    F              ......-++++###+-.-            F
G        .-+++#+++-...         .          G    G              ... ----++###++..             G
H       ..-++-+--.-..                     H    H              .. ..-++#++#+#+-              H
I          .-.-.-  ...                    I    I          .     .. ...-.++++##+-..          I
J                                         J    J                                           J

25 of 25 speakers searched; 25 used term      25 of 25 speakers searched; 25 used term
```

Notes

1 Maffi (1991) provides relevant bibliography.

2 Several studies in addition to Rosch's are cited in Kay (1975) as supporting the idea of color term evolution involving category boundaries as well as foci.

3 A fuzzy set is a function from a (standard) set of objects to a real interval, conventionally the interval between zero and unity inclusive.

4 These are called "fundamental neural response categories" in the K&McD model. At the time, the opponent hue primaries of Hering (red, yellow, green, blue) were considered by vision researchers to benefit from direct neurophysiological confirmation in the response characteristics of certain LGN cells of the rhesus macaque (De Valois, Abramov, and Jacobs 1966). This simple model of the neurological substrate for the perceptual phenomena of color categorization (e.g. Sternheim and Boynton 1966, Wooten 1970) has more recently been replaced by more complex models, based on spatial as well as spectral opponency, by interaction within cells of color and luminance information, and on the behavior of a wider range of neural structures, including the cones, the horizontal cells, and the bi-polar and ganglion cells (e.g. De Valois and De Valois 1996). It is now recognized that the 1966 model of De Valois *et al.* failed to account for as wide a range of the perceptual phenomena of color as was originally thought. The validity of the six perceptually salient Hering primaries retains broad consensus in the vision research community, as does the conviction that a fully satisfying neurophysiological derivation must eventually be forthcoming (Abramov this volume).

Jameson and D'Andrade (this volume, hereafter J&D) propose to drive a further wedge between the Hering primaries and their neurophysiological substrate. J&D argue, with regard to the psychophysical level, that neither cancellation experiments nor after-image facts support perceptually unique red, green, yellow, and blue as determinants of the axes of chromatic opponency. At the physiological level, they point to Abramov and Gordon's (1994) observation that the crossover points of recorded LGN cells do not correspond well to the phenomenal unique hue points, but rather suggest axes like bright red/greenish blue and yellow-green/dark purple (although this latter point is effectively answered by De Valois and De Valois 1993, which J&D also cite).

J&D locate the Hering primaries at the level of a conceptual (or semantic) "color space", a higher-level cognitive object, whose properties are inferred from the application of multidimensional scaling techniques to judged similarities among pairs of colors and whose relation to the psychophysics of color J&D acknowledge to be uncertain. Assuming, for the sake of brevity, that J&D are correct in all of this, the Hering primaries are deprived of significant psychophysical support.

Nevertheless, J&D accept the phenomenal reality of the Hering primaries. Indeed, they attempt to provide for them a different psychological substrate than that of standard opponent theory. The Hering primaries, whatever perceptual rationale they are finally accorded, remain a major interface between color vision and the semantics of color.

In unpublished work, Kemmerer (1995) argues that color *categories* cannot be represented at the ganglion/LGN level. Color constancy effects (modeled by Land, e.g. 1974) show that color categorization requires comparison of signals arising at points in the retina further separated than the diameter of the largest area represented by a ganglion or LGN cell. Based on the work of Zeki (most recently, 1993) and others, Kemmerer proposes a cortical model of the B&K findings. This model posits comparison and recoding of color signals at a series of cortical levels, including the V1, V2, V4 and TO areas.

5 A derived category is defined as twice the fuzzy intersection (that is, twice the minimum) of the fuzzy categories from which it is derived. Consider the case of red, yellow, and the derived category, orange. It follows from the fuzzy set implementation of the opponent process model that the red function and the yellow function sum to unity throughout the range in which they are both non-zero. The derived category, orange, has a fuzzy set function that rises from zero at the red and yellow unique hue points to unity at the point at which the red and yellow fuzzy categories both have ordinates of .5. This procedure expresses formally the observations (a) that the more equal the mixture of red and yellow perceived in a color, the more orange that color appears, and (b) that a color that consists perceptually of an equal (non-zero) mixture of red and yellow is as orange as you can get.

6 Funded by NSF grants BNS 76–14153, BNS 78–18303, BNS 80–06802, and SBR 9419702; also supported by the Summer Institute of Linguistics (SIL), the Anthropology and Linguistics Departments and the Institute of Cognitive Studies at University of California at Berkeley, and the International Computer Science Institute, Berkeley, California. All these sources of support are gratefully acknowledged.

7 Scientific challenges such as these merit serious attention. Epistemological and/or deontological critiques have also appeared, which empirical research is not equipped to address. For example, Saunders and van Brakel consider K&McD's "reductionist argument" according to which "six basic or atomic color categories … can be reduced to Fundamental Neural Response categories," as invalidated by the prior epistemological tenet that " there is no privileged discourse in which what is true is independent of our choices, hopes, and fears" (Saunders and van Brakel 1994: 8). The Western scientific tradition presupposes the existence of an objective world independent of human choices, hopes or fears. To suppose that the world exists independent of human sentiments is not, of course, to conclude that unbiased construals of that world are easy to achieve or that science provides a magic formula for avoiding bias. The empirical researcher believes that one can reduce (not eliminate) bias through the disciplined application of procedures of observation and inference designed specifically with the reduction of bias as their object and trusts that the exercise of this discipline can sometimes result in one type of understanding: scientific understanding. Saunders and van Brakel are not atypical of those post-modernists who leap from the observation that the attainment of scientific understanding is not trivial to the conclusion that it is not possible. We assume, contrariwise, that the existence of science provides strong evidence of its possibility. A comprehensive evaluation of the post-modern critique of research on color naming is beyond the scope of this chapter. (See Hardin 1993 and Stanlaw 1993 for careful appraisals of several points.)

8 See K&McD: 639. B&K and Kay (1975) had earlier noted a few exceptions to this rule with regard to grey and brown, but these cases were left unexplained by the generalizations embodied in the evolutionary sequence.

9 Figures 2.1 and 2.2 contain more information than is conveniently explained at their first introduction. All the features in the Figures will be fully explained in due course. The reader's patience is requested for the moment.

10 Column o presents the neutral white-to-black sequence.

11 All forty entries of row A denote a single pure white chip and all of row J a single pure black chip.

12 For example, if at least 81% of the speakers who name any chip with the term being mapped name chip *c* with that term, then *c* receives "#". If 61–80% of the speakers who name any chip with the term being mapped name

chip *c* with that term, then *c* receives " + ". If 41–60% of the speakers who name any chip with the term being mapped name chip *c* with that term, then *c* receives "–". And so on, as indicated in the legend above the term maps in part 2 of Figure 2.2.

13 See section commencing on p. 23 for details on maps.

14 Names in square brackets following a language name indicate the field linguist(s) who gathered data on that language for the WCS. We acknowledge with gratitude the work, not only of the SIL field linguists whose names appear here, but also of each of the over 100 such persons contributing to this study.

15 This is supported by their almost identical distributions in their respective term maps. Therefore, in the aggregate naming arrays, they are assigned the same symbol: [|].

16 MacLaury (1986) was the first to suggest this.

17 Heterogeneous categories are discussed below.

18 The use of the word "channel" here is motivated by the fact that the grammar of English requires that *some* noun be employed and a choice like "what's-its-name" or "thingamabob" could be distracting. In particular, no pretense of denoting a neurological entity is intended.

19 Some caveats apply. First, the reader is reminded that we have not yet introduced consideration of languages containing words for yellow/green categories (cf. Figure 2.4). Secondly, the WCS sample contains no examples of Stage I systems, although their existence is documented elsewhere, and therefore noted in Figure 2.3. Thirdly, our initial screening of the WCS sample discloses no unequivocal example of type III.Bk/Bu (but cf. description of Konkomba on pp. 41f.), although it indicates four languages at Stage IV with W, R, Y, G, and Bk/Bu, and three yellow/green languages at Stage III with W, R, Y/G, and Bk/Bu (see Figure 2.4).

20 That is, there are no evident generalizations, comparable to those summarized in Table 2.1, regarding yellow/green transitions.

21 Further analysis may show the peripheral red category to describe an "unbroken" region of the surface of the color solid in the sense that the surface of a lake with an island may be said to present an unbroken expanse of water. Thus the heterogeneous categories may turn out to be less bizarre than they appear at first sight.

22 The format described here reflects our current thinking on the monograph. These decisions are subject to revision as the work proceeds.

23 More information on speakers than this was gathered. The decision to restrict published information on individual speakers to age and sex stems from our initial evaluation of space constraints.

24 These are spelled out in some detail in KBM.

25 Consideration of the individual speaker data may also enter into this analysis.

26 The aggregate naming arrays also appear in the volume II entries, as illustrated in Figure 2.1 for Buglere. This redundancy has been thought desirable to make each volume relatively self-contained.

27 Here and in the following examples, geo-demographic data on individual languages, as well as their language family ascriptions, are derived from Grimes (1992).

28 In the case of the W category, this applies to the combined data for the terms *pipin* and *pipiin*, which are analyzed as variants and given the same symbol "o" in the aggregate naming arrays. The separate term maps for *pipin* and *pipiin* support this analysis by showing their overlapping distribution.

References

Abramov, I., and J. Gordon 1994. Color appearance: on seeing red – or yellow, or green, or blue. *Annual Review of Psychology* 45: 451–485.

Berlin, B., and P. Kay 1969. *Basic Color Terms: Their Universality and Evolution*. Berkeley and Los Angeles: University of California Press. 1st Paperback edn 1991, with a bibliography by Luisa Maffi.

De Valois, R. L., and K. K. De Valois 1993. A multi-stage color model. *Vision Research* 33(8): 1053–1065.
      1996. A three-stage color model—comment. *Vision Research* 36: 833–836.

De Valois, R. L., I. Abramov, and G. H. Jacobs 1966. Analysis of response patterns of LGN cells. *Journal of the Optical Society of America* 56: 966–977.

Greenfield, P. J. 1987. What is grey, brown, pink, and sometimes purple: the range of "wild-card" color terms. *American Anthropologist* 88: 908–916.

Grimes, B. (ed.) 1992. *Ethnologue. Languages of the World.* 12th edn. Dallas: Summer Institute of Linguistics.

Hardin, C. L. 1993. Van Brakel and the not-so-naked emperor. *British Journal for the Philosophy of Science* 44(1): 137–150; 44(2): 377 [correction].

Heider, E. R. 1972a. Universals in color naming and memory. *Journal of Experimental Psychology* 93(1): 10–20.

1972b. Probabilities, sampling and ethnographic method: the case of Dani colour names. *Man* 7(3): 448–466.

Hering, Ewald 1964 [1920]. *Outlines of a Theory of the Light Sense*. Cambridge, MA: Harvard University Press.

Kay, P. 1975. Synchronic variability and diachronic change in basic color terms. *Language and Society* 4: 257–270.

Kay, P., and C. K. McDaniel 1978. The linguistic significance of the meanings of basic color terms. *Language* 54(3): 610–646.

Kay, P., B. Berlin, and W. R. Merrifield 1991. Biocultural implications of systems of color naming. *Journal of Linguistic Anthropology* 1(1): 12–25.

Kemmerer, D.L. 1995. *Towards a Cognitive Neuroscience Analysis of the Meanings of Basic Color Terms.* Cognitive Science Technical Report 95–7. Buffalo: SUNY.

Land, E. 1974. The retinex theory of color vision. *Proceedings of the Royal Institution of Great Britain* 47: 23–58.

MacLaury, R. E. 1986. Color in Mesoamerica. Vol. I, A theory of composite categorization. Doctoral dissertation. University of California at Berkeley. UMI 8718073
      1987a. Color-category evolution and Shuswap yellow-with-green. *American Anthropologist* 89: 107–124.
      1987b. Coextensive semantic ranges: different names for distinct vantages of one category. In B. Need, E. Schiller, and A. Bosch (eds.), *Papers from the 23rd Annual Regional Meeting of the Chicago Linguistic Society*. Vol. I (pp. 268–282).
      1991. Exotic color categories: linguistic relativity to what extent? *Journal of Linguistic Anthropology* 1(1): 26–51.
      1992. From brightness to hue: an explanatory model of color-category evolution. *Current Anthropology* 33: 137–187.

Maffi, L. 1991. A bibliography of color categorization research 1970–1990. In B. Berlin and P. Kay, *Basic Color Terms: Their Universality and Evolution* (pp. 173–189), 1st paperback edn. Berkeley: University of California Press.

Saunders, B. A. C., and J. van Brakel 1994. Translating the World Color Survey. Ms. (18 pp.).

Stanlaw, J. 1993. Review of B. A. C. Saunders: *The invention of basic colour terms. American Anthropologist* 95(1): 183–184.

Sternheim, C.E., and R. M. Boynton 1966. Uniqueness of perceived hues investigated with a continuous judgmental technique. *Journal of Experimental Psychology* 72(5): 770–776.

Wooten, B. R. 1970. The effects of simultaneous and
    successive chromatic constraint on spectral hue.
    Doctoral dissertation. Brown University, Providence,
    RI.
Zadeh, L. A. 1965. Fuzzy sets. *Information and Control*
    8: 338–353.
Zeki, S. 1993. *A Vision of the Brain*. Cambridge, MA:
    Blackwell Scientific.

II VISUAL PSYCHOLOGISTS

3 The psychophysics of color

Bill Wooten and David L. Miller

General introduction

Properties of visual photopigments

The only way light can influence the eye is by something in the retina absorbing quanta. That something is the visual photopigment found in the outer segment of the photoreceptors, the rods and cones. When a molecule of photopigment absorbs a quantum, the molecule changes its shape. This is the only direct effect that light has on the eye. All subsequent events are chemical reactions that do not require light. One particularly important, but not well understood, reaction is the amplification of this tiny event into a definite change of the receptor's membrane potential, which in turn causes the synaptic activity exciting the next cell in the pathway.

One of the most important characteristics of any photopigment is the relative probability of its absorbing photons from different regions of the spectrum. This aspect of a photopigment may be called its spectral sensitivity – or better yet, its relative spectral absorption. The best-studied photopigment is rhodopsin, the one found in rods. Rhodopsins from different animals have slightly different relative absorption spectra although most have maximal sensitivity around 500 nanometers (nm). Figure 3.1 shows the curve for human rhodopsin. Notice that it is most sensitive at about 500 nm and falls off gradually on either side of that wavelength. For example, the probability of absorbing quanta at 448 or 536 nm is only half of what it is at 500 nm. A good way of thinking about the relative absorption curve is that it describes the relative efficiency with which a pigment can capture quanta.

If an eye has only rods, and if rhodopsin is really the substance that interacts with light, then that eye's spectral sensitivity should correspond with rhodopsin's relative spectral absorption curve. The human eye contains cones as well as rods, but under dim-light condi-

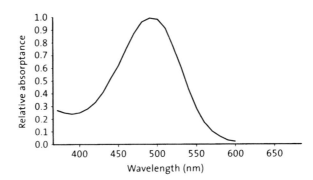

tions only the rod (or scotopic) system functions. Thus, if scotopic spectral sensitivity is determined by measuring (at each wavelength) the minimum amount of light required to just reach visibility, so that the less light required, the higher the sensitivity, it should match the relative spectral absorption curve of rhodopsin. Under the proper conditions and with appropriate corrections for pre-retinal absorptance, the spectral absorption curve and the spectral sensitivity measurements match quite well.

One of the most fundamental aspects of scotopic vision is that chromatic colors are not seen, i.e., under dim-light conditions we experience only shades of gray. The reason for this complete color blindness is inherent in a fundamental property of any given photopigment: the event of quantal fundamental absorption contains no information concerning which spectral (wavelength) region the quantum came from. The photopigment can only signal that a quantum has been absorbed. It cannot signal the wavelength associated with the absorbed quantum. This concept is referred to as the *Law of Univariance* and applies to all known visual photopigments.

An example illustrating the Law of Univariance may help to clarify its implication of total color blindness. Imagine observing two semi-circular patches of light as diagrammed in Figure 3.2. The left patch emits quanta of 500 nm at the rate of 1,000 per second. The right patch emits quanta of 536 nm also at the rate of 1,000 per second. Further assume that the lights stimulate only the scotopic system. Could the two patches be discriminated? One might be inclined to answer "no," on the basis of the Law of Univariance.

Consider, however, the relative spectral absorption of Figure 3.1. The rhodopsin in the rods is only half as efficient at absorbing 536 nm

Figure 3.2 Side-by-side
fields for matching
lights.

500 nm   536 nm

quanta as it is at absorbing 500 nm quanta. Thus, the rods corresponding to the right patch are being stimulated at only half the rate of
those corresponding to the left patch. The result is that the left patch
will appear brighter than the right patch. Therefore, the two halves
can be discriminated purely on the basis of brightness. However, this
effect does not violate the Law of Univariance since the discrimination
has nothing to do with wavelength *per se*. If the quantal emission rate
is doubled on the right side, the two patches will look identical since
the quantal absorption rate of the rods corresponding to the two sides
will be identical. This follows from the Law of Univariance. Thus, for
any single-pigment system, any two lights can be made to appear identical if their intensities are adjusted to give equal quantal absorption
rates. Hence, it can be said that any single-pigment system is totally
color blind in the sense that no wavelength information can be
extracted.

Multiple photopigment systems

If rhodopsin-like photopigments are found in all photoreceptors, and
if they cannot extract any wavelength information from light, then
how is color vision possible? The answer in general terms is quite
simple: have more than one photopigment with differing spectral
absorption curves. The simplest case is, of course, to have just two
photopigments. Consider the example of Figure 3.3, where the relative
spectral absorption curves of two hypothetical photopigments are
shown. The β photopigment is most sensitive at about 540 nm whereas
the γ pigment is most sensitive at about 570 nm. Notice that, roughly
speaking, the γ curve is simply shifted about 30 nm in the longwave
direction compared to the β curve. Thus, the γ pigment is relatively
more sensitive beyond the crossover wavelength of about 550 nm and

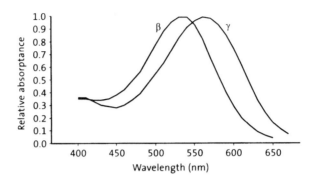

Figure 3.3 Relative spectral absorption for two hypothetical photopigments β and γ with maximum absorption at 540 nm and 570 nm.

vice versa below that point. The result is that almost all wavelengths will tend to give different quantal absorption rates for the two pigments. For example, compare the rates of the two pigments for 500 nm: β is roughly twice as sensitive as γ at the wavelength, so when stimulated by the same light source its quantal absorption rate will be twice as great. The situation is just the reverse for 590 nm: γ absorbs at twice the rate of β.

Consider again the split-field arrangement shown in Figure 3.2. This time the left side emits 500 nm and the right side emits 600 nm. Now assume that there are two classes of receptors being stimulated by each semi-circular field, i.e., one with the β pigment and one with the γ pigment. If each side emits 1,000 quanta per second, what is the quantal absorption ratio of the two pigments? From the discussion above it should be clear that for the receptors corresponding to the left side the ratio of β/γ is 2, whereas for the right side it is 0.5. Furthermore, if the quantal emission rate is doubled for one side, say the left half, the ratio of β/γ absorptions is unaltered, even though the rate in each pigment is doubled. Thus, for a given wavelength the ratio of quantal absorptions is independent of the absolute intensity level. The brain has some way of keeping track of these ratios, and it represents them as particular hue sensations. However, just how particular patterns of neuronal activity result in sensations at all is still a total mystery.

A two-pigment system certainly would provide some wavelength discrimination ability. It would not, however, be as good as that exhibited by normal humans. For example, notice that in the 400–450 nm region the β and γ photopigments have an approximately constant ratio of sensitivities, i.e., the curves are nearly parallel. This means that all of the wavelengths in that region would have the same hue, i.e., they could not be discriminated from one another. For the normal human many of these wavelengths have distinctly different hues, e.g. 450 nm is almost pure blue whereas 410 nm is violet. Another example also clearly demonstrates that such a two-pigment system is inferior to normal human color vision. Referring again to Figure 3.2, assume that the left half emits 550 nm light. (Remember that the two photopigments are equally sensitive at that wavelength.) Now, imagine that the right half emits all wavelengths equally, i.e., there is an equal number of quantal absorptions in each pigment; but, this would also happen with the 550 nm light on the other side. Thus, by adjusting the intensity of either light, it is possible to have an equal quantal absorption ratio for the two pigments on each side. From the Law of Univariance, we know that when such a condition obtains the two lights will look identical, even though their spectral distributions are quite different. So, for an animal with the two pigments in Figure 3.3, a light at a single wavelength of 550 nm will look the same as one containing an equal number of quanta of all wavelengths, providing the intensities are properly adjusted. This is not true for the normal human. More generally, no single wavelength can be made to match an equal-quantum light distribution. From these two examples alone, we can infer that the normal human must have a retina that contains more than just two photopigments.

But how many? Thomas Young, in 1803, pointed out that it could not be a large number because then spatial vision (acuity) would be poor. Each small region of the retina is devoted primarily to spatial resolution. Hence, two small points of light can be discriminated as distinct even if placed quite close together. This would not be possible if each small retinal region contained a large number of receptors (each with a slightly different photopigment) devoted to the analysis of wavelength. (Unless, of course, receptors were infinitely tiny, which they are not.) In reality, receptors serve simultaneously to extract wavelength and spatial information from the retinal image. Therefore, Young reasoned, there must be a compromise between having just two receptor types and having a large number. He guessed that the number is three. That may have been one of the best guesses in the history of science. After almost 175 years of debate, modern methods have verified Young's conjecture. Without detailing the rather complex techniques employed, we now know that the human retina contains three different photopigments that are the basis of color vision. Further, we know that they are found in the outer segments of cone cells and that each cone contains only one of the pigments. In addition, we know that they are similar to rhodopsin, differing primarily only in the relative spectral absorption curve. Two of them are similar to β and γ of Figure 3.3. The third one, α, is shifted to the short-wave region with peak sensitivity at about 420 nm. The relative spectral absorption curves of all three are shown in Figure 3.4.

It should be obvious that a three-pigment system is capable of better wavelength discrimination than a two-pigment system. It also follows that, since there are more ratios involved, such a system allows many more distinct hue sensations. For example, in the 400–450 nm region there are now ratio differences as a result of the differential sensitivity of the α pigment. Recall that in the two-pigment system (β and γ only) wavelengths of 420 and 400 nm were confused because the β/γ ratios were the same. They are also the same in the three-pigment system of Figure 3.4, but the two wavelengths stimulate the α pigment to different degrees: at 400 nm the sensitivity is 0.8, whereas at 430 nm the sensitivity is 0.95. Thus, in this spectral region many of the wavelengths can be discriminated simply by keeping track of the simultaneous relative activities (the ratios of quantal absorptions) of α, β, and γ. Somehow these ratios result in a violet hue for 400 nm and a violet-blue hue for 430 nm. Similar reasoning shows why a 550 nm light will no longer match an equal-quantum light, i.e., the former is not significantly absorbed by α whereas the latter is.

It is important to realize that although a three-pigment system is better than a two-pigment system, even a three-pigment system is not

Figure 3.4 Relative spectral absorption for two hypothetical photopigments β and γ with maximum absorption at 540 nm, with the addition of photopigment α with maximum absorption at 420 nm.

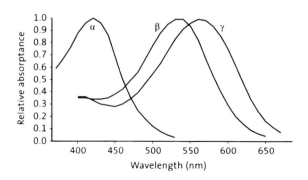

infallible. A perfect color-vision mechanism would allow all lights of different wavelength compositions to be discriminated. Such a system would be possible only if an infinite number of pigments (each with a slightly different spectral absorption curve) could be utilized. This was the very notion that Young correctly rejected, as we have already seen. A three-pigment system can be fooled, but to a lesser degree than a two-pigment scheme. Here is one way. Referring back again to Figure 3.2, assume that the left side emits a light with an equal number of quanta in each wavelength region (an equal-quantum light). It would appear approximately white to a normal (non-color-deficient) observer. Now assume that the right side emits three wavelengths homogeneously, i.e., from each point in the semi-circle. In addition, let the quantal emission rate of each wavelength be independently controllable. If the three wavelengths are properly chosen, it is possible to adjust their intensities so that the mixture looks identical to the light on the left, i.e. white. What must the three wavelengths be? There is some latitude, but the basic idea is that they must be chosen so that, when their intensities are properly adjusted, they activate α, β and γ in exactly the same ratio as the equal-quantum light on the left. Three good choices would be 470, 530, 640 nm. When seen alone these wavelengths appear blue, yellowish green, and yellowish red, respectively, but when mixed in the proper intensities the mixture appears white because the quantal absorption ratios are approximately equal, and that is the brain's code for white.

We have seen how an equal-quantum light may be matched with one composed of a mixture of three wavelengths. Here, then, is a failure of discrimination by a three-pigment system. Other lights may also be confused. As a general rule, for a three-pigment system, any light may be matched with a mixture of the proper intensities of three single wavelengths. A four-pigment system would be better. Why have we not evolved one? The answer would seem to be that, given the spectral reflectances of objects in our environment, what we have is adequate.

Neural processing of wavelength information

Up to this point we have considered in detail only events at the level of the visual photopigments. An understanding of photopigments is fundamental to an appreciation of color vision in general. Indeed, certain aspects of color vision are entirely explainable on the basis of the Law of Univariance and a limited number of photopigments (three). As we have seen, the fact that for the normal, three-pigment system any light can be matched by a suitable mixture of three wavelengths is based entirely on those two concepts. To this extent Young's speculation (later called the *Young–Helmholtz Theory*) has been entirely substantiated. But, there is much more to the phenomenon of color vision than determining which combinations of lights can be mixed to match with others. Psychologists in particular are also interested in the phenomenal aspect of light, i.e., why the different wavelengths look as they do.

The Young–Helmholtz Theory was really two theories. At one level it attempted, successfully, to explain why three wavelengths are needed to match any given light; but the theory was also applied at the perceptual level, i.e., to explain the appearance of different lights. The theory assumes that each receptor type has a simple, direct line to the brain. Further, it assumes that quantal absorptions in each type of receptor directly signal a hue percept. Specifically, Helmholtz believed that activity in what we have called the γ pigment directly results in the sensation of redness. In fact, he called this class of cones the Red (R) receptors. Similarly, he felt that activity in β and α signaled greenness and blueness, respectively: hence Green (G) and Blue (B) receptors. The model asserts that the relative activity in the R, G, and B receptors results in the hue sensation that we associate with the various wavelengths. A light of 465 nm, for example, would result in a blue-green sensation because B and G receptors are stimulated about equally by that wavelength (see Figure 3.4). Yellow comes about by an approximately equal activation of the R and G receptors.

The great nineteenth-century physiologist, Ewald Hering, challenged the Young–Helmholtz Theory's claim to be an adequate model of color perception. He attacked it purely on phenomenological grounds. His main thrust concerned its account of the sensations of blue-green and yellow. He argued that whereas blue-green can be conceived of as a psychological mixture of blueness and greenness, yellow cannot be considered a psychological mixture of redness and greenness. He simply appealed to our common experience in asserting that yellowness is a fundamental sensation that cannot be fractionated into redness and greenness, or into any other components. On this basis, Hering argued that the Young–Helmholtz Theory did not constitute an internally consistent description of color perception.

Hering formulated his own conception, which came to be called the *opponent-process theory*. It was based on the subjective appearance of the spectrum. He asserted that common experience tells us that there are four primary, indivisible hue sensations: blueness, yellowness, greenness, and redness. Further, he said that there are certain relations between these elemental sensations that are self-evident. Blueness, for example, may be perceptually mixed with greenness or redness. Hence, some wavelengths may be purely blue while others may appear green-blue or red-blue. However, blueness and yellowness may not be perceptually mixed, i.e., there is no light that appears yellow-blue. Similarly, greenness may be perceptually mixed with yellowness or blueness, but not with redness. To account for these perceptual relations, Hering hypothesized that yellowness and blueness are opposing manifestations of a single physiological process. In like manner, he said that greenness and redness are opposite aspects of another unitary physiological process. The hue sensation of any light depends upon how it influences the two processes. Figure 3.5 shows Hering's conception of the wavelength dependence of the red–green (R–G) and the yellow–blue (Y–B) processes. Take, for example, the Y–B process. Wavelengths longer than 505 nm cause the process to be excited (+) to the degree indicated by the curve labeled "Y." These wavelengths result in the sensation of yellowness. Wavelengths shorter

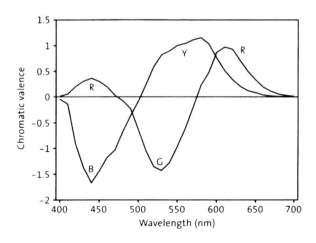

Figure 3.5 Opponent chromatic cancellation functions based upon seven observers. R, G, Y, and B refer to the red, green, yellow, and blue lobes, respectively. (Based upon Werner and Wooten 1979a.)

than 505 nm cause the process to be inhibited $(-)$ to the degree indicated by the curve labeled "B." These wavelengths result in the sensation of blueness. Notice that precisely 505 nm results in neither excitation nor inhibition; hence neither yellowness nor blueness. From Figure 3.5, it should be obvious why, according to Hering, no light can result in a yellow-blue sensation: the Y–B process cannot be excited and inhibited at the same time. The R–G process has precisely the same general features but in different regions of the spectrum. Notice that R has two lobes, one long wave (>570 nm) and one short wave (<470 nm) that give excitation in the R–G process. The total hue percept of any given wavelength depends upon the degree and the way $(+$ or $-)$ in which it simultaneously activates the Y–B and R–G processes.

Hering's theory was an attempt to formulate a complete and internally consistent description of the spectrum. Since it is a model of sensory process, it is difficult to prove (or disprove) because sensations cannot be directly measured like the weight of an object or the temperature of a solution. Its validity as a useful model must be evaluated largely on the basis of how much order it brings to all of the data of color vision. One important aspect is, of course, how well it accounts for hue sensations. The above description can be expanded within the confines of the theory. Many hue names can be applied to various portions of the spectrum and then analyzed on the basis of Hering's theory. As an example, let us take the seven hue names used by Newton to describe the spectrum and see how Hering would explain them. See table on next page.

In addition, the theory easily explains the blue-greens (480–500 nm) and the yellow-greens (510–560 nm). Notice that there is no place in the spectrum where R is activated and Y–B is neither $+$ nor $-$. This means that pure red, according to Hering, is not found in the spectrum, i.e., that no single wavelength gives the sensation of pure red. Red can, of course, be produced by the appropriate mixture of a long-wave light (yellowish red) and a short-wave light (blue).

An important aspect of Hering's theory is that his processes refer to neural mechanisms. Contrary to what many secondary sources claim, he did not imagine that his opponent processes were photochemicals. His theory was purposefully noncommittal with respect to what the receptors or photopigments might be since little was known about them at the time (1860–1915).

nm	Newton	Hering
400–430	violet	a range with lots of B and a moderate amount of R; reddish blue
440–460	indigo	similar to above but with somewhat less R; reddish blue
470	blue	occurs only where R–G is neither + nor –, but lots of B; hence pure blue
505	green	occurs only where B–Y is neither + nor –, but lots of G; hence pure green
575	yellow	occurs only where R–G is neither + nor –, but lots of Y; hence pure yellow
590–620	orange	occurs where there are approximately equal amounts of Y and R; yellow-red
>630	red	occurs where R is large and Y is relatively small; yellowish red

Achromatic colors

"Color" is defined as the appearance of light. So far we have been discussing aspects of appearance characterized by such terms as "violet," "magenta," "red," "yellow," "orange," etc. This aspect of the perception of light is called *chromatic color*. The other major dimension is called *achromatic color* and refers to such colors as black, white, and all the shades of grey. Just as Hering reduced all of chromatic color to a small number of elemental processes (four), he proposed that achromatic experience could be accounted for with just the elemental processes of black (Bk) and white (W). All of the other achromatic qualities, i.e., the shades of grey, are merely perceptual mixtures of black and white. A mid-grey, for example, is an achromatic color where the black and the white processes are activated to about the same degree. A light grey, to take another example, results when the white process is much stronger than the black process. Thus, the entire series of achromatic colors from pure black, through all shades of grey, to pure white is accounted for by the relative activity of two underlying processes.

How are the black and white processes activated? According to Hering, the white process is driven by receptor activity, feeding directly (in line) to the white channel. The black process, is, however, organized quite differently. It is not activated directly (in line) by receptor activity. Rather, it is responsive to receptor activity from neighboring retinal regions. In a functional sense, black is a contrast color, i.e., the percept of black corresponding to a given region of visual space arises from light stimulating an adjacent area of visual space. Blackness, then, is not merely the absence of light. It is an elemental quality that arises from adjacent, stronger stimulation. This does not make black different from the chromatic qualities, since they too may be aroused by adjacent stimulation, i.e., simultaneous chromatic contrast. What makes black different is that it can *only* by aroused by adjacent stimulation. White, on the other hand, is activated by direct stimulation.

The modern view of the achromatic channels is similar to Hering's, but an attempt is made (as for the chromatic channels) to relate them more specifically to activity of the three photoreceptors. The white channel is thought to result from the summed ($+$) activity of the three receptors, with β and γ weighted about equally and α weighted nearly zero. The black channel is driven by the adjacent white response and is thus related to the three receptors by the same weight, albeit indirectly.

When the spectral energy of a stimulus is such that the R–G and Y–B channels are in equilibrium, only the Bk and W channels are excited. The resulting colors, from pure black, through the shades of gray, to pure white, are properly referred to as the dimension of *lightness*. Most stimuli do not, however, produce perfectly silent chromatic channels. Most stimuli result in the activation of one or both chromatic channels as well as the black and white channels. The simultaneous activation to varying degrees of chromatic and achromatic channels provides the basis for the perceptual dimension of *saturation*, which is an attribute of colors, with pure chromatic colors (e.g. pure red) at one extreme, pure achromatic colors (black or white or both) at the other extreme, and intermediates such as pink (red-white) and maroon (black-red) in-between. Colors, then, are perceptual blends resulting from varying degrees of chromatic (red or green and blue or yellow) and achromatic (black and/or white) activation.

Relation to physiology

Does Hering's theory have any physiological reality? It seems to have been essentially verified by single-cell recordings (see Abramov this volume for a fuller account of this issue). It would be wrong to say that the theory has been proven, but the discovery of opponent color cells over fifty years after Hering's prediction is certainly impressive. In addition, most psychologists feel that it does provide a valid and economical description of color perception. Such converging evidence lends support for its usefulness as a model of color perception.

How can both Young–Helmholtz and Hering be right about color vision? The answer is rather simple and pleasing. The Young–Helmholtz theory was correct about there being three types of receptors. Where the theory went astray was in the simple kind of relation it proposed between the pigments and the hue sensations. Hering seems to have had it right in relating hue to the activity of opponent processes. We now have a good idea about how the pigments and the opponent processes may be related. In general terms, it now appears that the opponent processes are built up by the interplay of excitation and inhibition initiated by the three types of receptors. Figure 3.6 shows a hypothetical scheme that is considered highly plausible by many psychologists and physiologists. To know the effect of quantal absorptions in a given pigment (α, β, and γ) on the opponent processes (B–Y, or G–R), follow the arrows. For example, absorption in β causes inhibition (−) in the R–G process and excitation (+) in the Y–B process.

Figure 3.6 The functional relation between the three receptors and the opponent stage.

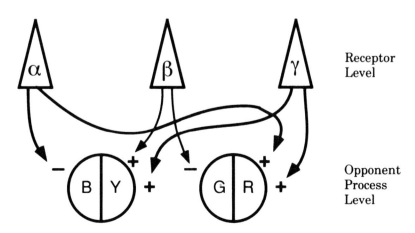

At the same time, however, the γ pigment may be absorbing quanta. It promotes excitation $(+)$ in both processes. The net result $(+$ or$-)$ for either opponent process depends upon simultaneously considering the quantal absorptions of each pigment and how $(+$ or $-)$ it affects the process. Thus, the activity of the opponent processes depends upon the relative spectral absorption curves of the three pigments, the wavelength of the stimulating light, and how $(+$ or $-)$ each pigment tends to drive the opponent processes.

Summary

Hering proposed that the millions of discernible colors can be explained as arising from the relative activity of a small number of physiological processes. Specifically, these material processes result in emergent red, green, blue, yellow, black, and white perceptions. These qualities are sufficient to describe all of color space. Hue is determined by the ratios of activity in the chromatic channels with the restriction that yellow–blue and green–red are mutually exclusive. Achromatic color is determined by the relative activity of the black and white channels with the provision that black is solely a contrast color. Saturation is determined by the relative activity of the chromatic and achromatic channels.

Opponent cancellation

Jameson and Hurvich (1955) quantified Hering's formulation by explicit algebraic expressions that relate perceived hue to opponent channel activities. Their model is as follows:

$$H_{(r,g)_\lambda} = \frac{|r\text{-}g|_\lambda}{|r\text{-}g|_\lambda + |y\text{-}b|_\lambda}$$

$$H_{(y,b)_\lambda} = \frac{|y\text{-}b|_\lambda}{|r\text{-}g|_\lambda + |y\text{-}b|_\lambda}$$

$H_{(r,g)\lambda}$ represents the perceived hue, either red or green, resulting from a given narrow-band light. Similarly, $H_{(y,b)\lambda}$ refers to the perceived yellowness or blueness associated with a spectral light. The terms $|r\text{-}g|_\lambda$ and $|y\text{-}b|_\lambda$ correspond to the absolute amount of opponent channel activity generated by a specific colored light. Thus, the hue of a light is determined by the ratio of the activity in each channel to the total amount of chromatic activity. The percentage of blue, for example, associated with a particular wavelength, can be calculated by taking the ratio of blue activation at that wavelength to the sum of all chromatic activity at that wavelength. In this model, the sum of $H_{(r,g)\lambda}$ and $H_{(y,b)\lambda}$ is always equal to 1.0. Furthermore, since each opponent channel can be excited in only one direction at a time two of the terms in the denominator and one of the terms in the numerator will always be zero.

In order to evaluate Hurvich and Jameson's model it is necessary to obtain empirical estimates for both the opponent response mechanisms and perceived hue. Opponent functions were first determined by Hurvich and Jameson using a hue cancellation task. Their procedure capitalized on the antagonistic mode of response of the chromatic channels. They assumed that the strength of an opponent channel is reflected by the relative radiance of an added light that brings that channel to equilibrium. For example, the degree of red activity in the R–G channel is proportional to that amount of green-appearing light that must be added so that the mixture appears neither red nor green. Similarly, the strength of yellow in a yellowish light is assessed by determining the amount of blue-appearing light that must be added to just cancel yellowness. The degree of green and blue activation is determined by the amounts of red and yellow, respectively, required to cancel the opponent hue. The blue, green, and yellow canceling lights were chosen to correspond to each observer's unique (pure) hues. Since unique red is extra-spectral it was not convenient to use it as a canceling light. Thus, Jameson and Hurvich used a predominantly red long-wave light for green cancellation. As they point out, it is convenient, but not necessary, to use unique hues as the canceling stimuli. Romeskie (1978) and Werner and Wooten (1979a) have used the same technique on several more observers. Werner and Wooten (1979b) have averaged the data from these three studies. Figure 3.5 shows the average cancellation functions for a total of seven observers.

How well do these cancellation functions predict hue? Werner and Wooten (1979b) specifically evaluated the issue by determining cancellation functions and hue estimates from the same observers. Perceived hue was determined by simply asking the subjects to report the percentage of red, green, blue, and yellow that they saw in randomly presented monochromatic lights. After a few trials subjects found the task easy. Consistent with the proposed antagonisms, no subject reported red-greens, or yellow-blues. There is a high concordance between hue reports and hue predicted from the cancellation functions. The mean absolute difference between the predicted and obtained points was 5.73%; 96% of the group average variance in hue naming is attributable to the opponent ratios. The only systematic departure between predicted and obtained points is at long wavelengths, where the average opponent response would predict about 9% more yellow than was obtained. Werner and Wooten noted that, over the course of the hue-naming practice sessions, prior to data collection, the reported amount of yellowness progressively increased. Perhaps if more sessions were allowed this trend would have continued and the obtained points would be in closer agreement with the opponent ratios in the long-wave region.

Figure 3.6 shows qualitatively how the opponent channels are related to the photopigment input. Assuming that the cancellation functions define the opponent channels, we can now ask what quantitative model satisfactorily relates the two sets of functions. Hurvich and Jameson proposed a linear model:

$$(r\text{-}g)_\lambda = k_1\gamma_\lambda - k_2\beta_\lambda + k_3\alpha_\lambda$$
$$(y\text{-}b)_\lambda = k_4\gamma_\lambda + k_5\beta_\lambda + k_6\alpha_\lambda$$

where the k's represent weighting factors. Note that in this scheme each photopigment-receptor system contributes to each channel as indicated by a + or − sign and a weighting factor. Werner and Wooten (1979a) have evaluated the expressions using well-agreed-upon estimates for γ, β, and α and their averaged opponent cancellation functions. They concluded that the R–G channel is well described by the model with k_1, k_2, k_3 set at 0.45, −2.79, and 1.89. The Y–B channel is best fit with k_4, k_5, and k_6 set at 1.79, 0.22, and 0.85. There are, however, systematic departures between the cancellation data and the yellow lobe of the opponent–response curve. This implies that a non-linear model is required to fit the Y–B function, as Larimer, Krantz, and Cicerone (1975) concluded using another method. Unfortunately, there are an indefinite number of non-linear models and no one has provided experimental evidence showing which one is best. This non-linearity of the yellow lobe remains an unsolved puzzle. Note, however, that, while in some subjects the non-linearity is severe, in others the linear expression is excellent.

Elemental and basic colors

The central assumption of the Hering opponent-process theory is that all of the approximately 7 million distinguishable colors reflect the activity of six underlying sensory processes. These basic processes, in some yet unknown way, each give rise to a unique, indivisible perceptual quality, i.e., red, green, blue, yellow, black, or white. These qualities are unique, indivisible sensations that cannot be analyzed into further components. For instance, every person has a unique "best" yellow that is neither a reddish nor a greenish yellow. Unique colors are also called elemental colors to suggest that all other non-unique colors are compounded of them. (Notice that psychological color elements should not be confused with physical color-mixing primaries; these constructs apply to separate domains.) At the psychological level, orange is a compound of yellow and red, and purple a compound of red and blue, etc. The achromatic colors, black and white, may be combined with each other (producing greys), or with the chromatic elements, producing such colors as pink (white/red), or maroon (black/red).

The early color models of Aubert, Mach, and Hering were based on the theorist's own introspection and were supported by internal consistency and parsimonious explanation of a wide variety of color phenomena. While neurophysiological studies are consistent with, and may provide converging evidence for, the opponent colors model, phenomenological evidence remains the basis for the study of elemental colors. From such evidence, it has been concluded that Hering's set of elemental colors are both necessary and sufficient to account for all of color space.

Early investigation of elemental colors used unconstrained free-naming of selected color samples. These hue-naming tasks usually sampled a portion of the visible spectrum, with observers naming isolated stimuli of monochromatic light. Observers were allowed to respond to a given color with a first and second (qualifying) color term (e.g. Beare 1963; Boynton and Gordon 1965). In such a hue-naming procedure, an observer might classify a 490 nm light as "blue, green." Unfortunately, these responses were often susceptible to the observer's idiosyncratic usage of color terms, and raw data had to be filtered for consistency and consensus. In later studies reliability was improved because observers were restricted to a given set of color names. Even so, hue-naming is a process which can be susceptible to conflicting *post hoc* analyses.

The first quantitative method for describing color appearance was devised by Jameson and Hurvich (1959) who used direct percentage estimates of perceptual qualities of hue and saturation. Sternheim and Boynton (1966) applied a similar method of hue scaling to the study of elemental hues, which has become the most popular method used for investigating color elements. Their technique also established criteria for assessing the elementalness of a given hue. In this method observers are given a set of hue terms with which to describe spectral lights. After being presented with a disk of light, the observer assigns relative proportions of the hues perceived from the permitted hue-term set. Observers assign a percentage of each hue "directly experienced" in each light, e.g. a 490 nm stimulus disk might be described as "50% blue, 50% green."

An example of hue scaling can be seen in Figure 3.7 (Miller 1985). In one condition of that experiment observers were given four hue terms (blue, green, yellow, red) to describe spectral lights ranging from 470 to 640 nm. Observers were not required to make their

Figure 3.7 Hue-scaling responses from 470 nm to 640 nm. Observers were allowed to use the elemental categories blue, green, yellow, and red. (Average of five observers.)

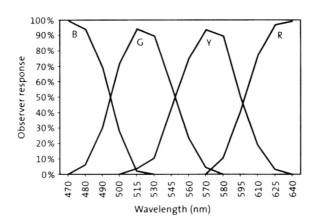

responses add to 100%. The data presented are from five observers. Because of repeated trials and slight individual differences, responses usually average to less than 100% at any given point along the spectrum. Nevertheless, the results show a remarkable agreement among observers, e.g. the average "blue" response at 470 nm is 99%, the average "yellow" response at 570 nm is 94%. In accordance with the opponent process theory, there is no "yellow" response at 470 nm, and no "blue" response at 570 nm. Intermediate points along the spectrum show hues to be composed of various proportions of neighboring hues (the 545 nm response averages 57% "green" and 43% "yellow"). This experiment shows that the four hue terms are sufficient to describe spectral hues. However, the question remains whether all these hue terms are *required* to describe spectral hues. For instance, could red and green be used to describe a 570 nm ("yellow") light?

The unabridged method of Sternheim and Boynton (1966) requires more than solely sufficient use of a color term to describe a given color. A color term must be both sufficient *and necessary* to describe a color for it to be declared elemental. The criterion of sufficient and necessary usage requires use of multiple-term color-name sets. Various color-term sets are tested by including, then excluding, the color terms of interest. If the terms are *sufficient* to describe a given color, observers will be able to describe the stimulus fully with some combination of terms. The *necessary* test for an elemental color can only be determined by its exclusion from a color term set. If a color term is necessary, then observers without it will be unable to describe a stimulus fully. When presented with a stimulus light that would normally be labeled with a color term that has been excluded from the color-term set, the observer can respond only with the residual (remaining) colors. For instance, consider an observer for whom a "yellow" response is not permitted, and who has been given the hue-term set of blue, green, and red. Upon seeing a yellowish-orange light, the observer might respond with "25% red." Such an inadequate description (less than 100%) indicates that the hue terms allowed during that experimental session were not enough to fully describe the color; therefore some excluded hue term was necessary. The unassigned hue portion is treated in subsequent data analysis as a "computed" hue. A computed hue at a given wavelength is determined by subtracting the hue % response from 100%, in this case $100\% - 25\%$

=75% computed hue. By convention the computed hue is assigned the omitted hue term that normally describes that part of the spectrum, e.g. computed yellow.

In practice the dual criteria of necessary and sufficient usage have proved arduous, so relatively few studies use these most stringent criteria across the full spectrum. Usually studies have been undertaken to investigate the status of a single putative elemental color. The impetus for the original Sternheim and Boynton (1966) study was to examine the status of orange as an elemental hue. Examining a spectral range from 530 to 620 nm with several hue-term sets, Sternheim and Boynton concluded that orange was not an elemental hue because it failed the necessary condition, i.e., observers were able to fully describe the appropriate hues as compounds of yellow and red, with no need for the term "orange."

The Sternheim and Boynton (1966) procedure can also be used with nonspectral colors. Several theorists have suggested that purple is an elemental hue. Indeed, the Munsell system implies an elemental purple because it is given equal status with the other four elemental hue terms forming a five-sectioned hue circle. To address the question of purple's status Fuld, Wooten, and Whalen (1981) investigated hues ranging from red, through the blues, to green. They included spectral stimuli from 420 to 510 nm and extraspectral stimuli between red and blue on the hue circle. The extraspectral stimuli, often described as purples or violets, were physical mixtures of various ratios of 400 and 700 nm light. In one condition, observers were permitted the hue-term set of red, blue, and green. The results in Figure 3.8 show that those hue terms are sufficient to describe the hues across the extraspectral and short-wave part of the hue circle. There was no computed function for that hue-term set, indicating that purple is not a necessary hue term.

To determine if blue is a necessary hue term for the same region, a second condition used the hue term set of red, green, and yellow. The results in Figure 3.9 show the computed blue function, indicating that blue is a necessary hue term. Figure 3.10 is a comparison between the actual blue response function of Figure 3.8, and the computed blue response function of Figure 3.9. The close similarity between actual and computed blue functions indicates that a blue category is used implicitly even when a blue response is not permitted. The similarity

Figure 3.8 Hue-scaling responses in the short-wave region (440 nm to 510 nm) and the extra-spectral region (mixtures of 400 nm and 700 nm). The x-axis is plotted in Farbton (DIN color system), which divides the hue circle into 24 perceptually equal intervals. (Farbton 8 is a monochromatic 700 nm; Farbton 13.5 to 21.5 correspond to monochromatic stimuli from 400 to 510 nm; Farbton between 8 and 13.5 are mixtures of 400 nm and 700 nm light.) Red, blue, and green (circles, triangles and squares, respectively) were the allowed categories.

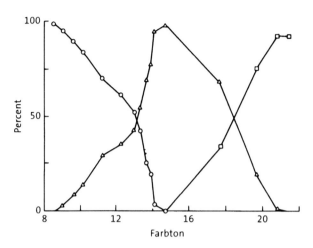

Figure 3.9 Hue-scaling responses with red, green, and yellow allowed categories. Red and green responses are indicated by circles and squares, respectively. Triangles represent computed values, as explained in the text.

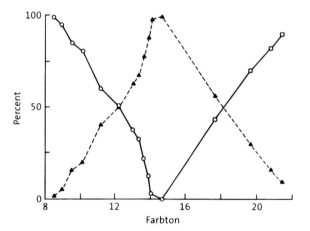

of both blue functions shows that such usage is not dependent on hue-term set composition.

That purple is sufficient to describe the stimuli is shown in Figure 3.11. In the purple condition, observers were permitted the hue-term set of red, purple, blue, and green. As can be seen, the purple hue function slightly displaces the red and blue functions, but does not replace them nor move their peaks. This mild displacement is characteristic of many nonelemental colors; they are used when available (they are sufficient), but are not missed when omitted (they are not necessary).

Several studies have examined various sets of elemental and compound (nonelemental) colors with the most rigorous criteria of

Figure 3.10 Comparison between the computed values (Figure 3.9) and the blue responses (Figure 3.8). Circles and triangles refer to computed values and blue responses, respectively.

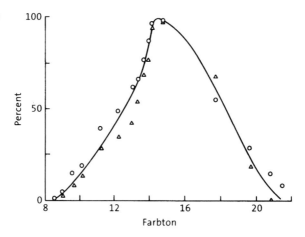

Figure 3.11 Hue-scaling responses with red, purple, blue, and green allowed categories (circles, crosses, triangles, and squares, respectively).

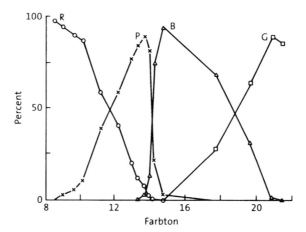

Sternheim and Boynton (1966). Blue, green, yellow, and red have been demonstrated to be elemental across diverse studies (see Miller, this volume, for the special case of green). Other colors, in addition to orange and purple, were shown to be nonelemental. The remaining elemental studies using the method of Sternheim and Boynton involve achromatic (black/white) colors.

Achromatic colors are non-spectral, and must always involve spatial contrast (see above). Spatial contrast can produce a range of lightnesses with black at one extreme, white at the other extreme, and grays in-between. Note that brightness is independent of lightness, and refers to perceived stimulus intensity, ranging from dim to bright (Sewall and Wooten 1991). Experiments on achromatic colors require the use of two stimulus fields to achieve a spatial contrast. The first field is a broadband (color-neutral) disk of light, and the second is a surrounding ring (annulus) of another neutral light. The luminance ratio between disk and annulus is varied for different stimuli which are judged for "blackness" or "whiteness." Quinn, Wooten, and Ludman (1985) investigated achromatic colors with such an arrangement. Observers used the Sternheim and Boynton method to describe a series of twelve stimuli whose appearance ranged from black, through grey, to white. This series was created by manipulating the relative luminance of central and annulus fields. Observers were permitted to respond with different color-term sets: black and white; black only; white only; black, grey, and white. Computed functions were obtained for black and white, but not for grey, indicating that only black and white are elemental. Although grey was used when available, it was not necessary in the series ranging from black to white. Observers were able to describe all greys as ratios of black and white. Unlike the chromatic elemental pairs, red/green and blue/yellow, which do not form compounds, black and white were not mutually exclusive, and hence are not organized as opponent colors.

Other studies used an achromatic color compounded with a chromatic color. This combination gives light or dark colors which lie outside the spectrum and the hue circle. Conceptually, these compounds inhabit all of the Natural Color System color space not on the equator or polar axis (see Sivik this volume). (These compounds are modeled less well in Munsell space. Optical Society of America space [see Boynton this volume] contains no pure black or white samples.) For instance, at some point along an achromatic/red continuum there is a white/red called "pink," and a black/red called "maroon."

Among the dark chromatic colors, brown has most frequently been named as a potential elemental color. Indeed, using a method similar to that described above, Fuld, Werner, and Wooten (1983) concluded that brown might be an elemental color. However, as they pointed out, the results may have been an artifact of color-term set order. After controlling for potential order effects, Quinn, Rosano, and Wooten (1988) found brown to be non-elemental. Their observers were able to fully describe brown as a compound of black and yellow. In addition, although used mainly as an experimental control, maroon was also shown to be nonelemental (compounded of red and black).

Lastly, pink was shown to be nonelemental by Ludman (1983). Her observers were able to classify all relevant stimuli as compounds of red and white; the term "pink" was unnecessary. Collectively these studies show the color elements to be: black, white, blue, green, yellow, and red. Brown, purple, pink, orange, grey, maroon, and violet have been demonstrated to be compounds from the six elements.

There has been a variety of color appearance studies using less stringent criteria than Sternheim and Boynton (1966). These studies allow the observer to give a quantitative response without the requirement of necessary usage. These experiments use a scaling method with a single standard color-term set. Fuld and Alie (1985) used this method with the four terms blue, green, yellow, and red across fifteen observers to confirm the conclusions of previous studies using more traditional methods.

However, most recent single-set studies are not designed primarily to investigate elemental colors, but other aspects of color appearance. Gordon and Abramov (1988) applied hue scaling to make a quantitative version of the hue-naming method of Boynton, Schafer, and Neun (1964). Gordon and Abramov used a single four-unique-hue-term set, plus a saturation judgment, to derive hue and saturation functions across most of the spectrum. This method, which they call "4+1," was used to generate data which were analyzed in several ways. With multidimensional scaling they derived a uniform appearance diagram, confirming and expanding earlier work (Ekman 1954, 1970). Gordon and Abramov were also able to show links to the classic wavelength discrimination function, and to various color phenomena such as the Bezold–Brücke hue shift. Further study (Gordon, Abramov, and Chan 1994) has shown their technique to be robust and efficient. The analyses of the 4+1 single-set method show good correspondence with several classic color psychophysical functions derived by other quite different methods. The connections among single-and multi-set scaling techniques with so many other psychophysical functions provide confidence in the basic findings of research on elemental colors.

Although the elementalness of black, white, blue, green, yellow, and red has been shown across many studies and methods, it is not completely without problem. Observer instruction and hue-name-set effects have been demonstrated by Beare (1963) and Beare and Siegel

(1967). Potential order effects of hue-set availability have been found in Quinn, Rosano, and Wooten (1988). Prior to Miller (1985), no single study using the stringent criteria of Sternheim and Boynton had included more than two presumed elementals. To address these methodological problems, Miller (1993) undertook a series of experiments with several new methods. These methods also cast elemental color research in a paradigm more hospitable to the contemporary methods of cognitive psychology (see Miller this volume).

The search for a minimal set of colors also took place in a wholly different research tradition – linguistic anthropology. Soon after the first anthropological color-naming data were collected there were attempts to link informant naming in the field with psychophysical laboratory color-naming (e.g. Woodworth 1910; Titchener 1916). In general, the psychologists favored a biological determinism, while anthropologists favored a linguistic determinism. There seemed little to recommend collaboration, and a long period of dormancy followed. This sleep was broken as psychology regained interest in color appearance and elemental hues in the late 1950s. Beare (1962, 1963) took up the question of linkage with some surprisingly contemporary concerns, e.g. linguistic influences, term-set composition, boundary reaction times. However, such concerns awaited a breakthrough on the anthropological side. It came with the work of Berlin and Kay (1969) (see the Introduction to this volume and Kay, Berlin, Maffi, and Merrifield, this volume, for further refinements). Their finding of a universal minimal set of basic color terms and an evolutionary term sequence precipitated several attempts at linkage between anthropological and psychological perspectives.

The first linking study found an equivalence between the unique hues and the corresponding basic color terms. In experiments with Wooten, McDaniel (1972) found the focal Munsell chips for twelve observers in the Berlin and Kay array. Each observer's focal blue, green, and yellow chips were then matched to spectral lights. The matching method allowed comparison between Munsell chips and monochromatic lights. The wavelength of each unique hue and the wavelength matching each focal color were determined (this provides a more accurate measure than relying on Munsell's published dominant wavelength). McDaniel's observers demonstrated a close correspondence between their focal chip selection and their unique hues.

It was concluded that focal colors are essentially unique hues. The observers' unique hues were quite similar to classic findings such as Dimmick and Hubbard (1939), which also match closely those in Figure 3.7.

Kay and McDaniel (1978) reconceptualized the Berlin and Kay evolutionary sequence as a successive differentiation of color space into three types of basic color terms. Kay and McDaniel used fuzzy-set theory to model color category structure. Fuzzy sets allow for degrees of membership in which there is a continuum from highly representative members to rather poor members. The degree of membership in a fuzzy set is equivalent to the hue coefficient (percentage response) in color scaling.

The first fuzzy-set category (fuzzy identity) contained the six elemental colors, labeled "fundamental neural responses." The second type of fuzzy set (fuzzy union) was formed by aggregating among the six elemental colors, e.g. red OR yellow OR white. These aggregates were labeled "composite categories." Composite categories are used in smaller lexicons having fewer than the six elemental hue terms. The third type of set (fuzzy intersection) is formed by compounds between the elemental colors, e.g. red AND yellow = orange. These compounds were labeled "derived categories." Derived categories are used in larger lexicons having more than the six elemental hue terms.

The naming of the fuzzy identity set "fundamental neural responses" was an unfortunate confounding of phenomenology with physiology (see Abramov this volume, and below); but however premature the attempted reduction to neurophysiology, these elemental basic terms still provide an inescapable point of reference for theorists across disciplines.

Psychophysics can shed little light on composite categories. With rare exceptions, elemental color research is done with American English speakers who have large color lexicons. These observers show little propensity to make composite categories. Usually lack of an elemental hue term will result in a gap in a hue response function, i.e., a computed hue. It is therefore difficult to conjecture about composite categories from the behavior of our typical experimental populations. One might speculate that no composite category would completely cross one of the Hering channels. We know of no composite categories that span both black and white, nor both unique red and unique green, nor unique yellow and unique blue (but see Kay, Berlin, Maffi, and Merrifield, this volume – Ed.).

Beyond the six elements are the derived color categories. These colors are the nonelemental compound colors of psychophysics. The colors found to be compounds with the Sternheim and Boynton method: brown, purple, pink, orange, grey (setting aside the controls, maroon and violet) flesh out the rest of the basic color terms. It is remarkable that collectively these, and only these, colors were tested as potential elements over many years by different researchers independent of any explicit connection with the set of basic color terms.

One other convergence between empirical elemental color research and the model of Kay and McDaniel (1978) should be mentioned. They predict non-contracted (stable) membership functions for elemental colors when derived colors are added to a lexicon. They cite as a possible example the orange function of Sternheim and Boynton (1966). The stability of elemental color response functions is exactly what is demonstrated when a color fails the *necessary* test. The nonelemental color produces no computed hue (see Figure 3.8 for the case of purple). This can be seen in all compound colors (which fail the necessary test). Taking the elemental hue literature as a whole, the Kay and McDaniel model has been demonstrated for all eleven basic color terms. Furthermore, the simple intersection model for chartreuse, the only non-basic color term tested with an elemental method, has been verified by Miller (1993) (see Miller this volume).

Cast in the terminology of elemental colors we can say the following about basic color terms: the elemental colors (fuzzy identity) pass both the necessary and sufficient criteria. Compound basic colors are sufficient, but fail the necessary criterion – they will displace (but not replace) elemental color functions. Non-basic colors are truly redundant, failing both necessary and sufficient criteria – they never displace color response functions.

Given the elegant structure of both the phenomenology of elemental and compound colors and the basic color terms, it is not surprising that there has been a search for mechanisms. There have been several attempts to link the order of basic-color-term appearance with psychological or physiological mechanisms. Physiological explanations have been elusive. Certainly, most would argue that light/dark distinctions should emerge first since they are essential to every known visual system. Why red should emerge before the other colors is more difficult. Simply stating that red is more salient, as is done in much anthropological speculation, seems tautological.

Ratliff (1976) approaches the order problem by asking why the blue term comes last. He observes that short-wave cones are relatively sparse in the central fovea (central area of vision), and macular pigment reduces short-wave sensitivity somewhat. However, although both these factors contribute to a lowered short-wave sensitivity, Ratliff believes their effect is minimal. Rather, he assigns the causal role in ordering to the facts that short-wave cones interact relatively late in neural integration and that the short-wave photopigment is weak and has a narrow absorption band. One must wonder, however, if these speculations are borne out in everyday activity; we seem to have little difficulty seeing blue objects. Ratliff claims that red has priority for exactly the opposite reasons: the long-wave pigment is highly represented in the fovea, and is by far the most sensitive photopigment in the longer wavelengths. However, it has been observed by Regan (1987) that "the relationship between [cone] color mechanisms and color categories is somewhat distant" (p. 450). Ratliff offers no explanation for the original Berlin and Kay ordering of yellow and green following red, but prior to blue. He mentions that brown may "complement" yellow, and does not even guess about the causes for the orderly emergence of other later color terms.

One might wonder where an extension of Ratliff's (1976) analysis could lead. He observes that the remaining basic terms for chromatic colors, brown, orange, pink, and purple, all refer to colors that appear to have some redness to them. Perhaps whatever mechanism gives red primacy as a basic color is also involved in the remaining terms. It is curious that no basic terms exist for the compound colors involving red's opponent, green: yellow-green and blue-green (Miller 1993).

In any case, the last five terms of the Berlin and Kay sequence, and, additionally, those predicted by various models, e.g. Kay and McDaniel (1978), may serve as phenomena to be accounted for in future research. Ratliff (1976) suggests that the compound (derived) basic color terms may have, "specific and distinct underlying physiological processes – although perhaps more subtle than those we believe to be related to the more basic categories and terms" (p. 325). Most likely the anatomical locus for the phenomena of interest will lie at much higher levels than previously thought, in all likelihood beyond the primary visual cortex.

Over the years the Hering opponent-process theory has survived any number of physiological models. It is robust, and has been crucial in guiding neurophysiological research. Unfortunately, neurophysiology still tells us precious little about perception, thought, or language. Rather, it is understanding the elements and compounds of color perception which most often serves to illuminate both neurophysiology and cognitive-linguistic theory.

References

Beare, A. C. 1962. Frequencies of color names as functions of wavelength. Ph.D. thesis, Columbia University.

——— 1963. Color-name as a function of wavelength. *American Journal of Psychology* 76: 248–256.

Beare, A. C., and M. H. Siegel 1967. Color name as a function of wavelength and instruction. *Perception and Psychophysics* 2(11): 521–527.

Berlin, B., and P. Kay 1969. *Basic Color Terms: Their Universality and Evolution*. Berkeley: University of California Press. 1st paperback edn. 1991, with bibliography by Luisa Maffi.

Boynton, R. M., and J. Gordon 1965. Bezold–Brücke hue shift measured by color-naming technique. *Journal of the Optical Society of America* 55: 78–86.

Boynton, R. M., W. Schafer, and M. E. Neun 1964. Hue–wavelength relation measured by color-naming method for three retinal locations. *Science* 146: 666–668.

Dimmick, F. L., and M. R. Hubbard 1939. The spectral location of psychologically unique yellow, green, and blue. *American Journal of Psychology* 52: 242–254.

Ekman, G. 1954. Dimensions of color vision. *Journal of Psychology* 38: 467–474.

——— 1970. Comparative studies on multidimensional scaling and related techniques. *Reports from the Psychological Laboratories*, University of Stockholm, Supplement 3.

Fuld, K., and A. M. Alie 1985. Hue naming: a test of the validity of Werner and Wooten's average observer. *Perception and Psychophysics* 37(2): 145–147.

Fuld, K., J. S. Werner, and B. R. Wooten 1983. The possible elemental nature of brown. *Vision Research* 23(6): 631–637.

Fuld, K., B. R. Wooten, and J. J. Whalen 1981. The elemental hues of short-wave and extraspectral lights. *Perception and Psychophysics* 29(4): 317–322.

Gordon, J., and I. Abramov 1988. Scaling procedures for specifying color appearance. *Color Research and Application* 13(3): 146–152.

Gordon, J., I. Abramov, and H. Chan 1994. Describing color appearance: hue and saturation scaling. *Perception and Psychophysics* 56(1): 27–41.

Jameson, D., and L. M. Hurvich 1955. Some quantitative aspects of an opponent-colors theory. I. Chromatic responses and spectral saturation. *Journal of the Optical Society of America* 45(7): 546–552.

——— 1959. Perceived color and its dependence on focal, surrounding, and preceding stimulus variables. *Journal of the Optical Society of America* 49(9): 890–898.

Kay, P., and C. K. McDaniel 1978. The linguistic significance of the meanings of basic color terms. *Language* 54(3): 610–646.

Larimer, J., D. H. Krantz, and C. M. Cicerone 1975. Opponent process additivity – II. Yellow/blue equilibria and nonlinear models. *Vision Research* 15: 723–731.

Ludman, E. J. 1983. An investigation of the perceived colors pink and gray. BA honors thesis, Brown University.

McDaniel, C. K. 1972. Hue perception and hue naming. Unpublished BA thesis, Harvard University.

Miller, D. L. 1985. The elemental hues of short and medium-wavelength spectral lights. Sc.M. thesis, Brown University.

1993. An investigation of elemental, basic, and categorical color perception. Ph.D. thesis, Brown University.

Quinn, P. C., J. L. Rosano, and B. R. Wooten 1988. Evidence that brown is not an elemental color. *Perception and Psychophysics* 43(2): 156–164.

Quinn, P. C., B. R. Wooten, and E. J. Ludman 1985. Achromatic color categories. *Perception and Psychophysics* 37(3): 198–204.

Ratliff, F. 1976. On the psychophysiological basis of universal color terms. *Proceedings of the American Philosophical Society* 120(5): 311–330.

Regan, D. 1987. Evoked potentials and color-defined categories. In S. Harnad (ed.), *Categorical Perception* (pp. 444–452). Cambridge University Press.

Romeskie, M. I. 1978. Chromatic opponent-response functions of anomalous trichromats. *Vision Research* 18: 1521–1532.

Sewall, L., and B. R. Wooten 1991. Stimulus determinants of achromatic constancy. *Journal of the Optical Society of America A* 8(11): 1794–1809.

Sternheim, C. E., and R. M. Boynton 1966. Uniqueness of perceived hues investigated with a continuous judgmental technique. *Journal of Experimental Psychology* 72(5): 770–776.

Titchener, E. B. 1916. On ethnological tests of sensation and perception with special reference to tests of color vision and tactile discrimination described in the reports of the Cambridge Anthropological Expedition to Torres Straits. *Proceedings of the American Philosophical Society* 55: 204–236.

Werner, J. S., and B. R. Wooten 1979a. Opponent chromatic mechanisms: relation to photopigments and hue naming. *Journal of the Optical Society of America* 69(3): 422–434.

1979b. Opponent chromatic response functions for an average observer. *Perception & Psychophysics* 25: 371–374.

Woodworth, R. S. 1910. The puzzle of color vocabularies. *Psychological Bulletin* 7(10): 325–334.

4 Physiological mechanisms of color vision

Israel Abramov

Color vision in general

Our world appears brightly colored, the colors – "natural" or artificial – drawn from huge palettes of pigments, dyes, and lights. But despite the ubiquity of color and the many studies of it, our knowledge of color is still filled with surprising gaps and misconceptions. Part of the problem is that there is no one "correct" way to ask about color: we each approach it with the preconceptions of our different disciplines. To bolster our "givens," we show how they accord with "facts" from neighboring disciplines. For example, linguists have been known to justify some of their conclusions by showing that they agree with the known categories of neuronal responses delineated by physiologists (e.g. Berlin and Kay 1969; Kay, Berlin, and Merrifield 1991), and physiologists have returned the compliment by referring to the universal color categories discovered by the linguists (e.g. Ratliff 1976, 1992). Unfortunately each of the many approaches to color vision has its own set of unvoiced problems. My role is both to describe some of the physiological mechanisms that might underlie color vision and to uncover some of the skeletons hidden in my discipline's intellectual closets. (See Abramov and Gordon 1994 for a detailed treatment of many of these issues.)

Since color is a response of the nervous system to certain stimuli, the goal is to answer the question, "How does the *human* nervous system encode those aspects of the stimulus that elicit color sensations?" Obviously much of the work I describe is done on nonhuman species. I shall focus on findings from macaque monkeys, even though many of the principles seem to hold across the vertebrates. Humans and macaque monkeys have very similar color vision, as measured psychophysically for a variety of wavelength-dependent sensitivity and discrimination functions (De Valois, Morgan, Polson, Mead, and Hull 1974).

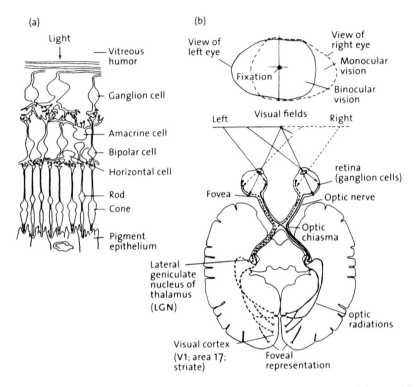

Figure 4.1 Anatomy of the visual system. (a) Retina (extrafoveal). (b) Top: view of the visual field seen by each eye. Bottom: horizontal section of brain showing projections of each optic nerve to left and right cerebral hemispheres.

Retinal anatomy

The optical apparatus at the front of the eye serves to focus an image of the world onto a thin layer of neural tissue at the back of the eye, the retina, where the interactions between light and the nervous system begin. Although the retina is thin (about ¼ mm in a human eye), it contains a large number of neurons interconnected in quite complex fashion; the details have been gleaned from a multitude of studies using both light and electron microscopy (see Dowling 1987 for a comprehensive review). Figure 4.1 shows a much-simplified schematic.

The transduction of light energy takes place at the receptors. Each of these cells contains a photopigment; when a molecule of photopigment absorbs a photon, an electrical response is initiated in the receptor. The information from the receptors is then transmitted through bipolar cells to the retinal ganglion cells. The axons of the ganglion cells course over the retina, come together on the nasal side of the retina to form the optic nerve, exit from the eye, and continue to the brain.

Some important details must now be added. There are several varieties of receptors: there are rods and cones, and of the cones, as we shall see, there are several sub-types. The common, simple story is that we have a "duplex" retina: the rods are associated with a "scotopic visual system" that does not have color vision and is optimized for low light levels; the cones are the receptors for a "photopic visual system" that has color vision and high acuity, but requires good light intensity. These co-existing visual systems are not uniformly distributed across the retina. While cones exist everywhere across the retina, they are maximally concentrated in the fovea, the central retinal region that is best capable of resolving fine detail. Rods are largely absent from the fovea and are maximally concentrated in an annulus about the fovea. Note also that the receptors are the most distal units in the retina; in order to reach them, light must first pass through all the other layers of neurons. To maximize the optical quality of the image of the world at the fovea, the proximal layers of neurons connected to the receptors are pulled to the side, thereby allowing unimpeded transmission of light to the foveal cones. (Of course, these cones still make all the usual connections to bipolar cells, and so on.)

At all levels where there is a synapse between one neuron and the next in the chain, there also exist lateral interconnections mediated either by horizontal or amacrine cells. Furthermore, except in the central fovea, the bipolar cells typically connect to several receptors. This means that the rule across the retina is that information from several (even many) receptors is pooled by the ganglion cells whose responses are the output of the retinal processing. Since the receptor types are often intermixed, this also means that the pooling cannot be random, especially in those situations in which the responses of neurons in the brain appear to be driven by one type of receptor. Before describing the visual pathways beyond the retina, I must reconsider in detail the initial events in the process – the responses of the receptors.

Figure 4.2 (*Opposite*)
Spectral sensitivities
of cones and color
matching (additive
mixtures). The graphs
show the proportion
of incident photons
(quanta) absorbed by
the different cone types
from the wavelengths
of light indicated in the
bipartite stimulus fields.
The tables next to the
graphs show how many
photons are absorbed
by each cone type from
stimulus flashes that
deliver the indicated
numbers of photons at
the given wavelengths.
(Note: the numbers of
photons shown are only
for illustration and are
not meant to give the
numbers that might
actually be present in
a real experiment.) (a)
Only L-cones are
present; the two halves
of the stimulus field can
be equated for photon
absorption, if the
stimuli are adjusted as
shown in the bottom of
the table. (b) L- and M-
cones are both present;
stimuli can be adjusted
for equal photon
captures by one or other
cone type, but not
simultaneously by both.
(c) L- and M-cones are
both present; using the
indicated additive
mixtures of lights in the
right half of the field,
both cone types respond
equally to both sides of
the field.

Cones: univariance

Color vision is the ability to distinguish wavelengths of light regardless of their relative intensities. What, then, are the spectral properties of the receptors and how do they relate to this?

The curve in Figure 4.2a is the spectral sensitivity of a single receptor's photopigment, which describes the ability of the photopigment to capture photons that pass through the receptor; for example, this receptor is almost three times more sensitive to light whose wavelength is 590 nm than to light at 630 nm. At any wavelength, however, increasing the light intensity (delivering more photons) will increase the rate at which photons are absorbed. It is generally accepted that when a photopigment molecule absorbs a photon of visible light, the effect is exactly the same regardless of the wavelength. (Strictly, a photon's energy is proportional to its vibrational frequency, which is inversely proportional to its wavelength; thus, across the range of visible wavelengths photons have different energies, but each photon has sufficient energy to elicit a fixed response from a receptor once it is absorbed.) This is the "principle of univariance," according to which a receptor can only report the rate at which its pigment is absorbing photons (Naka and Rushton 1966; Sirovich and Abramov 1977; Zrenner, Abramov, Akita, Cowey, Livingstone, and Valberg 1990). The electrical response of the receptor need not be proportional simply to the number of photons absorbed from any stimulus – for example, a receptor's responses might begin to saturate when light intensity, and therefore the rate of photon absorption, is high. Formally, univariance only requires that a receptor's response, R, be some function, f, of light absorbed by its photopigment at a given wavelength, λ, such that:

$$R = f\{IA(\lambda)\},$$

Where I is the number of photons and $A(\lambda)$ denotes the fraction of incident photons absorbed by the photopigment at each wavelength. Thus, $A(\lambda)$ acts simply as a scale factor on intensity and the receptor's responses to wavelength variations are completely confounded with its responses to intensity variations.

(a)

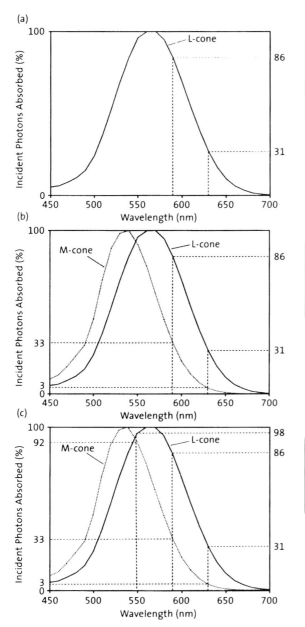

Stimulus		Photons absorbed by cones	
Wavelength (nm)	Photons	L	M
590	1,000	860	
630	1,000	310	
590	1,000	860	
630	28,667	860	

Stimulus

(b)

Stimulus		Photons absorbed by cones	
Wavelength (nm)	Photons	L	M
590	1,000	860	330
630	2,774	860	83
590	2,606	2,241	860
630	28,667	8,887	860

Stimulus

(c)

Stimulus		Photons absorbed by cones	
Wavelength (nm)	Photons	L	M
590	1,000	860	330
550	299	293	275
+		567	55
630	1,830	860	330

Stimulus

Cones: color mixing

In the strictest sense, a single receptor is color blind. A corollary is that visual receptors are not color receptors: there is no such thing as a "red cone," or a "blue cone," but only cones that may differ in their sensitivities to different wavelengths.

Let us look at some of the consequences of this. Assume one is dealing with a subject who has only receptors of the sort in Figure 4.2a. If we present that subject with a bipartite field, illuminating one side with 630 nm and the other with 590 nm, initially the two halves will appear different for the trivial reason that the subject is much less sensitive to the 630 nm light, which will appear darker. However, if we readjust the intensities as suggested in the Figure then the receptors will absorb the same number of photons from each half of the field and the responses to each wavelength will be identical and that subject can no longer distinguish these lights. A subject whose receptors are all spectrally the same is completely color blind and can exactly match the appearance of any light by adjusting the intensity of a single "primary"; such a subject is referred to as a *monochromat*. Note also that any wavelength can be chosen as the primary.

But what if the subject has receptors of two different spectral types (as in Figure 4.2b) and we present the same bipartite field? Now, there is no way to adjust the intensity of one or other wavelength so that the responses of *both* receptors are simultaneously equated for each wavelength. One or other receptor will always respond more strongly to one half of the field. Conclusion: the minimum requirement for any form of color vision is that a subject should have receptors of two different spectral types.

Even with two spectrally different receptors, however, it is still possible to match two halves of a field that differ in spectral content. This can be achieved by additively mixing two wavelengths on one half of the field, as shown in the Figure. In general, such a subject can exactly match the appearance of any light by adjusting the relative intensities of two "primaries"; such a subject is a *dichromat* (a category that seems to include most non-primate mammals: Jacobs 1993). A dichromat's color vision, however, is degraded in the sense that there will be a spectral neutral point. For a dichromat, this is a wavelength that is indistinguishable from white. The reason is that white light (usually a mixture of all wavelengths) stimulates both receptors to some extent; the response to the white can be represented as the ratio of the responses of the two receptors and the single wavelength that produces the same ratio of responses will appear the same as that white.

To have continuous variation in hue across the spectrum, a subject must have more than two spectrally different receptor types. In fact, we have known for quite some time that human color vision is trichromatic. That is, given any light, you can add together, in the other half of a bipartite field, not two, but three, specific lights whose intensities are independently adjustable. If this is done properly, the two halves will exactly match. This is one of the few facts about color vision that is considered "rock-solid" and is taken for granted.

Cones: spectral sensitivities

Trichromacy has usually been interpreted as showing that we have three different types of receptors, which are probably cones, since even the largely rod-free fovea is trichromatic. Unfortunately, the finding that three independent lights can be mixed to match any other light implies only that color vision is describable by a space with three independent dimensions.

The fovea, which has few rods, is trichromatic, and so must have at least three types of cones – it is not possible to start with fewer types and still have the three independent dimensions shown by color mixing; but we have, across the retina, at least four different receptors, if we include the rods. We are often led to believe that we can ignore rods when dealing with color vision: they are said to operate only at night, or in similar scotopic conditions, and so do not contribute to our color vision. This is most misleading. Rods respond well into daylight, or photopic, levels of illumination. Furthermore, even at absolute threshold, there is one part of the spectrum where rod and cone systems are equally sensitive.

Figure 4.3a shows the spectral sensitivity of the human eye under conditions of dark-adaptation (scotopic; rod-driven) and light-adaptation (photopic; driven by some amalgam of responses of the different cones). Usually these curves are plotted such that each is relative to its own maximum; here they are plotted so that both are referred to the same value and their sensitivities can be meaningfully compared to each other. Note that at the longest wavelengths both systems have the same thresholds, so that rods could in principle contribute to color vision under low illumination. Even under daylight conditions, when the responses of rods might be saturated, driven to a ceiling, they may still contribute to color vision. When responses are pinned at some ceiling, they cannot signal variations among stimuli, but they can still modify the responses, bias the sensitivities, of other mechanisms. Strictly, rods are precluded from directly participating in color vision only in the rod-free center of the fovea. While this region, the one we use when we look directly at a target, is extremely important, its area is only about one hundred-thousandth of the entire visual field. Across all the rest of the visual field rods and cones co-exist and it is entirely possible, and indeed likely, that rods influence color appearance. Nonetheless, having just argued for a color role for rods, I shall adopt the customary simplification and ignore them.

There are difficult methodological problems in measuring sensitivity functions such as those in Figure 4.3a. Sensitivity is defined as the reciprocal of the stimulus intensity needed to elicit some criterion level of response, such as adjusting intensity to threshold. However, intensity can be measured either as total energy or as the number of photons delivered by a stimulus. Psychophysicists usually measure energy, although, when dealing with photopigments and receptors it may be more useful to count photons (see univariance, above); the reader has to be alert to cavalier changes in axes and units of measurement. More importantly, we can only measure the light delivered to the front of the eye, and not the amount that reaches the receptors. Unfortunately, some of the light is absorbed by intervening structures, such as the lens, and this absorption varies with wavelength, as shown in Figure 4.3b. Returning to the scotopic curve in Figure 4.3a, we see that it is well described by the sensitivity of the rod photopigment (rhodopsin), except at the shorter wavelengths. Although the discrepancy can be fully accounted for by pre-retinal absorption (Figure 4.3b), the needed corrections vary considerably with age and skin pigmentation (Werner 1982; Abramov and Hainline 1991).

The photopic curve in Figure 4.3a is a combination of individual cone curves. The spectral sensitivities of the separate cone types are

Figure 4.3 (a) Spectral sensitivities of the human eye under dark-adapted (scotopic, rod-driven) and light-adapted (photopic, cone-driven) conditions. The points are all shown as multiples of the same reference value. The curve marked "rhodopsin" gives the relative sensitivity of the rod photopigment. (b) Proportion of light incident on the cornea that passes through the ocular media to the retina. Pre-retinal absorption (low transmittance) at the shorter wavelengths accounts for the discrepency between the sensitivities of rhodopsin and the scotopic system, as shown in (a).

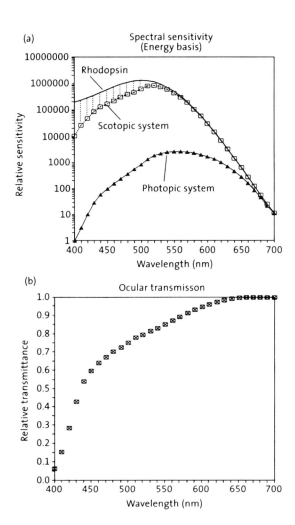

shown in Figure 4.4; they are denoted as "L-," "M-," and "S-" cones to specify which is more sensitive than the others to long, middle, and short wavelengths, respectively, even though all have some sensitivity to most parts of the spectrum. Three basic approaches have been used to obtain these curves (see MacNichol 1986 and Zrenner *et al.* 1990, for general reviews). In the first, microspectrophotometry (introduced in the mid-1960s), a single cone is isolated under a microscope and light is passed through its photopigment-containing region to a photocell. At each wavelength one measures the ratio of the intensity passing through the cone to the intensity of a comparison beam passing through a blank region outside the cone. This tells the amount that was absorbed in the passage through the cone. A second and more recent method records the electrical responses of single cones isolated from excised retinas of both humans and macaques; light intensities are adjusted until each wavelength elicits a criterion response (Schnapf, Nunn, Meister, and Baylor 1990). This method has the advantage that it measures directly the response of the entire receptor. The third, classical approach is psychophysical, in which subjects adjust intensities to reach threshold. The problem is that there is no simple stimulus manipulation that allows stimulation of just one cone type at a time. The spectral sensitivities of the different cones overlap considerably and heroic measures must be used to separate them, including using intense adaptation to specific spectral regions chosen to desensitize preferentially one or more types, and so leave responses to be driven by the one type that has been more or less functionally isolated. A widely accepted set of "fundamentals," derived in part from these sorts of experiments, is shown in Figure 4.4 (Smith and Pokorny 1975). Incidentally, the overlapping of the cone spectra reemphasizes another fundamental point: cones are not color receptors, but are simply light receptors.

The agreement among all the measures for any one cone is not astoundingly good, even allowing for the fact that only the psychophysical curves include the light losses due to pre-retinal absorption (Figure 4.3b). Partly, this is due to the difficulty of these experiments and to limitations inherent in them; but another reason may be that we have more than three cone types. Using the newly developed techniques of genetic marking, it seems that we each carry several different versions of the genes that code for the production of the L- and M-cones (Nathans, Thomas, and Hogness 1986; Nathans, Merbs, Sung, Weitz, and Wang 1992). Additionally, many individuals express more than one of each type, so that a retina could have four or more cone types, rather than the canonical three (Winderickx, Lindsey, Sanocki, Teller, Motulsky, and Deeb 1992; Neitz, Neitz, and Jacobs 1993; see Abramov and Gordon 1994 for a review). This means that the cones cannot be imposing the limitation of three dimensions for color vision, and disposes of the mythic correspondence between the dimensions of color vision and the number of receptor types. The limitation must come from the ways in which the nervous system combines responses of the cones.

Figure 4.4 Spectral sensitivities of the three cone types measured with different techniques. (a) Physiological recordings of the responses of single, excised cones. (b) Microspectrophotometry of light absorption by single, excised cones. (c) Psychophysical measures from human observers. All sensitivities are referred to number of photons delivered either to the receptor (a & b) or to the cornea (c). (Re-drawn from Zrenner *et al.*, 1990.)

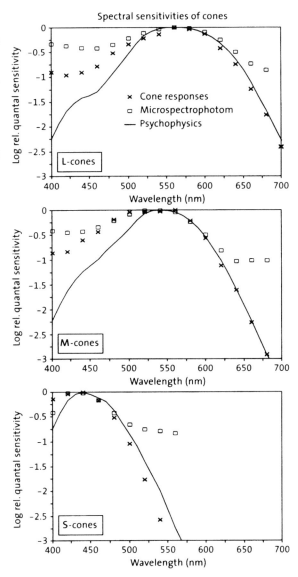

Spectrally opponent and non-opponent neurons

We have noted that, because of the univariance of photopigments, color vision must be based on the presence of at least two receptors of different spectral sensitivities. In fact, we possess more than two types, but the processing of their responses must be such as to reduce color vision to three dimensions. One widely accepted dimensional trio is: *hue*, *saturation*, and *brightness*, each term representing an independent way in which the sensation elicited by a light can be described. Hue is the quality described by terms such as red, orange, green, purple, and so on; saturation refers to the strength or concentration of hue relative to the rest of the sensation; and brightness denotes the intensive domain from dark to light. Obviously the nervous system beyond the receptors must process the receptors' responses so as to yield these sensory qualities. Thus, the next major topic is how this is achieved.

Hue is really the defining characteristic of color vision. To preserve any wavelength-dependent differences in the responses of the various cones, the nervous system must compare responses of different cones. For example, if some neuron can report that L-cones responded more strongly than M- or S-cones, then the stimulus must have been of a long wavelength (or something that is the visual equivalent, to allow for the facts of color mixture). On the other hand, the intensive dimension could be satisfied by simply pooling the responses of all the cones. In terms of neuronal processes, spectral differences could be preserved by trading excitation with inhibition – one cone type excites the next neuron in the chain, while another cone type inhibits it, and the resulting spectral output function is the difference between the cones' spectral response functions; but locating and recording from such neurons is not enough to "explain" color vision. There must also be a testable hypothesis linking the physiology with the psychological sensation (Teller 1984). I shall begin by describing what seem to be appropriate neuronal responses, mostly from macaques, and defer until later the question of how well they are linked with sensation.

Starting in the retina (Figure 4.1a), light is absorbed by the cones, whose responses are then pooled in various ways and transmitted to the ganglion cells, which respond with the well-known action potentials of the nervous system. The axons of the ganglion cells exit the eye, forming the optic nerve, and enter the brain where they terminate in a region of the thalamus devoted to vision, the lateral geniculate nucleus, or LGN (Figure 4.1b). Neurons in the LGN, in turn, send their axons to the primary visual cortex, area V1, and from V1 the information ramifies to all other regions of the brain associated with vision (in primates one might argue that this encompasses at least half of the cerebral cortex). My central point, for the moment, is that the LGN is a way-station on the transmission line from ganglion cells to cortex.

The responses of the LGN embody the results of all the retinal processing and show what is presented to the cortex for further analysis. Each LGN (the brain is generally bilaterally symmetrical and has a left and right exemplar of each component) has six layers of neurons, three associated with each eye, with each layer receiving inputs from only one eye. The top four layers are termed *parvocellular* (P-cells) since their neurons have small cell bodies and receive synapses from axons of retinal ganglion cells that are similarly small-bodied. The bottom two layers have fatter cells and are termed *magnocellular* (M-cells). These two cell types represent distinct streams of information emerging from the retina, streams that are thought to determine different aspects of vision (Livingstone and Hubel 1988; Shapley 1990; Merigan and Maunsell 1993).

The great majority, if not all, of the P-cells in a macaque (about 80 percent of the total LGN population) have responses that are spectrally opponent, while M-cells are generally spectrally non-opponent (De Valois, Snodderly, Yund, and Hepler 1977; Lee, Martin, and Valberg 1989; Kaplan, Lee, and Shapley 1990). Figure 4.5 shows an example of an opponent cell's responses to different wavelengths of light. In the dark, preceding the stimulus, the cell is spontaneously active, firing action potentials in a random pattern in the absence of a specifiable stimulus. At stimulus onset one of two responses occurs: for some wavelengths there is an increase in firing rate (excitation), while for other parts of the spectrum there is a decrease (inhibition). In addition to being spectrally opponent, the responses of these P-cells are also linear. That is, responses of a P-cell are directly proportional to variations in the intensity of the stimulus. A P-cell simply adds together (with appropriate sign) the responses of the various cones scattered across its receptive field (the region of the retina whose receptors can drive the responses of the neuron of record).

In contrast, most M-cells respond qualitatively in the same way to all wavelengths – they are either excited or inhibited by all parts of the spectrum. Additionally, it is often said that M-cells have nonlinear response functions. Caution is called for when talking about response linearity, especially if theories hang on this. The concept of a neuron that simply sums the responses contributed to it by a set of receptors

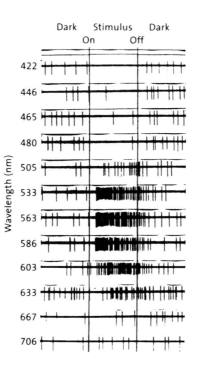

Figure 4.5 Responses of a so-called +Y-B spectrally opponent neuron in the parvocellular layers of the lateral geniculate nucleus of a macaque monkey. Each trace shows three seconds of responses, before, during, and after a stimulus flash whose wavelength is indicated to the left of the trace. (From De Valois, Abramov, and Jacobs 1966.)

was first stated for the cat. In cats, P-cells are indeed linear, while M-cells are not, a distinction that was enshrined as the dichotomy of *X*- and *Y-cells* (Enroth-Cugell and Robson 1966). In macaques, all P-cells are spectrally opponent and X-like; M-cells are mostly spectrally non-opponent, but only about 30 percent are Y-like, the others having X-like linear properties (Kaplan *et al.* 1990).

Spectrally opponent cells: four different types

One of the earliest analyses of the responses of spectrally opponent cells in the macaque LGN reported that they could be subdivided into four classes, whose mean response functions are shown in Figure 4.6 (De Valois *et al.* 1966). Even though this classification is "old" on the time scale of neurophysiology and the details may be open to question, the basic classification has been amply validated (Derrington, Krauskopf, and Lennie 1984; Shapley 1990). I reproduce the original data because they are the ones that have so often provided the point of contact with theories stemming from linguistic descriptions of color

Figure 4.6 Mean responses of the four types of spectrally opponent neurons in the lateral geniculate nucleus of the macaque monkey. The three curves shown in each graph depict the responses to different intensity levels; the numbers next to the curves give the logarithmic values relative to the highest intensity that was used. The dotted horizontal lines represent the spontaneous response rates in the periods preceding the stimulus flashes. (From De Valois *et al.*, 1966.)

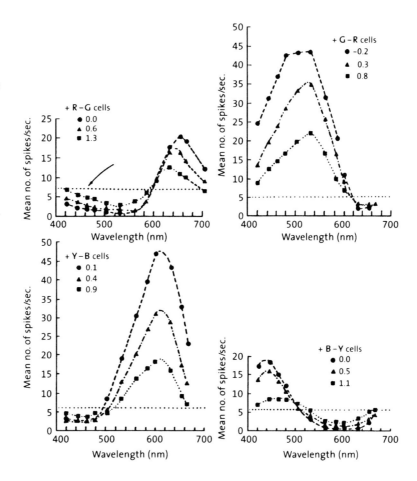

(e.g. Berlin and Kay 1969; Ratliff 1976). In the original LGN paper, the neuronal classes were referred to with terms such as +R–G – cells excited by wavelengths that appear red and inhibited by wavelengths that appear green – or +Y–B, excited by yellow and inhibited by blue (Figure 4.5 is an example of a +Y–B cell's responses); there are also the mirror images, +G–R and +B–Y.

One question about these four spectrally opponent cell types is why are there so many? The spectral information carried by +R–G and +G–R cells would seem to be the same, except for sign. A possible reason for this redundancy is that cortical neurons cannot overtly report an inhibitory response – they are notorious for having very low, often nonexistent, spontaneous rates and so can only increase their firing rate, which would report only the excitation remaining after any trade-offs between excitatory and inhibitory inputs.

A much more important question deals with how responses of three cone types result in four spectrally opponent cell types. Any spectrally opponent cell must receive inputs from a minimum of two cone types, where one cone type provides the excitatory signal and the other the inhibitory; the cell reports the difference between the spectral response functions of these cones. Clearly, different combinations of cone inputs can produce different opponent response patterns. However, identifying the cone inputs to a particular cell is far from trivial (Sirovich and Abramov 1977; Zrenner *et al.* 1990).

I shall touch briefly on the two most widely used techniques for deciphering the cone inputs. The first uses chromatic adaptation (e.g. De Valois *et al.* 1966). Consider the +G−R cell in Figure 4.6. Clearly, the cone type that contributes to its inhibitory input is more sensitive to the long wavelengths. One can use, therefore, a relatively intense light of long wavelength (to which this inhibitory input will be more sensitive than the excitatory input) to adapt or desensitize preferentially the inhibitory input; in the presence of such adaptation, the responses of the cell will be determined by the isolated (at least partially) excitatory input. Of course the reverse experiment can also be done: desensitize the excitatory input and uncover most of the inhibitory input. The other technology assumes knowledge of the spectral functions of the cones in order to design specific stimuli that are distinguishable by some combinations of cone inputs but not by others (e.g. Abramov 1968; Derrington *et al.* 1984). For example, stimuli could be given spectral distributions such that they all activate L- and M-cones equally, but do not activate S-cones equally. Any neuron receiving inputs only from L- and M-cones will respond equally to all such stimuli, whereas a neuron with an input from S-cones will respond differently to these stimuli. Results from all these studies can be summarized as follows (Abramov and Gordon 1994): a +R−G cell receives excitatory inputs from L-cones and inhibitory inputs from M-cones; a +G−R cell has the same inputs except that the signs are reversed; +Y−B and +B−Y cells have inputs from all three cone types, although, as is generally the case in this field, the details are not always clear.

So far I have described exclusively the spectral antagonisms seen in the responses of these cells. However, the different cones that provide the inputs are not uniformly intermixed across the cell's receptive fields – the fields also have a spatial structure. Ganglion and LGN cells are usually said to have concentric receptive fields in which small stimuli confined to the field center elicit one sort of response (say, excitation), while annular stimuli on the surround elicit the opposite sort of response; in spectrally opponent cells, these regions also differ in their spectral sensitivities. The import of such an organization for responses that might be related to color can be illustrated by the response functions of the +G–R cell shown in Figure 4.7 (De Valois and De Valois 1975). The filled data points are the responses to bars of white light of different widths, all centered on the receptive field. (Note that these responses of this spectrally opponent cell are to an *achromatic* stimulus.) As the bar is expanded, response grows because more of the excitatory center is being covered; but as the stimulus increases in width beyond the boundary of the center, it begins to encroach on the antagonistic surround thereby causing responses to decline. If, instead, we use a chromatic stimulus, such as a green bar flanked by red bars (open symbols), then as we expand the green bar responses keep on growing and reach an asymptote only when the entire field is covered by the green bar.

Figure 4.7 Receptive fields of a +G-R spectrally opponent neuron in the lateral geniculate nucleus of a macaque monkey. One curve (filled symbols) shows the responses of the neuron to a pattern of a white (W) bar flanked by dark (D) bars at each of the bar widths given on the horizontal axis; this pattern is achromatic and varies only in luminance. The other curve shows responses to a pattern of a green (G) bar flanked by red (R) bars; all bars equated for luminance so that the variation across the pattern is only chromatic. (Re-drawn from De Valois and De Valois 1975.)

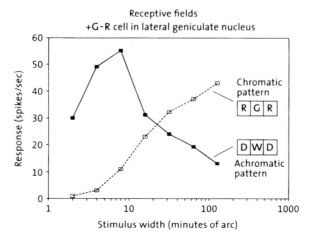

Spectrally opponent cells: psychophysiological linkages

Adding spatial stimulus variations to spectral ones greatly increases the complexity of the cell's responses – what exactly is such a spatially and spectrally opponent cell signalling? This raises the issue of the psychophysiological linking postulates. Implicit in the labels (e.g. +R–G) originally attached to the responses of spectrally opponent cells was the hypothesis that, when these cells responded, they signalled particular hue sensations. However, most P-cells behave like the one in Figure 4.7; they respond equally well to chromatic or achromatic stimuli and response often depends on spatial configuration of the stimulus. It has been suggested, therefore, that cells that carry hue information should not also carry spatial information, and should not have antagonistic surrounds (Rodieck 1991). However, were that the case, there should be large numbers of cells with spectral, but not spatial, opponencies. Unfortunately, careful measurements of the center and surround diameters of many LGN P-cells show that the overwhelming majority are both spatially and spectrally opponent (Croner and Kaplan 1995).

I favor the psychophysiological linking hypothesis that any unique (unitary, not subdividable) category of sensation corresponds to the responses of a specific neural mechanism, and the response properties of this mechanism match the psychophysical functions of the related sensory category. We experience the given sensation only when that mechanism responds. From this viewpoint, the first step in identifying some set of neurons as the immediate substrate of a sensation must be identification of what constitutes the unique sensations. For color vision, we must start by specifying the unique hue sensations.

It is widely accepted that hue can be represented by a pair of axes: red–green, or R–G, and yellow–blue, or Y–B. The connecting dashes can be looked on as negative signs, since the axes are bipolar: the paired qualities are mutually exclusive; we cannot experience simultaneously a sensation of R and G, and similarly for Y and B. Several lines of evidence, not the least of which is introspection, converge on the basic nature of R, Y, G, and B (Abramov and Gordon 1994). Any other hue can be described as a combination of these basic sensations; for example, orange is some combination of R and Y, and violet or purple is R and B (Sternheim and Boynton 1966). Also, any stimulus that elicits some amount of one of these sensations (e.g. some G) can be added to one eliciting some of the opposed sensation (e.g. R) so as to cancel it; the intensity of the canceling light providing a measure of the strength of the canceled sensation (Hurvich 1981). In such studies, a light that appears solely G can cancel R, but has no effect on any co-existing sensations of Y or B, showing that these form an orthogonal dimension.

In the above framework, hue could be based on the responses of two sets of spectrally opponent mechanisms, such as +R−G and +Y−B (together with their inverses, to allow for the low spontaneous firing rates of cortical neurons, as already described). A precise question can now be formulated: "Are the four unique hue sensations directly determined by the four types of spectrally opponent neurons in the LGN?" Regrettably, the answer must be, "No." To take a concrete example: if +R−G LGN cells are the R mechanism, then whenever these cells fire we should experience R and should not experience it under any other conditions; but +R−G cells, and indeed all the spectrally opponent P-cells, respond well to achromatic, white stimuli (see Figure 4.7). Also, the wavelength at which a +R−G's responses cross from excitation to inhibition should correspond to a sensation that is neither R nor G − the sensation should be determined only by the remaining opponent responses, which would be excitation from +Y−B cells, and hence this wavelength should correspond to a sensation that is uniquely Y. In many cases, especially in the more recent and precise measurements, this cross- or null-point is at a wavelength much shorter than that of unique Y; the null-point of most of these cells is at a wavelength that typically appears GY or chartreuse (Derrington *et al.* 1984). Furthermore, none of these +R−G cells exhibits a secondary excitatory zone in the short wavelengths and yet the short end of the spectrum elicits sensations that include some R (as in violet).

Spectrally opponent LGN cells cannot, by themselves, constitute the hue mechanisms. However, lest we throw out the baby with the bath-water, we must remember that they are a vital link in the chain that leads to color sensations. In some parts of the spectrum humans are exquisitely good at detecting changes in stimulus wavelength; wavelength discrimination of single LGN cells is often as good (De Valois, Abramov, and Mead 1967). Additionally, selective destruction of either P- or M-cells confirms that only when P-cells are destroyed is color vision severely compromised (Schiller, Logothetis, and Charles 1990; Merigan and Maunsell 1993). However, this does not mean that P-cells are the sole contributors to color, which includes hue, saturation, and brightness. Both P- and M-cell types are probably involved in all three functions.

Expanding the argument, brightness is not determined solely by the nonopponent M-cells. M-cells encode intensive aspects of stimuli and they do seem to underlie our perception of luminosity in that their spectral sensitivity matches the standard photopic sensitivity curve (Lee, Pokorny, Smith, Martin, and Valberg 1990). The standard function is typically obtained from heterochromatic flicker photometry in which we rapidly alternate two lights, a standard and some other test light, and have the subject adjust the intensity of the test light so as to minimize apparent flicker; the physical intensity (radiance) of each test wavelength needed to equate responses to it with those to the standard measures the threshold for each test light (see Figure 4.3). This function does not delineate "brightness." A brightness function can be obtained by asking subjects to adjust intensity of a static, bipartite field until the test side appears as bright as the standard or comparison side. The resulting function is quite different from the photopic luminosity curve and shows three distinct peaks; it has been modelled as a mechanism that derives not from M-cells but from a pooling of the responses of all the spectrally opponent P-cells (Sperling 1992). Similarly, M-cells may contribute to hue and, in some peculiar circumstances, may encode a particular hue (Abramov and Gordon 1994); and any comparison of chromatic and achromatic response magnitudes, a comparison which would correspond to the dimension of saturation, will involve all cell types.

The main point is that, at the level of the LGN, the responses of the different cells do not correspond exclusively to different categories of sensation. Each cell responds to some extent to many aspects of a stimulus – its responses are intrinsically ambiguous with respect to sensation. At higher, presumably cortical, levels of the nervous system the responses of LGN cells must be combined and recombined in many ways in order to disambiguate their responses, to extract the information corresponding to each sensory function.

Neurons in the diverse "visual" areas of the cortex are often described as "color coded" (see Dow 1991 for a recent review). However,

a word of caution is in order for the unwary consumer of this volumi-
nous literature. In many cases, spectral responses may be poorly
specified, either because the spectrum was coarsely sampled or stimuli were not controlled precisely; linking physiological and psychophysical studies becomes questionable. What is clear is that as yet we
have not found neurons whose responses unequivocally correspond
to color sensations. For example, at the level of primary visual cortex
(V1), and even in area V4 (an area touted as the locus of true "color
coding": Zeki 1983), most of the spectrally opponent neurons also
respond to achromatic stimuli (Thorell, De Valois, and Albrecht 1984;
Schein and Desimone 1990). Chromatic and achromatic streams of
information have not yet been completely separated, something
which a human observer can readily do when sensory experiences
are examined psychophysically.

Hue mechanisms

Even though we have not encountered neurons that determine hue
sensations directly, we can still place constraints on the properties
such neurons must have. I shall refer to these "neurons" as hue mechanisms, since they need not even refer to single neurons – the different
hue sensations may reflect the joint activity of ensembles of neurons.

At its most ambitious level, this "top-down" approach starts by
asking, "What is color vision used for?" or "Why did it develop?"
Descriptions of visual perception typically start with the need to
locate similar sensory elements in a complex visual image and then
to assemble or group these into related regions that correspond to
objects "out there." Virtually all current models emphasize intensity
or luminance boundaries in the image, since these are probably
related to changes in reflectance of real objects. Unfortunately, the
emphasis on intensity boundaries makes it very difficult to deal with
things like shadows, which pose real problems for parsing a scene.
An important factor may be that any object has a certain color and
all that a shadow does is to reduce light intensity in part of its image
without changing the characteristic wavelengths reflected by that
object. Another important aspect of color vision is that colors can
signal specific properties (Jacobs 1993). Many species use color vision
to recognize other members of their species. Color may also play a

vital role in foraging for food. Indeed, it has been seriously proposed
that primate color vision co-evolved with fruit coloring. Primates
developed in an arboreal environment, which is characterized by a
bewildering and random array of leaves and shadows. It is no mean
feat to locate a ripe fruit or edible flower in such surroundings. (See
Mollon 1989 for a striking example of the consequences to a human
of losing color vision.)

Obviously, color makes it much easier to identify elements in the
world, especially those that are important to a particular species. This
suggests that color vision should be designed to segregate stimuli into
a small set of categories – it is more important to know that a given
thing is yellowish and therefore probably ripe and good to eat than
it is to be able to make many very fine discriminations. Similarly, the
color category of an object should be stable under a wide range of
viewing conditions: a fruit should be seen as ripe whether it is seen
under the noonday sun or "by dawn's early light"; also, its color
should be roughly the same when seen from afar as from close up;
and so on.

These sorts of considerations provide our first constraints. Species
with only two cone types are dichromats: they can only split the spectrum into two categories. This is the case with the great majority of
mammals. It helps to be trichromatic; trichromatic color vision
requires the presence of at least three cone types. The next constraint
is that the different cone types must exist in roughly comparable numbers; if one type is in the great majority, the system is so lop-sided that
color discrimination becomes poor and is probably no longer a salient
aspect of that species' life, as is probably the case for the domestic cat.

Hue mechanisms: Gedanken physiology

Let me now formalize our current approach in which we use the
behavioral capabilities of the organism to constrain the physiological
models (Abramov and Gordon 1994). Note that from psychophysics
alone we cannot determine how the nervous system actually carries
out some function – all we can specify is the set of operations that it
must be carrying out. That is, we are currently studying Gedanken,
or Imaginary, physiology.

Hue can be subdivided into four separate categories, referred to in English by their initials, R, Y, G, and B. These terms, assuming they are linguistic universals, probably refer to fundamental sensory categories that are the same for all humans. Note that the existence of these four unique hue sensations does not clash with the three-dimensionality of color: since R and G are mutually exclusive, as are Y and B, RG and YB can be represented as two independent dimensions that cover hue and saturation. The axes of this color space are the bipolar hues and saturation is simply the distance from the origin (the intersection of the RG and YB axes), which still leaves one dimension free to represent brightness (Hurvich 1981; Gordon and Abramov 1988; Gordon, Abramov, and Chan 1994). Since each chromatic mechanism signals a pair of mutually exclusive sensations, each can be represented by a spectrally opponent mechanism. For example, +R–G; the linkage is that we experience R when, and only when, this mechanism is excited; when this mechanism is inhibited, we experience G. Similarly, excitation of the other mechanism leads to Y and inhibition to B. In fact, we have evidence that there are really four such physiological channels, but the other two are simply the spectral inverses of the first pairs: +G–R and +B–Y. At a conceptual level, this still allows us to talk about only two opponent hue mechanisms.

Model.

Figure 4.8 shows a general form of a model of these two opponent hue mechanisms (Abramov and Gordon 1994). For each mechanism, we start with the well-accepted spectral responses of the three cones (Smith and Pokorny 1975; see Figure 4.4). These are then combined in spectrally opponent fashion. For example, Figure 4.8a illustrates the +R–G mechanism; as shown in the schematic on the right, this mechanism's responses are the result of combining excitatory inputs derived from L- and S-cones, with inhibitory ones derived from M-cones. Note that the mechanism has two spectral null points – wavelengths at which the opposed cone inputs exactly cancel each other. At these points this mechanism cannot contribute to hue sensation. Thus at the null point near 580 nm the sensation can be neither R nor G; however, the other mechanism (Figure 4.8b) is excited and so the sensation is one only of Y. This null point of the RG mechanism defines the position in the spectrum of unique Y. Similarly, the absence of R or

Figure 4.8 A general model of the spectrally opponent hue mechanisms. (a) +R-G mechanism. The amplitudes of the spectral response curves of the three cone types depict their relative weights when combined to produce the responses of the opponent hue mechanism; the schematic at the right shows the signs with which the inputs from each cone type are combined. Excitation is denoted with "+" and inhibition with "-." (b) +Y-B mechanism. Details as above. The null points of each opponent function define the wavelengths at which only one opponent hue mechanism is active– these are the stimuli that elicit unique hue sensations. Note that neither of these mechanisms responds to an achromatic (white) stimulus that consists of all the visible wavelengths all at the same energy. (From Abramov and Gordon 1994.)

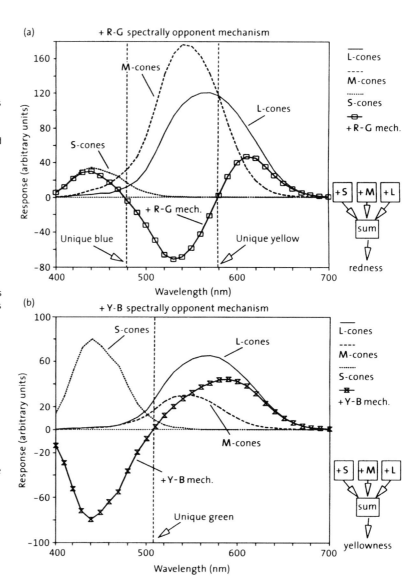

G at this mechanism's other, short-wavelength null point defines the spectral locus of unique B. Sensations that are uniquely Y or B occur only when R and G are absent. In similar fashion, the null point of the +Y–B mechanism defines the wavelength that elicits a unique G sensation.

Clearly the detailed spectral responses of these hue mechanisms depend on the relative weights assigned to the cone inputs to each mechanism. Psychophysical measurements of where in the spectrum the unique hues typically occur were used to constrain the choice of weights assigned to the different cones: they were chosen so that the unique hues fell in the correct places. Another vital constraint also had to be observed: a hue mechanism should not respond to a white light; if it did respond, we would experience a hue sensation and not the achromatic sensation of whiteness. An acceptable psychophysical definition of an achromatic stimulus is a white light that has the same energy at all wavelengths (see Sternheim and Drum 1993). Thus, the cone weights chosen for each model mechanism had not only to place the null points in the right places, but also to ensure that, when presented with an equal-energy white, the excitatory and inhibitory responses completely canceled each other.

Gedanken physiology

From the generic model we see that the spectral loci of the *unique hues* depend only on the relative responses of the separate cone types. More correctly, this applies to the cone inputs to each mechanism and not necessarily to the magnitudes of the cone responses themselves or to the relative numbers of each cone type. This is emphasized by the very different weights associated with each hue mechanism (see Figure 4.8). Therefore, psychophysical studies of how and when these loci change inform us about the inputs of the cones to the hue mechanisms. For example, the loci of the unique hues are largely unaffected by changing stimulus intensity (see Schefrin and Werner 1990). This is useful (the spectral boundaries of color categories remain stable across viewing conditions) as well as providing an important clue about the responses of the cones. The responses of individual cones grow with increasing light intensity, although the function need not be linear. Whatever the function is, however, the invariance of the unique hue loci tells us that the different cone types must have the same sort of intensity-response function. Strictly, they can only differ from each other by fixed, multiplicative scale factors; otherwise responses of one cone type would grow faster than those of another and the wavelength that elicited the equal but opposite inputs to the opponent mechanism would no longer be the same – the locus of the unique hue would shift.

The *intermediate* or *non-unique* hues are determined at the next level of the system. These sensations arise from simultaneous activity of both hue mechanisms and require some comparison of the responses of one mechanism to those of the other. Finally, *saturation* involves yet another level of comparison: part of the total sensation derives from the opponent hue mechanisms and part from achromatic mechanisms – how much of the total sensation came from achromatic as opposed to chromatic mechanisms? When none of the hue mechanisms respond, sensation is entirely achromatic and saturation is zero. The rules governing this level of processing can be examined by deliberately varying the purity of the stimuli – that is, by adding various amounts of white light to monochromatic flashes while keeping everything else the same.

In short, the goal is to understand the mechanisms that determine color appearance by specifying the properties that any candidate mechanism must have. However, the linear models presented in Figure 4.8, while they may be a useful framework, are still excessively simplified (see Abramov and Gordon 1994). Also ignored is the problem of how to assemble such cortical mechanisms from the responses of LGN neurons, which provide the only possible inputs. For example, none of the LGN's opponent neurons are excited both by long and by short wavelengths, which is a necessary feature of a +R–G hue mechanism. In our model, the short-wavelength excitation is determined by excitatory inputs to this mechanism from S-cones, which, incidentally, reinforces the point that the cones are not color receptors – in this case S-cones are contributing an R signal. The problem is that there are no pathways to the cortex that are driven exclusively by one cone type and yet responses from S-cones must be isolated and recombined with opponent responses from L- and M-cones in order to create this +R-G hue mechanism. One attempt to show how this might be achieved has recently been provided by De Valois and De Valois (1993).

Peroration

We have been studying color vision for several centuries. Many facts are known; but the entire picture still eludes us. This is especially true when we ask: "What determines color appearance?" or "Do we all share common color experiences, regardless of our cultural backgrounds?" Physiology, by itself, cannot provide answers. Physiological responses need interpretation – there must be an agreed set of postulates that link sensory phenomena and physiological responses. I have attempted a necessarily brief outline of some of the salient physiological findings and have shown where they fall short of "explaining" color sensations. I have also tried to erect a conceptual framework within which we might explore the constraints that must be imposed on any candidate mechanism claimed to determine color perceptions – somewhere, somehow, the nervous system carries out the equivalent manipulations. Eventually someone may actually locate cells that carry out these operations. With a little luck, this ensures continuing research careers for many of us for the foreseeable future.

Acknowledgments   Preparation of this chapter was supported in part by PSC/CUNY Faculty Research Award Program Grants 662224 and 664238.

References

Abramov, I. 1968. Further analysis of the responses of LGN cells. *Journal of the Optical Society of America* 58: 574–579.

Abramov, I., and J. Gordon 1994. Color appearance: on seeing red – or yellow, or green, or blue. *Annual Review of Psychology* 45: 451–485.

Abramov, I., and L. Hainline 1991. Light and the developing visual system. In J. Marshall (ed.), *Vision and Visual Dysfunction*. Vol. XVI, *The Susceptible Visual Apparatus*. General ed. J. R. Cronly-Dillon. Boca Raton, FL: CRC Press.

Berlin, B., and P. Kay 1969. *Basic Color Terms: Their Universality and Evolution*. Berkeley: University of California Press.

Croner, L. J., and E. Kaplan 1995. Receptive fields of P and M ganglion cells across the primate retina. *Vision Research*, 35: 7–24.

Derrington, A. M., J. Krauskopf, and P. Lennie 1984. Chromatic mechanisms in lateral geniculate nucleus of macaque. *Journal of Physiology* 357: 241–265.

De Valois, R. L., and K. K. De Valois 1975. Neural coding of color. In E. C. Carterette and M. P. Friedman (eds.), *Handbook of Perception*. Vol. V (pp. 117–166). New York: Academic Press.

1993. A multi-stage color model. *Vision Research* 33(8): 1053–1065.

De Valois, R. L., I. Abramov, and G. H. Jacobs 1966. Analysis of response patterns of LGN cells. *Journal of the Optical Society of America* 56: 966–977.

De Valois, R. L., I. Abramov, and W. R. Mead 1967. Single cell analysis of wavelength discrimination at the lateral geniculate nucleus in the macaque. *Journal of Neurophysiology* 30: 415–433.

De Valois, R. L., D. M. Snodderly, E. W. Yund, and N. K. Hepler 1977. Responses of macaque lateral geniculate cells to luminance and color figures. *Sensory Processes* 1: 244–259.

De Valois, R. L., H. Morgan, M. C. Polson, W. R. Mead, and E. M. Hull 1974. Psychophysical studies of monkey vision – I. Macaque luminosity and color vision tests. *Vision Research* 14: 53–67.

Dow, B. M. 1991. Colour vision. In A. G. Leventhal (ed.), *Vision and Visual Dysfunction*. Vol. IV, *The Neural Basis of Visual Function*, (pp. 316–338). J. R. Cronly-Dillon. general ed. Boca Raton, FL: CRC Press.

Dowling, J. E. 1987. *The Retina, An Approachable Part of the Brain*. Cambridge, MA: Harvard University Press.

Enroth-Cugell, C., and J. G. Robson 1966. The contrast

sensitivity of retinal ganglion cells of the cat. *Journal of Physiology* 187: 517–552.

Gordon, J., and I. Abramov 1988. Scaling procedures for specifying color appearance. *Color Research and Application,* 13(3): 146–152.

Gordon, J., I. Abramov, and H. Chan 1994. Describing color appearance: Hue and saturation scaling. *Perception and Psychophysics* 56(1): 27–41.

Hurvich, L. M. 1981. *Color Vision.* Sunderland, MA: Sinauer Associates.

Jacobs, G. H. 1993. The distribution and nature of colour vision among the mammals. *Biological Reviews* 68: 413–471.

Kaplan, E., B. B. Lee, and R. M. Shapley 1990. New views of primate retinal function. In N. N. Osborne and G. J. Chader (eds.), *Progress in Retinal Research.* Vol. IX. (pp.273–336). New York: Pergamon.

Kay, P., B. Berlin, and W. R. Merrifield 1991. Biocultural implications of systems of color naming. *Journal of Linguistic Anthropology* 1:12–25.

Lee, B. B., P. R. Martin, and A. Valberg 1989. Nonlinear summation of M- and L-cone inputs to phasic retinal ganglion cells of the macaque. *Journal of Neuroscience* 9: 1433–1442.

Lee, B. B., J. Pokorny, V. C. Smith, P. R. Martin, and A. Valberg 1990. Luminance and chromatic modulation sensitivity of macaque ganglion cells and human observers. *Journal of the Optical Society of America A* 7: 2223–2236.

Livingstone, M., and D. Hubel 1988. Segregation of form, color, movement, and depth: anatomy, physiology, and perception. *Science* 240: 740–749.

MacNichol, E. F., Jr. 1986. A unifying presentation of photopigment spectra. *Vision Research,* 26: 1543–1556.

Merigan, W. H., and J. H. R. Maunsell 1993. How parallel are the primate visual pathways? *Annual Review of Neuroscience* 16: 369–402.

Mollon, J. D. 1989. "Tho' she kneel'd in that place where they grew..." The uses and origins of primate colour vision. *Journal of Experimental Biology* 146: 21–38.

Naka, K. I., and W. A. H. Rushton 1966. An attempt to analyse colour perception by electrophysiology. *Journal of Physiology,* 185: 556–586.

Nathans, J., S. L. Merbs, C.-H. Sung, C. J. Weitz, and Y. Wang 1992. Molecular genetics of human visual pigments. *Annual Review of Genetics,* 26: 403–424.

Nathans, J., D. Thomas, and D. S. Hogness 1986. Molecular genetics of human color vision: the genes encoding blue, green and red pigments. *Science,* 232: 193–202.

Neitz, J., M. Neitz, and G. H. Jacobs 1993. More than three different cone pigments among people with normal

color vision. *Vision Research* 33: 117–122.

Ratliff, F. 1976. On the psychophysiological basis of universal color terms. *Proceedings of the American Philosophical Society* 120(5): 311–330.

——— 1992. *Paul Signac and Color in Neo-Impressionism.* New York: Rockefeller University Press.

Rodieck, R. W. 1991. Which cells code for color? In A. Valberg and B. B. Lee (eds.), *From Pigments to Perception* (pp. 83–93). New York: Plenum Press.

Schefrin, B. E., and J. S. Werner 1990. Loci of spectral unique hues throughout the life span. *Journal of the Optical Society of America A* 7: 305–311.

Schein, S. J., and R. Desimone 1990. Spectral properties of V4 neurons in the macaque. *Journal of Neuroscience* 10: 3369–3389.

Schiller, P. H., M. K. Logothetis, and E. R. Charles 1990. Role of the color-opponent and broad-band channels in vision. *Visual Neuroscience* 5: 321–346.

Schnapf, J. L., B. J. Nunn, M. Meister, and D. A. Baylor 1990. Visual transduction in cones of the monkey *Macaca fascicularis. Journal of Physiology* 427: 681–713.

Shapley, R. 1990. Visual sensitivity and parallel retinocortical channels. *Annual Review of Psychology* 41: 635–658.

Sirovich, L., and I. Abramov 1977. Photopigments and pseudopigments. *Vision Research* 17: 5–16.

Smith, V. C., and J. Pokorny 1975. Spectral sensitivity of the foveal cone photopigments between 400 and 500 nm. *Vision Research* 15: 161–171.

Sperling, H. G. 1992. Spatial discrimination of heterochromatic stimuli: a review and a new experimental approach. In B. Drum (ed.), *Colour Vision Deficiencies.* Vol. XI., (pp.35–50). Dordrecht, Netherlands: Kluwer.

Sternheim, C. E., and R. M. Boynton 1966. Uniqueness of perceived hues investigated with a continuous judgmental technique. *Journal of Experimental Psychology* 72(5): 770–776.

Sternheim, C. E., and B. Drum 1993. Achromatic and chromatic sensation as a function of color temperature and retinal illuminance. *Journal of the Optical Society of America A* 10: 838–843.

Teller, D. Y. 1984. Linking propositions. *Vision Research* 24: 1233–1246.

Thorell, L. G., R. L. De Valois, and D. G. Albrecht 1984. Spatial mapping of monkey V1 cells with pure color and luminance stimuli. *Vision Research* 24: 751–769.

Werner, J. S. 1982. Development of scotopic sensitivity and the absorption spectrum of the human ocular media. *Journal of the Optical Society of America* 72: 247–258.

Winderickx, J., D. T. Lindsey, E. Sanocki, D. Y. Teller, A. G. Motulsky, and S. S. Deeb 1992. Polymorphism in red photopigment underlies variation in colour matching. *Nature* 356: 431–433.

Zeki, S. 1983. Colour coding in the cerebral cortex: the reaction of cells in monkey visual cortex to wavelengths and colours. *Neuroscience* 9: 741–765.

Zrenner, E., I. Abramov, M. Akita, A. Cowey, M. Livingstone, and A. Valberg 1990. Color perception: retina to cortex. In L. Spillmann and J. S. Werner (eds.), *Visual Perception: The Neurophysiological Foundations* (pp. 163–204). San Diego, CA: Academic Press.

5 The neuropsychology of color

Jules Davidoff

This chapter focuses on the neuropsychology of color. It considers the theme of this volume, the categorization of colors, by first discussing the category of color, a somewhat different topic which has been the subject of some important research in neuropsychology. This approach allows us to address questions concerning the relationship between color and other aspects of an object. In particular, I consider the relationship between color and shape, because we can only talk about color itself after we have disentangled the connections between the two.

Despite any possible associations between them, color and shape are quite different from each other. They are distinct, for example, in the way we talk about them: color terms are different parts of speech from shape terms. In ordinary speech, we talk about seeing a sphere; we do not talk about seeing a red. Now, this may seem to be a trivial distinction; but I think it is an important one. Colors are attributes of something else; they are qualities of surfaces or surface appearance. So if we wish to talk of color, we must disentangle talk of the surface appearance from talk of the boundary within which it is contained.

Theoretical approaches to the mental representations of objects have placed different emphases on the roles of shape and the surface held by that shape. At the extreme of complete separation between the two is nineteenth-century phrenology. The phrenological diagrams of the brain show that those bump readers of that century believed in the existence of a separate faculty of color. As it turns out, they were somewhat mistaken, in that most phrenological diagrams placed this faculty in a bump just above the eyebrow. As we now know, if there is a locus for a color center it is likely to be in the back of the brain, somewhere in the visual cortex.

If the phrenologists erred, it was for a very good reason: they went by correlations. Any scientist who pays much attention to correlations eventually makes a blunder; this particular one arose because the phrenologists related color skill to being Japanese. In the nineteenth century, the Japanese were considered to be the arbiters of color taste. As they had pronounced eyebrows, here was evidence of where the color center was to be found. The phrenologists located the separate faculty of shape appreciation not very far away.

The opposite extreme approach is represented by Kandinsky, the painter and teacher at the Bauhaus in Germany in the twenties. Kandinsky believed that colors and shapes were intrinsically linked rather than intrinsically separate – that every shape had a color naturally associated with it. Yellow was intrinsically linked to a triangle, red to a square, and blue to a circle, and there was no argument about it. The colors of intermediate shapes were based on the colors of their constituent shapes. A pentagon, for example, was a shape midway between a triangle and a square, so its color was orange (red and yellow). Kandinsky also had the same idea about angles. Each angle in any picture should have a particular color associated with it. Current neuropsychological thinking can be seen as leaning more to the side of the phrenologists.

Neuropsychological investigations often report on patients with disorders of color processing. I would like to examine these data in greater detail in order to consider whether they provide sufficient evidence for a separate neurological instantiation of color. There is a specific impairment in which it appears that patients have lost the ability to perceive color *and* have not lost the ability to perceive anything else. This particular complaint is known as *achromatopsia*. From a neuropsychological point of view, an achromatopsia has to be acquired and cortical rather than innate or retinal. Since this impairment was first reported, there have been a number of cases in the neurological literature. The number of ascribed cases varies from one reviewer to another. Some provide extensive lists (Meadows 1974; Zihl and Von Cramon 1986; Zeki 1990), based on their view of how reliable these cases were or how well they had been tested, whereas others restrict their list to a number less than one (Teuber, Battersby, and Bender 1960). There certainly have been very few reliable cases.

Most of the American/British literature reports the first case of achromatopsia to be that studied by Verrey (1888), whose patient lost color vision in one visual field (hemiachromatopsia). The German literature (see Zihl and Von Cramon 1986) considers the first case to be the one described by Teitel in 1879. The majority of the cases that have been reported as achromatopsia, perhaps amounting to fifty or so, are really dyschromatopsia: patients have impairments, but not a complete loss, of color vision. The number of cases in which people report total loss of color perception is very small. Indeed, it was the view of the distinguished neurologist Holmes (see Davidoff 1991) that all reported cases were of dyschromatopsia. He studied thousands of people in the First World War who had bullet wounds in the brain. Holmes contended that, on careful examination, one always found at least a loss of brightness as well as of hue. During the Second World War, again not a single case of achromatopsia emerged from a wound to the brain. Thus, Holmes' opinion was taken as gospel until recently. The revival of interest has come about largely because we now think of the visual system as consisting of modular pathways in which different visual properties are processed in parallel. One of these visual properties, investigated by neurophysiological research into the action of the various types of neurons (see Abramov this volume), is color. That approach has made it more fashionable to believe in achromatopsia.

Usually, achromatopsic cases are associated with some visual field loss. That is to say, when the patient's visual field is examined, it is found not to be completely intact. The most common lesion site produces visual field loss in the left upper quadrant; this led people to suggest, because of the crossed nature of the optic pathways, that the color center must be in the right hemisphere. I do not believe this can be true, since there have been rare reports of patients who are hemiachromatopsic (e.g. Verrey 1888). That is to say, they can see color in one visual field but the world appears in black-and-white on the other side. There have only been two or three reliable cases of such a deficit, but it does so happen that the lesions have been on either side of the midline between the cerebral hemispheres.

The most likely reason, I think, for the continuation of the belief that the color center might be in the right hemisphere is that patients with right posterior lesions do have enormous problems making hue discriminations (DeRenzi and Spinnler 1967). The normal way in which a conscientious investigator will look for achromatopsia is by placing the patient in front of a collection of Munsell chips. In selected sections of the total range, say going from red to green in about twenty equal steps of hue change, the patient is asked to arrange the chips so that they systematically change in hue from red to green. This is a particularly difficult task for many of these patients with right-hemisphere damage who also have a spatial disturbance (Zihl, Roth, Kerkhoff, and Heywood 1988). I think that, in order to verify the cortical locus for color, we ought to wait until we can obtain some PET (positron emission tomography) scans for patients performing hue discrimination tasks. It would be interesting if it turned out that we have bilateral color centers but one of them is more finely tuned than the other.

What is it that is lost in achromatopsia? First of all, it must be something very early in visual processing, since the loss is topographically mapped. However, it is not a retinal loss. There have been quite a few good recent studies showing that, in achromatopsic patients, there is normal cone function (Mollon, Newcombe, Polden, and Ratcliff 1980; Heywood, Cowey, and Newcombe 1991). One can tell that the lower-level opponent processes (see Abramov this volume) are working by adapting the eyes to a white light and noticing that the thresholds for the different wavelengths vary in a way that one would predict from the operation of opponent processes. So, although the patient says that the lights are not colored, the thresholds for those lights are precisely what one might expect from the adaptation of opponent processes. Alternatively, one can adapt an area of the retina with red light and find the threshold for green. In this way, we can verify that the retina is functioning normally.

Achromatopsic patients may also be able to use wavelength information to form boundaries. The "color-coded" parvocellular cells of the LGN (see Abramov this volume) also carry information used for boundary formation. Heywood, Cowey, and Newcombe (1991) showed that patients may detect the difference between a red and a green area because they can tell that there is a boundary between the two colored surfaces. One interpretation of their findings is that the parvocellular cells provide input into the boundary-forming mechanisms. The patient is detecting the difference between red and green because he can see an edge; if one separates the two surfaces slightly, then the ability to discriminate the colors disappears.

Damasio, Yamada, Damasio, Corbett, and McKee (1980) claimed that their patients showed no other significant defects besides achro-

Figure 5.1 Two sections from a CT scan of a patient in the study by Damasio *et al.* (1980). The hatching shows the lesioned areas that produced the full field achromatopsia. (Adapted from Davidoff 1991.)

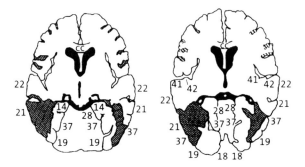

matopsia, although they did not systematically test for brightness discrimination. However, in a subsequent but less clearcut case, Heywood, Wilson, and Cowey (1987) have shown brightness discrimination to be quite good, though not, as the report claims, perfect. Heywood and colleagues used Munsell grays and asked the patient to arrange them in order going from black to white. The patient made very few mistakes, although he did make some.

Where is the lesion that causes achromatopsia? This is the main problem for any simple account that attempts to transfer data from monkeys to humans. Figure 5.1 shows a cross-section through the skull of a person who has one of the purest cases of achromatopsia that has come to radiological examination. This is a CT (computer tomography) scan taken from Damasio *et al.* (1980) for a stroke victim. The patient is an almost perfect case; she exhibited no acuity loss or topographical loss, no neglect or language disturbance. However, she did have a problem recognizing faces, and there was a loss of vision in her right visual field. In a case of hemiachromatopsia presented in the same publication, the patient's other skills were even better preserved. The sites of the lesions shown by the cross-hatchings (see Figure 5.1) are bilateral, but they would appear to be too far away from the visual receptive center (V1 – see Figure 4.1) to affect color perception (the visual field loss of the patient could easily be due to the lesions cutting the optic radiations rather than damage to V1). This same doubt was raised by Holmes (1918) about the early cases. In his opinion, it is impossible that a lesion so far forward in the brain could cause a loss of such a simple perceptual attribute as color vision. These lesions (see Figure 5.1) are in the temporal lobe; they are in the posterior part of it, in the lingual and fusiform gyri.

Now, if we do have a center for color in the lingual and fusiform gyri of the temporal lobe, what is its function? It is not to register color constancy, a function that some have claimed for V4 (see Abramov this volume). These patients do not report that they are unsure of the true color of objects presented to them; they report that there is no color at all. Indeed, there is some controversy about the function of V4. When some of the neurophysiologists remove V4 in animals, they observe a color constancy impairment (Wild, Butler, Carden, and Kulikowski 1985; Zeki 1990) others observe a loss of shape discrimination (Dean 1979; Heywood and Cowey 1987). There is, therefore, a distinct disagreement about the function of V4 in monkeys. We do not really know if the color center in Figure 5.1 is the analogue of V4 in monkeys but located differently. To be sure, it has nothing to do with color memory, since the patient in Figure 5.1 reported being able to dream and imagine in colors. Is it concerned with some sort of language disorder? Zeki, who has carried out PET studies on this particular disorder, denies that it is (Lueck *et al.* 1989). The PET studies are done by asking people to look at a colored array (a "Mondrian" composed of different colored patches) while recording the brain activation. Then, the same normal person is asked to look at an achromatic version of the same array. By subtracting one PET scan from the other, one should be able to identify the color center. Lueck, Zeki, Friston, *et al.* (1989) did just that, and found that it falls right where Damasio believes it should be in humans (Figure 5.1). My only, slight, concern is that the PET scans show a more pronounced color center on the left hemisphere than the right. Because of the connections between the two hemispheres, something happening on the left will drive a homologous area on the right. Therefore, one does wonder whether, during the time the patients were spending looking at these colors, it might not have occurred to them to call the colors "red" and "green" and "blue," etc. Is what Lueck *et al.* discovered the center for color appearance, or has it something to do with color categorization?

Let me discuss some further evidence for color being separate from shape. Figure 5.2 shows some results from a patient seen some years ago (Davidoff and Ostergaard 1984). This patient (P. L.) seemed to have a particular problem with color recognition, but there was no problem with object recognition and, very importantly, no problem with color vision as tested on the Farnsworth–Munsell color deficiency

Figure 5.2 Recognition memory for colors (a) and shapes (b) in a task not involving a verbal component. Chance level would be one-third correct. P.L. 5s exposure (■——■). Controls 5s exposure (●– – –●). Controls 1s exposure (○– – –○).

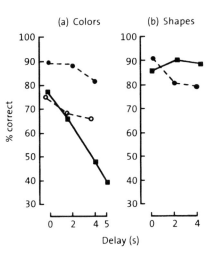

test. In other words, the patient had normal color vision. We asked the patient to remember shapes. He was first given a nonsense shape and then, shortly afterwards, three similar alternatives from which to choose. We asked the patient: "Which one did you see before?" We contrasted his ability to pick out shapes to that shown on a comparable task with Munsell chips. We first presented him with a Munsell chip and then showed an identical one and two others very similar and asked, "Which one of these did you see before?" We went to considerable trouble to make sure that the tasks could not be carried out by naming the first stimulus. The results were really quite dramatic, as seen in Figure 5.2. On the right of the Figure, in the solid line, is the patient's ability to remember shapes. He performed as well as same-age normal controls. On the left is shown the patient's ability to remember colors. It can be seen that there was some drop even at "zero" seconds delay. The stimuli were mounted on cards and were put in front of the patient, with the choice card on top, so "zero" might not be quite that. However, for all purposes, this patient could not maintain the color (the surface appearance) in memory, although he could remember the boundary shape.

The patient of Davidoff and Ostergaard (1984) also could not name colors. The lesion responsible for a loss of color naming is shown in Figure 5.3, taken from Damasio and Damasio (1983). Figure 5.3a shows, in cross-sections through the brain, the lesion for the combination of color anomia and alexia (inability to read); Figure 5.3b shows the

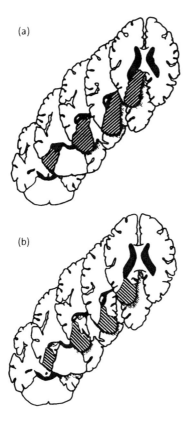

Figure 5.3 Slices of the brain of a patient, from Damasio and Damasio (1983), revealing the lesion sites for (a) color anomia and alexia, and (b) alexia without color anomia. (Adapted from Davidoff 1991.)

(a)

(b)

lesion for alexia alone. By subtraction, one can find the color naming center. The inability to name colors while preserving the use of other categories of words is actually a rather rare occurrence. The first reliable cases were reported in a large study carried out in Boston of the particular categories of names that are lost in aphasic disturbances (Goodglass, Klein, Carey, and Jones 1966). The authors compared patients for preservation and impairment with respect to different categories of words (digits, letters, verbs, nouns), but no adjectives besides those for colors. There were patients who were specifically impaired in, or preserved all of, these categories. The patient of Davidoff and Ostergaard (1984) could name "metronome" and "stethoscope" perfectly well but he could not name "red" or "blue." Such a dramatic discrepancy clearly cannot be explained by the frequency of the words.

There is a further dissociation shown by the same patient. We

asked him to color in – an expression he understood – a line drawing
he could name. The patient went grossly wrong (e.g. blue hair, green
lips). Here we have a dissociation between loss of object-color knowledge and preserved object-shape knowledge. Goldenberg and Artner
(1991) investigated this dissociation in greater detail. They asked
patients with left posterior lesions questions concerning objects.
Some could not answer questions of the form: "Try to picture a carrot,
can you tell me its color?"; others could not answer questions such as:
"Imagine a bear, does it have long, pointed ears or round ones?"

Gathering these threads together, I suggest that we consider these
dissociations between color and shape as analogous to the ways cognitive psychologists model the production of names of objects. I propose
a scheme by which we introduce color naming into the model for the
production of these names. What I propose is that there is some sort of
temporary representation (a "pictorial register"), perhaps at V4, that
recovers a boundaried surface from the visual input. In order to name
the boundaries (shapes) that we have recovered from the world, we
have to match those shapes to some memory store. The memory
description for an object is somewhat abstract, because it is not
sufficient to know that one particular view or aspect of a shape is
called a "dog." We need to know all such aspects, and take note of variations in size and orientation, position in the field, etc. All of these
have to be ignored in order for us to give the same object-name, e.g.
"dog," to all views. Experiments suggest that the memory description
is of a boundary-edge type (Ostergaard and Davidoff 1985; Biederman
and Ju 1988), for which the surface quality, that is to say color, is
not critical. However, somewhere along the line, we might make use
of the object-color information in order to produce the object's name.

The system for the separation of an object-shape from the object-
color is shown in Figure 5.4. What I am proposing is that from the
boundaried surface held at the pictorial register we may extract
information relating only to color or only to shape. A patient may be
able to extract one but not the other type of information. For example,
there could be a complete inability to recognize a single object, yet
perfect color vision and color naming (Wechsler 1933). Thus, in part,
the boxes in the model may be justified by the dissociations of functions found after brain damage. Figure 5.4 is part of a model whose
main aim is to distinguish color representations from object repre-

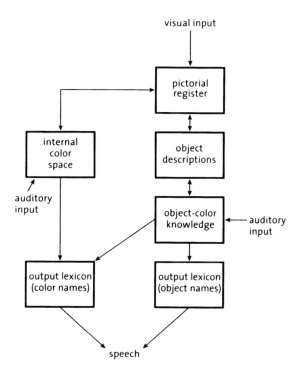

Figure 5.4 Flow chart for a separation of object-shape from object-color.

sentations. A novel aspect of the model is that it contains the important difference between color and object-color. Recent research has verified the distinction between the two abilities (Davidoff and Mitchell 1993). Retrieval of color and object-color are logically distinct operations that have empirically separate consequences. Whereas color naming is in essence a categorization labeling task, reporting an object-color is a paired associate task that might benefit from both visual and verbal experience (a similar distinction is made by Bialystok and Olson [1987] between roundness and the knowledge that a ball is round). Thus, the same response, e.g. "red," can arise from two largely separate operations. Indeed, it could be the lack of distinction between color labels and object-color labels that has resulted in some apparently "universal" aspects of color naming now being disputed (see Lucy this volume). A language low on the Berlin and Kay (1969) hierarchy might nevertheless have a rich vocabulary of object-color terms.

Intervening between the pictorial register and the lexicon for color names I have posited the internal color space, a stage for the (long-term) memory for color (see Figure 5.4). A particular colored surface produced at the pictorial register (say a cerise shade of red) will have a corresponding representation in memory at the internal color space. The internal color space has a categorical structure in which each category will have represented more or less typical examples of a color of that category. Thus, an important aspect of perceived surface colors is that they have a systematic relationship to each other; that is to say, the individual colors fall into categories (reds, oranges, blues, etc.) with a systematic structure. It is the internal color space that is the functional locus for most of the material in this volume; it is the locus of the full range of color categories. There is a great deal to be known about the internal color space but, unfortunately, little research has come from neuropsychology.

As this volume makes clear, color categorization is a task of considerable theoretical importance to many disciplines in the social and natural sciences (Berlin and Kay 1969; Ratliff 1976; Kay and Kempton 1984; Thompson, Palacios, and Varela 1992). At one extreme, the cross-linguistic study of color categorization has shown support for the Sapir–Whorf view (cultural relativism) that language can determine thought (Kay and Kempton 1984; Lucy 1992). At another extreme, the study of color names has emphasized universal aspects of human behavior providing a possibly unique link from neurophysiology to language (Berlin and Kay 1969; Ratliff 1976; Thompson *et al.* 1992). The prevailing belief since Berlin and Kay (1969) has shifted from extreme cultural relativism towards belief in color "universals." Berlin and Kay proposed that, rather than varying without constraint, basic color-term inventories were drawn from a severely constrained subset represented in a hierarchy, and that all languages evolved from a stage with just two basic terms through to a possible eleven terms by taking "permissible routes" through the hierarchy.

Some aspects of the underlying neurophysiological basis of color categories have been discovered. We know that the category within which a surface appearance is located derives, to a large extent, from the categorical output of opponent-process mechanisms. However, there are many aspects of color categories that are still underspecified. In particular, despite our considerable knowledge of wavelength-coded cells (see Abramov this volume), we do not know how color *categories* are produced from the underlying neurophysiology. Indeed, we are a long way from understanding the categorical relationships between individual color samples (let alone what it means to *experience* color) because we are unable to produce a computer simulation that generates a common output for surfaces that we wish to label with the same color name. At the moment, there are many systems for unambiguously coding color samples (see Sivik this volume), but none would satisfy that aim. Moreover, no coding system is psychologically perfect in that all include samples with a color name (e.g. "red"), to which we would not normally give that name. A further aspect of our ignorance of color categories is the extent to which cultural pressures might push a color into one category rather than another (e.g. cerise might be a "red" to one person and a "purple" to another).

Inspection of Figure 5.4 shows that one might expect some relationship between the ability to categorize color and color-naming ability. According to one contemporary account, there is a tight link between the possession of color words and the output of general learning mechanisms (e.g. those proposed by Rumelhart and McClelland 1986). In support of this position, it has been found that children without color terms are not able to sort by color (Rice 1980; Smith 1984). On another account, the difficulty is restricted to lexicalization. Consequently, subjects are able to perform some categorization tasks by color even knowing no color names (Au and Markman 1987; Macario 1991; Soja 1994). Whatever the proper linkage between color categorization and color naming, this issue should not be confused with another important developmental issue: the tardiness of color naming.

Despite some universal aspects of color categorization, children appear to have a peculiar difficulty with color name acquisition. Even when English-speaking children have acquired 500 object names, they cannot correctly apply any color words (Modreski and Goss 1969). The tardiness of color name acquisition continues into the school years. In what now seems a surprising statement, Binet and Simon (1908) gave the naming of 4 colors as the average achievement for an 8-year-old. My own studies suggest that we might expect today's 3.5-year-old child to have the same color-naming ability. If color naming is an intellectual marker, as Binet thought, the present norms are very surprising. There is considerable flexibility in the age at which color names are acquired and it is clear that the phenomenon of tardy color naming requires a better explanation than the delay in myelinization of callosal fibers (Bornstein 1985). In fact, today's norms are probably a result of color being used by the young child to make distinctions between objects that were not made by children of previous generations. However, even if future research were to find better explanations, the tardiness of color naming would have no necessary status in an argument against universality.

The best experimental evidence that some aspects of color categorization are universal comes from the research of Heider with the Dani of New Guinea (Heider 1972; Heider and Olivier 1972). Heider proposed that the Dani, despite having only two basic color terms, had an internal representation of color space identical to that of English speakers. She argued that the mental representation of colors was the same for the speakers of both languages; they were organized around the same focal colors and it was easier, in both languages, to associate previously unconnected words with focal colors rather than with other colors. The research of Heider on the representations of color in the Dani was both stimulating and innovative. However, there are at least three areas (see also Ratner 1989) where either the methodology or interpretation is unclear, or the results would support alternative interpretations.

First, there is concern about whether the Dani really showed greater accuracy for memory for focal rather than nonfocal colors. They achieved an average of only 2.05/8 correct for focal colors (Heider 1972); this is a very low success rate, and suggests that the task was not a suitable one for use with the Dani. Of equal concern was that the Dani produced this low success rate with very fast responses compared to the American sample. Here there are potential problems for the interpretation favoring universality. The poor performance of the Dani could reflect the difficulty in performing the memory task without the availability of color labels, thus supporting relativism rather than universalism. However, any interpretation is difficult given the possibility of a speed–accuracy tradeoff.

Second, Heider's evidence in support of the Berlin and Kay evolutionary order is very weak. It came solely from latency data and then only to a limited extent. American subjects showed a difference in latency of memory response between the four Hering elementary colors and four nonelementary focal colors; there was no reliable evidence that this was the same for the Dani (Heider 1972, exp. 3). For the paired-associate learning experiment (Heider 1972, exp. 4), the order of learning "did not correlate significantly with Berlin and Kay's proposed evolutionary order" with only a marginal relationship when grouped into primary and nonprimary focal colors. Thus, although Heider interpreted her results as supporting universalism, they only weakly support the version of Berlin and Kay.

Third, a serious weakness in Heider experiments, when viewed from the perspective of the linguistic relativists, is that her stimuli were not culturally appropriate for the Dani. In Dani, color terms are typically bound to objects rather than to isolated patches (to the object-color knowledge box in Figure 5.4 rather than to the internal color space). Therefore, color-term inventories may be inadequately sampled if only isolated color patches are used. These considerations make it clear that Rosch's important experiments need to be replicated and, if possible, extended.

To return to the neurophysiological evidence for the mechanisms underlying color categorization, selective damage within the route to the color lexicon could spare the internal color space; that is to say, there are patients who cannot name colors but who can nevertheless categorize them (e.g. into reds, blues, and browns). Thus, Sittig (1921) drew a distinction between *Farbenagnosie* and *Farbennamenamnesie*. Sittig's use of the term "color agnosia" (*Farbenagnosie*) is more precise than that of many who have used the term since his day. In his terminology, a pure agnosia for color meant an inability to categorize colors and need not necessarily be accompanied by an impairment in the memory of object-color nor a loss of color names Farbennamenamnesie).

Using techniques capable of more precision, color categorization was recently investigated in two patients who successfully passed the Ishihara color blindness test but had difficulty naming colors. Fukuzawa, Itoh, Sasanuma, Suzuki, and Fukusako (1988) employed a multidimensional scaling procedure in which objects reliably associated with a color (in Japan this would, for example, mean an apple for red and a persimmon for orange) were presented in three separate studies. The objects were presented as color patches, color names, and line drawings. The subject's task was to select, from three stimuli, the two colors, color names, or imagined colors of objects that were more similar. From these data, Fukuzawa *et al.* plotted a color space for their patients. The results of the multidimensional scaling were compared to tasks in which patients were asked for a binary categorization of colored patches (green vs. yellow, and purple vs. blue) and to sort seventy colors into as many color groups as desired. The patients were found to have atypical color spaces.

The Fukuzawa *et al.* technique for investigating color space is considerably more sophisticated than those used in previous studies. However, it may not be an effective way of recovering the color space for all subjects. It is less likely to be effective if judgments are requested from disparate typical areas of the color space. Some subjects, without good access to an internal space which arranges hues in the conventional circle, would find such similarity judgments hard to comprehend. Typical examples of red, yellow, and green would be equidistant in their color space and it might make no sense whatsoever to say that one of them was more different from the other two than they were from each other.

Neuropsychological research has provided evidence for a considerable number of dissociations involving the discrete stages shown in Figure 5.4. A particularly important one has been the dissociation between a color agnosia and the memory of object-colors. This dissociation has been confirmed in only a few cases (Kinsbourne and Warrington 1964; Beauvois and Saillant 1985) because color categorization is so infrequently examined. There is also an important dissociation between color anomia and memory for object-colors. The two disorders normally occur together, and it has been possible to attribute the latter to irrepressible and wrong color naming. However, Luzzatti and Davidoff (1994) recently reported two patients who had difficulty retrieving the colors of objects but demonstrated perfect color naming. The separate status of the boxes in Figure 5.4, including that for color categorization, can therefore be guaranteed from neuropsychological findings.

The yellow color of a ripe banana appears to us as an integral part of its surface. The yellowness helps to define its shape, and to make it stand out from a clutter of other things. When we are asked to think of something yellow, we readily think of bananas, and when we imagine a banana, we find it hard to imagine it without imagining it as yellow. We readily name its color, and cannot help but see that color as more akin to the color of oranges than to the color of blueberries. So easily do we move from one of those aspects of the banana's yellow to another that we may fail to appreciate that each involves a distinct perceptual or cognitive task. Thanks to those unfortunate people whose grasp of color has been compromised by insult or nature, we are able to get a firmer grasp in our understanding of the mental representations for color.

References

Au, T. K., and E. M. Markman 1987. Acquiring color names via linguistic contrast. *Cognitive Development* 2: 217–236.

Beauvois, M.-F. and B. Saillant 1985. Optic aphasia for colours and colour agnosia: a distinction between visual and visuo-verbal impairments in the processing of colours. *Cognitive Neuropsychology* 2: 1–48.

Berlin, B., and P. Kay 1969. *Basic Color Terms: Their Universality and Evolution.* Berkeley: University of California Press. 1st paperback edn. 1991, with bibliography by Luisa Maffi.

Bialystock, E., and D. R. Olson 1987. Spatial categories: the perception and conceptualization of spatial relations. In S. Harnad (ed.), *Categorical Perception* (pp. 511–531). Cambridge University Press.

Biederman, I., and G. Ju 1988. Surface versus edge-based determinants of visual recognition. *Cognitive Psychology* 20: 38–64.

Binet, A. and T. Simon 1908. Le développement de l'intelligence chez les enfants. *Année Psychologique* 14: 1–94.

Bornstein, M. H. 1985. On the development of color naming in young children: data and theory. *Brain and Language* 26: 72–93.

Damasio, A. R., and H. Damasio 1983. The anatomic basis of pure alexia. *Neurology* 33: 1573–1584.

Damasio, A. R., T. Yamada, H. Damasio, J. Corbett, and J. McKee 1980. Central achromatopsia: behavioral, anatomic and physiologic aspects. *Neurology* 30: 1064–1071.

Davidoff, J. 1991. *Cognition Through Color.* Cambridge, MA: MIT Press.

Davidoff, J., and Mitchell, P. 1993. The color cognition of children. *Cognition* 48: 121–137.

Davidoff, J., and A. L. Ostergaard 1984. Color anomia resulting from weakened short-term memory.

Brain 107: 415–431.

Dean, P. 1979. Visual cortex ablation and thresholds for successively presented stimuli in rhesus monkeys. II. Hue. *Experimental Brain Research* 35: 69–83.

DeRenzi, E., and H. Spinnler 1967. Impaired performance on color tasks in patients with hemispheric damage. *Cortex* 3: 194–217.

Fukuzawa, K., M. Itoh, S. Sasanuma, T. Suzuki, and Z. Fukusako 1988. Internal representations and the conceptual operation of color in pure alexia with color naming defects. *Brain and Language* 34: 98–126.

Goldenberg, G., and C. Artner 1991. Visual imagery and knowledge about the visual appearance of objects in patients with posterior cerebral artery lesions. *Brain and Cognition* 15: 160–186.

Goodglass, H., B. Klein, P. Carey, and K. Jones 1966. Specific semantic word categories in aphasia. *Cortex* 2: 74–89.

Heider, E. R. 1972. Universals in color naming and memory. *Journal of Experimental Psychology* 93(1): 10–20.

Heider, E. R., and D. C. Olivier 1972. The structure of the color space in naming and memory for two languages. *Cognitive Psychology* 3: 337–354.

Heywood, C. A., and A. Cowey 1987. On the role of cortical area V4 in the discrimination of hue and pattern in macaque monkeys. *Journal of Neuroscience* 7: 2601–2617.

Heywood, C. A., A. Cowey, and F. Newcombe 1991. Chromatic discrimination in a cortically blind observer. *European Journal of Neuroscience* 3: 802–812.

Heywood, C. A., B. Wilson, and A. Cowey 1987. A case study of cortical color "blindness" with relatively intact achromatic discrimination. *Journal of Neurology, Neurosurgery and Psychiatry* 50: 22–29.

Holmes, G. (1918). Disturbances of vision by cerebral

lesions. *British Journal of Ophthalmology* 2: 353–384.

Kay, P., and W. Kempton 1984. What is the Sapir–Whorf hypothesis? *American Anthropologist* 86(1): 65–79.

Kinsbourne, M., and E. K. Warrington 1964. Observations on colour agnosia. *Journal of Neurology, Neurosurgery and Psychiatry* 27: 296–299.

Lucy, J. A. 1992. *Language Diversity and Thought: A Reformation of the Linguistic Relativity Hypothesis.* Cambridge University Press.

Lueck, C. J., S. Zeki, K. J. Friston, M.-P. Deiber, P. Cope, V. J. Cunningham, A. A. Lammertsma, C. Kennard, and R. S. J. Frackowiak 1989. The color centre in the cerebral cortex of man. *Nature* 340: 386–389.

Luzzatti, C., and J. Davidoff 1994. Impaired retrieval of object-colour knowledge with preserved colour naming. *Neuropsychologia* 32: 933–950.

Macario, J. F. 1991. Young children's use of color in classification: foods and canonically colored objects. *Cognitive Development* 6: 17–46.

Meadows, J. C. 1974. Disturbed perception of colors associated with localised cerebral lesions. *Brain* 97: 615–632.

Modreski, R. A., and A. E. Goss 1969. Young children's initial and changed names for form-color stimuli. *Journal of Experimental Child Psychology* 8: 402–409.

Mollon, J. D., F. Newcombe, P. G. Polden, and G. Ratcliff 1980. On the presence of three cone mechanisms in a case of total achromatopsia. In G. Verriest (ed.), *Color Vision Deficiencies* (pp. 130–135). Bristol: V. Hilger.

Ostergaard, A. L., and J. Davidoff 1985. Some effects of color on naming and recognition of objects. *Journal of Experimental Psychology: Learning, Memory and Cognition* 11: 579–587.

Ratliff, F. 1976. On the psychophysiological basis of universal color terms. *Proceedings of the American Philosophical Society* 120(5): 311–330.

Ratner, C. 1989. A sociohistorical critique of naturalistic theories of color perception. *Journal of Mind and Behavior* 10: 361–372.

Rice, M. 1980. *Cognition to Language Categories: Word, Meaning and Training.* Baltimore: University Park Press.

Rumelhart, D. E. and J. L. McClelland 1987. On learning the past tenses of English verbs. In J. L. McClelland, D.E. Rumelhart, and the PDP Research Group (eds.), *Parallel Distributed Processing: Explorations in the Microstructure of Cognition.* Vol. II, *Psychological and Biological Models* (pp. 216–271). Cambridge, MA: MIT Press.

Sittig, O. 1921. Störungen im Verhalten gegenüber Farben bei Aphasischen. *Monatsschrift für Psychiatrie und Neurologie* 49: 63–68, 169–187.

Smith, L. B. 1984. Young children's understanding of attributes and dimensions: a comparison of conceptual and linguistic measures. *Child Development* 55: 360–380.

Soja, N. N. 1994. Young children's concept of color and its relation to the acquisition of color words. *Child Development* 55: 360–380.

Teuber, H.-L., W. S. Battersby, and M. B. Bender 1960. *Visual Field Defects after Penetrating Missile Wounds of the Brain.* Cambridge, MA: Harvard University Press.

Thompson, E., A. Palacios, and F. J. Varela 1992. Ways of coloring: comparative color vision as a case study for cognitive science. *Behavioral and Brain Sciences* 15: 1–74.

Verrey, D. 1888. Hemiachromatopsie droite absolue. *Archives d'Ophthalmologie* (Paris) 8: 289–300.

Wechsler, I. S. 1933. Partial cortical blindness with preservation of color vision. *Archives of Ophthalmology* 9: 957–965.

Wild, H. M., S. R. Butler, D. Carden, and J. J. Kulikowski 1985. Primate cortical area V4 important for color constancy but not wavelength discrimination. *Nature* 313: 133–135.

Zeki, S. 1990. A century of cerebral achromatopsia. *Brain* 113: 1721–1777.

Zihl, J., and D. Von Cramon 1986. *Zerebrale Sehstörung.* Stuttgart: Kohlhammer.

Zihl, J., W. Roth, G. Kerkhoff, and C. A. Heywood 1988. The influence of homonymous visual field disorders on color sorting performance in the FM 100-hue test. *Neuropsychologia* 26: 869–876.

6 Insights gained from naming the OSA colors

Robert M. Boynton

Introduction

By the time the year 1985 rolled around, I had already been working in the realm of color vision for thirty years, with a clear focus on the psychophysiological aspects of adult human vision – the kinds of phenomena for which a genetic basis seems likely, and for which individual differences are minor. That is, I deliberately avoided working on developmental or comparative aspects of color vision, and with some exceptions I also tried to steer clear of cognitive complications. In most of my experiments, usually carried out in collaboration with graduate students or postdoctoral fellows, we used noninvasive psychophysical techniques and human subjects. (For a while I was inserting microelectrodes into monkey eyes as well.) For many years I never suspected that linguists or anthropologists had any interest in the fundamental aspects of color vision, although I was familiar with (and, I must say, unimpressed by) the Whorfian hypothesis, and it was my understanding that anthropologists considered that the naming of colors was an arbitrary affair, fully under the control of cultural influences. Perhaps most vision scientists felt that way too, because, compared to threshold measurements and matching procedures, color naming was not considered to be a very respectable psychophysical technique for getting at the fundamental aspects of color perception.

I first became aware of Berlin and Kay's *Basic Color Terms* (1969) when the monograph was mentioned in a 1973 *Annual Review of Psychology* article (Trandis, Malpass, and Davidson 1973). The account intrigued me and so, for purposes of recreational reading, I borrowed the book from the UCSD library. I found the book fascinating and delightfully easy to read. Although it was clear to me that the experimental portions of the study would not pass muster if judged according to the standards upon which experimental psychologists insist, I was somehow convinced that the major conclusions reached by Berlin and Kay were probably correct.

Despite the large number of people who have been inspired by this slim book, it has not been of much interest to most color-vision researchers with my kind of pedigree. A significant exception is Floyd Ratliff, who sent me an unsolicited copy of his 1976 review article (Ratliff 1976) published in the *Proceedings of the American Philosophical Society*. Floyd and I are old friends. We were graduate students together in Lorrin Riggs's laboratory in the Department of Psychology at Brown University around 1950. Floyd subsequently made an enormous reputation for himself in the area of spatial vision, working initially with Keffer Hartline, who had been the first person to record single-unit neural activity in any visual system. The experimental animal from which they recorded, the lowly horseshoe crab *Limulus,* does not possess any form of color vision. However, Ratliff's interests are much broader than his published experimental work might suggest, and color has been of more than passing interest for him, particularly as it relates to his deep concern with representational painting. Floyd told me recently that the Berlin and Kay monograph was also the launching pad for his interest in basic color terms, and that after he read it, he immediately began to think about the relevant underlying visual physiology. When invited to give a lecture to the American Philosophical Society, of which he is a member, he spoke on the psychophysiological basis of universal color terms, which led to his excellent paper in their journal. (Recently, Ratliff's interests in color and art have been brought together in a book [Ratliff 1992] entitled *Paul Signac and Color in Neo-Impressionism.*)

Orange and the spectral colors

Many years ago, Charles Sternheim and I published a study (Sternheim and Boynton 1966) in which we examined the color naming of monochromatic lights, from which we concluded that the category orange was unnecessary for rating the appearance of long-wavelength spectral lights, although both red and yellow categories were essential for this purpose. To my knowledge, neither the logic of our study nor the conclusion we reached has ever been challenged, and the method we developed has been employed by Fuld, Wooten, and Whalen (1981) to ask the same question about purple, with the same result. Therefore, when I learned of the Berlin and Kay work, it seemed odd to me that orange, which so obviously contains both red and yellow coextensively, could be a basic color. Obviously, this has been a source of concern for others, as is reflected, for example, by the division of chromatic basic color terms into primary and derived groups, as proposed by Kay and McDaniel (1978).

Color naming by colorblind subjects

Horst Scheibner and I (1968) used a color-naming procedure to examine the behavior of classical dichromats (the red–green colorblind) and we were able to show, for example, that the probability of their using the name "red" increased with wavelength for equally bright monochromatic lights, whereas all of these should have appeared identical according to accepted accounts of red–green color deficiency. This led us to conclude that a weak residual red–green chromatic system was retained in most dichromats. Few believed our conclusion at first, but our interpretation has since been verified using other methods and other investigators, including two participants in the Asilomar conference (Abramov [Gordon and Abramov 1977] and Wooten [Fuld *et al.* 1981]) who have done excellent work using color-naming procedures similar to ours. As already noted, it was unusual for visual scientists of my ilk to use color-naming procedures when we began our studies. Although this early work may not bear directly on issues related to basic color terms, I mention it here because it helps to explain why, after having my curiosity piqued by reading the Berlin and Kay book, I was eventually motivated to do color-naming experiments related to their conclusions.

Color-naming experiments at University of California San Diego

Background

Prior to 1975, I had never worked with surface colors. For the most part we had used monochromatic stimuli delivered by Maxwellian view, a method that provides isolated ethereal lights that appear suspended in space and utterly devoid of any object properties even when a second channel provides a surround. As we all know, the real world of color depends importantly upon the nature of surfaces as these selectively absorb and reflect the spectral components of incident light, and the difference between the appearances of aperture and surface colors is so great that making color matches between them is virtually impossible.

Neither Berlin and Kay, nor most of those who have used a similar methodology, seem to have been concerned with the nature of the light illuminating their materials, or the possible problems introduced by chromatic context. The mechanisms of color constancy work so well that, within limits, the intensity and spectral distribution of the light used to illuminate the experimental materials make surprisingly little difference. Yet it seemed to me that these variables should be better controlled, there being no reason for them not to be if one is working in the laboratory, rather than out in the field somewhere. Contextual problems relate to the well-established fact that the chromatic appearance of any given part of the visual field depends not only upon the physical properties of the light coming from it, but also upon the surround. Therefore a focal green, say, that an informant might select from the Berlin and Kay ordered array may well be a different sample than the one that would be selected if the samples appeared in pairs, or sequentially in isolation. Berlin and Kay tended to choose the color terms to be examined a priori, rather than allowing each subject to make an independent selection, and we wished to avoid this. Other variables, including viewing time, response time, and the exact distance between the observer and the experimental materials also had not been fully controlled. So I decided to design a study to remedy these possible deficiencies (Boynton and Olson 1987, 1990).

Choice of stimuli: the OSA set

The first decision that we had to make concerned the choice of color samples. It would be possible in principle to create a set of 1 million color chips, no two of which would match if viewed side by side under good viewing conditions. There would be about 500 billion possible nonmatching pairs that could be drawn from such a set. This observation is testimony both to the exquisite sensitivity of the human visual system to small color differences, and to the impossibility of using a separate name to communicate about each discriminable color. It also means that the researcher working with a palpable set of color chips must deal with a severely restricted subset of the million or so discriminably different colors that potentially could be used, and it may well matter which set is selected for experimental purposes. I did not favor the set of Munsell colors used by Berlin and Kay. By avoiding the use of all but the most saturated chromatic colors in the set, Berlin and Kay kept the number of colors within reasonable bounds, but otherwise I could see no logical reason for doing this. Also, the cylindrical arrangement of specimens in the Munsell system guarantees that the perceptual distance between adjacent colors must vary markedly from one region to another, meaning that calculations of distances between colors in this space, which some people have done, are not very meaningful.

Ten years prior to the start of our research, the Optical Society of America had made available a new set of color chips, called the OSA Uniform Color Scales Samples (Nickerson 1981). The committee that developed this, which had supervised the relevant psychophysical observations that went into it, was attempting to produce an ordered set of colors that would sample three-dimensional color space with the requirement that the perceptual distance between each color and its nearest neighbors would be constant throughout the metric of that space. If this could be achieved, it would furnish equally spaced specimens in an isotropic color space, within which a linear distance would imply the same number of just-noticeable color steps regardless of the starting point or the direction traversed. It cannot be claimed that the final product met this criterion exactly, nor that it is even possible to achieve it exactly in Euclidean space, but it can be claimed that the OSA colors come closer to meeting this objective than do any of the other sets of color chips.

There are 424 color samples in the OSA system, in which the central axis runs from near black at the bottom through grey to near-white at the top (see Figure 6.1). The two chromatic axes, orthogonal to one another and to the achromatic axis, are very roughly red–green and yellow–blue. The middle grey of the set is called 0,0,0, and the others are designated plus or minus as one moves outward, upward, or downward along the three dimensions.

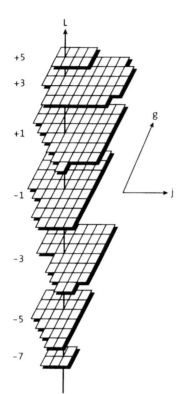

Figure 6.1 Arrangement of the OSA colors. The lightness axis "L" runs from near-black at the bottom to near-white at the top, with a neutral gray sample at each of the even-numbered lightness levels, which have been left off the diagram for clarity. At each lightness level, there are 2 chromatic axes, labeled "j" and "g", which are perpendicular to each other and to the lightness axis. Each of the 424 color chips of the system is intended to be equidistant from its 12 nearest neighbors.

Because of an interest in the relation between color discrimination and color order as these relate to color naming, I chose the OSA colors for our investigation despite knowing that doing so would complicate comparisons of our results with those of previous investigators. (Later we [Boynton, MacLaury, and Uchikawa 1989] would specify the matching samples of the OSA and Berlin–Kay Munsell sets of color chips.)

Experimental procedures

Our experimental setup was the following. The subject sat in a booth painted inside with a spectrally flat grey paint matching Munsell #5. An aperture on a slanted grey table, into which color samples could be slid from behind, was covered most of the time with a grey shutter blade. Lighting was provided indirectly by a single photoflood lamp, which produced a luminance of 40 cd/m² of the background grey at

3,000 K. The specular component of reflectance was negligible. Subjects were instructed to be prepared on signal to expect the shutter to open, exposing a uniform square of color. They were told to name each color using a single color term ("no modifiers or compounds are allowed") and to do so within 5 seconds. They were instructed that if they used an incorrect compound name, or delayed their response beyond the 5-second limit, they would be informed of their error and the trial would have to be repeated later, which would prolong the experimental session. These errors very seldom occurred, and no further mention of speed was made to induce time pressure. Unknown to the subjects, we recorded their response times, but we wanted the data to reflect what came naturally, rather than what they might be able to do in a hair-trigger reaction-time situation.

The experimental design was very simple. For each subject, a random order of the 424 color samples was determined. The colors were individually presented in this sequence, and the elicited names and response times were recorded for later analysis. At this point the subject's job was half completed. We continued by presenting the samples again, this time in the reverse of the initial random order. To control for possible sequential effects, each subject had his or her own random order. Our data set for each subject then consisted of 848 monolexemic color terms – 2 for each of the 424 samples, and the response times for each. Usually about 4 experimental sessions of an hour or more were needed to obtain these data.

Results: use of basic color terms

All subjects, including the dichromats, used all eight basic chromatic color terms. (There are only poor examples of white and black in the OSA set of colors, and some dichromats also avoided gray [Montag and Boynton 1987].) There was no non-basic color term that was used by all subjects. The frequency of use of non-basic color terms was wildly idiosyncratic: we have had subjects who used as few as four, and others who used more than fifty. We examined the consistency of color usage, which relates to the probability that a color name, if used by a given subject on the first presentation, will be used again on the second one. No overlap was found for mean data between basic and non-basic color terms; that is, all basic color terms were used more consistently than

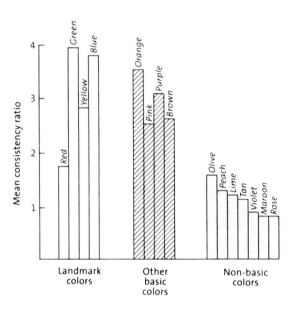

Figure 6.2 Consistency of color naming. The ordinate shows the ratio of consistent to inconsistent color naming when each of the color terms is used. The most consistently used non-basic colors are shown at the right, and the basic colors (left and center) are separated into the fundamental (landmark) and derived (other) categories. All basic colors are used more consistently than any of the non-basic ones.

any non-basic term. Moreover, the results for basic color terms were about the same for fundamental and derived basic colors. We also looked for consensus of color naming across subjects. Again, there was greater consensus for the use of all basic color terms than for any of the non-basic ones. There are some non-basic terms used by most adult subjects, such as peach, tan, and olive, but none of these was used by all of them. By contrast, we found that all color-normal adult subjects use all basic color terms. We examined one American two-year-old and two four-year-olds, one of them a Japanese child. (Only the Japanese four-year-old would tolerate the booth; the others were tested with Munsell colors lent by MacLaury.) Except for the use of the word "peach" on three occasions by the American four-year-old, and the word *mizu* (light blue) by the Japanese one, only basic color terms were used. Both four-year-olds used all of the basic color terms of their respective languages. The two-year-old never called any of the chips brown or red, although he was already fully capable of describing the colors of natural objects using these words (Boynton, *et al.* 1989).

Centroids of basic colors in the OSA space

We proceeded to examine the arrangement of basic colors in the OSA space. To do this, we calculated, both for individual and group data, the centroid location of each color. This is simply the average, across trials, for each of the three coordinate values of the color samples that elicited that color name, weighted according to the number of times it was used. Again I emphasize that such a calculation only makes sense for an isotropic space. The proper way to think about these centroids, and the color space in which they are imbedded, is the following. Take yellow as an example. The centroid is the middle of the region of color space in which the term "yellow" is used. It is not quite the same as the focal yellow, which is a bit more saturated, but it is in the region where the probability of the name "yellow" being used is greatest. The probability of any other basic color term being used in this mid-region approaches zero. Although very definite at its focus, the yellow region represents a fuzzy subset of all color chips that might be called "yellow," because the region overall lacks sharp edges. Instead, the probability of the name "yellow" being used decreases as one moves away from the middle of the region, and other basic color names begin to creep in, along with an increased use of non-basic terms. Approximately midway between the yellow and green centroid locations, for example, the two names are used with roughly equal frequency to name samples that appear coextensively yellow and green.

Need for bridges between certain basic colors.

With a few exceptions that mostly involve brown and grey, we found that the basic colors whose fuzzy sets overlap have centroids that plot less than 7.5 OSA units apart, whereas centroids for regions whose sets do not overlap are separated by distances greater than this. A very significant observation is that the red and yellow regions do not overlap at all. That is, there are no samples that are called red on one occasion and yellow on another, whereas red and orange, and yellow and orange, are frequently linked in this sense. Orange is therefore an essential bridge between red and yellow, just as yellow is an essential bridge between orange and green. This is surprising because of the derived nature of orange in contrast with the unique character of yellow: colors intermediate between red and yellow are seen as containing components of both, whereas yellow, when acting as the bridge between orange and green, does not seem to contain components of either. A bridge is also needed between red and blue.

Figure 6.3 Linkages. Basic colors are said to be "linked" when there are intervening color chips that are sometimes named with one of the basic color terms, and sometimes with the other one. Connectors are shown between the centroid locations of colors linked in this sense. Note that there are no linkages between red and yellow, or between red and blue. In this diagram, the larger spheres should be visualized as being closer to the observer, representing lighter colors.

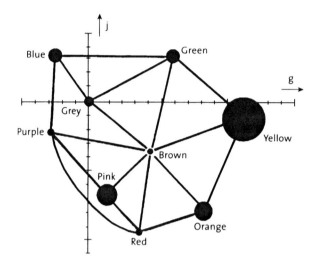

Despite their non-elementary nature, the so-called derived basic colors, in addition to meeting the criteria of consistency and consensus (and, as we will see below, short response times), serve essential bridging functions and are equally as essential for filling the basic color space as are the primary ones. (We speak of two colors as being linked or unlinked, depending upon whether or not a bridge color is necessary to move between them.) Figure 6.3 attempts to summarize the locations of and linkages among the basic colors. The lightness dimension is encoded by the size of the symbols.

No basic color exists between green and its nearest chromatic neighbors, blue and yellow, which are much closer to green than red is to yellow. There is no suggestion that a new basic color term representing a blue-green or yellow-green is needed or is likely to evolve. GRUE could describe an early cognitive stage for the two linked primary basic colors green and blue. A single term for the yellow–green region is similarly possible. Single categories embracing red and yellow, or red and blue, seem unlikely because their separation is too great, although red–orange–yellow and red–purple–blue would seem to be likely possibilities because they include the necessary bridges.

A missing basic color?

Our use of desaturated colors, as well as saturated ones, leads to an interesting result near the middle of the color space. Here there is a region, variously called "peach," "tan," and by other non-basic names (including *hada* by our Japanese subjects [Uchikawa and Boynton 1987]) that is much more than 7.5 OSA units across in any direction between flanking basic-color centroids. The one sample of the 424 which is the most difficult to name is located near the middle of this region. Basic color terms are seldom used to identify this sample and, to a progressively lesser extent, its neighbors. Response times are long; consensus and consistency are poor. This situation suggests that another basic color *ought* to exist in this region, but that for some reason it does not. If another emergent basic color sensation were to evolve, I think it ought to have its centroid here, but any physiological basis for it is apparently lacking, and it is difficult to imagine the new chromatic sensation that would elicit the use of a new basic color term for its description.

Response times

As already noted, we examined response times for the use of basic color terms in comparison with those for non-basic terms. In their 1981 review article concerned with the categorization of natural objects, Mervis and Rosch (1981: 96) conclude that: "Response times are shorter for verification of the category membership of representative exemplars than nonrepresentative exemplars; these effects are robust and appear in a variety of experimental paradigms."

In Figure 6.4, the color names are again divided into three groups. The primary basic colors are at the left, the other derived or secondary basic colors are shown in the middle, and data for the six most popular non-basic colors are shown at the right. This chart, like the one for consistency in Figure 6.2, again illustrates the lack of overlap between data for basic versus non-basic colors, with all non-basic color names being used more slowly, and by the criterion of response time also there is no difference between the primary, or landmark, basic colors and the other basic colors.

Lightness locations of basic colors

It is very important not to overlook the importance of the lightness dimension in the arrangement of color centroids, because centroids alone cannot tell the full story about the shapes of the fuzzy sets they

Figure 6.4 Response times. The ordinate shows the mean response time for the use of the color names depicted on the bars. Note that one second has been subtracted from the response times; this is approximately the shortest response time recorded for any individual color sample. The groupings are the same as in Figure 6.2.

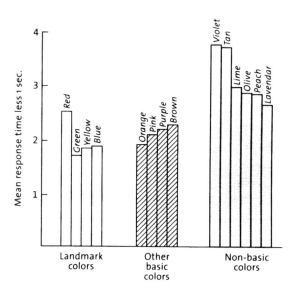

Figure 6.5 Lightness ranges. For each of the curves and at each lightness level, the shortest mean response time recorded (nine subjects combined) at that level is plotted. Where no points are plotted, the indicated color name was very seldom, if ever, employed. The plots show the range over which the basic color terms are used, and the minima of the plotted functions can be taken to indicate, by this criterion, the lightness levels for the best exemplars. The curves have been displaced arbitrarily in the vertical direction. Minimum response times are indicated for each color.

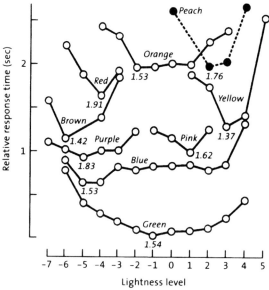

represent. Of all the plots we have created to represent our results, Figure 6.5 is my favorite. Each curve shows the shortest response time for any color sample used in each of the categories of chromatic basic color naming, plotted as a function of lightness level. There are points on a given curve only for lightness levels at which that color name was used at least ten times by the nine subjects included in the analysis, so

for all practical purposes each name was used only over the range plotted. (Note that the separate curves have been arbitrarily displaced vertically from one another.) These curves summarize the important facts
about basic colors as a function of lightness level, which are the following:

(a) Unlike the other colors, green and blue are seen at virtually all
lightness levels. The darker blues appear to be slightly more
prototypical, yielding the shortest response times. The best greens
are seen at the middle lightness levels.

(b) Red, brown, and purple are reported only at the lower lightness levels.
Optimal brown is the darkest, followed by purple and then red.

(c) Next to blue and green, the use of orange covers the broadest range
of lightnesses, optimally so at intermediate levels. The lightness of
the best pink is intermediate between those for the best orange and
the best yellow.

It is interesting to speculate concerning why the centroid locations of the basic colors are where they are. Looking down on the array
from the top, and ignoring the achromatic spindle, it is clear that each
centroid occupies a unique location when projected to the chromatic
plane. This is not surprising because it reflects the relative excitations
of the L-, M-, and S-cones of the visual system which are fundamental
to chromatic variation. However, the important proviso must be added
that there is no chromatic plane at any lightness level that includes all
of the basic colors. Yellow, orange, and pink simply do not exist at the
lower levels, and purple, brown, and red are absent at the lighter ones.
Brown requires a lighter surround for its very existence. The low-
lightness position of the centroid for red, unlike that for brown, is
dependent instead upon the nature of reflecting pigments. To get a
good red, all but the longest wavelengths of incident white light must
be absorbed. The remaining long wavelengths are ones to which the
eye is relatively insensitive, and it is for this reason alone that the red
centroid plots at low lightness. A source that emits long-wavelength
light and which appears red does not lose its redness at high brightness levels, even without any surround (as we all know from our
experience with red stop lights at night). Brown signal lights, on the
other hand, are impossible to produce, even though brown is as useful
as any other basic color for coding purposes in reflecting displays.

Some other color-naming studies at San Diego

We have used our color-naming method to examine a number of other areas that I have not mentioned because they do not bear directly on the issues under discussion in this volume. These include the color rendering of light sources (Boynton and Purl 1989; Boynton, Fargo, and Collins 1990), color memory (Boynton, Fargo, Olson, and Smallman 1989), the influence of surrounds (Uchikawa, Uchikawa, and Boynton 1989a), color constancy (Uchikawa, Uchikawa, and Boynton 1989b), and the role of basic colors in visual search (Smallman and Boynton 1990).

Final remarks

In thinking about basic colors, as these relate to the kinds of concerns that seem to motivate anthropologists, I would suggest that it would be much more useful to consider our color space than to refer to opponent-color diagrams, and that one should accept our conclusion that there are no differences between primary and derived basic colors except for the compound sensory aspect of the latter, which really does not seem to matter. I would argue that all eleven basic colors are perceptual fundamentals, and that the concept of fundamental neural responses, as defined by Kay, Berlin, and Merrifield (1991), should be expanded to include all eleven. Their appeal to the early research of DeValois and his colleagues is misguided, if only because sensations surely do not arise from the lateral geniculate nucleus, which was the site of their recordings. Moreover, DeValois's use of the names red, yellow, green, and blue to classify groups of data was entirely arbitrary and ignored a virtual continuum of opponent responses that exists as a function of crossover wavelength in the data of individual units (see Boynton 1979: 234–236).

We simply do not yet know what kind of activity in the brain generates our color sensations. I feel it reasonable to suppose that there may be eleven categorically separate varieties of activity, corresponding to each of eleven kinds of color sensations that are identified by the eleven basic color terms. It might be productive, I think, to consider these as the pan-human perceptual fundamentals, and to keep their fuzzy-set locations in mind when speculating about the cultural evolution of basic color terms. I also feel hopeful that physiologists or physiological psychologists may eventually find the basis in the brain for the eleven basic color sensations. Some progress in this regard has been made by Yoshioka, Dow, and Vautin (1996).

Acknowledgments Those who have participated with me in our color-naming research are Lynn Bailey, Geoffrey Boynton, Lee Fargo, Ethan Montag, Conrad Olson, Kathleen Purl, Harvey Smallman, Hiromi Uchikawa, and Keiji Uchikawa. I am greatly indebted to all of them.

References

Berlin, B., and P. Kay 1969. *Basic Color Terms: Their Universality and Evolution*. Berkeley: University of California Press. 1st paperback edn. 1991, with bibliography by Luisa Maffi.

Boynton, R. M. 1979. *Human Color Vision*. New York: Holt, Rinehart, and Winston.

Boynton, R. M. and C. X. Olson 1987. Locating basic colors in the OSA space. *Color Research and Application* 12(2): 94–105.

1990. Salience of chromatic basic color terms confirmed by three measures. *Vision Research* 30(9): 1311–1317.

Boynton, R.M., and K. F. Purl 1989. Categorical color perception under low-pressure sodium lighting with small amounts of added incandescent illumination. *Lighting Research and Technology* 21: 23–27.

Boynton, R. M., L. Fargo, and B. L. Collins 1990. Categorical color rendering of four common light sources. *Color Research and Application* 165: 222–230.

Boynton, R. M., R. E. MacLaury, and K. Uchikawa 1989. Centroids of color categories compared by two methods. *Color Research and Application* 14: 6–15.

Boynton, R. M., L. Fargo, C. X. Olson, and H. Smallman 1989. Categorical effects in color memory. *Color Research and Application* 14: 229–234.

Fuld, K., B. R. Wooten, and J. J. Whalen 1981. The elemental hues of short-wave and extraspectral lights. *Perception and Psychophysics* 29(4): 317–322.

Gordon, J., and I. Abramov 1977. Color vision in the peripheral retina II. Hue and saturation. *Journal of the Optical Society of America* 67: 202–207.

Kay, P., and C. K. McDaniel 1978. The linguistic significance of the meanings of basic color terms. *Language* 54(3): 610–646.

Kay, P., B. Berlin, and W. R. Merrifield 1991. Biocultural implications of systems of color naming. *Journal of Linguistic Anthropology* 1(1): 12–25.

Mervis, C. B., and E. Rosch 1981. Categorization of natural objects. *Annual Review of Psychology* 32: 89–115.

Montag, E., and R. M Boynton 1987. Rod influence in dichromatic surface color perception. *Vision Research* 27: 2153–2162.

Nickerson, D. 1981. OSA color scale samples: a unique set. *Color Research and Application* 6: 7–33.

Ratliff, F. 1976. On the psychophysiological basis of universal color terms. *Proceedings of the American Philosophical Society* 120(5): 311–330.

1992. *Paul Signac and Color in Neo-Impressionism*. New York: Rockefeller University Press.

Scheibner, H. M. O., and R. M. Boynton 1968. Residual red–green discrimination in dichromats. *Journal of the Optical Society of America* 58: 1151–1158.

Smallman, H. S. and R. M. Boynton 1990. Segregation of ten basic colors in an information display. *Journal of the Optical Society of America A* 7(10): 1985–1994.

Sternheim, C. E., and R. M. Boynton 1966. Uniqueness of perceived hues investigated with a continuous judgmental technique. *Journal of Experimental Psychology* 72(5): 770–776.

Trandis, H. C., R. S. Malpass, and A. R. Davidson 1973. Psychology and culture. *Annual Review of Psychology* 24: 355–378.

Uchikawa, K., and R. M. Boynton 1987. Categorical

color perception of Japanese observers: comparison with that of Americans. *Vision Research* 27(10): 1825–1833.

Uchikawa, H., K. Uchikawa, and R. M. Boynton 1989a. Influence of achromatic surrounds on categorical perception of surface colors. *Vision Research* 29: 881–890.

1989b. Partial color constancy of isolated surface colors examined by a color naming method. *Perception* 18: 83–91.

Yoshioka, T., B. M. Dow, and R. G. Vautin 1996. Neuronal mechanisms of color categorization in areas V1, V2, and V4 of Macaque monkey cortex. *Behavioural Brain Research*. 76: 51–70.

7 Beyond the elements: investigations of hue

David L. Miller

There is a long tradition in philosophy, art, and science of attempting to reduce color to its essential elements. In the past forty years this quest has advanced with a greater analytic precision made possible by quantitative color psychophysics. This chapter describes research extending the quantitative approach, building bridges between venerable experimental techniques and new approaches that allow assessment of hypotheses about color usage raised by cognitive psychology and anthropology.

This research sought to move beyond the identification of elements, to examine how elements might be arranged and combined into more complex entities (the original aspiration of elemental analysis). In the chasm between the elemental hues and the millions of perceivable colors, there may be orderly structures that will inform us about complex colors, categorization, and, possibly, thought and language.

Elemental (unique) hues are those which cannot be perceptually analyzed into more basic hue components, and thus cannot be further described by other hue names – for example, each person has a unique yellow that is neither reddish nor greenish. The psychophysical investigation of elemental hues has been approached by several methods, the most popular of which is that of Sternheim and Boynton (1966). In this method observers describe the appearance of colored samples by assigning percentages from a specified hue term set. A given sample stimulus might be described as, for instance, 50 percent green, 50 percent yellow. The results are averaged across many trials and observers, and are presented as hue-scaling functions plotted by wavelength. If a hue term is both *necessary* and *sufficient* to describe a range of color samples, the hue is determined to be elemental. This technique serves as both method and criterion for assessing elementalness (see Wooten and Miller, this volume).

Hue-scaling experiments typically sample the spectrum with

single-wavelength patches of light produced by a monochromator and presented in Maxwellian view. The sample stimuli appear as equally bright, saturated disks of uniform hue centered in a darkened field. Each stimulus is 1° of visual angle in diameter, moderately bright (1000 Trolands), and viewed for a fraction of a second (300–500 msec). These viewing conditions assure a rigid standardization and comparability across similar experiments in different laboratories.

Multi-term hue scaling

Several studies have examined portions of the spectrum using hue-scaling methods (e.g. Sternheim and Boynton 1966; Fuld, Wooten, and Whalen 1981). Across various studies, blue, yellow, and red have been demonstrated to be elemental. However, no single study using the stringent criteria of Sternheim and Boynton (both necessary and sufficient usage) included more than two presumed elementals. Furthermore, green had never been specifically studied, although it has long been presumed to be elemental. To remedy this situation, Miller and Wooten (1990) conducted a hue-scaling study with spectral stimuli ranging from 470 to 640 nm. Each unique spectral hue (blue, green, and yellow) was determined by a computed function (the residual percentage hue left unscaled). This study was intended to be an agglutination of previous limited spectral range multi-term studies.

Computed hue functions for red, blue, and yellow did replicate earlier findings: when the four terms ("blue," "green," "yellow," and "red") were available, all observers found the terms *sufficient* to describe spectral stimuli. This also agrees well with other studies that employ only the set of terms (B, G, Y, R).

However, when the term "green" was not allowed (hue set = BYR), meeting the more stringent condition of *necessary* usage was problematic. Two types of response were observed. Only five of eight observers performed as expected (Figure 7.1), producing a normal computed function which resembled the BGYR condition. The remaining three observers produced anomalous results with stimuli ranging between 490 and 570 nm (Figure 7.2), showing no computed green function. Instead, these three observers used a combination of "blue" and "yellow" responses (e.g. "50 percent blue, 50 percent yellow") for a "green" stimulus. (Note that observers were instructed to judge

Figure 7.1 Mean hue scaling of five subjects with computed green.

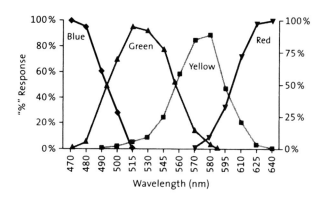

Figure 7.2 Mean hue scaling of three paint-bias subjects.

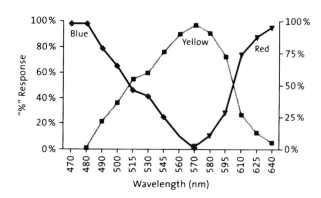

appearance, not mixture.) Observer responses indicate an untenable "bluish yellow" appearance.

This pattern was interpreted as a "paint bias." It was presumed that observers responded to green as a mixture of blue and yellow because of training in, or experience with, subtractive color mixing. Further sessions were run with the three paint-bias observers to explore this interpretation. In these follow-up sessions, observers were restricted to one hue term per session with which to describe the stimuli. It was assumed that it might be more difficult to maintain the paint bias when the summation of blue and yellow was not an allowed response, but no change in response to green stimuli was observed. However, it should be noted that these observers had already been exposed to the prior multi-term method and had already established a response to green stimuli as blue/yellow.

Miller and Wooten (1990) had expected to confirm earlier, more restricted findings across the full spectrum, but instead were left with the larger question of whether the traditional method of Sternheim and Boynton was flawed, or whether there was an underlying anomaly in the perception and/or naming of green stimuli. Miller and Wooten argued that if a widely accepted elemental hue (i.e., green) could not be reliably classified, then the validity of other elemental and non-elemental hue classifications might also be questioned. However, rather than questioning the elemental nature of green, they suggested changes in the methods and criteria currently used to assess elemental hues.

Single-hue scaling

A single-hue scaling task (Miller and Wooten 1992), similar to the follow-up study of paint-biased observers, was developed to assess the hypothesis that task demands (requiring observers to compose a 100 percent summation from a set of hue terms) had influenced the earlier results. Establishing a single-hue methodology was also important to future research for the following reasons:

(a) there were known problems with the traditional method (e.g. Beare and Siegel 1967; Miller and Wooten 1990) ;
(b) it is more efficient, because it is not necessary to use a computed hue for every presumed elemental – a necessary elemental hue is indicated by a gap between hue functions; and most importantly,
(c) if it could be shown that a single-hue scaling technique was equivalent to the traditional method, then future research could be recast into even more rigorous quantitative analyses.

Ten naive observers were used to provide an unprejudiced evaluation. Stimuli were the same as described earlier and ranged across the whole spectrum (430–660 nm). Each session used a different single hue name ("blue," "green," "yellow," or "red") with which to describe the test stimuli. Observers were instructed to assign a percentage to that single hue for each stimulus (e.g. 50 percent yellow).

The results from this experiment show that only one observer exhibited a paint bias. Data from the other nine observers were averaged; hue-scaling functions for blue, green, and red have minima and maxima consistent with previous studies (Figure 7.3).

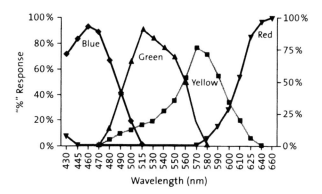

Figure 7.3 Hue scaling for nine subjects, single-hue method.

The function for yellow deviates from what might be expected in five of ten observers. However, since the blue function reaches minimum at the green maximum (and does not extend beyond peak green), these data do not exhibit the symmetry of both blue and yellow functions needed to support the paint-bias hypothesis. The lowered intersection of red and yellow functions is caused by three observers exhibiting little red or yellow response at 600 nm, perhaps hinting at the presence of an implicit orange category.

These data indicate that this simplified method is capable of revealing the same information as the more elaborate method of Sternheim and Boynton. The single-hue method is more sensitive to non-probed hue terms because it removes the task demand of multiple hues summing to 100 percent. Furthermore, it appears to have prevented right-skewed blue functions, thus eliminating paint bias as a problem for all but one observer.

The 2AFC method

With the single-hue scaling method established, a more rigorous experiment was designed to explore further the nature of elemental hues and their simple compounds. A new single-hue method was developed to derive both hue-naming functions and choice reaction times (RTs) across the whole spectrum (Miller 1993).

In this experiment, a single-hue response was used, but scaling was eliminated. In this procedure only a "present" or "absent" hue response was allowed. The detection of the presence or absence of a hue component is taken as being logically prior to the assignment of percentages in a scaling task. The process of merely recognizing "is there any?" of a given hue in the stimulus occurs before the process of magnitude assignment, thus the elimination of a linguistic response from the forced-choice yes/no response should yield a more sensorially based judgment. The use of brief stimulus presentations and standard two alternative forced-choice (2AFC) button presses was an improvement to earlier written response methods (Heider 1972), covert RT measures (Boynton and Olson 1990), or unrestrained stimulus viewing (Beare 1962).

Another advantage of this method is that multi-hue term sets and scaling responses are eliminated. By restricting the observer's response to a 2AFC design, accurate reaction time data may be taken and used to assess any color order effects. Furthermore, this design probes the whole spectrum with all hue-term pairings. Earlier studies confounded the hue name and the stimulus by using only short segments of the spectrum, thus providing little comparison of inappropriate term/stimulus relationships (which serve as controls). All wavelengths and hue-term combinations were investigated in a factorial design. Choice reaction times were also recorded, allowing the separation of reaction time influences contributed by hue-term usage from those of wavelength. This method allowed:

(a) separation of the effects of wavelength and hue term, leading to questions such as, "is there any 'green' in the red light?";
(b) psychophysical assessment of elemental, basic, and non-basic hues, as well as focal (center) vs. boundary stimuli;
(c) replication of elemental-hue-term usage across the spectrum, to see if anomalies observed in previous work were eliminated by new methodologies.

Berlin and Kay's (1969) evolutionary color-term sequence included four elemental hue terms ("blue," "green," "yellow," "red") out of eleven basic terms. For this experiment, six color names were selected so that: four referred to colors that are elemental (unique) *and* basic in the Berlin and Kay sequence (blue, green, yellow, red); one ("orange") referred to a color that was *not* unique, but was basic and binary (made up of two elemental hues, red and yellow); and one ("chartreuse") referred to a a color that was *neither* elemental nor basic, although it was binary (composed of green and yellow).

Predictions about category structure are made possible by the inclusion of orange and chartreuse. Since no current theory holds orange to be elemental, nor chartreuse to be either basic or elemental, their inclusion gave an opportunity to see if responses to them could be objectively distinguished from those to elemental hues. If the non-elementalness of orange and chartreuse could not be distinguished with this method, then color naming might be confounded with higher-level processes, challenging the straightforward sensory report model dear to classical psychophysics.

Chartreuse is typically a binomial; that is, it is usually described using two hue names ("yellowish green" or "greenish yellow"). Although the most common monolexemic term for yellow-green is "chartreuse," it is unknown to many naive subjects due to its low frequency of usage. Its inclusion allowed observation of hue naming without the overlearning characteristic of linguistically common elemental hue terms. No term was used to represent the blue-green portion of the spectrum, thus that region could serve as a control for the other two spectral binaries (chartreuse and orange).

This design also allowed an initial assessment of hypotheses generated by diverse theories of color usage. From the basic color term work of Berlin and Kay, it can be hypothesized that the evolutionary sequence of color terms will be reflected in a rank ordering of reaction times. RTs to the four elementary hues should be faster than those to orange; those to orange should be faster than those to chartreuse. Prototypic categorization theory predicts that RTs should be slower at the boundary between categories and faster within categories, producing an M-shaped function.

Of the 8 observers serving in this experiment, 7 were naive (data were also collected on the experimenter). The stimuli were the same as in the single-hue scaling experiment. Each of the 20 stimuli was randomly selected and was paired with 1 of the 6 hue terms. Observers were presented with 6 blocks of the 20 stimuli, for a total of 120 trials per session (each observer repeated the session 7 times). Observers were instructed that after a warning tone they would receive a single hue term and then must push one of two buttons indicating whether that hue was "present" or "absent" in the stimulus. Observers were told to maximize both speed and accuracy. The hue terms tested were the four elemental hue terms (BGYR), "orange" (a basic term that refers to a non-elemental hue) and "chartreuse" (a non-basic term).

Figure 7.4 Mean identification functions for six hue terms.

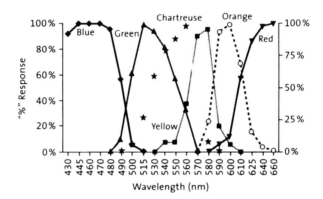

Although half of the observers reported knowing the term "char-treuse," they were all told it referred to a "greenish yellow or yellowish green about halfway between green and yellow." Curiously, all observers who did not know the meaning of "chartreuse" guessed it to fall between pink and purple. This is in line with my informal observation that, when presented with an unknown hue term, most people assume a mixture involving redness (and almost never greenness).

The hue identification results can be seen by plotting the mean identification response (percentage of trials in which "any of the hue" was detected in the stimulus) against wavelength (Figure 7.4). These results are quite similar to those in the single-hue scaling experiment, showing good translation from the scaling method to the identification task. Unlike the scaling study, hue-naming functions did not reveal a skew towards the shorter wavelengths for yellow. Identification functions for some individual observers were mesa-shaped (spectral spans of 100 percent hue response) as is common with single-term identification.

RTs for each wavelength were first averaged across hue names. Overall, RTs were faster to red and blue stimuli and slower for the middle wavelengths. Slower RTs at 490–500 nm and 560–570 nm indicate that those two category boundaries followed the pattern predicted from prototypic organization. In contrast, RTs at the yellow–red boundary at 590–600 nm showed no marked elevation.

When the individual RT data are plotted as a function of hue term and stimulus wavelength, the findings are more complex. Five observers showed more rapid responses (400–600 msec) to all stimuli, and had little differentiation among their responses. For three observers,

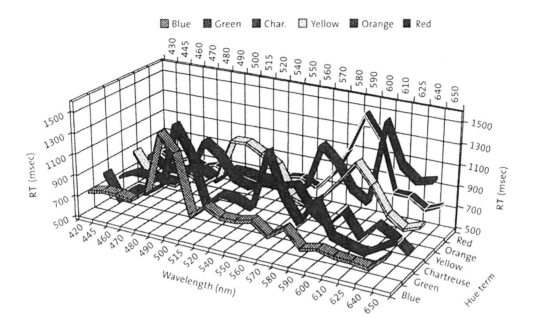

Figure 7.5 RT for wavelength x hue term interaction, single subject.

responding was slower overall (700–1000 msec), although still faster than response times found in other research. For these slow responders, the M-shaped pattern predicted from prototypic organization tended to emerge for each hue term: two peaks (indicating slower RTs), one at each boundary of a hue category (Figure 7.5). These individual differences suggest that slower responses might be more influenced by linguistic factors (hue terms), and that categorization effects found in previous research are also likely to be higher-level phenomena.

Differential responding appeared when hue-term RTs were combined across wavelength. Responses were fastest for detection using the term "red," and "blue" was the next fastest term for subject identification response; these were followed by "orange." "Green," "yellow," and "chartreuse" did not differ as dramatically from each other as they did from "red" and "blue."

Ratliff's (1976) assertion, based on Berlin and Kay's work, that red has primacy over all other hues was supported. When examined separately, RT data showed that the hue term "red" produced the fastest responding. Likewise, responses to long-wavelength (red) stimuli were among the two fastest responses, along with responses to short-wavelength (blue) stimuli. However, a perusal of the hue-by-wavelength individual RT data does not reveal any interaction between hue term and wavelength. "Red" responses to long-wavelength stimuli are not faster than other comparable combinations. The fact that responses to short-wavelength stimuli and hue terms were nearly as fast casts some doubt on a simple rank ordering of RT based on the Berlin and Kay sequence.

The primacy of red over the other basic hues is in contradiction to Boynton and Olson (1990), who found no hue differentiation *within* the basic color terms. This may be due to their long response times (3–5 sec) which can be expected to reflect linguistic factors.

Two important patterns emerged in the hue identification functions for chartreuse and orange. The function for chartreuse was largely redundant with the green and yellow identification functions, and the presence of "chartreuse" as a term option had little effect on observers' green and yellow hue functions. In contrast, "orange" produced a peak near the yellow–red boundary (slightly shifted towards red), with a marked depression in yellow and red identification functions. Thus orange was not redundant with yellow and red.

Examination of both hue identification functions and RTs sheds light on classification systems applied to hues. "Chartreuse," a non-elemental and non-basic term, is distinguishable from the other hue terms on both dependent variables. Redundancy is observed with green and yellow hue functions, and "chartreuse" also has the longest reaction time of any hue term.

With this method, "orange" is shown to be indistinguishable from the terms for the elemental hues – their hue functions and RT patterns are comparable. "Orange," which has previously been considered non-elemental but basic, also falls in the middle of the four unique hue terms in overall RT. This pattern suggests that the term "orange" is a useful and reliable descriptor of the corresponding wavelengths, and that observers will use it given the opportunity. The fact that this pattern is different from that observed for "chartreuse" demonstrates that "orange" has a basic, if not elemental, status.

Conclusion

The hue-identification functions derived from the present single-hue detection paradigm are comparable to classically derived functions, and thus demonstrate the validity of this method. The hue-term set is open-ended, and without the additivity constraints imposed by summation of permitted hue terms. Since this technique also allows collection of reaction-time data, it may be viewed as a more powerful alternative to the traditional hue-scaling and hue-naming techniques.

To the psychophysicist, these data demonstrate that the construct of "basic color term" is meaningful and has quantifiable properties. The microstructure within the basic color terms, the primacy of red, and the strength of orange present a challenge to extend the underlying mechanisms. For the anthropologist, these data show that the evolutionary structure of basic color terms compiled across cultures can be assessed in the perception of individuals, further bolstering psychological determinism. These data also provide support for the theoretical constructs based on fuzzy-set analysis (Kay and McDaniel 1978). For the cognitive scientist, prototypic category organization is upheld, but appears better fitted to language than to wavelength. This suggests that patterns observed in earlier research reflect higher levels of processing rather than low-level categorical perception.

This series of experiments has taken the first step in looking beyond the elemental hues with traditional psychophysical methods. Our findings suggest that the distinctions between elemental hues, basic, and non-basic colors are useful and measurable. The new methods show great promise for future research – where more complex color cognition requires more exacting research tools.

References

Beare, A. C. 1962. Frequencies of color names as functions of wavelength. Ph.D. thesis, Columbia University.

Beare, A. C., and M. H. Siegel 1967. Color name as a function of wavelength and instruction. *Perception and Psychophysics* 2(11): 521–527.

Berlin, B., and P. Kay 1969/91. *Basic Color Terms: Their Universality and Evolution*. Berkeley: University of California Press. 1st paprback edn. 1991, with bibliography by Luisa Maffi.

Boynton, R. M., and C. X. Olson 1990. Salience of chromatic basic color terms confirmed by three measures. *Vision Research* 30(9): 1311–1317.

Fuld, K., B. R. Wooten, and J. J. Whalen 1981. The elemental hues of short-wave and extraspectral lights. *Perception and Psychophysics* 29(4): 317–322.

Heider, E. R. 1972. Universals in color naming and memory. *Journal of Experimental Psychology* 93(1): 10–20.

Kay, P., and C. K. McDaniel 1978. The linguistic significance of the meanings of basic color terms. *Language* 54(3): 610–646.

Miller, D. L. 1993. An investigation of elemental, basic, and categorical color perception. Ph.D. thesis, Brown University.

Miller, D. L., and B. R. Wooten 1990. The elemental hues

of spectral lights, and the occasionally anomalous
nature of green. *Investigative Ophthalmology and
Visual Science* 31(4): 262.

    1992. Application of the single-hue naming method
to the determination of elemental hues. *Advances in
Color Vision, 1992 Technical Digest (*Optical Society of
America) 4: 164–166.

Ratliff, F. 1976. On the psychophysiological basis of
universal color terms. *Proceedings of the American
Philosophical Society* 120(5): 311–330.

Sternheim, C.E., and R. M. Boynton 1966. Uniqueness
of perceived hues investigated with a continuous
judgmental technique. *Journal of Experimental
Psychology* 72(5): 770–776.

8 Color systems for cognitive research

Lars Sivik

How many colors?

While some researchers claim that there are eleven basic colors, others claim that there are several million colors. By that I do not refer to the merry advertisements from the computer screen manufacturers promising 16 million colors (most of these have one and the same color: black), but rather to the number of colors (calculated – not counted) that the normal human eye can distinguish. If two identical surfaces are first presented adjacent to each other and then one of them is slightly varied until a "just noticeable difference" (jnd) can be seen, it is possible, by extrapolating from the stimulus difference to the entire "visible wavelength- and intensity-range," to get an estimate of the number of possible color nuances. Whether these are 3 million or 10 million could only be of academic interest.

To arrive at this large number of distinguishable colors requires that the colors be *juxtaposed*. If we move them apart by even a few centimeters, the two color surfaces, which when juxtaposed are seen as clearly dissimilar, immediately appear identical. If we hold color samples even farther apart from each other rather large color differences are necessary if we are to see surfaces as different. Suddenly the number of perceptually distinct colors has dropped to a couple of thousand, or less.

Although it is an intricate task to determine just how many colors there are, even for a "normal observer," we can at the very least state that there are many. But how are we to describe them? We obviously have some need to do this, even if this need varies for different cultures and subcultures. The color terms and their corresponding color categories which have emerged through history may, of course, also be seen as color reference systems, and it is a color system of this kind that average people use in all cultures in their everyday speech. (This includes me and other so-called color experts [Sivik & Hård 1983a].)

After all, it is only for certain rather special purposes that it is important to be able to describe colors and color differences with greater precision. It is my intention to discuss first some principles for the construction of such systems.

Some dimensions for color order

It is important to distinguish between systems for the arrangement of colors that are based on the physical attributes of stimuli and those systems we can call *phenomenological* or purely psychometric, i.e., systems which are based solely on color sensations and their interrelations. It is the latter that conceptually ought to be of greater relevance than the others in research on human cognitive categorization of color sensations, which is a psychological aspect of the truly multi-disciplinary realm of color research.

Unfortunately, in many languages the word "color" has come to mean both the color stimulus and the color sensation itself. In what follows I intend to use the word "color" exclusively in the meaning of sensation, the color percept. There is in fact a variety of different ways to structure all possible colors. Many color-naming studies have, without further clarification, referred to *the* color space (which, furthermore, has been taken for granted to be the same as Munsell's Hue, Value, and Chroma). This is not justified: the color-perceptual reality is more complex than that and the parameters mentioned are hardly the only possible ones.

If we wish to illustrate graphically the interrelationships of colors we can present them as a "color space." We should, however, be aware that at the very moment we imagine such a space we have in some way defined its dimensions, and we have formed an idea about the metric and the scaling of these dimensions. As a rule, what most people first think of when asked to describe in what way colors differ is *variation in hue*: the colors are yellow, orange, red, purple, blue, blue-green, green, yellow-green. If "color-naive" persons are asked to order, in whatever way they wish, a number of color samples differing by small steps in hue, they all lay out a color circle, even if not all of them realize until they are through that it is possible to connect the two ends of the row they made. Most color appearance systems have a hue circle, but its scaling and partitions may differ from system to system. To this I shall return.

Next we come to the difference between the chromatic colors (those colors in which it is possible to see a hue) and the achromatic colors, which are somewhat carelessly called *neutral* (in the sense of color-meaning they are far from "neutral"). As far as the gray scale is concerned, there is also considerable concordance among the various systems: white is at one end, black at the other, and in-between, a continuous scale of all shades of grey. A controversial question, however, is how to define the endpoints. Are they to be the whitest and blackest imaginable or the whitest and blackest possible to produce with samples? Which metric to apply is another open question.

The chromatic colors may also vary continuously in relation to the attribute light–dark, but contrary to what many believe and take for granted, it is not at all easy to judge colors on the variable lightness (Munsell Value) scale unless one makes comparisons between juxtaposed samples. Compare, for example, a light blue color (NCS 2020 B30G) with a strong yellow (NCS 0070 Y10R) while holding them far apart. Most people will say that the light blue looks far lighter than the yellow color – until they see the samples juxtaposed and find that the light blue was darker than the strong yellow (which nobody would call light yellow). In this case, was it the lightness that was estimated or the *whiteness*?

In Ewald Hering's proposal for a "natural color system" (1878) there are, instead of the lightness parameter, the qualitatively descriptive attributes of whiteness and blackness. These attributes are color-characterizing whereas the lightness variable is comparative, discriminative. Whiteness can be defined as "how much the actual color resembles the concept of absolute white," and blackness can be defined as "how much the actual color resembles the concept of absolute black." However, the lightness of a given color can only be defined by how much it is lighter or darker than another color. There is no inner reference of absolute lightness, unless one thereby means white, and then the variable is whiteness.

Ewald Hering's model, which was based on his analysis of the phenomena of color – as he *saw* the colors – formed the basis of his opponent-color theory of the physiology of color vision. Although it is widely known today, it was not until well into the twentieth century that this theory was recognized by the official scientific community. There were not many who dared, as Hering did, to rely on what they could see with their own eyes. It was safer to rely on recognized theory and facts about Young and Helmholz's three kinds of receptors in the retina. Hering did not question the validity of these empirical results, but since he saw four different chromatic and two achromatic color qualities he drew the conclusion that both he and Young and Helmholz must be right. He simply stated that science did not yet know everything. Physiologists were later able to show neurophysiologically how the impulses from the three kinds of receptors interconnected in a structure that is consistent with the opponent-color theory. So Hering's theories were given scientific validation, even if he did not live to see it.

It is noteworthy that Hering, who lived between 1834 and 1918, also made pioneering discoveries in the areas of heart–lung functions, the structure of the liver, temperature sense, and nerve and muscle physiology, along with many other achievements. In spite of the fact that many of his theories were not accepted during his lifetime, he was very famous even then and was successively appointed professor in Vienna, Prague, and Leipzig.

Long before the opponent-color theory was recognized by the physiologists of perception, in Sweden there emerged an interest in his model for ordering colors. With Hering's opponent-color model as a basis the NCS was developed, and in its present form, it entirely conforms to Ewald Hering's text. Even the name is Hering's ("das natürliche Farbensystem"), but since English is the dominant international language the name had to be Natural Color System (NCS).

In the introduction I identified five possible parameters for color description: hue, lightness, whiteness, blackness, chromaticness (or Chroma). I shall now discuss these in greater depth by way of a comparative description of the NCS and the Munsell system. For a theoretical discussion of other systems there are many good reviews, for example Derefeldt (1991) and Tonnquist (1993).

The Munsell system was created by an American artist, Albert Munsell (Nickerson 1940). One of the reasons why he took an interest in color systematics was to "find a systematic color scheme for painters, so as to determine mentally on some sequence before laying the palette." As he counted many scientists among his friends he wanted to include current theories of psychophysics. He accepted Fechner's law for the relation between stimulus intensity and perceived value (lightness), but used it beyond its range of validity (note that this was long after Hering had rejected it for its inadequacy). He also built his own photometer and a Maxwell disk, which he used for his scaling experiments. Another example of his "technical" thinking was his preference for decimal scales, something that can partly explain his choice of how the hue circle was to be partitioned.

Munsell's variables

In studying some historical comments on the early development of the Munsell system I have not found any discussions concerning the choice of variables for the systematization of colors. The color world was evidently *one* and it could unambiguously be described by the dimensions Hue, Value, and Chroma as a Euclidean space. This monotheistic view of the color world also seems to permeate a great deal of Anglo-Saxon color research (including color-naming studies), and this is perhaps due to the fact that the Munsell system became the unquestioned predominant reference system. The behavioral scientists who were primarily interested in, for example, color meaning and color categorization of course grabbed the "tools" that were nearest at hand for color notation.

Based on Munsell's original definitions (which were strictly phenomenological), the cognitive model may be illustrated by Figure 8.1. There is a vertical axis for Value (lightness), against this a perpendicular axis designating Chroma (color strength) for a particular hue, and as the third variable in a three-dimensional model, the Hue circle. Due to the fact that the colors of maximal strength for the different Hues vary in both Chroma and Value, the graphical representation becomes irregular and skewed (Figure 8.1). When Munsell later realized his cognitive model with color samples he abandoned the phenomenological attitude and placed his trust in the methods and psychophysical relationships known at the time. This was described by Tyler and Hardy (1940) in their analysis of the Munsell system as follows:

> The definitions of hue, value and chroma are unambiguously
> established by the operations involved in constructing the system
> by means of additive mixtures on a Maxwell disk.

Hue.   When a chromatic color is mixed additively with a neutral (white, grey or black) the Hue of the mixture is the same as that of the chromatic color.

Value.   When two colors whose values are Va and Vb occupy relative areas a and b on a Maxwell disk, the Value of the mixture is given by the equation $V2 = aVa2 + bVb2$.

Chroma. When two complementary colors occupy areas on a Maxwell disk which are inversely proportional to the product of value by Chroma, a neutral grey results.

By comparison, ... it is evident that Hue is synonymous with dominant wavelength, that Value is the square root of luminous apparent reflectance, Y, expressed in percent, and that, for a given hue and value, Chroma is proportional to colorimetric purity in psychophysical systems.

Commenting on this Tonnquist (1994) finds that

these definitions – and their corollaries – are more psychophysical than perceptual, reflecting an attitude to "color" unfortunately prevailing among scientists until recent days. Instead of direct visual observations, Munsell made extensive use of his photometer and the

Figure 8.1 The Munsell color solid.

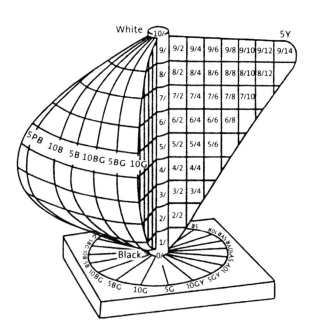

Maxwell disk in spacing the color solid according to colorimetric rules. In these operations "color" is used not in the sense of appearance but for color samples and color stimuli. Such psychophysical definitions occur in several color order systems, like DIN, Coloroid and CIELAB. Only NCS and color-naming systems as ISCC-NBS [a.k.a. the OSA system – Ed.] give strict preference to color appearance.

The Value scale.

Both conceptually and operationally Munsell equated the Value scale with the physical correlate reflectance. He adopted Fechner's law as a principle and defined Munsell Value as reflectance in percentage terms. The zero-point of the scale equals lack of reflected light, and 100 percent reflectance equals Value 10; but neither Value 0 nor Value 10 is possible to produce as a color sample; the darkest and the lightest samples of the scale have Values 0.5 and 9.5, respectively.

In the later revisions of the atlas the steps of the gray scale were determined by a number of thresholds (jnds) produced by means of differences in reflectance. These results were then checked using a psychological supraliminal direct estimation method, where equal steps in Value were determined by having observers directly estimate equal differences in brilliance ("an attribute of any color in respect of which it may be classed as equivalent to some member of a series of grays"). A similar ratio estimation method was also used as a basis for the scaling of Chroma and Hue in equal steps.

Chroma.

Chroma designates the visual distance from the grey axis for a given value. Munsell wanted the Chroma scale to have the same visually equal steps as the Value scale. This goal was, however, not achieved. One Value step corresponded to two steps on the Chroma scale which is open-ended, i.e., it is only limited by *real colors* as specified by color samples.

The partition of Hues.

The "dimension" of Hue in the Munsell system is that attribute which, in light of current theories of color vision, appears the most alien and peculiar. As Newton once wanted at all costs to accommodate the "sacred" number seven (for the number of colors in the rainbow), Munsell wanted to have ten major colors, in accord with the decimal basis of the then recently introduced metric system. Whether it was because of the difficulty of finding names for all of these major colors, I do not know, but he reduced the number to five. His praiseworthy intention was now to partition the hue circle into as many equal steps as possible and he did this in the following way.

He started with a green color which was supposed to be neither warm nor cold (sic! – I have been unable to find the theoretical motive behind this particular choice). Then he divided his Maxwell disk into five equal sectors of which one was clad with this green, neutral-tempered color, the Value/reflectance of which was determined with a photometer. Then he determined, by trial and error, the four other color samples (reflectance determined in the same way) which together with the original green looked neutral gray when the disk was spinning. The result was, in addition to the initial color, a red, a yellow, a purple, and a blue. (I have not found any attempt to explain theoretically why the experimental procedure produced just these colors.)

On the basis of this method of additive stimulus-mixing the Munsell system considers the hue circle to be partitioned in five visually equal parts (a postulate which should at least be open for discussion). How close his four first-mentioned colors – green, yellow, red, and blue – are in Munsell's early edition to the so-called unique hues in the opponent-theory and the NCS definitions can probably not be determined today. In later revisions, however, these positions have been adjusted somewhat and in the current version of the *Munsell Book of Color* 5G, 5Y, and 5R are quite close to the unique hues/NCS elementary colors; 5B, however, is quite far from unique blue – it is rather a blue-green. (This is of course a serious handicap if Munsell's is supposed to be a color descriptive system in the sense that one should be able to imagine the color from the notation.)

Munsell denotation

Hue

By inserting 5 intermediate hues between the 5 mentioned colors (which he called principal hues) he achieved the desired number of 10 major hues around the circle: R–YR–Y–GY–G–BG–B–PB–P–RP. For each of the major hues there are 10 hue-steps. These were also determined by a method of direct estimation. The circle is thus divided into 100 steps, but in the *Book of Color* there appear only 40 hue charts, chosen to represent 4 steps (2.5, 5, 7.5, and 10) of each of the 10 major hues. Hues may be denoted by either just a numeral, referring to the 100–hue circuit, or with a letter–digit combination, where the letter refers to one of the ten major hues and the numeral is either 2.5, 5, 7.5, or 10. All major hues are denoted by the number 5.

Value

Values are denoted by Figures from 0 to 10, where 0 is said to represent absolute black and 10 absolute white. (In the original definition, however, Value 0 was 0 reflectance and a Value of 10 was 100% reflectance. These two definitions are not easily alignable.) In the *Munsell Book of Color* the Value scale is exemplified with Values from 0.5 to 9.5.

Chroma

Chroma notations indicate the degree of departure of a given Hue from a neutral grey of the same Value. The Chroma scales extend from /0 for a neutral grey to /10, /12, /14, or farther (*Munsell Book of Color, 1929* 1976).

According to Billmeyer (1987) it is possible to distinguish four stages in the development of the Munsell atlas. The first includes the development of the notation system by Albert Munsell himself and its publication in 1905, followed by the first physical exemplification, the *Atlas of the Munsell Color System*, in 1915. Shortly after Mr. Munsell's death in 1918, the Munsell Color Company began research leading to improvements in the spacing, resulting in the *Munsell Book of Color* of 1929.

After the introduction of Hardy's spectrophotometer in the mid-1930s, several measurements were performed on the entire Munsell atlas. All revealed serious irregularities when the results were plotted onto the graphics of the CIE system. The Committee of Colorimetry of the Optical Society of America then carried out the third phase, which was reported in 1943 as the "Munsell Renotation." Billmeyer, the chief editor of *Color Research and Application* for many years, claims (1987) that "this study was an enormous undertaking, involving hundreds of thousands of visual observations aimed at judging the equality of spacing and thus the conformance of the guiding principles of the system. *That it is largely successful is evidenced by the absence of serious studies to repeat the work in the four decades since its completion.*" (Sic! The italics are mine, intended to suggest that an alternative reason for the lack of repetition could be that those who wanted a better color system abandoned the Munsell concept altogether and created new ones; DIN and NCS are actually good examples of this.)

Billmeyer's laudatory statements are somewhat contradicted by the sources he is referring to, which describe the renotation work. In one (Newhall 1940), the experimental procedure is described (though rather vaguely) as follows: a set of charts was sent to the subjects for estimation: "7 constant-Value charts and 20 constant-Hue charts were used in the survey, and since each of these 27 charts was prepared with the three backgrounds, a total of 81 charts were to be examined … and those who returned complete sets of data … usually took a year or so to do so." Forty-one named persons returned the data, amongst whom the five (possibly ten) participating experimental psychologists were strongly critical of the psychometric methods. Also, the well-known color researcher D. L. MacAdam objected on psychological grounds.

Regardless of whether the experimental procedure can be judged as scientifically sound or not by today's criteria, there are other questions to be raised, particularly from the standpoint of the phenomenological paradigm used in Sweden. As I understand it, the new data from the visual judgments were plotted onto the CIE diagrams as curves for equal Chroma, equal Hue, etc. These curves were then smoothed, a method that was also used in the development of the NCS atlas; but that which is held up as a merit by the Munsell advocates is seen in Sweden as a handicap, namely its dependency on the CIE *par definition*:

> One of the major purposes of the OSA Committee on Colorimetry, in addition to smoothing and adjusting the spacing of the Munsell colors, was to relate the results to the 1931 CIE system, *and it is these relationships that are usually referred to as the Munsell Renotation*

system. Since their publication, they have been the fundamental definition of the Munsell system. The notations are specified for the 1931 CIE standard observer and standard illuminant C. (cf. Billmeyer 1987; italics added)

Further it is claimed that "The guiding principle of the Munsell system is the equality of the visual spacing between adjacent notations *in each* of the three attributes of Hue, Value and Chroma, insofar as the geometry allows." (Billmeyer 1987). This may be true although it is by no means peculiar to the Munsell atlas, but probably holds for any color atlas.

We turn now to the Natural Color System. In the color theory behind the NCS, it is not self-evident, for example, that what is called the hue variable is one single variable rather than four. Conceptually and cognitively the bipolar relationship between yellow and red is different from the bipolar relationship between red and blue and therefore constitutes another scale. At the inflexion point at unique red something happens: the yellow–red scale ends and the red–blue scale begins. In the graphical model we have, however, kept the conventional continuity of an unbroken arc of a circle.

In the preparation for this chapter I reread the cited sources of the Munsell system as well as the source of the present NCS, namely Jameson and Hurvich's translation of Ewald Hering's Outlines of a Theory of the Light Sense (1964). I have been struck by the tremendous differences between them in sophistication and awareness of perceptual psychology as well as physical and physiological knowledge. For those who consider this statement biased and exaggerated I recommend that they do the same reading. The work of the artist Albert Munsell is greatly to be admired, but I am convinced that if he had read Hering's writings the NCS atlas would have been of American origin.

Natural Color System

It should perhaps be pointed out that the NCS color descriptive system and atlas (Hård 1966; Hård and Sivik 1981) were developed in Sweden as a result of a general dissatisfaction with the color systems then available, including Munsell's, which was well known there. Its lack of theory and incomprehensible notation system were questioned, even if in these respects it was an improvement over other systems. It was a physicist, Tryggve Johansson (1905–1960), employed at the National Defence Research Laboratory, who, through his interest in color, found Ewald Hering's works. His ability to read German provided him access to an alternative perspective on what was at that time the sanctioned (mainly physical) view of the nature of color

One of the fundamental theoretical points of departure that differentiates Hering from the Young–Helmholz school that then prevailed, and even from present-day technicians, is that, rather than clinging to a quantitative stimulus-response thinking, he clearly recognizes a characteristic of the visual system: it transforms quantitative variable stimuli to qualitative variables. In Hering's book (1964) a chapter entitled "The natural color system," concerned with principles for the classification of colors, begins as follows:

> What we want is to classify the great multiplicity of colors to get a systematic perspective of them, and designations for them such that the reader is given a comprehensible expression as precise as possible for every color, so that he can mentally reproduce any color with some exactness. To do this we must at first disregard altogether the causes and conditions of their arousal. For a systematic grouping of colors the only thing that matters is *color* itself. Neither the qualitative (frequency) nor quantitative (amplitude) physical properties of the radiations are relevant. For, as we have already said, exactly the same radiation can elicit now one color and now another, depending on the circumstances, and on the other hand, exactly the same color can be seen as the effect of quite different radiations.

Cognitive references.

While the Munsell system today is a stimulus-based system, defined by its color samples as fixed by their CIE-measurements, the NCS system is primarily a theoretical/cognitive system for estimation and identification of colors in any situation. As references for such an estimation we are able, according to Hering, to use the built-in images that we all have of ideal yellow, red, blue, green, white, and black. The phenomenological basis of Hering's postulates, to which we all have access, is that all colors can be described in terms of resemblances to these six elementary colors. Further, each of us can say that "this color is not a perfect red," which actually implies that we have an image of what a perfect red is. (In addition, today there are, of course, the neurophysiological empirical data that support Hering's phenomenological analysis of colors.) A graphically illustrated model of the interrelationships between these elementary colors in a Euclidean space is depicted in Figure 8.2.

Figure 8.2 The NCS.

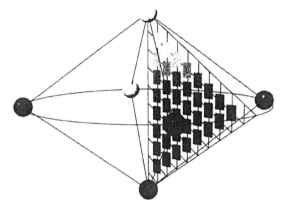

The NCS variables

Resemblances to the cognitive references.

The phenomenological–empirical basis for the NCS is thus that all colors (here I refer to percepts of surface colors) more or less resemble these elementary colors. Hering's term was "Urfarben" and we have chosen the term *elementary colors* because they are not further divisible. The opponent-color theory says, however, that a color cannot resemble more than four of these at a time (which anybody can observe), and that the color is then either

  red *or* green plus white *and* black

or

  blue *or* yellow plus white *and* black.

The unit of measurement chosen for the variable "visual resemblance to the elementary color A" was *percent*.

The hue circle and the hue partition.

NCS has adopted the traditional form of a circle for the variations in hue. This was, however, not at all self-evident. As I pointed out earlier, conceptually and cognitively we are here dealing with four separate scales, namely one variation between yellow and red, one between red and blue, one between blue and green, one between green and yellow.

For each of these the variation of the visual content can be illustrated as a bi-polar diagram (Figure 8.3). The endpoint of one scale is, however, identical with the starting-point of the next, but this is a completely new scale and a more correct illustration would actually have been a square; but since the hue circle is such a well established concept, everybody yielded to this convention. One should, however, be aware of the fact that the hue circle is conceptually not one scale but four (see Figure 8.4). The partition into four chromatic elementary colors is given directly by the opponent-color theory as are the positions of these colors on the circle, namely, as endpoints of perpendicular diameters. This illustrates graphically the mutual

Figure 8.3 The "hue dimension" consists of four bi-polar scales.

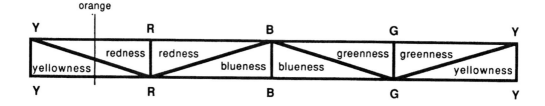

Figure 8.4 NCS color circle.

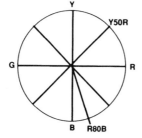

exclusiveness of the attributes of opposite colors. The arc of each circle quadrant, which designates all the imaginary maximal hues of this hue scale, is divided into 100 equal steps. For example, a color that looks equally yellowish and reddish, i.e., has as much of the visual component yellowness as it has of redness, is to be marked in the middle of the arc between Y and R. According to the NCS notation system for hue this will be Y50R, which means 50 hue steps

from Y towards R. The notation R8oB consequently means a red-blue
color situated 8o/100th of the way from red towards blue, that is, 80%
relative bluishness (20% relative reddishness). The markings on the
hue circle referred to here do not represent single colors but *all* imaginable colors of the particular hues, i.e., all colors with the same *pro-*
portion of yellowness–redness and redness–blueness, respectively for
the two examples.

NCS color triangle.

The graphical illustration of all colors of a given hue is in the NCS (as
in Hering's original model) an equilateral triangle, where each point
represents a certain *nuance*. (See Figure 8.5.) The unidimensional
"dimension" nuance is thus the locus for all colors, of all hues, with a
specific relationship between the parameters of whiteness, blackness,
and chromaticness.

Figure 8.5 NCS color
triangle.

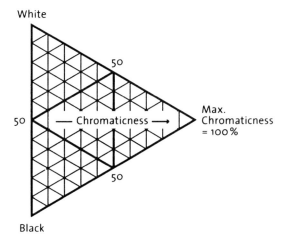

Chromaticness

Chromaticness corresponds to the dimensional direction of Munsell's
Chroma, but not to the scaling. Munsell's Chroma is an open-ended
scale which is defined by color samples which are determined by
means of a so-called production method of estimation, i.e., the subject
chooses a color sample which deviates in Chroma as much from the
target sample as it does from the previous sample.

On the other hand, NCS chromaticness has, as do all the NCS parameters, two end-points and the scale between these is divided into 100 equal steps defined as "resemblance to the reference-points." Chromaticness in the color triangle is "the resemblance (in per cent) to the *maximal color*," by which is meant the color with the given hue which is devoid of whiteness and devoid of blackness. In the NCS color triangle this maximal color is represented by the corner point C.

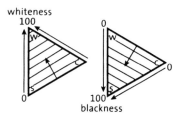

Figure 8.6 NCS whiteness and blackness.

NCS whiteness and blackness.

The other corner points W (white) and S (after the Old English word "swarthy," German "schwarz," Swedish "svart," etc.) represent correspondingly the imaginable elementary colors white and black according to Hering's phenomenological color model. The variable whiteness (w) is defined as "the degree of resemblance to the imagination of the elementary white" (W), and the variable black (s) is defined as "the degree of resemblance to the imagination of the elementary black" (S). The scaling is, as mentioned, an equispacing in 100 steps.

NCS color space.

If we now combine the hue circle with the color triangles for each of all possible hues we get the three-dimensional NCS color solid. (See Figure 8.7.) Each point within it thus represents the perception of a surface color whose relative resemblance to one or two chromatic elementary colors and to white and black is given by the relative distances to these points in the color solid.

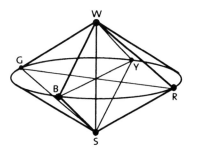

Figure 8.7 The NCS color space.

Color assessment with the NCS method.

In its theoretical structure as described above, the NCS is also a method for color assessment. Hering's simple discovery was that any color can be described in terms of the six elementary colors – as people have done for ages, if we accept Berlin and Kay's (1969) scheme for the development of the basic color terms. These are the six terms that seem to appear first in development, and it is also obvious that the so-called secondary colors can be described in terms of visual content of the other six. This was the phenomenological observation that formed the basis for Hering's opponent-color theory.

When estimating colors by the NCS method one is simply following a spontaneous color description by asking the person to estimate *how much*, relatively, there is, for example, of yellowness, redness, whiteness, and blackness in an orange color. One easy way to do this is by using the NCS graphical symbols, the color triangle and the color circle (Figure 8.8). The first step is to decide upon the hue. Let us keep to the orange color: mark the hue on the arc between Y and R. If the color is equally reddish and yellowish the marking comes in the middle, if it is more yellowish it comes nearer the yellow reference point (Figure 8.9). After the hue is determined, we proceed to the color triangle, which represents the particular hue we have assessed. It is convenient to begin with the chromaticness, which in the triangle is represented by the distance from the gray axis towards, and proportional to, the maximal color C. If one marks the chromaticness with a vertical line it is possible to assess on that line the relative resemblances to white and black, respectively (Figure 8.10). At this point, in combination with the marking on the hue circle, the color estimation in the NCS space is completed. Anybody can do this color estimation and see that it works.

If a group of, say, 25 subjects perform such an estimation of a color with instructions of about the same length as the one given above, and their answers are plotted together, these will of course form a cluster. A statistical analysis of the dispersion of this cluster will, however, show that the confidence interval on the .95-level seldom exceeds 3–5 NCS

Figure 8.8 NCS graphical symbols.

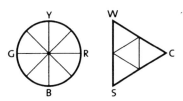

Figure 8.9 Assessment of proportions of chromatic elementary hue-content.

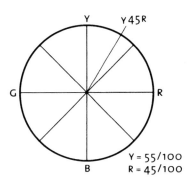

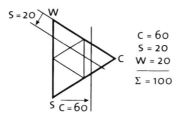

Figure 8.10 Assessment of chromaticness, blackness, and whiteness.

C = 60
S = 20
W = 20
———
Σ = 100

units, i.e. 3–5% in any direction. If a narrower confidence interval is required it is, of course, possible to increase the number of observers. It may be mentioned that this dispersion gets neither larger nor smaller if the experiment is repeated and the observers are asked to estimate the resemblances to "elementary colors" in the form of color samples instead of comparing with their inner conceptions of elementary white, black, yellow, red, blue, and green. The absolute values come out somewhat differently, but the dispersions are the same.

An NCS color notation

An NCS color notation (Swedish Standards Institution 1990) consists of a digit–letter combination denoting the color's blackness, chromaticness, and hue, in that order. If we go back to the description of how to estimate the *nuance* of a color, i.e., its relative whiteness (w), blackness (s), and chromaticness, by means of the color triangle, then we find that such a triangular coordinate system is overdetermined. It is sufficient with two of the variables w, s, and c, and for the definition of a color in the triangle blackness (s) and chromaticness (c) have been chosen. The whiteness then can be inferred as s+c+w=100, which means that w=100-(s+c). The construction of the hue notation (ϕ) was described in connection with the description of how to estimate the hue. R6oB, for example, is a purple whose visual content is 60% blueness and 40% redness. The total symbol is thus s c ϕ with two digits. (Try to imagine a 10 80 Y50R.) The elementary colors are denoted only by the letters Y, R, B, G, W, and S. White (W) could just as well have been written oo oo, i.e., no blackness and no chromaticness, and elementary black (S) could have been 100 oo. The grey colors in-between are denoted 10 oo, 20 oo, 30 oo, and so on, with other values for the blackness (s). The chromaticness oo denotes achromatic colors.

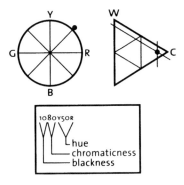

Figure 8.11 The meaning of NCS color notation.

The NCS atlas

The theoretical color system and method for color estimation that has been described has also been illustrated – or exemplified – with a color atlas (Swedish Standards Institution 1989). It was built up according to the model with 40 pages representing each tenth of the 4×100 steps around the hue circle. The atlas samples were determined in experiments which were nearly identical with the NCS method of color assessment: a large number of color samples over the whole gamut of hue, chromaticness, whiteness, and blackness that could be produced were judged, one by one, by a number of observers. From the data the variable means for each sample were calculated and these were related to the measured spectrophotometric attributes of the samples. finally, new samples were produced for positions at the intersections of the NCS triangles' coordinate system.

The results of such a work will seldom be entirely perfect, but studies have shown that the agreement between the nominal values of the samples and their targets is comparable with that of other atlases, e.g. Munsell's. In the NCS atlas there are, however, some color samples with notations that deviate somewhat from their "true" values, namely the ones at two of the triangle sides, with zero blackness and zero whiteness respectively. These zero-values were not possible to obtain with available pigments and here the samples deviate up to 5 NCS units from the nominal notation positions where they have been placed in the atlas. This deviation is generally not important for most practical applications and for any usage where more precise values are required it is of course better to use the exact NCS notations. These are published in a separate list with the atlas.

In returning to the NCS–Munsell comparison it should be noted that the NCS by definition *is* the perceptually based color descriptive system, with its references to the cognitive images of the elementary colors. The NCS atlas is only an illustration of this, under a specific viewing condition. The Munsell system, on the other hand, *is* the

Munsell Book of Color, and this color system is thus explicitly defined by its CIE values. For both the NCS *atlas* and the Munsell atlas (and all other atlases and collections of color samples) their color notations (when they are referring to how colors look) are valid only under the specified light and viewing conditions in which they were developed. But this restriction is, of course, not necessary for the NCS *system* which is independent of outer conditions. All persons with normal color vision carry with them their cognitive references. The Munsell system is thus dependent on its atlas, but NCS is not.

It has been claimed that a direct estimation method, such as the NCS method, which does not use external standards, could be applied equally well with the Munsell parameters of Hue, Value, and Chroma. Some serious problems arise here, however. It is perhaps possible that Value can be fairly well assessed – at least along the grey scale because this has two end-points; but as I mentioned in my introduction, it has proven to be very difficult to assess the lightness/Value variable for chromatic colors, unless one makes a comparison with the samples adjacent to one another. In that case it is easy to assess the discriminative variable lightness. If the samples are kept apart, however, one tends instead to compare the whiteness of the colors, which is a qualitative attribute, even if we often consciously *call* this lightness, just as we call colors "light blue" and "light green" when we actually refer to blues and greens near white.

As regards the assessment of hue it could have been just as easy to judge the relationships of a color to the neighboring unique hues along the Munsell hue circle as along the NCS circle. The problem is, though, that principal blue in Munsell is quite far from unique blue. It is also difficult to relate to the point "purple" which is not a unique hue, nor is the Munsell principal purple a color midway between red and blue; but not even to green, yellow, and red is it conceptually correct to relate the Munsell Hue of a given color, although in Munsell these are fairly close to NCS elementaries. The reason is that the principal Hues in the Munsell system have nothing to do with the Hering definition of unique hues. A proportional estimation of hue resemblance to these principal Hues, comparable to hue estimations in the NCS, is therefore theoretically wrong. A *post-hoc* adaptation of the theory of the Munsell atlas to the opponent hues, which is now planned (MacCamy, personal communication), is for the same reason illogical and in violation of the underlying theoretical principles.

The most serious problem with applying direct estimation to the Munsell parameters arises, however, in relation to Chroma. This scale is open-ended, the "equal steps" in the atlas are defined to be equal to steps along the Value scale, and such estimations can only be done with such a scale available. Even if most people are surprisingly good in performing direct psychometric judgments, it is indeed too complicated a task for them to "first imagine a tenth of the perceptual distance between black and white, then cognitively translate this lightness difference to a Chroma difference, and then estimate how many such distances the given color is in Chroma from the gray axis."

Now it should be added that color atlases are certainly also often appropriate for direct ocular comparisons of colors. Almost all architects in Scandinavia use the NCS atlas for that purpose along with others. The human visual system has an amazing ability to adapt to various lighting conditions and thus object colors look much the same, which makes this use of color atlas samples appropriate, at least if the lighting has a sufficiently smooth spectral emission curve.

NCS lightness

The fact that the perceptual concept of lightness is not used as a variable for the construction of the NCS certainly does not mean that it is not important. Lightness is a very relevant concept in for example the perception of contrasts between colors (Hård and Sivik 1986). However, in line with Hering's statements we have, in the development of the NCS, pointed out that the color parameter lightness is of a different kind than the ones that constitute the NCS space. It is discriminative rather than qualitatively descriptive and cannot unambiguously be comprehended as an attribute of a single color but rather as a color difference attribute, which requires that two colors be compared. To specify *NCS lightness*, we adopted the following operational definition: for an achromatic color the lightness is proportional to whiteness/blackness; *the lightness of a chromatic color is the same as the lightness of the particular achromatic color against which it has a minimally distinct border in a juxtaposed position.*

When we performed this experiment with the NCS atlas colors, juxtaposing each sample with the gray scale and determining where it had the least distinct border, we found that the lightness, defined in this way, was linearly proportional to (|), i.e., the luminance/reflectance factor. In the NCS atlas the values for equal lightness conform to straight lines which are inscribed on the atlas pages. The exact lightness values for each sample are also provided in a special publication. The equal lightness lines in the NCS converge at a point whose position varies with hue. See Figure 8.12.

Figure 8.12 Lines of equal NCS lightness.

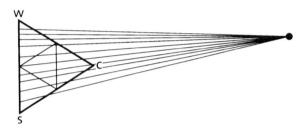

Examples of research applications of the NCS in Sweden

A prototype for the NCS color atlas was ready in 1970, but it took almost a decade before all economic and technical problems connected with the publication were solved. It was, of course, possible right from the beginning to use the system as such as well as the results from the research and development of the atlas: any color sample could be measured spectrophotometrically and the values transferred to NCS notations. With support from the government the work with color research has continued in cooperation with the University of Göteborg and the University of Technology in Stockholm. One of the main purposes of the development of the NCS had been that it be used in color research.

The main supplier of grants has been the Swedish Building Research Council and many of the questions they wanted investigated could be classified under environmental psychology. One example is "how colors change as a function of viewing distance": houses are seen both from a short distance and from long distances. (See Figure 8.13.) This is a typical example of how to use the NCS: one performs direct estimations with the NCS methods. An atlas is not as useful for this purpose (Sivik and Hård 1977).

Another color research problem, for which we could show that direct estimation is appropriate, is that of color rendering – that is,

Figure 8.13 Perceptual changes of colors from 0.5 to 80 meters.

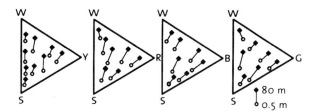

"how surfaces change colors under different lighting conditions." Here it is not possible to apply a system like the Munsell as this is defined by its atlas, and color samples cannot be used for comparison since these also change with the change of lighting. We want to measure the net result of the various visual functions of color change and color constancy, and that is what we actually see, namely, colors qualitatively perceived in comparison with our inner standards (Sivik 1980).

A third example of color change, of which many are aware although they do not always know exactly how to describe it, concerns the general notion that the color of a small sample does not look the same when it is applied on a whole wall. Most people guess that it becomes more chromatic, but that is actually not the case; often a strong color becomes somewhat less chromatic due to less simultaneous contrast. But it becomes *much more* of whatever color it is, and that can be quite overwhelming if it is, for example, a strong red.

Studies of color meaning

An area of research which for a long time has been of interest in Sweden is that of color connotations. Our research team started such studies in the mid-1960s and the basic aim has been to map out, in the NCS space, how various semantic, color-connotative variables, such as warm–cold and active–passive, vary systematically over the color space. This variation is not necessarily linear and that is the reason why the relationships between color dimensions and semantic variables should be illustrated in a graphic color space. Linear regression equations, which have been popular among experimental behavioral researchers, are likely to conceal more complex relationships which may very well be revealed by direct mapping (Sivik and Hård 1983b).

There are, however, many aspects of color meaning. A list of some of the basic and researchable ones can include the following:

- generality
- context
- dimensions of colors – color space
- structure of color meaning
- dimensions of color combinations

It is often said that color preferences and other associations with colors "are cultural or even completely individual" (Sivik and Taft 1991; Taft and Sivik 1991, 1992). At the same time, however, people assume that others share their opinions about color. The truth is that the degree of agreement lies somewhere in between these two extremes, and that it varies. On closer inspection the question of generality of color connotations could be a research area of its own. The degree of conformity thus varies depending on which association- or connotation-variable we are talking about, and, of course, the context. People are relatively concordant about which colors are, for example, "warm" or "cold." On the other hand, more emotionally evaluative variables such as "like–dislike" show a much smaller degree of generality which also is very much dependent on the context. However, in the most common context for color preference experiments, i.e., judging paper color samples, the conformity between people appears to be considerable.

In our first studies a large number of color samples were judged one by one and by means of the conventional semantic differential method:

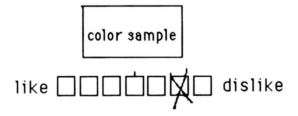

The average judgments of the different color samples vary for most variables successively and systematically over the color space. On the basis of these mean values it is possible to plot, as in a weather chart, the varying semantic loadings in a color space. An example from the semantic scale "masculine–feminine" is given in Figure 8.14. The

Figure 8.14
Associations between colors and the semantic variable "masculine – feminine." Isosemantic mapping in the NCS color triangle of elementary blue showing how "masculinity" increases with increasing blackness. The pattern is similar for all the other hues regarding this semantic variable.

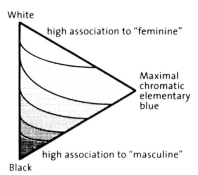

White

high association to "feminine"

Maximal chromatic elementary blue

high association to "masculine"

Black

choice of color space model for this mapping is arbitrary, but an appearance-based model seemed to us most relevant as specific positions and relationships in such a space have meaningful correlates in a perceptual sense, which would not be the case with, for example, the CIE space and its derivates.

There are many words in common use to describe the character and associative meanings of colors. Besides such attributes as yellow, blue, strong, weak, deep, and saturated, colors can also have connotations like cold, joyful, depressing, sick, healthy, dirty, feminine, masculine, etc. Such color-relevant adjectives can add up to a rather long list. It is now possible to make a semantic map from the average judgments for each of all imaginable words, or for pairs of opposites if we choose to use bi-polar scales as in the masculine–feminine example above. In our first studies (Sivik 1970), twenty-seven such antonyms were mapped out in the NCS.

A conspicuous result, perhaps astonishing for many, was that the color parameter *hue* had less influence on the semantic variance than the other color parameters chromaticness, whiteness, lightness, and blackness. The connotative variable "active–passive," for example, was thus primarily dependent on the chromaticness of the color. Whether it was red or green was less important. An exception to this general finding was the variable "warm–cold," along which the associated colors clearly varied by hue, with the warmth maximum in the yellow–red region and the cold maximum in the blue–blue-green. But also here the variation across color triangles with constant hue was considerable. Judgement of the masculinity–femininity of a color was a function mainly of its blackness and to a much lesser extent of hue, although the strong colors in the "warm" hue region were somewhat more associated with the concept of femininity.

But many such bi-polar semantic scales seem to be more or less synonymous with respect to color and therefore we tried to compress the data by means of a principal components analysis (Sivik 1974a). Four factors, or semantic dimensions, were extracted. On the basis of the meaning of their most typical variables we labeled them: Excitement/Activity, Evaluation, Energy/Forcefulness, and Warmth. Those who are familiar with the original work with the semantic differential method by Osgood and his collaborators will recognize the first three as their general semantic factors. The variable "warm" usually merges with the evaluative factor (a warm person, for example, is positively evaluated), but as an attribute of color it forms a factor of its own. Whether a color is perceived as warm or cold does not influence judgments of its beauty, and this makes the warmth factor emerge as an independent, orthogonal dimension of meaning.

In order to demonstrate the influence of context, a number of semantic scales were also tested against a set of photographic pictures in which the color "belonged to" buildings (Sivik 1974b). Such experiments, with judgments of simulated environments, were rather cumbersome at that time. Today they are much easier with the help of computers. This study showed, as expected, that some variables of meaning changed their pattern radically in comparison with the judgments of color samples, in particular for evaluative variables such as "beautiful–ugly."

Other variables, e.g. "warm–cold," did not change at all. As the form of the house was the same in all the pictures (only the color was changed) it was evident that it was only the color that accounted for the difference in ratings, even if we asked for the global appearance of the house in the picture. A special aspect of the results of these architecture-related studies demonstrated that color has a substantial effect on the perception of spaciousness.

Another area we have started to investigate concerns the appearance and evaluation of *color combinations* (Sivik and Hård 1994). Colors never appear alone, but always together. Even if seemingly alone a single color must have a surround, which also has a color. Irrespective of whether there are thousands or millions of colors a human can see, the number of possible color combinations is practically infinite. In order to study meaningfully people's attitudes to, and the associations of, and evaluations of all these it is necessary to have a descriptive language and a structural model for the color combinations as such (in addition to recognizing the earlier-mentioned factors of context, texture, subject population, etc.). It is virtually impossible to investigate all the billions of possible combinations, and an arbitrary selection is

of limited value. In our team we have proposed such a descriptive combinatorial model (Hård and Sivik 1979) and, based on this, also carried
out a series of preliminary studies to investigate some semantic loadings of color combinations (Sivik and Taft 1990).

Here we also started with a large number of semantic variables
(130 adjectives) with questions such as, "Does the combination look
happy, sharp, brutal, warm?" The results were then compressed by
means of factor analysis. Five bi-polar factors or dimensions emerged
which were named: General evaluation, Articulation, Light–dark,
Warm–cold, and Originality.

When we later investigated how the color combinations were
ordered in relation to the semantic structure it appeared that the
latter had clear relationships to the dimensions of the color combinatorial model with its parameters of interval, color-chord, color similarity, etc. A picture of the semantic structure from these studies is given
in Figure 8.15. From this it is possible to imagine the types of color
combinations that belong to different areas of the space (here compressed to only two dimensions).

For this kind of study it seems as though it would have been
equally appropriate to use another color atlas, e.g. the Munsell, for
the mapping. We still consider NCS better, however, because Munsell
in "the vertical" color directions is only based on the discriminative
variable of lightness (Value) and consequently does not account for
the qualitative color attributes of blackness and whiteness. It has
been shown, both by ocular inspection and by analyses of correlations,
that these two color variables have, for many semantic connotations,
better explanatory value than lightness has.

The same may also be true as regards the question which is the
main theme of this volume: color categorization. In the late 1960s we
had already mapped the thirteen most common Swedish color terms in
the NCS. These data were first published only in Swedish, but a shorter
version appeared in the proceedings of the AIC conference in Monaco
(Sivik 1985). The reason why we did this work was that we had not seen
any similar mapping in any other color space. When Berlin and Kay's
very interesting work came to our attention it was clear that their primary interest was not the intricate complexity of color dimensions.
We were somewhat astonished by their choice of colors. This was not
because they had chosen Munsell samples, since this system had

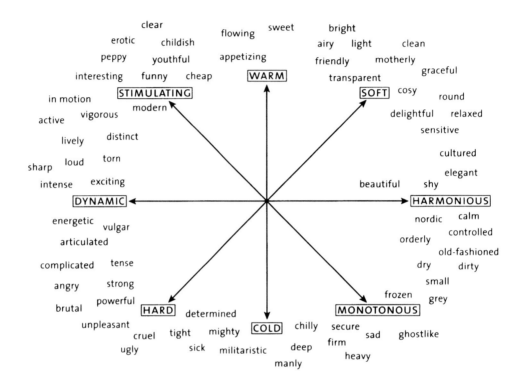

Figure 8.15
Configuration of the
semantic scales in
two dimensions from
multidimensional
scaling (ALSCAL).

been the dominant one and few behavioral researchers were aware of
the existence of alternatives. It was rather because they just used the
"surface" of the color solid plus the mid-axis of black–grey–white. Is
it not interesting to know whether the inner color nuances have
specific names in the various cultures? (These colors are more
numerous than the ones from the surface of the color solid.)

A different approach was used by Boynton and Olson (1987), who
mapped the color categories in the OSA–UCS, a system which was created with the aim of equal spacing. The problem with the color sample
collection illustrating this color space is, however, that it only represents the inner parts of a space with all possible colors and thus it
lacks the "surface" of a more complete color space (like the Munsell or
NCS). It was therefore difficult to compare their focal point or category
area data with ours because for many color categories these had no
color representative in the OSA–UCS. Boynton's method of using reaction time as a measure of salience is interesting and can be validated
against other methods (cf. Boynton this volume).

Figure 8.16
"Isosemantic map"
of brown.

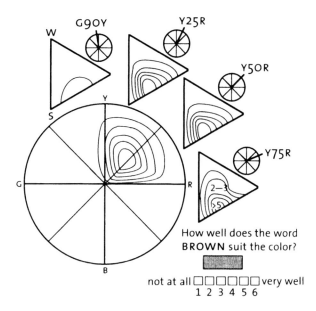

How well does the word
BROWN suit the color?

not at all ☐☐☐☐☐☐ very well
     1 2 3 4 5 6

The first investigations we performed were with the so-called semantic differential (SD) technique, which has proven useful and reliable in similar data collections, even if it is rather time-consuming (Sivik and Taft 1994). It offers a possibility of showing a rather continuous gradation from high agreement among the respondents for the "focal colors" for which everyone considered the actual color term appropriate, over the intermediate SD means, to the colors with means of zero for the color term, indicating that nobody accepted the term for those colors.

As a follow-up to this first investigation we have now started a cross-national study with, as we believe, a better and more expedient method. The whole array of over 1,500 colors in the NCS atlas are presented to the subjects. To date we have data from Croatia, Sweden, Poland, Italy, India, and the USA. By this method we are able to record, for each color in the atlas, the frequencies of acceptance of the particular term studied. The concept of "focal point" then can be operationally defined as, say, 90 percent acceptance (or another frequency; we have not yet decided upon this). Then it is possible to draw iso-lines for decreasing acceptance of the term, as in Figure 8.16. These maps look more or less the same as the ones obtained from the SD method.

We believe that this method will be a valuable complement to the

Berlin and Kay paradigmatic procedure for cross-cultural comparison, as it provides a more complete picture of how the various color categories are spread out in the color world. It should perhaps be pointed out that so-called desaturated colors are by no means "inferior," or "lesser" colors; they are as much colors as the more saturated ones. All color percepts, including the achromatic ones, are 100 percent of themselves and "whole", in a qualitative sense. They are certainly not less important to investigate than the highly chromatic ones, since they actually constitute the majority of colors we perceive as our visual world.

References

Berlin, B., and P. Kay 1969. *Basic Color Terms: Their Universality and Evolution*. Berkeley: University of California Press. 1st paperback edn. 1991, with bibliography by Luisa Maffi

Billmeyer, F. W. 1987. Survey of color order systems. *Color Research and Application* 12: 173–186.

Boynton, R. M., and C. X. Olson 1987. Locating basic colors in the OSA space. *Color Research and Application* 12: 94–105.

Derefeldt, G. 1991. Color appearance systems. In P. Gouras (ed.), *Vision and Visual Dysfunction*, Vol. VI, *The Perception of Colour*. General ed., J. R. Cronly-Dillon. London: MacMillan.

Hård, A. 1966. Philosophy of the Hering–Johansson Natural Color System. *Die Farbe* 15: 287–295.

Hård, A., and L. Sivik 1979. Outlines of a theory of colors in combination. *Man–Environment–Systems* 9(4 & 5): 217–228.

1981. NCS – Natural Color System: a Swedish standard for color notation. *Color Research and Application* 6(3): 129–13.

1986. Distinctness of border: an alternative concept for a uniform color space. *Color Research and Application* 11(2): 169–175.

Hård, A. Sivik, L., and Tonnquist, G. (1996). NCS, Natural Color System – from Concept to Research and Applications. Part I and Part II. *Color Research and Application*, 21(3):180–220.

Hardin, C. L. 1988. *Color for Philosophers: Unweaving the Rainbow*. Indianapolis, IN: Hackett Publishing Co.

Hering, E. 1964[1920]. *Outlines of a Theory of the Light Sense, (Zur Lehre vom Lichtsinne)*, trans. L. M. Hurvich

and D. Jameson. Cambridge, MA: Harvard University Press. (Translation of *Zur Lehre vom Lichtsinne*. Vienna: Gerolds Sohn.)

Munsell Book of Color 1929, 1976. Baltimore, MD: Munsell Color Company, Macbeth Division of Kollmorgen Corporation.

Newhall, S. M. 1940. Preliminary report on the OSA subcommittee on the spacing of the Munsell colors. *Journal of the Optical Society of America* 30: 617–645.

Nickerson, D. 1940. History of the Munsell color system and its scientific application. *Journal of the Optical Society of America*. 30: 575–586.

Sivik, L. 1970. Om färgers betydelser. *Färgrapport* C9 (Stockholm: Scandinavian Color Institute).

1974a. Color meaning and perceptual color dimensions: a study of color samples. *Göteborg Psychological Reports* 4(1).

1974b. Color meaning and perceptual color dimensions: a study of exterior colors. *Göteborg Psychological Reports* 4(11).

1980. Direct psychometric scaling of color rendering. *Acta Chromatica* (Tokyo).

1985. Mapping of color names in NCS. In *Mondial Coureur 85, Proceedings of the 5th AIC Congress 1985*, 2:5. Paris: Centre Francais de la Couleur.

Sivik, L., and A. Hård 1977. Methodological studies of color changes due to distance and lighting: direct assessment using the Natural Color System. In *Proceedings of the 3rd AIC Congress, Color 77*. Bristol: Adam Hilger Ltd.

1983a. Is color naming the most natural color system? Proceedings of the Forsius Symposium on

Color Order Systems (AIC), Kungälv, Sweden. *Color Report No F26* (Stockholm: Scandinavian Color Institute).

    1983b. On the appearance of color order spaces. Proceedings of the Forsius Symposium on Color Order Systems (AIC), Kungälv, Sweden. *Color Report No F26* (Stockholm: Scandinavian Color Institute).

    1994. Some reflections on studying color combinations. *Color Research and Application* 19(4): 286–295.

Sivik, L., and C. Taft 1990. Semantic variables for the evaluation of color combinations – an analysis of semantic dimensions. *Göteborg Psychological Reports* 19(5).

    1991. Cross-cultural studies of color meaning. In *Proceedings of AIC conference on Color and Light '91.* (pp. 93–96). Sydney: Colour Society of Australia.

    1994. Color naming: a mapping in the NCS of common color terms. *Scandinavian Journal of Psychology,* 35: 144–164.

Swedish Standards Institution 1989. Swedish Standard SS 01 91 02, *Color atlas.* Stockholm: SIS.

    1990. Swedish Standard SS 01 91 00, *Color notation system.* Stockholm: SIS.

Taft, C., and L. Sivik 1991. Stability and variability of color meaning associations: a cross-national comparison. *Göteborg Psychological Reports* 21(1).

    1992. Cross-national comparison of color meaning. *Göteborg Psychological Reports* 22(3).

Tonnquist, G. 1993. 25 years of colour with the AIC – and 25,000 without. *Color Research and Application* 18(5): 353–365.

    1994. Reference points in colour systems. *Die Farbe* 40:83–94.

Tyler, J. E., and A. C. Hardy 1940. An analysis of the original Munsell color system. *Journal of the Optical Society of America* 30: 508.

III ANTHROPOLOGISTS AND LINGUISTS

9 Establishing basic color terms: measures and techniques

Greville G. Corbett and Ian R. L. Davies

Introduction

This is an unusual type of chapter.[1] We are looking at the notion of basicness of color terms by comparing various tests. To do this, we are using languages that are well studied. Often this means the basic color terms in those languages can be taken as given, so that we can then see how well particular types of tests perform in identifying the basic color terms. There are two reasons for doing this. One is that it may tell us something about the different types of tests and therefore about the notion of basicness. The second is a practical point. Given the difficulties of fieldwork in particular places, it is worth looking for tests that are easy to run, quick, and efficient, as opposed to those that are more elaborate. So this chapter is about testing the tests. In addition, it has been found that languages which have a full set of basic color terms may still preserve a color hierarchy. That is to say there is not simply a division between basic and non-basic color terms but rather the terms higher on the hierarchy can still be seen to be "more basic" than those lower on the hierarchy. We shall be looking for tests which can reveal that type of structure.

First we outline the Berlin and Kay hierarchy. Then we look at the types of measure available and the statistical techniques for establishing how well they fit with the predictions derived from Berlin and Kay. We then give examples of the tests in turn, referring briefly to the results obtained and the degree of correspondence with the hierarchy. This leads to an investigation of the interrelation between the measures,[2] and to examining consistency across investigators and across languages; certain measures give considerably better results than others. We conclude that, while the indicators point in the same direction, supporting Berlin and Kay to varying degrees, different measures serve different functions. For instance, elicited lists are quick and effective at separating basic from non-basic terms, but not very good at fine-grained distinctions within the hierarchy. On the other hand, frequency in texts is better at discriminating amongst the basic terms, but cannot reliably distinguish basic from non-basic terms.

The hierarchy

As originally formulated by Berlin and Kay (1969: 5), the hierarchy consists of the following positions:

								purple
white			green					pink
	<	red	<		<	blue	<	brown	<
black			yellow					orange
								grey

The hierarchy constrains the possible inventories of color terms: the presence of any given term implies the existence of all those to the left (thus a language with a basic term for yellow will have basic terms for white, black, and red). It makes diachronic predictions, since languages must move from one state allowed by the hierarchy to another. Kay (1975: 257–262; see also Kay and McDaniel 1978: 638–640) revised the hierarchy, claiming that the earlier evolutionary stages involve the decomposition of composite categories. This is not directly relevant for our purposes. It is also claimed that grey may occur as a "wild card," rather earlier than was originally thought, though this is believed to happen only infrequently. We shall not include this relaxation of the hierarchy in what follows for two reasons: first, if grey can occur at various points, this makes it easier to find data matching the order of the hierarchy;[3] and second, we wish to draw comparisons with earlier analyses which retained grey only as one of the four terms at the right end of the hierarchy. Not all basic terms have the same status: the first six terms are treated as the *primary* basics (Kay and McDaniel 1978: 626; see also MacLaury 1991: 42). These correspond to the labels for the landmark colors of Miller and Johnson-Laird (1976: 344). The remaining five basic terms we shall call "*secondary* basic."

Assessing the tests

Tests of basicness vary in their resolving power. The main requirement of a test is to sort out the basics from the non-basics; we call this *the level one criterion*. In addition, a test may be able to make distinctions within the basic terms. Firstly, the primary basic terms may be distinguished from the secondary basic terms – *the level two criterion*. Secondly, rather than just dividing the basic terms into two groups, a test may reveal regularities in the orderings of the basic terms – *the level three criterion*. This ordering can then be compared to the Berlin and Kay hierarchy discussed in the previous section.

Now, we might think that those three criteria are hierarchically organized. If a test reveals a consistent ordering of the terms (level three), we may expect that it will also distinguish between primary basic and secondary basic terms (level two), and between basic and non-basic terms (level one). And a test which discriminates between primary basic and secondary basic terms (level two) is also likely to distinguish basic from non-basic terms (level one). Although this is plausible, it is not logically necessary. It is possible that a test might be effective at revealing a consistent order within the basic terms, but be poor at distinguishing basic from non-basic terms. If the relationship between the three levels of resolving power were not hierarchical, it would mean that different tests would serve different purposes, and the choice of test would depend on whether the primary aim was to establish the inventory of basic terms, or to compare the ordering of basic terms to the Berlin and Kay hierarchy, or whatever. And, interestingly, as we shall see, the tests do give quite different results.

We should consider next how to establish whether a test meets any of the three criteria just described: firstly, by considering the patterns of data which would indicate that the criteria were met, and secondly, by considering what statistical tests might establish objectively to what extent the criteria were met.

First, let us consider the level one criterion. If a measure met the level one criterion perfectly, then there would be a sharp cut-off between the basic terms and the non-basic terms. That is, there should be no overlap between the sets of scores for the two groups of terms, and the difference between the scores of the closest of the basic and non-basic terms would be large. However, failure to reach this perfect degree of separation does not mean the measure achieves nothing; it may achieve some degree of partial separation. Formal statistical procedures cannot be applied to most of the data we report here, because they require the scores for each of the non-basic terms, and these have not usually been published. We therefore concentrate mostly on the degree of overlap between the basic and non-basic sets by comparing scores for the "worst" basic terms with the "best" non-basic terms. Where possible we give the scores for the three best non-basic terms for a given language and test to compare these with the scores for the basic terms.

Second, establishing whether a test discriminates primary basic from secondary basic terms (the level two criterion) requires conceptually the same procedures as for distinguishing basic from non-basic terms. That is, we analyze the degree of overlap between the two sets of scores, and the difference between the "average" score for each set. In this case however, the data for each of the eleven terms are available and we are able to apply formal statistical procedures. Here we have used procedures testing for a statistically significant difference between the mean scores of the primary and secondary terms such as t and Mann-Whitney's U.[4]

Finally, if a test satisfied the level three criterion perfectly, the rank orders of the terms on the test would correspond exactly to the rank order of the terms on the Berlin and Kay hierarchy. However, this is rare, and we need some measure of degree of correspondence or association, to tell us how close the association is to perfection, and whether it is statistically significant. In general the appropriate statistical assessment of the strength of an index of basicness is some kind of measure of association between the rank order of color terms on the index and the Berlin and Kay rank order. In this chapter we report Kendall's tau as the preferred measure, when correlating measures with the Berlin and Kay ranks, and Pearson's r for correlations between measures.

Behavioral tests

The behavioral measures we describe here are all predicated on Berlin and Kay's notion of psychological salience (1969: 6).[5] We have identified five measures: reaction time (RT) as recommended by Hays, Margolis, Naroll, and Perkins (1972: 1120); the frequency with which terms are used in naming experiments; the consistency of use of color terms; and the frequency of occurrence and the order of occurrence of terms in elicited lists. Here we present just the data on reaction time in color naming and frequency of occurrence in elicited lists. Summary data on the other means are included in Tables 9.5, 9.6 and 9.7 on pp. 212–214 (and the full data are in Corbett and Davies 1995).

Reaction time (RT)

This measure was used as part of four recent studies: Boynton and Olson (1987, 1990) using English speakers, Uchikawa and Boynton (1987) for Japanese speakers, and Moss, Davies, Corbett, and Laws (1990) for Russian speakers.

These studies measured the time taken to name a large sample of colors: each of the 424 OSA colors[6] in Boynton and his coworkers' studies and the 219 color samples of the Color Aid Corporation's range[7] in the Russian study. Each of the colors was presented singly and the subject was required to name the color with a monolexemic term as quickly as possible. The time from the onset of the color display to the beginning of the vocalization was recorded, and this was the RT for that trial. The entire set of colors was presented twice in different random sequences.

The data in Table 9.1 are the mean RTs across every use of a term – that is, across both repetitions of the set of colors and across respondents. Thus, 1949 ms (1.949 seconds) in Table 9.1 is the mean RT across all occurrences of the Russian term *belyj* "white." Although all four studies used equivalent procedures, there is some variation in the measures reported. We have derived comparable measures where possible from each study, and these are shown in Table 9.1. This gives the means across subjects and color samples for:

(a) each of the basic terms, except black for Boynton and Olson (1987) – American sample 1 – and black, white, and grey for Boynton and Olson (1990) – American sample 2 – where these data are not given. The scores for the three non-basic terms with the fastest RT in each study are also shown, except for Boynton and Olson (1987) where data for individual non-basic terms are not given.

(b) the mean scores $\overline{X}$ for basic and non-basic terms.

(c) the mean scores $\overline{X}$ for primary and secondary basic terms.[8]

Table 9.1   Response times (milliseconds) to color stimuli in Russian, Japanese, and American English

	Russian	Japanese	American 1	American 2
PRIMARY				
white	1949	1900	1900	–
black	1892	2250	–	–
red	1776	2140	1440	2550
green	1596	2010	1450	1780
yellow	1503	2190	1360	1920
blue	1520	2180	1420	1940
SECONDARY				
brown	1628	2210	1470	2360
purple	1916	2000	1500	2220
pink	1991	2310	1570	2140
orange	1958	2260	1540	1970
grey	1578	2510	1490	–
THREE FASTEST				
NON-BASIC TERMS	2024	2350		2690
	2059	2350		2880
	2061	2360		2920
basic $\bar{X}$	1646	2150	1736	2110
non-basic $\bar{X}$	2169	2480	2380	3170
primary $\bar{X}$	1706	2112	1510	2050
secondary $\bar{X}$	1814	2258	1510	2170

For each language, the mean RT for basic terms is less than for non-basic terms; with the single exception of grey for Japanese, the slowest basic term is faster than the fastest non-basic term for each language. This corroborates Boynton's claim (this volume). Furthermore, within the basic terms, the mean score for the primary terms is faster than the mean for secondary terms for Russian, Japanese, and the second American sample, and they are equal for the first American sample (but remember the first American sample scores are just consensus scores, and the mean for primary terms does not include the score for black). However, the separation between the primary and secondary terms is much less clearcut than for basic and non-basic terms; the primary/secondary difference is not significant in either language ($t=.92$, $p=.38$ for Russian; $t=1.5$, $p=.16$ for Japanese). For each language, three of the primary terms tend to be the fastest overall, whereas some of the secondary terms are faster than the remaining primary terms in each language.

Kendall's tau was calculated between the RTs and the Berlin and Kay rank order, for Russian and Japanese only, because of the missing data for the American samples. The correlation was significant for Japanese (tau $=.41$, $p < .05$), but not for Russian. The Pearson correlation (r) was calculated for the RTs between the two languages; it was statistically non-significant.

In summary, response time serves to discriminate basic from non-basic terms well (the level one criterion); but it does not distinguish primary from secondary terms, nor does it correspond to the full Berlin and Kay hierarchy very well.

Elicited lists

In describing their fourth criterion, psychological salience, Berlin and Kay suggest three indices (though these are not exclusive); the first is "a tendency to occur at the beginning of elicited lists of color terms" (1969: 6). The example we take here is a study of Russian, chosen because the language has received considerable attention as a possible exception to Berlin and Kay. It is exceptional because it appears to have two basic terms for blue. We believe this exception is well established (see appendix 1, Davies and Corbett 1994a and Corbett and Davies 1995, for more detail). Morgan and Corbett (1989) report an experiment in which thirty-one native speakers of Russian were asked, in Russian, to write down as many color terms as they could think of within five minutes. After each minute subjects were asked to draw a line across their paper before continuing to add color terms, so that results could be calculated for each successive minute. Note that the measure is not exactly that envisaged by Berlin and Kay. We compare across subjects, expecting that basic terms will occur on more lists than non-basic terms.

Table 9.2 shows the number of respondents who had produced each term after one minute, the number who put each term first in their lists, the rank order of these frequencies, and the frequencies after five minutes together with their ranks.

It can be seen that, with the exception of *rozovyj* "pink" and *seryj* "grey," after one minute, both frequency measures separate the basic from non-basic terms (the level one criterion). By five minutes the separation is complete: there is no overlap now between the frequencies with which basic and non-basic terms occur. Note that *sinij* "dark blue" and *goluboj* "light blue" both pattern with the basics.

Furthermore, both frequency measures and the number of first places are higher for the primary than for the secondary basic terms (t=3.09, p<.01 for frequency after one minute; t=2.2, d.f.=5.1, p<.03 for the first places; t=2.1, p<.04 for frequency after five minutes). The degree of correlation with the hierarchy after one minute is tau=.32 (not significant) and that after five minutes is tau=.52, p<.02. The data on first position (given in parentheses) significantly correlate with the hierarchy (tau=.51, p<.025), but it seems this is primarily due to a clear difference between primary and secondary terms; of the secondary terms, only *rozovyj* "pink" ever appears first on a list, and of the primary terms, only *želtyj* "yellow" never appears first on any lists.[10] However, the precise value of tau needs treating with caution because of the relatively small sample, and the large number of tied scores.

Linguistic tests

There are three linguistic tests available: frequency in texts, word length, and the number of derived forms. We shall consider the most important, frequency in texts, which Hays *et al.* (1972) used as an index of psychological salience. The best data available are for Russian and English.

Table 9.2   **Number of Russian informants offering each term in the list experiment (31 subjects)**

term	1st minute			5th minute	
	occurrences	(first)	rank (within basics)	occurrences	rank (within basics)
PRIMARY					
belyj "white"	18	(9)	9	28	7
černyj "black"	21	(1)	5.5	30	2.5
krasnyj "red"	24	(11)	3.5	31	1
zelenyj "green"	25	(2)	2	30	2.5
želtyj "yellow"	21		5.5	27	10
sinij "dark blue"	24	(4)	3.5	28	7
goluboj "light blue"	27	(1)	1	29	4.5
SECONDARY					
koričnevyj "brown"	17		10	29	4.5
fioletovyj "purple"	20		7	27	10
rozovyj "pink"	12	(1)	11	26	12
oranževyj "orange"	19		8	28	7
seryj "grey"	10		12	27	10
HIGHEST NON-BASIC[9]					
beževyj "beige"	13	(1)		22	
bordovyj "claret"	13			20	
sirenevyj "mauve"	12			20	
primary $\bar{X}$	22.4	(4.9)		29.1	
secondary $\bar{X}$	15.6	(0.2)		27.4	

Russian

Russian was one of the languages considered by Hays *et al.* (1972). Since their work, better sources of data have become available, notably Zasorina (1977), an investigation of over 1 million words of twentieth-century Russian. From this we can obtain the data given in Table 9.3.

Table 9.3   **Frequency of basic color terms in Russian texts**

term	number of occurrences	rank (basic terms)
PRIMARY		
belyj "white"	471	2
černyj "black"	473	1
krasnyj "red"	371	3
zelenyj "green"	216	4
želtyj "yellow"	109	8
sinij "dark blue"	180	5
goluboj "light blue"	137	6
SECONDARY		
koričnevyj "brown"	23	10
fioletovyj "purple"	22	11
rozovyj "pink"	49	9
oranževyj "orange"	15	12
seryj "grey"	116	7
HIGHEST NON-BASICS		
belosnežnyj "snow-white"	67	
ryžyj "ginger"	59	
buryj "brown"	31	
primary $\bar{X}$	299.8	
secondary $\bar{X}$	45.0	

The three highest non-basic terms outscore four of the basic terms, and so the measure does not reliably pass the level one criterion. However, the difference between primary and secondary basic (the level two criterion) is almost complete; the exception is *seryj* "gray" ($t=3.8$, d.f.$=5.8$, $p <.005$). The degree of correlation with the hierarchy is high – tau$=.77$, $p < .001$ – but three basic colors are "out of order" and deserve comment. First, *želtyj* "yellow" occurs less frequently than would be suggested by its position on the hierarchy. We have no explanation for this, but it seems to be a common problem; Hays *et al.* (1972: 1112) found yellow lower in frequency than expected in English, French, German, and Spanish, as well as in Russian. *Koričnevyj* "brown" is also low; this is because it is in the process of taking over from an earlier term for brown, namely *buryj* (Corbett and Morgan 1988: 45, 48, 51–52). In other counts of twentieth-century

Russian, reported in Corbett and Morgan (1988: 47), *koričnevyj* is the
more frequent. *Seryj* "grey" is higher than expected; this perhaps
should be connected with its status as a "wild card."

English

Good data on English are available for comparison in Johansson
and Hofland's (1989) analysis of the Lancaster – Oslo/Bergen (LOB)
corpus.[11] The LOB corpus consists of a million words of modern
British English. It has been tagged, so that frequencies of color
terms functioning as adjectives can be separated from other uses
(thus allowing more reliable comparison with other languages). The
data are as in Table 9.4.

Table 9.4 **Frequency of basic color terms in English texts**

term	number of occurrences	rank (basic terms)
PRIMARY		
white	247	1
black	144	2
red	142	3
green	85	4
yellow	31	8
blue	83	5
SECONDARY		
brown	61	7
purple	16	10
pink	28	9
orange	7	11
grey	80	6
HIGHEST NON-BASICS		
silver	22	
bronze	14	
scarlet	14	
primary $\bar{X}$	122.0	
secondary $\bar{X}$	38.4	

As with Russian, the three most frequent non-basic terms have scores higher than at least one basic term, *orange*; and the highest non-basic term, *silver*, also outscores *purple*. The frequencies of *silver* and *bronze* are probably overestimates of their use as color adjectives, however.[12] It appears that frequency in texts does better in English than in Russian in terms of the level one criterion.

With the exception of *yellow*, the primary basic terms all score higher than the secondary terms (t=2.5, p < .03), and the correlation with the hierarchy is high: tau=.77, p < .001.

There are some striking points of comparison with Russian. First the number of occurrences of color terms in a corpus of comparable size is markedly lower in English.[13] This deserves investigation, but probably results from the composition of the corpora, literature having a larger place in the Russian corpus. When we turn to the ranking of the individual terms, two surprising similarities are found. First there is the unexpectedly low position of *yellow* as with Russian *želtyj* (a recurring problem as mentioned earlier). And second, like *seryj*, *grey* again shows evidence of its "wild card" status, occurring much higher than would have been expected from the original hierarchy.

In general, word frequency does not separate basics from non-basics completely but it is a strong separator for primary versus secondary basics (the level two criterion).

The interrelationship between measures and languages

So far we have considered examples of a measure in operation on a single language. Overall we have data on thirty-six combinations of languages and measures in which we can explore the relationship between measures and between languages. These combinations consist of a partial sample of language–measure pairs. The languages are English (various sources), French, Hebrew, Japanese, Russian, and Spanish, and the measures are behavioral (RT, frequency of naming, consistency of naming, frequency in lists, number of first places in lists, and mean position in lists) and linguistic measures (number of derived forms, frequency in texts, number of phonemes, and number of syllables). (See appendix 2 for the actual combinations.) These data were subjected to a correspondence analysis (Greenacre 1984; Weller and Romney 1990), which is a technique for exploring patterns of association in large data matrices. In brief, it attempts to discover a

number of "vectors" – structures underlying the patterns of covaria-
tion – and each case (color) and variable (measure) has a value (weight)
on each vector. The analysis provides a measure of "percentage of inertia" for each vector, which in essence is a measure of the strength, or
degree of influence, of that vector,[14] and a measure of the degree of statistical significance of each vector. There is a spatial metaphor underlying the product of the analysis. Each element (colors and measures)
is plotted in a graph whose axes are the vectors which are statistically
significant. The more similar a pair of elements, the closer together
they appear to be in the graph. Moreover, the distance apart of two elements can be seen to be due to component distances on each of the
vectors. By inspecting which elements differ on which vectors, it is
sometimes possible to interpret a vector in terms of some meaningful
property of the elements.

The analysis revealed two major vectors which are massively statistically significant. One accounted for 85% of the inertia (p<.00009),
and a second vector accounted for 7.6% of the residual inertia
(p<.00009); six other vectors, although statistically significant, had a
more or less negligible magnitude of effect on the structure. Figure 9.1
shows each measure plotted in the two-dimensional space of the first
two vectors; the major vector forms the horizontal axis, and the minor
vector the vertical.[15] It can readily be seen that the variables form clus-

Figure 9.1
Correspondence
analysis for each
measure and each
language.

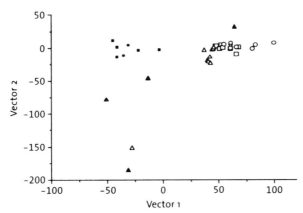

Behavioral measures
    □ = RT, frequency, and consistency
    △ = Lists – frequency and mean position
    ▲ = Lists – number of first places

Linguistic measures
    ■ = Frequency in texts and no. of derived forms
    ○ = Word length

ters; these clusters are generally groups of equivalent measures across languages. For example, measures of frequency in texts from different languages tend to cluster together (top left of the plot). At the other end of vector 1 (the right hand side in Figure 9.1) is a second large cluster, consisting of the measures of word length for each language and the behavioral measures (response time, frequency of naming, consistency, and elicited lists). However, first places in elicited lists surprisingly do not fit here, but appear as a dispersed group in the bottom left-hand quadrant. Within the large cluster on the right-hand side, word length tends to occupy the rightmost area, and the behavioral measures fall closer to the center, although there is some overlap between these two regions. The separation of word length measures from word frequency measures is interesting; it appears inconsistent with Zipf's Law (according to which more frequently occurring words tend to be shorter). On the other hand, the two sets of measures have similar values on vector 2; although this is less important than vector 1, it indicates that there is some partial relationship between the two sets of measures. The major vector seems to be characterized by the difference between frequency in texts and word length, and the minor vector something to do with the difference between the number of first places in lists and the remaining measures.

Figure 9.2 shows the color terms plotted in the same space as are the measures in Figure 9.1. The space divides approximately diagonally into two: the six primary basic terms lie in the left diagonal section and the five secondary basic terms occupy the right diagonal section. Could either of the two vectors be a good measure of the hier-

Figure 9.2
Correspondence analysis of the eleven basic terms.

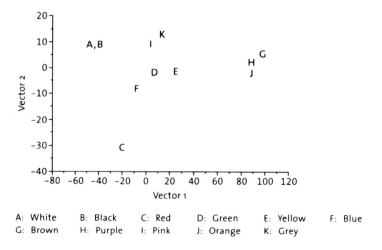

A: White	B: Black	C: Red	D: Green	E: Yellow	F: Blue
G: Brown	H: Purple	I: Pink	J: Orange	K: Grey	

archy? Vector 2 is clearly poorly related; for instance, pink and brown have similar values to white and black. The order on vector 1 is white, black, red, blue, pink, green, grey, yellow, purple, orange, and brown. Given the wild card status of grey, the primary deviation from the ranks of the hierarchy is the relatively high position of pink. The correlation with the hierarchy is $t = .51$, $p < .05$, but although this is a reasonably strong value, several of the correlations of the single measures are greater.

Combinations of measures within languages

We saw in the previous section that there were strong relationships between measures across languages. In this section we consider whether, within a language, the measures might be combined to provide a better measure of basicness than any measure on its own. We do this for Russian, English (British and American data), and French; it is only for these three that we have a reasonable spread of the measures listed in the preceding section (thus the number of combinations is lower than in appendix 2).

Tables 9.5, 9.6, and 9.7 summarize the performance of each basic term on each test in two ways. First, whether on a given measure that term scores better than the best non-basic term. If it passes this test, it is shown as $+$; if it fails, as $-$; and if the data are not available (as with RT for English) no indication is given. Second, we give the rank within the eleven basic terms, for each basic term on the measures for which we have data. In the case of English, we have used the first American sample for RT (as in Table 9.1), and for frequency of occurrence (Boynton and Olson 1987), as there was least missing data for this sample; but we have used the second American sample for the consistency measure, as the data for the highest non-basic terms were available. We have not used the syllable version of word length for the English sample because there was so little variation in the scores.

Finally, we combine the data within each language in three ways:

(a) the hurdles model – here we simply add the number of tests for which a given term scores better than the strongest non-basic term. That is, we sum the number of $+$ results in each row, and the total is shown in the column labeled "total hurdles."

(b) the mean rank – the mean of the ranks shown in a row is calculated and is shown in the next column.

	RT	Frequency of occurrence	Consistency	List frequency	List first places	Derived terms	Frequency in texts	Number of phonemes	Number of syllables	Total hurdles	Mean rank	Rank of weighted mean
belyj "white"	+ 9	− 10.5	− 10	+ 6.5	+ 2	+ 1	+ 2	− 1.5	− 3	5	5.1	1
černyj "black"	+ 7	− 10.5	− 11	+ 2.5	+ 5.5	+ 2	+ 1	− 4	− 3	5	5.2	2
krasnyj "red"	+ 6	− 9	− 9	+ 1	+ 1	+ 6	+ 3	− 7	− 3	5	5	3
zelenyj "green"	+ 4	+ 1	+ 1	+ 2.5	+ 4	+ 3	+ 4	− 7	− 7.5	7	3.8	4
želtyj "yellow"	+ 1	− 6	+ 3	+ 8.5	− 9	+ 5	+ 7	− 4	− 3	5	5.2	6
"blue"	+ 2	+ 3	+ 4	+ 5	+ 3	+ 4	+ 5	− 4	− 6	7	4.0	5
koričnevyj "brown"	+ 5	− 7.5	+ 7.5	+ 4	− 9	− 10.5	− 9	− 9.5	− 9.5	3	7.9	9
fioletovyj "purple"	+ 8	+ 2	+ 5.5	+ 8.5	− 9	− 9	− 10	− 9.5	− 11	4	8.1	10
rozovyj "pink"	+ 11	+ 4	+ 7.5	+ 11	+ 5.5	− 8	− 8	− 11	− 7.5	5	8.2	8
oranževyj "orange"	− 10	− 7.5	+ 2	+ 6.5	− 9	− 10.5	− 11	− 7	− 9.5	3	8.1	11
seryj "grey"	+ 3	+ 5	+ 5.5	+ 10	− 9	+ 7	+ 6	− 1.5	− 3	6	5.6	7

Table 9.5 Summary of all tests for Russian terms

(c) the weighted mean – this score is derived from a separate correspondence analysis for each of the three languages; this is described more fully later (see also Davies, MacDermid, Corbett, et al. 1992).

Hurdles model

There is a relatively weak trend for the primary basic terms to "jump" more hurdles than the secondary basic terms, but there are exceptions. In Russian, *seryj* "grey" does better than *černyj* "black," *belyj* "white,"

	RT	Frequency of occurence	Consistency	List frequency	List first places	Frequency in texts	Number of phonemes	Total hurdles	Mean rank	Rank of weighted mean
white	10	10	− 11	+ 1.5	− 6	+ 1	− 2.5	2	6.7	1
black	?	11	+ 8	+ 6.5	− 6	+ 2	− 8	3	6.9	3
red	3	8	+ 9	+ 4.5	+ 1	+ 3	− 2.5	4	4.4	2
green	4	1	+ 1	+ 1.5	+ 3.5	+ 4	− 8	4	3.3	6
yellow	1	6	+ 5	+ 4.5	+ 3.5	+ 8	− 8	4	5.1	8
blue	2	2	+ 2	+ 1.5	+ 2	+ 5	− 2.5	4	2.4	5
brown	5	7	+ 6	+ 10.5	− 9.5	+ 7	− 8	3	7.6	7
purple	7	3	+ 4	+ 8	− 6	− 10	− 8	2	6.6	10
pink	9	4.5	+ 7	+ 10.5	− 9.5	+ 9	− 8	3	8.2	9
orange	8	4.5	+ 3	+ 3	− 9.5	− 11	− 8	2	6.7	11
grey	6	9	− 10	+ 9	− 9.5	+ 6	− 2.5	2	7.4	4

Table 9.6 Summary of all tests for English terms

želtyj "yellow" and *krasnyj* "red", and in English, *pink* and *brown* do better than *white*. However, in French there is a tendency for the primary basic terms to score higher than the secondary basic terms, and this is reflected in a significant correlation with the hierarchy (tau = −.64, p < .009). No other correlation with the hierarchy is significant.

Mean rank

In this case, the separation of primary basics from secondary basics is complete for Russian and French. It is almost complete for English: the

	List frequency	List first places	Derived terms	Frequency in texts	Number of phonemes	Number of syllables	Total hurdles	Mean rank	Rank of weighted mean
blanc "white"	+ 7	+ 3	+ 1.5	+ 2	− 3.5	− 4.5	3	3.4	1.5
noir "black"	+ 1	+ 7	− 6	1	− 9	− 4.5	2	4.8	1.5
rouge "red"	+ 4	+ 2	− 5	3	− 3.5	− 4.5	2	3.5	3
vert "green"	+ 4	+ 6	+ 1.5	6	− 3.5	− 4.5	3	4.3	6
jaune "yellow"	+ 2	+ 4.5	− 3	8	− 3.5	− 4.5	2	4.3	8
bleu "blue"	+ 4	+ 1	− 7	4	− 3.5	− 4.5	2	4.0	4.5
marron "brown"	+ 10	− 10.5	− 11	11	− 9	− 10	1	10.3	11
violet "purple"	+ 9	− 10.5	− 9	10	− 11	− 10	1	9.9	10
rose "pink"	+ 7	+ 4.5	− 8	5	− 3.5	− 4.5	2	5.3	4.5
orange "orange"	+ 7	+ 8	− 10	9	− 9	− 10	2	8.8	9
gris "grey"	+ 11	+ 9	− 4	7	− 3.5	− 4.5	1	6.5	7

Table 9.7 Summary of all tests for French terms

only exceptions are *purple*, which has a marginally higher rank than *black* and *white*; and *orange*, which scores the same as *white* and is marginally higher than *black*. The correlations with the hierarchy are significant for Russian (tau = .52, p < .02) and for French (tau = .54, p < .02), but not for English. However, these correlations are mostly attributable to the difference between primary and secondary basics.

Weighted mean

For each language, the original test data summarized in Tables 9.5–9.7 were subjected to correspondence analyses. In each case, there was one major vector which accounted for a substantial proportion of the inertia. The minimum was 78%. We have used the scores for each color term on this vector as weighted scores in that they reflect the contributions of each measure in accord with how much each measure contributes to that vector score. We have then ranked the vector scores and these are shown in the final columns of the tables.

On this measure, the primary basics are well separated from the secondary basics in Russian and English; the only exception is that *grey* in English does better than several primary basic terms. The separation in French is partial in that *jaune* "yellow" does worse than *rose* "pink" and *gris* "grey"; and *bleu* "blue" is equal to *rose* "pink." The correlations with the hierarchy are significant for all three languages: tau = .81, p < .0009 for Russian; tau = .56, p < .02 for English and French.

In summary, the mean rank and the weighted rank do well at separating the primary basics from the secondary basics; better in general than any measure on its own. However, although the correlations with the hierarchy are generally significant, they are of the same order as for the best single measure; the weighted rank correlates tau = .81 for Russian compared to tau = .77 for frequency in texts, which is the best single measure for Russian; and tau = .57 for French compared to tau = .56 for frequency in texts, the best measure for French.

Discussion

Several clear patterns emerge. First, there is clear consistency over languages. By and large the efficacy and range of a test is independent of the language it is applied to. This contention is supported by the correspondence analysis (Figure 9.1), where the uses of the same measure across languages tend to cluster together.

Second, there are broadly just three superordinate groups of measures with perhaps a fourth less clearcut group. This again is seen most easily in the correspondence analysis (Figure 9.1). The groups are:

(1) frequency in texts and number of derived forms;
(2) word length;
(3) the behavioral measures – RT, frequency of naming, consistency of naming, and frequency in elicited lists (but not the number of first places in elicited lists).

The possible fourth group is the number of first places in elicited lists. This group is rather more diffuse than the others; but it is clear that this measure is very different from frequency in elicited lists and the other behavioral measures.

The three groups fall on both sides of the linguistic–behavioral distinction that we drew in the introduction and the results section. The first two are linguistic, but are also very different from each other in terms of what they appear to be measuring. They are maximally different on vector 1 in the correspondence analysis. The third group consists of all the behavioral measures, except the number of first places on elicited lists, and is closer to word length than to frequency in texts.

This superordinate structure can also be seen when we consider what each measure achieves. We have summarized the main patterns in the results in Table 9.8. There, for each measure and language, we have considered whether a measure achieves each of our three measurement criteria. That is, if a measure helps distinguish basic from non-basic terms, this is indicated by a plus in column 1; if it fails the level one criterion it receives a minus. If no data are available, then we indicate this with a question mark. Similarly, if a measure helps distinguish primary from secondary basic terms it receives a plus in column 2, otherwise a minus. Finally, if it helps discriminate the ranking within the basic terms over and above the level two criterion, it receives a plus, otherwise a minus. We have adopted this relatively coarse pass-or-fail procedure in order to summarize a large set of results succinctly, and to help reveal general patterns.

The rules we have adopted for passing and failing the three criteria are as follows:

(a) level one: if no more than one non-basic term ranks higher than some basic terms or no more than two non-basic terms rank higher than just one basic term, then that measure passes the level one criterion;

(b) level two: if either no more than one secondary basic term is higher than some primary basic terms, or the difference between the mean scores is significant at more than the .025 level (that is, $p < .025$), then it passes the level two criterion;

(c) level three: if the correlation is (i) statistically significant at < .025, and (ii) this is not just due to the level two criterion, then it passes the level three criterion.

Table 9.8 Assessment of each test according to the three criteria

Measure	Language	Criterion Level 1 Basic/ non-basic	Level 2 Primary/ secondary	Level 3 Correlation with hierarchy
Behavioral				
RT	Russian	+	–	–
	Japanese	+	–	–
Frequency of	Russian	–	–	–
occurrence	Am. Eng.	?	–	–
Consistency of	Russian	–	–	–
naming	Japanese	–	–	–
	Am. Eng. 1	?	–	–
	Am. Eng. 2	–	–	–
Elicited lists				
(a) Frequency	Russian (5 mins)	+	–	–
	Am. Eng.	+	+	–
	Brit. Eng.	+	+	–
	French (5 min)	+	+	–
b) First places	Russian	+	+	–
	Am. Eng.	+	+	–
	Brit. Eng.	–	+	–
	French (5 min)	+	–	–
Linguistic				
Number of	Russian	–	+	+
derived forms	French	–	+	–
Frequency in	Russian	–	+	+
texts	English	?	+	+
	French	?	+	+
	Hebrew	?	+	+
	Spanish	?	+	+
Word length				
(a) Phonemes	Russian	?	+	–
	English	?	–	–
	French	?	–	–
	Spanish	?	–	–
(b) Syllables	Russian	?	+	–
	English	?	–	–
	French	?	+	–
	Spanish	?	–	–

Table 9.8 shows that only measures from groups (1) and (3) identified by the correspondence analysis are useful for establishing basicness or making discriminations within basic terms. Group (1) measures (that is, frequency in texts and numbers of derived forms) generally pass the level two and three criteria. This means that they are useful for discriminating within the basic terms; but their level one status is less clear. There are three cases for which we have data (for non-basic as well as basic terms). These are the number of derived forms for Russian and French, and frequency in texts for Russian. All three instances fail the level one criterion; that is, they do not reliably separate the basic and non-basic terms. It would be interesting to learn whether frequency in texts did serve this function in other languages.

By and large, the elicited list procedure succeeds at both levels one and two but fails level three. It is effective in establishing the basic terms, and it can differentiate between the primary and secondary terms, but it does not correlate with the Berlin and Kay hierarchy. Of the rest of the behavioral measures, only RT appears at all useful, and then only for distinguishing basic and non-basic terms. Finally, word length in general appears to have only limited use. In Russian and French, the primary and secondary terms do differ on one or both measures of word length, but neither of these measures meets the level three criterion.

The implication of Table 9.8 for future work is that the elicited list procedure and frequency in texts are the two most useful measures. Further, there is some suggestion that they complement each other. Only the elicited list measure reliably distinguishes basic from non-basic terms; and only frequency in texts discriminates within the basic term inventory and correlates with the hierarchy. The list procedure has the further advantage that it is quick to perform, whether respondents write down the forms themselves or give oral responses.[16] The text-frequency measure is more laborious, but, given a corpus of texts, spoken or written, there are various software packages which will produce the required concordance information.

Appendix 1

The basic color terms of Russian

We consider here the basic color terms of Russian, since Russian seems to be an exception to the Berlin and Kay hierarchy. It has two basic terms for blue (a possibility noted by Berlin and Kay 1969: 99) which gives an inventory of twelve basic terms:

> *belyj* "white," *černyj* "black," *krasnyj* "red," *zelenyj* "green," *želtyj* "yellow," *sinij* "dark blue," *goluboj* "light blue," *koričnevyj* "brown," *fioletovyj* "purple," *rozovyj* "pink," *oranževyj* "orange," *seryj* "grey".

While several of these are straightforward, others require comment. Our research suggests very strongly that both terms for blue are indeed basic (see, for example, Corbett and Morgan 1988;[17] Davies and Corbett 1994a; for instrumental data on referents of the two terms see Morgan and Moss 1988/89).[18] Our list varies in two respects from that provided by Slobin for Berlin and Kay (1969: 98–99): first the basic term for orange is certainly *oranževyj*, and not that given by Slobin. The second difference is more contentious: Slobin gives *purpurnyj* for purple. Corbett and Morgan (1988) showed that there are considerable problems with *purpurnyj* and that *fioletovyj* has a better claim to be considered a basic term. At that stage we were unsure whether to claim it was basic; the list experiment reported in Morgan and Corbett (1989), discussed on pp. 203–208, suggests very strongly that *fioletovyj* is indeed basic. For confirmation see Davies and Corbett (1994a), and for instrumental data on the referent of *fioletovyj* see Moss (1989).

Appendix 2   Correspondence analysis: coordinates for each measure

Source	Measure	Vector 1	Vector 2
Russian	RT	46.17	3.25
Japanese	RT	47.16	3.32
Russian	Frequency of naming	67.12	0.88
American 1	Frequency of naming	65.33	−9.55
Russian	Consistency	59.53	−1.39
Japanese	Consistency	51.40	4.50
American 1	Consistency	50.00	−1.24
American 2	Consistency	52.91	0.40
Russian	Frequency in lists (1 min)	41.69	−12.90
Russian	No. first places in lists	−51.22	−78.13
Russian	Frequency in lists (5 min)	44.58	−1.01
Illinois	Frequency in lists	42.17	−22.46
Maryland	Frequency in lists	39.23	−18.89
Ill. + Maryland	Frequency in lists	40.34	−20.23
Ill. + Maryland	No. first places in lists	−30.97	−184.07
Brit. English	Frequency in lists	43.43	−2.04
Brit. English	No. first places in lists	63.67	31.74
Brit. English	Mean position in lists	−27.56	−151.14
French	Frequency in lists	36.36	−2.71
French	No. first places in lists	−13.49	−45.55
French	Frequency in lists (5 min)	44.77	0.91
Russian	No. of derived forms	−31.26	4.27
French	No. of derived forms	−3.55	−2.52
Russian	Frequency in texts	−40.87	−13.14
English	Frequency in texts	−22.16	−2.93
French	Frequency in texts	−40.90	1.89
Hebrew	Frequency in texts	−35.19	−11.28
Spanish	Frequency in texts	−45.12	11.30
English	No. of phonemes	54.09	5.37
English	No. of syllables	59.80	−0.63
French	No. of phonemes	60.08	4.92
French	No. of syllables	82.35	4.61
Russian	No. of phonemes	79.50	−1.33
Russian	No. of syllables	98.67	7.74
Spanish	No. of phonemes	60.13	7.64
Spanish	No. of syllables	65.15	1.27

Notes

1 The support of the Economic and Social Research Council (ESRC) is gratefully acknowledged (grant numbers R000 23 1958 and R000 23 3978). We are also very grateful to Sean Hammond for useful discussions on statistical matters. This chapter was presented as a paper at the Conference on Color Categorization held at Asilomar, October 1992 – we wish to thank the National Science Foundation for funds enabling us to attend; the convenor, Professor C. L. Hardin, and our fellow participants for interested and illuminating discussion. A more extended account of this research is given in Corbett and Davies (1995).

2 An interesting investigation of the interrelation between measures, particularly those relevant to salience, can be found in Bolton (1978). He, however, restricted himself to a single language.

3 Bolton (1978: 310) also retained the earlier formulation because of the increased indeterminacy of the revision, which makes it "difficult to find an appropriate statistical technique for correlating the sequence with other variables." See Kay, Berlin, and Merrifield (1991) and Kay, Berlin, Maffi, and Merrifield (this volume) for recent reformulations of the hierarchy.

4 These are the standard statistical tests for the situation we are investigating. For assessing the strength of association between two variables, tau and r are appropriate, as discussed shortly. A full account of the statistical procedures is given in Corbett and Davies (1995).

5 Note the recent discussion by MacLaury (1991: 56).

6 The OSA (Optical Society of America) sample attempts to sample color space in equal perceptual steps.

7 Based on the Ostwald color solid; for a technical description see Foss, Nickerson and Granville (1944), and for a more accessible account see Smith (1965).

8 The sources for our data are as follows. For the individual terms, the Russian data are taken from Moss et al. (1990: 319, Table 2); the score for "blue" is the mean of *sinij* "dark blue," and *goluboj* "light blue." The Japanese data are from Uchikawa and Boynton (1987: 1828, Table 4). The first American English sample is based on Boynton and Olson (1987: 96–7, Figure 1) which gives the RTs to individual color samples which were given the same name unanimously (consensus scores). This was because Boynton and Olson (1987) do not report the overall RTs for each term. Our scores based on the consensus items therefore almost certainly underestimate

what the overall means would have been, but probably reflect their relative speeds reasonably well. The second American English sample scores are derived from the graph in Boynton and Olson (1990: 1315, Figure 3). The Russian means are based on Moss et al. (1990: 322, Table 4) for basic and non-basic terms, and on Moss et al. (1990: 319, Table 2) for primary and secondary terms, using unweighted means. The Japanese mean scores are based on Uchikawa and Boynton (1987: 1829, Table 5), using weighted means for basic and non-basic, and on Uchikawa and Boynton (1987: 1828, Table 4) for primary and secondary, using unweighted means. The first American English Figures are taken from Boynton and Olson (1987: 95, Table 1) using weighted means for basic and non-basic terms, and are derived from Boynton and Olson (1987: 96–7, Figure 1) just using consensus terms for primary and secondary terms. The second set of American English scores is derived from the graph in Boynton and Olson (1990: 1315, Figure 3) for both sets of means.

9 The highest non-basics are given after 1 minute (for better comparison with studies for which only data from shorter time limits are available). If taken after 5 minutes they would be:

	occurrences after 1 minute	occurrences after 5 minutes
beževyj "beige"	13	22
malinovyj "raspberry"	11	22
salatovyj "light green"	10	22

10 The other first choices on the list were *beževyj* "beige" and *kremovyj* "cream," each put first by a single subject.

11 Moskovič (1969: 18) analyzed a somewhat larger corpus (1,452,000 words) of English prose, mainly recent; he does not give the actual number of occurrences, but does give the rank order, which shows a remarkable fit with Berlin and Kay, the more impressive since he was unaware of their work. It is: 1 *white*, 2 *black*, 3 *red*, 4 *green*, 5 *yellow*, 6 *blue*, 7 *grey*, 8 *brown*, 9 *purple*, 10 *pink* (11 *scarlet*), 12 *orange*. This also illustrates that the frequency test performs well in separating basics from non-basics (in the LOB corpus too, *scarlet* occurs more frequently than *orange*, being found 14 times as compared to 7 for *orange*). If we again consider just the basic terms, the degree of correlation of the rank order found by Moskovič with Berlin and Kay is tau = .89, p < .0009.

12 Though the information on tagging enables us to select only adjectival usage, we do not know how many examples of *silver* and *bronze* relate strictly to color.

13 This is particularly interesting since in early Russian writing, of the eleventh–twelfth centuries, but even as late as the seventeenth century, the use of color terms seems largely to be avoided (Baxilina 1975: 14, 56).

14 This is analogous to the percentage of variance accounted for in regression or factor analysis.

15 Appendix 2 gives the values of the two vectors for each measure.

16 We have taken the message to heart: in the work we have done on languages of Africa we use the list procedure as the warm-up, in order to get a handle on the possible basic terms of a language (see Davies et al. 1992; Davies and Corbett 1994b; Davies, Corbett, Mtenje, and Sowden 1995).

17 Unknown to Corbett and Morgan (1988), Vamling (1986) claimed that Russian has two basic terms for blue, on the basis of frequency in texts. She quoted the list of basic color terms proposed by Kulick and Vamling (1984) which corresponds exactly to the twelve given above, having been established independently. She noted, however, (Vamling 1986: 226) that *fioletovyj* "purple" and *oranževyj* "orange" seem to have a less certain status as basic color terms.

18 Whenever we correlate Russian data with the hierarchy or with other languages we take the mean of the values for the two blue terms. When checking whether a measure distinguishes primary from secondary basics we treat the Russian blues (mean value) as a primary term. For the development of the two blue terms see Baxilina (1975: 174–207) and Alimpieva (1982).

References

Alimpieva, R. V. 1982. Stanovlenie leksiko-semantičeskix grupp cvetovyx prilagatel´nyx v russkom jazyke pervoj poloviny XIX v. *Voprosy semantiki: Issledovanija po istoričeskoj semantike* 49–60. Kaliningrad.

Baxilina, N. B. 1975. *Istorija cvetooboznačenij v russkom jazyke.* Moscow: Nauka.

Berlin, B., and P. Kay 1969. *Basic Color Terms: Their Universality and Evolution.* Berkeley: University of California Press.

Bolton, R. 1978. Black, white, and red all over: the riddle of color term salience. *Ethnology* 17(3): 287–311.

Boynton, R. M., and C. X. Olson 1987. Locating basic colors in the OSA space. *Color Research and Application* 12: 94–105.

1990. Salience of chromatic basic color terms confirmed by three measures. *Vision Research* 30(9): 1311–1317.

Corbett, G. G., and I. Davies 1995. Linguistic and behavioural measures for ranking basic colour terms. *Studies in Language* 19(2): 301–357.

Corbett, G. G., and G. Morgan 1988. Colour terms in Russian: reflections of typological constraints in a single language. *Journal of Linguistics* 24: 31–64.

Davies, I. R. L., and G. G. Corbett 1994a. The basic colour terms of Russian. *Linguistics* 32: 65–89.

1994b. A statistical approach to determining basic color terms: an account of Xhosa. *Journal of Linguistic Anthropology* 4: 175–193.

Davies, I. R. L., G. G. Corbett, A. D. Mtenje, and P. Sowden 1995. The basic colour terms of Chichewa. *Lingua* 95: 259–278.

Davies, I. R. L., C. MacDermid, G. G. Corbett, H. McGurk, H. Jerrett, T. Jerrett, and P. Sowden 1992. Colour terms in Setswana: a linguistic and perceptual approach. *Linguistics* 30: 1065–1103.

Foss, C. E., D. Nickerson, and W. C. Granville 1944. Analysis of the OSTWALD color system. *Journal of the Optical Society of America* 34(7): 361–381.

Greenacre, M. J. 1984. *Theory and Application of Correspondence Analysis.* London: Academic Press.

Hays, D. G., E. Margolis, R. Naroll, and D. R. Perkins 1972. Color term salience. *American Anthropologist* 74: 1107–1121.

Johansson, S., and K. Hofland 1989. *Frequency Analysis of English Vocabulary and Grammar Based on the LOB Corpus.* Vol. I: *Tag Frequencies and Word Frequencies.* Oxford: Clarendon.

Kay, P. 1975. Synchronic variability and diachronic change in basic color terms. *Language in Society* 4: 257–270.

Kay, P., B. Berlin, and W. R. Merrifield 1991. Biocultural implications of systems of color naming. *Journal of Linguistic Anthropology* 1: 12–25.

Kay, P., and C. K. McDaniel 1978. The linguistic significance of the meanings of basic color terms. *Language* 54(3): 610–646.

Kulick, D., and K. Vamling 1984. Ryska. In T. Pettersson (ed.), *Färgterminologi: Seminarieuppsatser i allmän språkvetenskap* (=Praktisk lingvistik 9) (pp. 79–109). Lund. (Quoted from Vamling [1986].)

MacLaury, R. E. 1991. Social and cognitive motivations of change: measuring variability in color semantics. *Language* 67: 34–62.

Miller, G. A., and P. N. Johnson-Laird 1976. *Language and Perception.* Cambridge, MA: Harvard University Press.

Morgan, G., and G. G. Corbett 1989. Russian colour term salience. *Russian Linguistics* 13: 125–141.

Morgan, G., and A. E. Moss 1988/1989. The two blues of Russian: the referents of *sinij* and *goluboj*. *Die Farbe* 35/36: 353–357.

Moskovič, V. A. 1969. *Statistika i semantika: opyt statističeskogo analiza semantičeskogo polja*. Moscow: Nauka.

Moss, A. E. 1989. Basic colour terms: problems and hypotheses. *Lingua* 78: 313–320.

Moss, A. E., I. R. L. Davies, G. G. Corbett, and G. Laws 1990. Mapping Russian basic colour terms using behavioural measures. *Lingua* 82: 313–332.

Smith, C. N. 1965. *Student Handbook of Color*. New York: Reinhold.

Uchikawa, K., and R. M. Boynton 1987. Categorical color perception of Japanese observers: comparison with that of Americans. *Vision Research* 27(10): 1825–1833.

Vamling, K. 1986. A note on Russian blues. *Slavica Lundensia* 10: 225–233.

Weller, S. C., and A. K. Romney 1990. *Metric Scaling: Correspondence Analysis*. Newbury Park, CA: Sage. (Sage University Paper Series on Quantitative Applications in the Social Sciences, 07–075.)

Zasorina, L. N. (ed.) 1977. *Častotnyj slovar´ russkogo jazyka: okolo 40 000 slov*. Moscow: Russkij jazyk.

10 Color shift: evolution of English color terms from brightness to hue

Ronald W. Casson

In the evolution of English color terms, a gradual semantic shift occurred from largely brightness color concepts to almost exclusively hue concepts.[1] Brightness was the predominant sense of color words in the Anglo-Saxon, or Old English, period (c. 600–1150). Hue was only minimally conceptualized in Old English, and did not become salient in conceptualizations of color until the Middle English period (c. 1150–1500). The set of Old English terms that evolved into English basic color terms followed the same pattern: they were predominantly brightness terms in the Old English period and almost entirely hue terms in the Middle English period. In keeping with the basic color categories theme of this volume, the evolution of English basic terms will be highlighted in this chapter.

Secondary or non-basic terms, which were uniformly hue terms, did not occur in the Anglo-Saxon period, but entered the English color vocabulary for the first time late in the Middle English period (1350–1500). This was the turning point in the English color shift. Secondary color terms increased gradually during the Early Modern English period (1500–1700) and the Modern English period (1700–present) until the second half of the nineteenth century, after which they increased rapidly.

Brightness to hue

The color shift is evident in two sets of coordinated lexical innovations. The first concerns the evolution of Old English brightness terms to Middle English hue terms, and the second deals with the advent and development of secondary color terms. The former is discussed in this section of the chapter, and the latter is considered in the following section. With few exceptions, Old English color terms that had pure brightness senses became obsolete or lost their brightness senses in the Middle English period.[2] This trend is illustrated in the following terms.

Torht, for example, was an Old English pure brightness term that had the sense "light" and probably the sense "luminous" before 1000 (*OED*; Hall 1960: 346; Sweet 1981: 175). It occurred in compounds such as *rodortorht* "heavenly bright" (Hall 1960: 284; Sweet 1981: 142) and *heofontorht* "very bright, glorious" (Hall 1960: 178; Sweet 1981: 87), and in expressions such as *leoht torht ontyned* "light, bright fire" (*MCOE*). *Torht* survived with its brightness senses into the early medieval period, but became obsolete in the course of the thirteenth century (*OED*).

Scir was a pure brightness term that meant "bright, clear, gleaming" in Old English by about 750 (Bosworth and Toller 1882: 836; Hall 1960: 296; Sweet 1981: 148), derived from Indo-European root *ski-* "to shine, glimmer low," and from Germanic *skiraz* "glimmer low" (*OED*; Barnhart 1988: 995). Middle English *schir* had the sense "clear, pure, thin" (Barnhart 1988: 995), but lost its "bright, shining" sense in the medieval period (*OED*, cf. *shire*). Only the "thin, transparent" sense of *scir/schir* survives in Modern English *sheer*, which has the senses "thin, diaphanous (of fabrics), pure (of liquids), and steep (of inclines)" (*OED*, *shire*).

Hador, another Old English pure brightness term, had the senses "bright, clear, and luminous" in the Anglo-Saxon period (Hall 1960: 164; Sweet 1981: 80). It was used in such collocations as *hador segl* "bright sail," *hador swegl* "bright sky," *hador heofonleoma* "bright heavenly light," and *hador heofontungol* "bright heavenly star" (*MCOE*). *Hador* is not cited in *OED* or *MED*, and apparently did not survive into the medieval period.

Old English terms that had hue senses, even those whose hue senses were very minor, survived into the Modern English period and in the process experienced a shift in color emphasis from brightness to hue. Three terms can illustrate this color shift: *dunn*, which had a strong brightness sense and a moderately strong hue sense in Old English, maintained a strong hue sense into the modern period; *salu*, which had a prominent brightness sense and a minor hue sense in the Old English period, survived as a hue term into the modern period; and *fealu*, which had a major brightness sense and a strong hue sense in the Old English period, survived only marginally into the modern period.

Dunn derived from the Indo-European root *dheu-1*, meaning "to rise in a cloud, as dust, vapor, or smoke" (Watkins 1985: 14). Its path of descent was from suffixed extended zero-grade *dhus-no- to Welsh *dwn* "dull brown" and then to Old English *dunn* (*ODEE*; Watkins 1985: 14), which had the dominant brightness sense "dark, dull, dim" and the well-established hue sense "brown" (*OED*; Hall 1960: 90; Sweet 1981: 44; Wheelwright n.d.: 10). By about 1300, Middle English *don(n)e* had the dominant hue sense "brown or grayish brown" and the minor brightness sense "dim, murky" (*OED*; *MED*).

Salu derived from the suffixed form *sal-wo- of the Indo-European root *sal-2 and from Germanic *salwaz "dirty grey" (Watkins 1985: 56). Old English *salu* had the sense "dark, dark-coloured, dusky, sallow" (Hall 1960: 288; Sweet 1981: 144; Barnhart 1988: 952), combining strong dark and luminous brightness senses with a weak (probably yellowish) brown hue sense. Middle English *salowe* developed its modern hue sense "sickly yellow or brownish-yellow, discoloured, pallid (skin or complexion)" before 1400 (*OED*; *MED*; Barnhart 1988: 952).

Fealu descended from the Indo-European root *pel-2 "pale," by way of Germanic *falwaz (Watkins 1985: 48). In Old English, it denoted hues ranging from pale yellow to yellowish red and reddish brown, but was primarily a brightness term with the senses "pale, grey, dull, dusky, shining" (*OED*; Bosworth and Toller 1882: 271; Lerner 1951: 247; Hall 1960: 112; Sweet 1981: 55; Wheelwright n.d.) that was used predominantly in reference to the brightness of such differently hued entities as a well-groomed horse, a polished shield, a flame, and waves in the sunlight (Lerner 1951: 247). Middle English *falewe* or *falowe* had the somewhat narrower sense "sallow, faded, yellowish brown" and few if any remnants of luminosity or reflectivity. After about 1410, *falewe* and then *fallow* had the sense "pale, yellowish brown," and were used in reference only to animal coats, as in Modern English *fallow deer* (*OED*; Barnhart 1988: 367).

The color shift is also evident in the development of English basic color terms. Like *dunn*, *salu*, and *fealu*, the eight Old English terms that evolved into basic color terms were predominantly brightness terms that had minor hue senses (except *red*, which had a dominant hue sense). All eight terms – *black*, *white*, *grey*, *red*, *green*, *blue*, *yellow*, and *brown* – survived and became strictly or primarily hue terms by the late Middle English period. *Red*, *green*, *yellow*, *blue*, and *brown* retained only minor brightness senses or none at all, while *black*, *white*, and *grey* were largely hue terms but continued to have brightness senses in the Middle English period and after.

Basic color terms have been part of the vocabulary of English from its inception in the fifth century. Color terms were absent in Nostratic, the ancestral language recently reconstructed from Indo-European, Afro-Asiatic, Kartvelian, Uralic, Altaic, and Dravidian (Kaiser and Shevoroshkin 1988). Four basic color terms have recently been reconstructed for Indo-European: *white, black, red,* and *yellow* (Shields 1979). The first terms in the prehistory of the English color lexicon must, therefore, have emerged after Nostratic and before or during the Indo-European period. Seven basic color terms, all derived from Indo-European ancestral sources, were encoded in Old English: *white, black, grey, red, yellow, green,* and *blue.*

White derived from the Indo-European root *kweit-*, which meant "white, to shine" (Watkins 1985: 33). *Hwit,* the Old English reflex of *kweit-*, was primarily, but not exclusively, a brightness term. The *OED* provides both brightness and hue senses for *hwit* in the Old English period: the sense "colourless, uncoloured" is attested in 888, the hair and complexion sense in 900, and "the colour of snow or milk" in about 950 (*OED*). The majority of occurrences of *hwit* in Old English suggest luminosity or reflectivity – the shining of light, of a roof, a helmet, a gem, or silver – but the term also had a white-hue sense, e.g. in reference to wheat, a stone, and a lock of hair (Bosworth and Toller 1882: 577; Mead 1899: 178–179). Middle English *whit* still had a brightness sense, but it was used primarily in hue reference. It was used for the brightness of snow and foam but, more importantly, for the hue of milk, flour, salt; alabaster, marble and pearl; ivory, (whale) bone; chalk; paper; clothing; swan, horse and mule; sheep's fleece and boar's tusk; hair and beards in old age; skin and complexion; and pallor resulting from illness or fear (*OED*; Burnley 1976: 41).

Black descended from *bhleg-* "to shine, flash, burn," a variant form of the Indo-European root *bhel-1*, and from Germanic *blakaz* "burned" (Watkins 1985: 6). *Blaec,* the Old English basic black term, was predominantly a brightness term, but it also had the conventional hue sense "burnt, scorched," carried over from Germanic (*OED*). Old English *blaec* was used in this sense in describing sea roads, ravens, and adders (Mead 1899: 181–182). Middle English *blak* continued to have a significant luminous sense, as *black* still does, but its hue sense was primary during the period. *Blak* was applied to the darkness of night and clouds, but more extensively to the hue of soot, coal, and pitch; pigment and ink; hair, beard, and complexion; the pupil of the eye; the devil crow; raven's feather; sloe-berry; fur; cloth, clothing and mourning garb; and species of animals and plants (*OED; MED*; Burnley 1976: 40).

Grey derived from the Indo-European root *gher*-3 "to shine, glow; grey." *Gher*-3 was the source of Germanic *grewas*, which in turn was the source of Old English *graeg* "grey" (Watkins 1985: 22). *Graeg*, the basic grey term in Old English, had both hue and brightness senses. References to grey animals, animal fur and human hair, ash bark, wheat, stone and rock, and hill and valley indicate an established hue sense, while references to water, wave, iron, sword, spearhead, mail-coat, smoke, and hoar-frost point to reflective and luminous senses (Mead 1899: 189–199; Barley 1974; Biggam 1993). The brightness sense of Old English *graeg* was predominant. As Barley (1974: 24) states, *graeg* was "generally applicable to glossy things." Middle English *grei* continued brightness senses from Old English *graeg* and developed a general hue sense during the Middle English period. *Grei* maintained both the luminosity sense "dim, dull" (morning, twilight) and the reflective sense "bright, gleaming" (sea, stars, and eyes) throughout the Middle English period, and retained the luminosity sense, but probably not the reflectivity sense, into the Modern English period (*OED; MED*). Hue referents of *grei* include bread and porridge; horse, hound, and badger; hen, goose, and falcon; marble and ash; cloth and garments; monks, friars, and sisters (their habits and persons); hair and beards; and old persons (*OED; MED*; Burnley 1976: 42). (For extensive analysis of Old English and Middle English *grey*, see Biggam 1993.)[3]

Red derived from Germanic *raudaz*, which derived from Indo-European *roudh*, zero-grade form of the root *reudh*-1: "red, ruddy" (Watkins 1985: 55). This root is ancestral not only to Modern English *red* and *ruddy*, but also to *ruby, rust, russett, rouge*, and numerous other reflexes (Watkins 1985: 55). *Read*, the Old English red term, was a hue-dominated term referring, for example, to roses and the blood-reddened cross, but it also denoted reflectivity and luminosity in reference to flames, fire and lightning, dawn and sunset, gold, sword edges, and the waters of the Red Sea (Mead 1899: 195; Lerner 1951:

248–249). Middle English *reed* was also used for the brightness of fire, flames, dawn and sunset (as red still is), and lightning, gold, and armor (which red no longer is), but its red-hue sense was much more widely used in reference to pigments and dyes, complexion, skin and lips, hair and beards, the eye or iris, cloth and garments, blood, coral, rose, ruby, grapes, wine, ripe wheat, soil, and earth (*OED*; *MED*; Burnley 1976: 41).

Yellow derived from the Indo-European root *ghel*-2 "to shine" – with derivatives referring to colors, to brightness (probably "yellow metals"), and to bile or gall (Watkins 1985: 21). *Ghel-wo*-, the suffixed form of this root, became Germanic *gelwaz, which then became Old English *geolo* (Watkins 1985: 21). Whereas Indo-European *ghel-wo*- was a strictly brightness term, Old English *geolo*, although primarily a brightness term, also had an established hue sense, e.g. in reference to fine yellow silk cloth and linden wood shields (Mead 1899: 198; cf. also Bosworth and Toller 1882: 424; Hall 1960: 151; Sweet 1981: 73). Middle English *yelou* had minor reflectivity and luminosity senses in reference to the sun, gold, crystal, and, possibly, a newly scoured basin (Burnley 1976: 42–44), but was primarily a hue term referring to pigments, fabrics, the yolk of an egg, discolored paper, ripe corn, faded leaves, sulfur, wax, hair, the complexion in age or disease, and various flowers, fruits, and roots (*OED*; *MED*).

Green, together with *grow* and *grass*, descended from the Indo-European root *ghre*- "to grow, become green" (Watkins 1985: 23). All three came into English from Germanic: *gro(w)an "to grow" became Old English *growan*; *grasam "grass" became Old English *graes*; and *gronjaz "green" became Old English *grene* (Watkins 1985: 23). Old English *grene* was basically a hue term, but it also had significant brightness senses. *Grene* was used in reference to water, the shining head of the phoenix, Mass vestments of rich textiles, the jasper, the emerald, and a flash from another gemstone (C. P. Biggam, personal communication 1994). Among the hue referents of Old English *grene* are the earth, fields, grass, trees, and hills (Mead 1899: 200). In the Middle English period, *grene* became a predominantly hue term, referring to grass and foliage, grassy places, herbs, plants and vegetables; the earth; cloth and clothing; emerald, jasper; unripe corn and unripe pears; and skin and complexion of a "pale, sickly or bilious hue" (*OED*; *MED*; Burnley 1976: 41).

Blue, according to its earliest *OED* citation, first occurred as a basic term – Middle English *blew(e)* (or *bleu*) – a little before 1300. Old French *blau* (or *blo*), the source of Middle English *blew(e)*, descended from Common Romance **blavus*, which in turn derived from Germanic **blewaz* "blue", and earlier still, from Indo-European **bhle-wo-*, a suffixed variant form of the root **bhel*-1 (which is also ancestral to *black*, see above). If *blew(e)*, however, were the first basic blue term to enter the language, it would have been a surprisingly late addition to the basic color lexicon. In fact, it was not the first English blue term, but rather a replacement for an earlier Old English term. Most probably, this earlier term was *haewen*, which descended from Indo-European root **kei*, "referring to various adjectives of color," and probably from Germanic **hiwam* (Watkins 1985: 28). Although it initially had both luminous and hue senses, denoting "pale grey, pale blue, pale green," *haewen* was "increasingly used to denote blue specifically, and, furthermore, all types of blue, including vivid blue and dark blue, as well as pale blue" (Biggam in press). *Haewen* was used in reference to woad dye, sapphire, indigo, and blue-black cinders (Biggam in press; cf. also Biggam 1993). *Haewen* did not survive into Middle English, but was replaced by *blew(e)*. Apart from such brightness referents as the sky and the deep sea, Middle English *blew(e)* was predominantly a hue term. Its hue referents included flowers, pigment, dye and enamel, cloth and clothing, and skin or complexion affected by a blow or severe cold (*OED*; *MED*; Burnley 1976: 42).

Brown probably was not a basic color term in Old English, but was added to the basic color lexicon in the Middle English period. It was not a general color term, but rather a restricted term limited to specific sets of objects. *Brown* derived ultimately from the Indo-European root **bher*-3 "bright, brown" (Watkins 1985: 7). Its line of descent was from the suffixed variant form **bhru-no-*, to Germanic **brunaz*, to Old English *brun*. *Brun* was not a basic color term but a restricted term limited to horses, other animals, birds, metals, human skin, and water (Barley 1974: 23). Clearly, the meaning of Old English *brun* (and earlier brown forms) had two components, hue and surface reflectivity (Barley 1974: 24). The use of *brun* for numerous brown animals and birds suggests that the term had an established hue sense, but its brightness sense in reference to "things that flash in the sunlight," e.g. helmets, sword-edges and the waves of the sea, was primary

(Lerner 1951: 247; cf. Mead 1899: 193–195). Old English *brun*, according to Lerner (1951: 247), had not lost its primary reflectivity signification nor moved very far towards its modern hue meaning. Middle English *broun* developed its general hue sense (the earliest *OED* citation for hue is 1300), and became a basic color term referring almost exclusively to hue by the end of the Middle English period. Two *broun* brightness senses continued in the Middle English period: the luminous sense "dark, dusky" (sky, weather) was a secondary sense during the period and became archaic afterward, and the reflective sense "glistening, burnished" (steel, armor, glass) was a minor sense during the period and obsolete afterward (*OED*; *MED*). Among the many hue referents listed for *broun* are pigments; cloth and yarn; bread and jugs; grain and bran; hair, eyebrows, and beards; faces, complexions, and persons; and varieties of plants, animals, and minerals (*OED*; *MED*; Burnley 1976: 42).

The three remaining Modern English basic terms – *purple*, *orange*, and *pink* – were added later in the evolution of the basic color lexicon, and were always strictly hue terms.

Purple, unlike the basic color terms thus far discussed, did not descend from Indo-European or Germanic sources. It came into English as a loanword from Church Latin late in the Old English period. Latin *purpura* (from Greek *porphura*), which was the name of a shellfish, a dye obtained from the shellfish, and cloth colored by the dye, became Old English *purpure*, purple cloth, in about 893, and then *purple*, the color, in about 975 (*OED*). When it was borrowed into Old English, *purple* was a restricted hue term used for the purple clothing of royalty and, by extension, for royal personages "born to the purple." *Purple* was a restricted term from its initial appearance in Old English until the late Middle English period (*MED*). It did not become a basic color term with a general range of reference until about 1398 (*OED*; *MED*). In both the Old English and Middle English periods, *purple* was exclusively a hue term. There is no evidence it had a brightness sense at any time in its developmental history.

Orange was borrowed into Middle English in the fourteenth century (*OED* 13 – ; *RHD* 1300–1350) from Old French (from Arabic, Persian, and Sanskrit) (*OED*; Norris 1969; *RHD*). It was a fruit name in English for almost 300 years before it became a color term in the Early Modern English period before 1600 (*OED*; cf. Conklin 1973). *Orange* is the only basic color term that has a transparent entity sense. It never had a brightness sense.

Pink, the last basic color term to enter English, came into the language "of obscure origins" by 1573, as the name for a species of flower (*OED*). *Pink* did not become a basic color term until the Modern English period, by about 1720 (*OED*). It was never a brightness term.

Secondary color terms

Secondary color terms compose the second set of lexical innovations that define the English color shift. While the shift from Old English brightness terms to Middle English hue terms was culminating in the late Middle English period (1350–1500), the first simplex secondary color terms entered the language.

Basic color terms – for example *black*, *green*, *orange*, and *purple* – are "simplex" lexemes. That is, they are lexemes whose meanings are not determinable from the meanings of internal components. "Complex" lexemes are derived through word-formation processes of modification and compounding and do have paraphrastic meanings. Secondary color terms, or non-basic color terms, are simplex and complex lexemes. *Scarlet*, *blond*, *indigo*, *puce*, and *eggshell* are simplex lexemes, and *yellowish*, *light green*, *orange-red*, *wine red*, and *tea rose* are complex lexemes (cf. Bauer 1983: 29–30).

In a study of English secondary color terms, a sample of terms was collected using open-ended elicitation along with a backtest procedure to ensure that elicited terms were legitimate English color words. From a total sample of 514 color terms, 92 conventional (as opposed to novel) simplex secondary color terms were obtained. Of these conventional terms, 56 are semantically transparent, or synchronically analyzable, and 36 are semantically opaque, or synchronically unanalyzable (for details, see Casson 1994: 7–14).[4]

A clear pattern is apparent in these conventional simplex secondary color term data. Simplex secondary terms all have hue senses. There are no brightness terms such as *light* and *dark* in the sample. They all have (or had) noncolor physical-object senses in addition to color senses, and these entity senses all derived from five object domains: plants, animals, minerals, foods, and artifacts. The entity senses of transparent terms such as *fawn*, *salmon*, *ivory*, *pearl*, *coral*, are generally obvious to English speakers. Although the entity senses of opaque terms such as *buff*, *puce*, *teal*, *crimson*, and *vermilion* are not generally known to English speakers, they were once the names of animals or of animal parts or products.

These secondary terms also all have (or had) polysemous entity–color relationships. Transparent terms are synchronically polysemous, having both entity senses and color senses, whereas opaque terms are currently monosemous, their earlier entity senses now being obsolete. In all cases, entity and color senses are (or were) related metonymically. Metonymy is a figurative semantic relationship based on perceived contiguities (i.e., natural or contextual associations) between literal primary referents and figurative secondary referents. For example, *lemon*, which literally refers to a yellowish acid fruit, is extended metonymically to the yellow color that is characteristic of and associated with lemons.

The color senses of transparent and opaque terms all resulted from metonymic extensions of earlier entity senses to later hue senses. Dates of first citations in *OED* reveal that entity senses predate hue senses in the development of all transparent terms. For opaque terms that initially appeared in English with now-obsolete entity senses, *OED* evidence shows that entity senses always predated hue senses. No *OED* dates are available for entity senses of opaque terms borrowed into English with only hue senses, but pre-English etymological evidence shows that these terms also had earlier entity senses, prior to entering English. These data strongly support the priority of entity senses and the unidirectionality of metonymic development from entity sense to color sense (cf. Casson 1994: 9–14).

This unidirectional metonymic process operated in the semantic development of all secondary terms, but not at a single point in time. None of the ninety-two secondary terms in the Casson (1994) sample were color terms in the Old English period (*c.* 600–1150). The first secondary terms were incorporated into the language in the late Middle English period (between 1350 and 1500). Twelve terms developed hue senses at this time, of which nine were names for dyestuffs, pigments, and textiles (and earlier entities from which they derived): *gold*, *silver*, *violet*, *azure*, *crimson*, *russett*, *ocher*, *scarlet*, and *vermilion*. The three terms with non-colorant entity senses – *auburn*, *blond*, and *ash* – were specialized terms restricted to hair and facial coloring.

Gold and silver are examples of early transparent terms. Gold was an Old English word (from Germanic, from Indo-European) used for metal by about 725, for money by 870, for embroidered and woven textile fabrics by 1340, and for its color by about 1400. Silver was also an Old English word (from Germanic) used for metal by about 825, for money by about the same time, for embroidered and woven textile fabrics by 1423, and for its color by about 1481.

Violet, which is also a transparent term, entered Middle English (from Old French, from Latin) with both its plant sense and its flower sense in about 1330, and added its secondary hue sense ("in early use only of woven fabrics") by 1370 (OED).

Crimson, scarlet, and vermilion are examples of early opaque terms. Crimson, which is an opaque term with pre-English entity senses, came into Middle English from Medieval Latin and derived ultimately from Arabic girmiz "kermes," an insect or worm producing a red dye. The term was borrowed in connection with textile dyeing: it was "at first chiefly used in dyeing fine cloth and velvet . . . in connexion with which this shade of red was first distinguished in English" (OED). Crimson had its pigment and color senses shortly before 1400.

Vermilion, which also derived from the kermes insect but from Old French by way of Late Latin vermiculus (literally "little worm"), was a pigment name by 1296 and developed its now monosemic hue sense before 1400–1450.

Scarlet, which is also opaque and had obsolete English entity senses, referred to bright red cloth imbued with dye from kermes insects when it entered Middle English from Old French (from Medieval Latin, from Arabic) by 1250. It was the first term (in the sample) to become a secondary color term when it acquired its color sense by about 1386.

Only fifteen additional terms acquired hue senses during the Early Modern period (1500–1700). Colorants and textiles continued to be sources of secondary terms, but plants, animals, and minerals were more frequent sources. Rose, pearl, indigo, and amber are examples of Early Modern secondary terms.

Rose, which is a transparent term, came into Old English from Latin with its flower sense no later than 888. It added its bush sense by 1390 and its color sense by 1530. Pearl, which is also a transparent term, entered Middle English from Old French (from Vulgar Latin) with its animal product and gem senses sometime between 1300 and 1350. It did not achieve secondary color term status until 1688, though it was used paraphrastically in *pearl-colour* by 1611.

Indigo, which is an opaque term, came into Early Modern English from Spanish (from Latin, from Greek) as the name for an Indian plant and the blue-powder product of the plant that was used as a dyestuff by 1555. It became the name for the color of the dye by 1622. *Amber*, which is also an opaque term, came into Early Modern English from Old French (from Medieval Latin, from Arabic) with its fossil resin sense by about 1400. It developed its secondary color sense by about 1500.

The gradual incorporation of secondary hue terms continued in the Modern English period (1700–present). Eight secondary terms were added to the color lexicon during the eighteenth century, and forty entered in the nineteenth century. Only nine of these terms were the names of dyes, pigments, or textiles: *cobalt*, *charcoal*, *siena*, *sepia*, *beige*, *ecru*, *khaki*, *mauve*, and *magenta*. *Lemon*, *chocolate*, and *buff* are examples of eighteenth-century Modern English secondary terms, and *coffee*, *mahogany*, and *magenta* are examples of nineteenth-century Modern English terms.

Lemon, a transparent term, came into Middle English from Old French (from Arabic, from Persian) with its fruit sense by about 1400 and acquired its plant sense by 1615. It did not become a secondary color term until the Modern period in about 1796. *Chocolate*, another transparent term, entered Early Modern English (from Spanish, from Nahuatl) with both its bean and beverage senses in about 1604, but it did not acquire its secondary color sense until the Modern period, by about 1776.

Buff, an opaque term, came into Early Modern English from French (from Vulgar Latin) with its buffalo or wild ox meaning by 1552, and it extended its meaning to include buffalo hides and leather made from buffalo hides by 1580. It did not take on its secondary color sense until the Modern period, by about 1788.

Coffee, a transparent term, was borrowed into Early Modern English from Italian (from Turkish, from Arabic) with both its bean and beverage senses by about 1598. Its color sense developed later, first as a paraphrastic expression *coffee-coloured* by 1694 and then as a simplex secondary color term by 1815. *Mahogany*, another transparent term, appeared in Early Modern English (of obscure origins, probably from a non-Carib West Indian language) with its wood sense in about 1671 and its tree sense in about 1759. It occurred paraphrastically as *mahogany-colour* by 1737, but did not become a secondary color term until the Modern period in about 1834.

Magenta, an opaque term, is particularly noteworthy for its rapid and well-documented development. It was the name of the location in northern Italy where a (bloody) battle was fought in 1859. It was incorporated into Modern English (by metaphorical transfer) as the name for a newly discovered (red) coal-tar dye (fuchin) in 1859 and, almost immediately thereafter, as a secondary color term in 1860 (*OED*).

The development of dyeing and textile manufacture was a motivating factor, although certainly not the only one, in the evolution of English color categories. From the eleventh century, black (and white, as well as other natural colors) was favored in European cloth and color symbolism in an effort to resist the Byzantine and Arab monopoly in polychrome textiles and dyestuffs in the eastern Mediterranean (Schneider 1978). In the fifteenth century, Renaissance Italy became the European center for textile manufacturing and dyeing, and "exploded with color." In spite of the legislation favoring black cloth, Italian polychrome textiles, as well as gold and silver cloth, began to make their way into England (Schneider 1978: 427–428). As the Mediterranean and Italian monopolies declined and the center of dyeing and textile manufacture moved to northern Europe in the sixteenth and seventeenth centuries, England abandoned efforts to legislate clothing and color (Schneider 1978: 434–436). A slow-but-steady increase in secondary color terms continued until 1856, when the invention of coal-tar, or aniline, dyes provided a further impetus to the development of color concepts. The manufacture of synthetic dyes accelerated the development of secondary terms, but only a small minority of the terms added between the mid nineteenth century and the present derived from colorant or textile entity senses.

Culture members innovated secondary color terms on the basis of an ontological metonym, which can be stated as "Entity stands for entity's color" – that is, names for entities with characteristic color associations are converted metonymically to color terms. The entity names that became color names were drawn from the plant, animal, mineral, food, and artifact domains. These entity sources neither caused secondary color terms to be innovated nor determined the direction of their development. They were, however, innovated in a nonrandom order. In general, the earliest secondary color terms were the names of dyestuffs, pigments, and textiles, while later secondary terms were only infrequently the names of colorant and textile entity sources.

Colorant and textile names probably became the first secondary color terms because they were proximate and contiguous resources. The introduction of colorants and textiles in the late medieval period did not cause these early secondary terms to be innovated, but it did contribute convenient entity sources for color names. Culture members innovated these early terms in response to the increasing need for more secondary color names, and colorants and textiles, as ingredients in and products of color processes, could readily and naturally stand for their highly characteristic associated colors. Later, when variously hued synthetic dyes were invented in the late nineteenth century, culture members only occasionally turned to colorants or textiles as entity sources for new color terms. For the most part, they innovated secondary color names that derived from non-colorant and nontextile sources, the majority of which were not proximate or contiguous resources and had existed in English for many years (cf. Casson 1994: 17–19).

Conclusion

Culture and cognition are critical factors in the evolution of color categories. Berlin and Kay (1969: 16–17) point out that as cultures evolve and become more complex, they encode more basic color categories. Small-scale societies with minimal social and technical complexity generally have only two, three, or four basic color categories, whereas industrialized societies encode all eleven colors. Biology and environment do not provide the primary factors motivating the evolution of color terms. Human color vision has been the same since the origin of *Homo sapiens*, and our environment has always been rich in colorful entities. Culture members, responding to increases in societal complexity and diversity, restructure their systems of color categorization by differentiating new concepts and innovating new vocabulary (cf. Kay 1977: 30; MacLaury 1992: 141).

The color shift from brightness to hue in the evolution of English basic color terms can be seen as a response to an increasingly complex color world in the Middle English period (1150–1500). The development of secondary color terms, beginning in the late medieval period (1350–1500), can also be attributed to this increasingly diverse array of culturally significant colors. The response of culture members to these changes was a "cognitive refocusing."[5] Culture members restructured their systems of color categorization by shifting from brightness to hue, and then innovating simplex terms to encode numerous finely differentiated secondary hue categories.

Acknowledgments   I want to thank Larry Hardin for inviting me to the Color Categories conference and Luisa Maffi and Larry Hardin for urging me to submit this chapter to the conference volume. This chapter derives ultimately from a manuscript with the same title, which I circulated in 1991. The present chapter has benefited greatly from generous comments on the earlier version by Paul Kay and Rob MacLaury, to whom I am most grateful. I also owe a debt of gratitude to Carole Biggam for her careful scrutiny of, and helpful comments on, my Old English and Middle English color-term analyses, and to Richard Diebold for suggesting several important Old English and Middle English color-term sources. Oberlin College provided support for this project in the form of Dana Foundation grants to four hardworking student interns. Any errors or infelicities remaining in the chapter are entirely my own responsibility.

Notes

1 Color reference is generally specified in terms of three psychophysical dimensions: (a) hue or prismatic color, the property of light determined by spectral position (measured in wavelengths), for example, red, yellow, green, and blue; (b) brightness or value, ranging from light to dark, and including quantity of luminescence present (from light sources), and degree of reflectivity present (from reflecting surfaces); and (c) saturation or purity, the relative dullness–vividness of a hue, determined by the amount of its admixture with white or black (cf. Berlin and Kay 1969; Conklin 1973; Kay and McDaniel 1978; MacLaury 1987). "Hue" is here extended to include black and white in the sense of object or surface color, that is, the sense in which they are treated the same as red, yellow, green, and blue. The focus in this discussion is on the relationship between brightness and hue only.

2 In definitions, *OED* and *MED* stand respectively for *Oxford English Dictionary* (Murray 1933) and *Middle English Dictionary* (Kurath and Kuhn 1954). *MCOE*

stands for *Microfiche Concordance to Old English* (Healey and Venezky 1980), *RHD* for *The Random House Dictionary of the English Language* (Flexner 1987), and *ODEE* for *The Oxford Dictionary of English Etymology* (Onions 1966). *The American Heritage Dictionary of Indo-European Roots*, edited by Calvert Watkins (1985), was the principal resource for Germanic and Indo-European roots. Entries from these dictionaries are generally cited without page numbers in the text.

3 Accounts here of Old English and Middle English terms for gray, green, and blue have been significantly altered from my earlier accounts in Casson and Gardner (1992). These changes were made on the basis of data and suggestions provided by C. P. Biggam (personal communication 1994).

4 Data on provenance and etymological sequence were compiled from Norris (1969), *RHD*, and *ODEE*.

5 I owe this term and concept to Robert E. MacLaury (personal communication 1992).

References

Barley, N. F. 1974. Old English colour: where do matters stand? *Anglo-Saxon England* 3: 15–28.

Barnhart, R. K. (ed.) 1988. *The Barnhart Dictionary of Etymology*. New York: H. W. Wilson Company.

Bauer, L. 1983. *English Word-Formation*. New York: Cambridge University Press.

Berlin, B., and P. Kay 1969. *Basic Color Terms: Their Universality and Evolution*. Berkeley: University of California Press.

Biggam, C. P. 1993. A lexical semantic study of blue and grey in Old English: A pilot study in interdisciplinary semantics. 2 vols. Unpublished Ph.D. dissertation, Strathclyde University.

    in press. Sociolinguistic aspects of Old English colour lexemes. *Anglo-Saxon England*.

Bosworth, J., and T. N. Toller 1882. *An Anglo-Saxon Dictionary*. Oxford: Clarendon Press.

Burnley, J. L. 1976. Middle English colour terminology and lexical structure. *Linguistische Berichte* 41: 39–49.

Casson, R. W. 1994. Russett, rose, and raspberry: the development of English secondary color terms. *Journal of Linguistic Anthropology* 4(1): 5–22.

Casson, R. W., and P. M. Gardner 1992. On brightness and color categories: additional data. *Current Anthropology* 33(4): 395–399.

Conklin, H. C. 1973. Color categorization. *American Anthropologist* 75: 931–942.

Flexner, S. B.(ed.) 1987. *The Random House Dictionary of the English Language*. 2nd edn., unabridged. New York: Random House.

Hall, J. R. C. 1960. *A Concise Anglo-Saxon Dictionary*. 4th edn., with a supplement by H. D. Meritt. Cambridge University Press.

Healey, A. di Paolo, and R. L. Venezky (compilers) 1980. *Microfiche Concordance to Old English*. Newark: University of Delaware.

Kaiser, M., and V. Shevoroshkin 1988. Nostratic. *Annual Review of Anthropology* 17: 309–329.

Kay, P. 1977. Language evolution and speech style. In B. G. Blount and M. Sanches (eds.), *Sociocultural Dimensions of Language Change* (pp. 21–33). New York: Academic Press.

Kay, P., and C. K. McDaniel 1978. The linguistic significance of the meanings of basic color terms. *Language* 54(3): 610–646.

Kurath, H., and S. M. Kuhn (eds.) 1954. *Middle English Dictionary*. Ann Arbor: University of Michigan Press.

Lerner, L. L. 1951. Colour words in Anglo-Saxon. *Modern Language Review* 46: 246–249.

MacLaury, R. E. 1987. Color-category evolution and Shuswap yellow-with-green. *American Anthropologist* 89: 107–124.

    1992. From brightness to hue: an exploratory model of color-category evolution. *Current Anthropology* 33: 137–187.

Mead, W. E. 1899. Color in Old English poetry. *Publication of the Modern Language Association of America* 14: 169–206.

Murray, J. A. H., Sir (ed.) 1933. *The Oxford English Dictionary*. 13 vols. London: Oxford University Press.

Norris, W. (ed.) 1969. *The American Heritage Dictionary of the English Language*. Boston: Houghton Mifflin.

Onions, C. T. (ed.) 1966. *The Oxford Dictionary of English Etymology*. Oxford University Press.

Schneider, J. 1978. Peacocks and penguins: the political economy of European cloth and colors. *American Ethnologist* 5: 413–447.

Shields, K. 1979. Indo-European basic color terms. *Canadian Journal of Linguistics* 24: 142–146.

Sweet, H. 1981 [1896]. *The Student's Dictionary of Anglo-Saxon*. Oxford: Clarendon Press.

Watkins, C. (ed.) 1985. *The American Heritage Dictionary of Indo-European Roots*. Boston: Houghton Mifflin.

Wheelwright, J. n.d. Anglo-Saxon color words. Unpublished ms.

11 Two observations on culture contact and the Japanese color nomenclature system

James Stanlaw

Introduction

Color nomenclature has been an ongoing research problem in anthropology for over a century, ever since ethnographers discovered that
"quaint and exotic peoples" have equally intriguing ways of naming
the colors of their world. It was puzzling to find that so "natural" and
neutral a stimulus as the color spectrum could be divided up – that is,
named – in hundreds of different ways. This variety of color vocabulary was taken as the best argument for linguistic relativism; indeed,
it was the only real empirical evidence that seemed to indicate that
there is nothing inherent in either human perceptual faculties or the
physical world that would compel a language to name some domain
in any particular fashion.

In 1969, however, Berlin and Kay and others demonstrated cross-
culturally that there are some severe constraints on how color nomenclature systems operate and how they develop. In short, if certain
unanalyzable, monolexemic, and psychologically salient color terms
are taken to be "basic," there is a universal ordering to the color spectrum and limitations on the way colors can be labeled. These eleven
"basic" color categories – WHITE and BLACK; RED, YELLOW, GREEN,
BLUE, BROWN; and PURPLE, PINK, ORANGE, and GREY – are thought
to be universal across cultures, and as languages/cultures evolve and
develop new terms for colors, they will do so approximately in this
order. As is now well known, by the 1990s several hundred studies
(cf. Kay, Berlin, and Merrifield 1991; Kay, Berlin, Maffi, and Merrifield
this volume) have supported the general Berlin and Kay hypotheses.
Though modified and refined, the universalist arguments of Berlin
and Kay have remained principally intact.

Here I will discuss two results from recent research on Japanese
that offer contributions to color nomenclature theory, the specific
tenets of the Berlin and Kay findings, and notions of linguistic relativ-

ity. The first relates to language and culture contact. Because of their concern with making an overall cross-cultural comparison, Berlin and Kay – necessarily – neglected several crucial aspects of the Japanese color nomenclature system. They failed to examine the pervasive use of loanwords in the Japanese language in general and in the color-term vocabulary in particular. When loanwords are also brought into the picture, various intriguing findings result. For example, several English loanword color terms – *pinku* (PINK), *orenji* (ORANGE), and *guree* (GREY) – are more salient than their native Japanese counterparts (*momo-iro*, *daidai-iro*, and *nezumi-iro* or *hai-iro*, respectively).[1] It even appears that the Japanese color lexicon consists of two distinct sets of terms, one of native origin, the other borrowed from English. I suggest that English loanwords are often *replacing* native Japanese color terms, and that they seem to be doing so in reverse order with respect to the Berlin and Kay evolutionary sequence.

The second observation involves culture contact of a different kind. Japanese people who have lived abroad for some length of time often become confused when asked to find the "green" color of the Japanese traffic signal. One of the reasons for this, I suggest, is that Japanese people – for cultural and sociolinguistic reasons – label this color "blue" even though it differs very little from the color of green-lights found in most other places of the world. I argue that the "color" an object is for Japanese people, then, is something more than just denotatum, wavelength, or habit.

Japanese color nomenclature and English loanwords

While conducting research on the use of English loanwords in Japan (Stanlaw 1992a, 1992b), I also collected data on color terms because much of the color vocabulary in contemporary Japanese is borrowed from English. The methods I followed were similar to those described by Berlin and Kay, and generally used by most researchers on color nomenclature. I first collected a list of color terms by simply asking speakers to name what they thought to be the salient color terms in Japanese. If nothing else, I thought it might be useful to attempt to corroborate Berlin and Kay's original findings on Japanese (which were based on data collected in English from a single bilingual speaker living in California). The results for this first task are shown in Table 11.1.[2]

Table 11.1 presents the frequency counts for twenty-nine Japanese color terms given as responses, including both native Japanese vocabulary items and English loanwords. Ninety-one people of various ages were asked to write down those color terms they thought were most common or most important in everyday life in Japan. Participants were encouraged not to deliberate too long over this task (three to five minutes at most), and told that no more than the first fifteen terms would be examined. They were also informed that less than the maximum number of items was perfectly acceptable, and that they should use their own judgment regarding the number of terms they considered sufficient.

Participants in this survey ranged from 8 to 62 years of age. For tabulation, speakers have been divided into the following 5 groups: (a) elementary school students (aged 8, 9, or 10), (b) junior high and senior high school students, (c) university students or people in their early twenties, (d) adults aged 26 to 45, and (e) adults over 45.

Younger students generally completed the task in groups in a classroom, or class-like setting. Older students and adults often completed the task individually or in small groups, in locations suiting the convenience of the participants or researcher (e.g. an office, a private home, a university building). Discussion and instruction was generally conducted in Japanese, except in a few cases where the participants preferred using English.

Table 11.2 presents the number of times participants, broken down by age, cited a particular form as an important color term in Japanese. The percentages next to each number indicate the fraction of the speakers in that age-group who cited that term. For example, 96% of the elementary school students (or 22 out of 23 school children) believed *shiro* (WHITE) to be an important and basic color term. In the TOTAL column the percentages represent responses for all age categories taken in aggregate. For example, 97% (or 88 out of all 91 respondents) considered *shiro* (WHITE) to be an important color term. Note that all percentages have been rounded off and terms that appeared fewer than five times are not cited. To facilitate reading, the data in both Tables 11.1 and 11.2 have been grouped into three sections: the original basic color terms in Japanese given by Berlin and Kay (1969), other native Japanese color terms mentioned by participants, and English loanword color terms given by respondents.

Table 11.1   Most frequently cited Japenese color terms

Color term	Category	Frequency
shiro	WHITE	88
kuro	BLACK	84
aka	RED	86
ao	BLUE	83
ki-iro	YELLOW	74
midori	GREEN	70
cha-iro	BROWN	55
murasaki	PURPLE	46
momo-iro	PINK	4
daidai-iro	ORANGE	4
hai-iro	GREY	14
nezumi-iro	GREY	5
kon	dark blue	24
mizu-iro	light blue	22
ki-midori	yellow-green	23
kin-iro	gold	11
gin-iro	silver	13
hada-iro	flesh	6
koge-cha	dark brown	5
sora-iro	sky blue	5
pinku	pink	39
orenji	orange	36
guree	grey	11
buraun	brown	9
kaaki	khaki	8
beeju	beige	7
kuriimu-iro	cream	6
remon	lemon	6
emerarudo guriin	emerald green	6

Table 11.2   Percentages and frequencies of Japanese color terms by age groups

	elem. sch. (=23) %/#	hi sch. (=9) %/#	univer. (=35) %/#	post-univ. (=18) %/#	older (=6) %/#	Total (=91) %/#
shiro	96/22	88/8	97/34	100/18	100/6	97/88
kuro	91/21	88/8	91/32	94/17	100/6	92/84
aka	100/23	88/8	94/33	94/17	83/5	94/86
ao	100/23	88/8	91/32	89/16	66/4	91/83
ki-iro	83/19	77/7	80/28	77/14	100/6	81/74
midori	96/22	66/6	74/26	72/13	50/3	77/70
cha-iro	65/15	55/5	51/18	66/12	83/5	60/55
murasaki	83/19	55/5	17/6	61/11	83/5	50/46
momo-iro	4/1	0/0	0/0	5/1	33/2	4/4
daidai-iro	0/0	11/1	0/0	5/1	33/2	4/4
hai-iro	13/3	22/2	6/2	16/3	66/4	15/14
nezumi-iro	4/1	0/0	0/0	5/1	50/3	5/5
kon	26/6	33/3	26/9	11/2	66/4	26/24
mizu-iro	4/1	55/5	31/11	11/2	50/3	24/22
ki-midori	13/3	44/4	31/11	11/2	50/3	25/23
kin-iro	17/4	22/2	8/3	5/1	17/1	12/11
gin-iro	17/4	33/3	11/4	5/1	17/1	14/13
hada-iro	4/1	11/1	0/0	16/3	17/1	6/6
koge-cha	0/0	22/2	0/0	11/2	17/1	5/5
sora-iro	0/0	22/2	3/1	5/1	17/1	5/5
orenji	43/10	33/3	45/16	28/5	33/2	39/36
pinku	26/6	44/4	60/21	33/6	33/2	43/39
guree	4/1	22/2	17/6	11/2	0/0	12/11
buraun	0/0	22/2	14/5	11/2	0/0	10/9
kaaki	4/1	22/2	11/4	5/1	0/0	9/8
beeju	4/1	22/2	6/2	11/2	0/0	7/7
kuriimu-iro	0/0	11/1	11/4	5/1	0/0	6/6
remon	0/0	11/1	11/4	5/1	0/0	6/6
emerarudo guriin	4/1	11/1	6/2	11/2	0/0	6/6

Note: terms mentioned less than five times by informants are not listed;
percentages are calculated on that fraction of those terms appearing above,
ignoring terms not meeting the five term criterion.

Table 11.3   Rank ordering of Japanese color terms

shiro	WHITE	97%
aka	RED	94%
kuro	BLACK	92%
ao	BLUE	91%
ki-iro	YELLOW	81%
midori	GREEN	77%
cha-iro	BROWN	60%
murasaki	PURPLE	50%
pinku	pink	43%
orenji	orange	39%
kon	dark blue	26%
ki-midori	yellow-green	25%
mizu-iro	light blue	24%
hai-iro	GREY	15%
gin-iro	silver	14%
guree	grey	12%
kin-iro	gold	12%
buraun	brown	10%
kaaki	khaki	9%
beeju	beige	7%
kuriimu-iro	cream	6%
remon	lemon	6%
emerarudo guriin	emerald green	6%
hada-iro	flesh	6%
nezumi-iro	GREY	5%
sora-iro	sky blue	5%
koge-cha	dark brown	5%
momo-iro	PINK	4%
daidai-iro	ORANGE	4%

Table 11.3 lists the color terms given in Tables 11.1 and 11.2 in decreasing order of saliency for all speakers. This table takes the percentages given in Table 11.2 and puts them in rank order, highest to lowest, regardless of a term's status as "basic," loanword, or native Japanese color term.

As many fieldworkers have noted, it is not always easy to determine the real basic color terms in a language.[3] In Japanese, the difficulties in defining basic color terms are compounded by several factors. First, the Japanese morphological system regarding color terms is rather intricate. Every Japanese color term can, or must, interact with a number of productive morphemes. For example, there are many complexities regarding color adjectival forms, and the use of productive morphemes to indicate the degree of saturation of hue (e.g. *-gakatta* "tinged with," or *-ppoi* "-ish") is often problematic. In addition, almost any Japanese noun can be made into a color term by simply adding the suffix *-iro* "-colored" (Stanlaw 1987: 85–118).

These problems are exacerbated even further when we consider a second point: how color terms are used in the Japanese writing system. Simply put, the problem comes down to what actually constitutes a word in Japanese. Is it a spoken set of phonemes? Or is it a written character or set of characters that are the units of analysis? Because Sino-Japanese characters were borrowed more than a millennium ago over the course of several centuries, most Japanese characters today have a multitude of pronunciations. For example, if the BLUE color term is thought to be *ao-iro*, what is the status of the alternative pronunciation of the same characters, *sei-shoku*?

We see, then, that the traditional Berlin and Kay criteria of unanalyzability, productivity, and morphological complexity may not be sufficient to determine a lexeme's basic color term status in Japanese. However, two other criteria remain. Berlin and Kay claim that a candidate basic color term's signification should not be included in the range of any other term. They also argue that a basic color term must be psychologically salient for speakers. Evidence for this would include occurrence at the beginning of elicitation lists, and occurrence in the idiolects of all speakers (Berlin and Kay 1969: 6). Therefore, I used these two criteria as the main determinants of basic color term status in Japanese: frequency salience, and evidence of inclusion derived from mapping tasks.

The literature suggests that frequency salience is actually a very good indicator of basicness. For example, Hays, Margolis, Naroll, and Perkins (1972), in a statistical analysis of five literary languages (English, Spanish, French, German, and Russian, with additional evidence from Hebrew and Romanian) found that salience – when defined as frequency of use – correlates with the order of the Berlin and Kay evolutionary sequence. That is, in general, the most frequently used terms in these languages are those for WHITE and BLACK, the next most frequently used term is the one for RED, and so on, throughout the evolutionary order. Using later sets of English frequency tables (Carroll, Davies, and Richman 1971; Francis and Kucera 1982), I found support for Hays *et al.*'s conclusions (which used data gathered in the 1940s). Evidence, too, from Bolton (1978) and Bolton, Curtis, and Thomas (1980) is generally confirmatory.

In examining frequency data from Japanese newspapers and magazines gathered by the Japanese National Language Research Institute (Kokuritsu Kokugo Kenkyuujo 1964, 1971, 1972, 1973, 1974), I found that frequency/salience seems to correlate with the Berlin and Kay evolutionary sequence (Stanlaw 1987: 111–116).[4] Thus, there appears to be strong enough evidence to believe that the salience data given in Tables 11.1, 11.2, and 11.3 reflect basic color term status in Japanese to at least a fair degree.

Speakers were also asked to perform a mapping task using the most frequently found terms in Table 11.3. This was an extension of the Berlin and Kay data given for Japanese (Berlin and Kay 1969: 123), using both (a) a much larger number of speakers, and (b) a greater sample of candidate basic color terms (namely, English loanword color terms and some other native Japanese color terms that appear to satisfy many of the basicness criteria). Figures 11.1 and 11.2 give the modal focal colors for the eleven Berlin–Kay color categories in Japanese, both for native terms and English loanwords. Figures 11.3 and 11.4 do the same for category ranges.

An examination of these Figures shows several things. In particular, we should notice that English loanword color terms are not mapped synonymously with native Japanese color terms. This was common for most speakers interviewed. For example, Figures 11.5 and 11.6 show the native Japanese and English loanword color maps for one typical speaker, Y. K., a 25-year-old female. Both the focal colors (marked with a plus sign) and the ranges vary extensively. In general, the number of chips chosen as focals for the categories identified by native Japanese color terms is different from the number of focal chips chosen for English loanword-named color categories, and in the latter case most focals seem to be brighter by at least one step on the

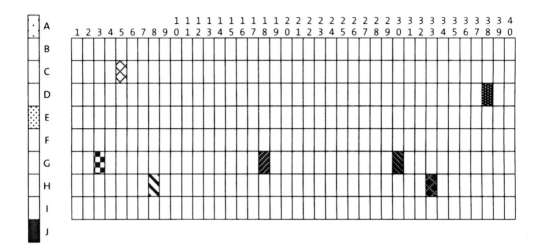

Key:

	Native Japanese color term	English loanword color term	Berlin/Kay category
	shiro	howaito	WHITE
	kuro	burakku	BLACK
	aka	reddo	RED
	ao	buruu	BLUE
	ki-iro	ieroo	YELLOW
	midori	guriin	GREEN
	cha-iro	buraun	BROWN
	murasaki	paapuru	PURPLE
	daidai-iro	orenji	ORANGE
	momo-iro	pinku	PINK
	hai-iro	guree	GREY

Figure 11.1 Modal focals for native Japanese color terms.

brightness level than their native Japanese counterparts. When considering the ranges of the color terms, a similar phenomenon is found. That is, in general, English loanword color terms seem to be thought of as referring to brighter examples than their native Japanese correspondents.

Using the mapping data above, and the salience data given in Tables 11.1, 11.2, and 11.3, a set of Japanese basic color terms might look like that found in Table 11.4. The first thing to notice about this list, or the data given in Table 11.3, is that the Berlin and Kay (1969) proposed order is closely followed, at least for the first eight color terms. The sole exception is that *aka* (RED) is just slightly more salient than *kuro* (BLACK). Aside from this very minor deviation, the rank order does nothing to contradict the theoretical evolutionary

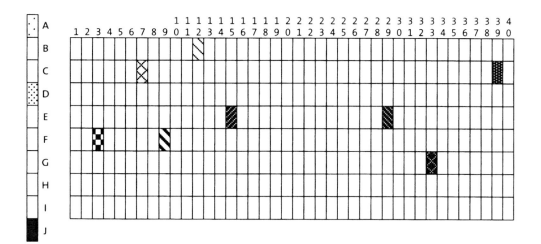

Key:

Native Japanese color term	English loanword color term	Berlin/Kay category
shiro	howaito	WHITE
kuro	burakku	BLACK
aka	reddo	RED
ao	buruu	BLUE
ki-iro	ieroo	YELLOW
midɒri	guriin	GREEN
cha-iro	buraun	BROWN
murasaki	paapuru	PURPLE
daidai-iro	orenji	ORANGE
momo-iro	pinku	PINK
hai-iro	guree	GREY

Figure 11.2 Modal focals for English downword color terms.

sequence. However, after this, from rank 8 on, the connections with the Berlin and Kay order are almost completely severed.

In places 9, 10, and 11 of Tables 11.3 and 11.4, the Berlin and Kay 1969 sequence predicts that we should find *momo-iro* (PINK; literally "peach-colored"), *daidai-iro* (ORANGE; literally "orange-colored"), and *nezumi-iro* (GREY; literally "mouse-colored") or *hai-iro* (GREY; literally "ash-colored") as the next color terms, in any order. Instead, in the next three ranks we find two English loanword color terms – *pinku* "pink" and *orenji* "orange" – and a native Japanese color term, *kon* (approximately "dark blue").[5] Interestingly, both loanwords, *pinku* and *orenji*, appear in the sequence where we would expect the PINK and ORANGE category terms to be. However, the native Japanese *momo-iro* (PINK) was only given by 4% of speakers, while the English loanword

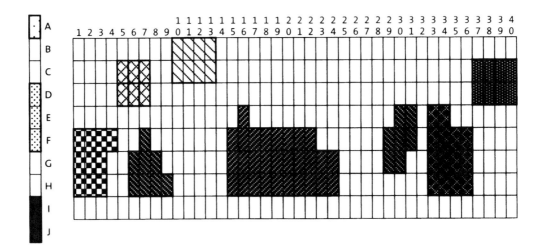

Key:

Native Japanese color term	English loanword color term	Berlin/Kay category
shiro	howaito	WHITE
kuro	burakku	BLACK
aka	reddo	RED
ao	buruu	BLUE
ki-iro	ieroo	YELLOW
midori	guriin	GREEN
cha-iro	buraun	BROWN
murasaki	paapuru	PURPLE
daidai-iro	orenji	ORANGE
momo-iro	pinku	PINK
hai-iro	guree	GREY

Figure 11.3 Native Japanese color terms (ranges at the 50% level).

pinku was given by 43%. Likewise, *daidai-iro* (ORANGE) was named by only 4% of speakers while the English loanword *orenji* was cited by 39%. Apparently, these two English loanword color terms are, in effect, substituting for the native Japanese terms as labels for the PINK and ORANGE categories.

The next five ranks in Table 11.3 are also in contradiction of the standard model. *Hai-iro* (Berlin and Kay's Japanese GREY term) appears, but so does *guree* (the English loanword "grey") shortly afterward; both were named by about 12 to 15% of participants. The other Japanese GREY term, *nezumi-iro*, was only named by 5% of respondents.

Several English loanword color terms, then, are highly salient in the minds of Japanese speakers. *Pinku*, *orenji*, and *guree* are used much more frequently than the corresponding Japanese terms *momo-iro*

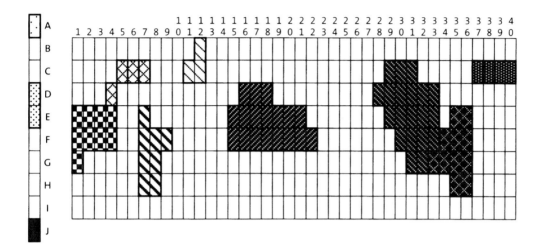

Key:

	Native Japanese color term	English loanword color term	Berlin/Kay category
	shiro	howaito	WHITE
	kuro	burakku	BLACK
	aka	reddo	RED
	ao	buruu	BLUE
	ki-iro	ieroo	YELLOW
	midori	guriin	GREEN
	cha-iro	buraun	BROWN
	murasaki	paapuru	PURPLE
	daidai-iro	orenji	ORANGE
	momo-iro	pinku	PINK
	hai-iro	guree	GREY

Figure 11.4 English loanword color terms (ranges at the 50% level).

(PINK), *daidai-iro* (ORANGE), and *nezumi-iro* (GREY) which are cited as basic by Berlin and Kay (1969). These native Japanese color terms do not appear until the very bottom of the list in Table 11.3. In other words, at least these three English loanword color terms – *pinku*, *orenji*, and *guree* – seem to be as basic as their native Japanese equivalents, and, in fact, may be replacing them for all practical purposes. Indeed, English loanword color terms may be in the process of replacing a number of native Japanese color terms. I suggest that Japanese may be substituting English loanword color terms for native Japanese forms in reverse order of the Berlin and Kay evolutionary sequence. For example, we might predict that native Japanese *murasaki* (PURPLE) or *cha-iro* (BROWN) could be the next color terms to be replaced (by *paapuru* and *buraun* respectively).

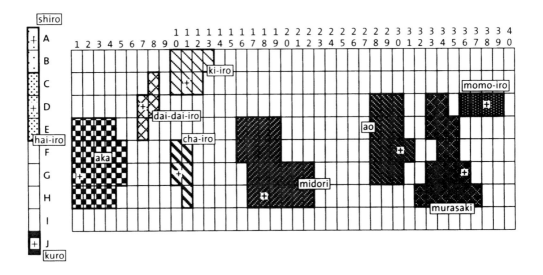

Key:

Native Japanese color term	English loanword color term	Berlin/Kay category
shiro	howaito	WHITE
kuro	burakku	BLACK
aka	reddo	RED
ao	buruu	BLUE
ki-iro	ieroo	YELLOW
midori	guriin	GREEN
cha-iro	buraun	BROWN
murasaki	paapuru	PURPLE
daidai-iro	orenji	ORANGE
momo-iro	pinku	PINK
hai-iro	guree	GREY

Figure 11.5 Native Japanese color terms (Y. K.).

The significance of Japanese color categories and language change

There are two fundamental questions regarding the Berlin and Kay evolutionary sequence: (a) why does the evolutionary sequence exist in the first place, and (b) what are the mechanisms that cause a language/culture to move along the sequence? As yet, no one has given a definitive answer to the first question, though some (e.g. Kay and McDaniel 1978) have argued for a physiological or neurological explanation. I will not go further into the first question here, although I have argued previously (Stanlaw 1987: 191–213) that languages encode color terms by alternating on extremes of brightness and hue. The second question, however, is no less vexing and equally

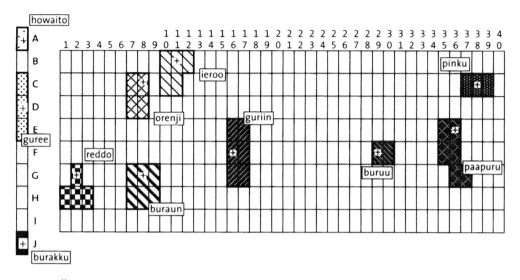

Key:

	Native Japanese color term	English loanword color term	Berlin/Kay category
	shiro	howaito	WHITE
	kuro	burakku	BLACK
	aka	reddo	RED
	ao	buruu	BLUE
	ki-iro	ieroo	YELLOW
	midori	guriin	GREEN
	cha-iro	buraun	BROWN
	murasaki	paapuru	PURPLE
	daidai-iro	orenji	ORANGE
	momo-iro	pinku	PINK
	hai-iro	guree	GREY

Figure 11.6 English loanword color terms (Y. K.).

important. The Japanese data again suggest that the standard Berlin and Kay model needs to be extended in several crucial ways.

Berlin and Kay have tried to explain the dynamics of the evolutionary color term sequence as due to cultural and technological complexity. They argue that in small societies, where the local environment is well known to everyone, secondary color terms are not only sufficient but actually advantageous. If all people know "plant X," then the secondary color term "color of plant X" carries more information than some hypothetical abstract color name. When technology and group size increase, general abstract color terms are required to convey information to people who may not have the same referent in their environment. Increasing technology, especially with regard to color-

Table 11.4   A possible set of basic color terms in Japanese

1.	shiro	WHITE
2.	kuro	BLACK
3.	aka	RED
4.	ao	BLUE
5.	ki-iro	YELLOW
6.	midori	GREEN
7.	cha-iro	BROWN
8.	murasaki	PURPLE
9.	*pinku*	pink
10.	*orenji*	orange
11.	hai-iro/*guree*	GREY

processing such as dyeing, would also require more emphasis on abstract color terms.

These arguments no doubt contain some truth. The Berlin and Kay data (1969: 16) indicate that cultures with small populations and limited technologies have few basic color terms, while complex and highly industrialized societies have the largest number of them. But what happens when a culture reaches a certain level of technological sophistication and linguistic development with respect to basic color terms? Do they stop evolving? There is no reason to assume so, though it might be hard for, say, English speakers at the pinnacle of the sequence to imagine how subsequent stages would appear. It is probably equally bizarre, however, for the Dani of Papua New Guinea – with only two basic color terms in their language – to imagine how the Europeans construct their color world, and for what purpose.

The Japanese data suggest at least three techniques which could encourage further development of the evolutionary sequence: (a) a language/culture could create new basic color categories (such as a dark blue or a yellow-green); (b) a language/culture could increase the number of terms available for basic color term status through extensive borrowing of loanwords; and (c) a language/culture could replace native terms in the evolutionary sequence with loanwords. All three processes are found in the tables.

The first case would posit the existence of unanalyzable, monolexemic, basic terms labeling a distinctly defined color space. Native

Japanese terms such as *kon* "dark blue," and possibly a few others, indicate that Japanese may have twelve or more basic color categories (as opposed to the maximum of eleven cited by Berlin and Kay 1969).

The number of English loanword color terms found in Japanese is extensive. Besides some of the basic English labels, even several borrowed English secondary color terms, like *kaaki* "khaki," *beeju* "beige," *remon* "lemon," *kuriimu-iro* "cream-colored," or *emerarudo guriin* "emerald green," are more salient than many Japanese basic or secondary color terms. Thus, a pool of abstract terms (i.e., those not as strongly connected to a referent as are many native Japanese labels) could be available for use in creating new color descriptions or creating new color categories.

The third mechanism, replacing native Japanese color terms by English loanwords, could let the native terms become relexified, possibly taking new denotative and connotative meanings. They might even eventually come to label new basic color categories.

Obviously, the presence of every English loanword color term – basic or secondary – will not imply the existence of a new category in the Japanese color nomenclature system; but considering the length of time required for languages to evolve, availability might increase probability. An awareness of English loanword color terms – presumably known by speakers to be different somehow from native Japanese color terms – might prompt people to experiment with these auxiliary terms in a wide variety of ways.

The colors of the Japanese go-light

A second observation about Japanese color nomenclature and the Berlin and Kay research concerns GREEN and BLUE terms, and the historical separation of the GRUE category. Perhaps as late as 800 years ago, the modern Japanese term for BLUE, *ao*, included most of the green hues – that is, colors which today would be called *midori* (GREEN).

However, there are still many differences in connotation between these terms. While *midori* has relatively few special referents or associations, *ao* has many. *Midori*, for the most part, means green colors or verdure. *Ao*, on the other hand, is also associated with notions of "freshness," "youth," or being "unripe." By extension, *ao* is also associated with being inexperienced or naive. More semantic extensions include *ao* referring to being "pale" or "sickly." In fact, most of the English "green"-metaphors – such as "He's still a green recruit" or "This apple is too green to eat" or "Your face looked pretty green after that roller coaster ride!" – would use *ao* in Japanese. What the Japanese seem to be encoding in their use of *ao* is the idea of "starting," or "beginning-ness." As several speakers told me, when the Japanese are talking about things plainly grown, they use *midori* (GREEN) or *aka* (RED), but "when we want to indicate things that are in the process of growth we use *ao*."[6].

For the most part, both historical and contemporary stoplights in Japan have had hues and shades very similar to those found in the United States or Europe. Today, the colors of the stoplight in Tokyo look pretty much the same as the ones in Tulsa. However, the "green" go-signal in Japan is called the *ao-shingoo* (lit. "blue light"), as in *shingoo ga ao ni natte kara, michi o watate-kudasai* "please cross the street after the light has turned green [BLUE])."

It is likely that the Japanese people were cuing in on this notion of "starting" or "freshness" when they decided to use *ao* as the name for the green light in their traffic signal. To put it in structuralist terms, a car must *begin* to accelerate when the light changes. This notion of process and change was probably even more of a central factor than hue itself when a label was chosen for the go-light. Thus, neither the native Japanese green term *midori*, nor the English loan-word *guriin*, were selected.

This choice of color labels has several interesting implications. On the Berlin and Kay color chart, I presume that most Japanese go-lights in most cities would be mapped to rows E or F between columns 19 and 22. This is well within the range that most speakers label as *midori* (GREEN) on the mapping and naming tasks described above. If colors were just pure denotata, then, the term *midori* should have been used to label this light. Cases such as this also make us question "natural-ist" or biological explanations of color naming (e.g. that perceptions corresponding to RED and GREEN are opposite neurologically or psychophysically, and therefore their categories enjoy some privileged linguistic position). However, there is one other aspect of this Japanese "blue light" phenomenon that is of note: the way in which color label affects memory and recall.

I have conducted a number of pilot studies asking overseas

Figure 11.7 Selections of stop-light terms for twenty-one Japanese speakers (a–u).

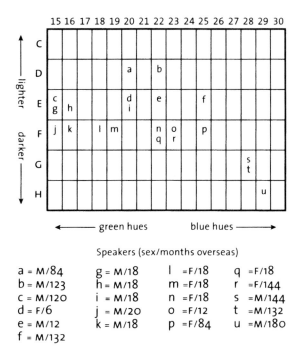

Speakers (sex/months overseas)

a = M/84   g = M/18   l =F/18   q =F/18
b = M/123   h = M/18   m =F/18   r =F/144
c = M/120   i = M/18   n =F/18   s =M/144
d = F/6   j = M/20   o =F/12   t =M/132
e = M/12   k = M/18   p =F/84   u =M/180
f = M/132

Japanese speakers to pick the best Berlin and Kay chip which matches the color of the go-light in the Japanese traffic signal. The results of one such study are seen in Figure 11.7.

Here, a section of the Berlin and Kay array is given for the middle brightness rows (C through H) and the green-to-blue hue columns (numbers 15 through 30). The responses of 21 speakers (named "a" through "u") are mapped for when they were asked to choose the best chip that they *remembered* as the color of the *ao-shingoo* "go-light." Each speaker had been residing in the United States for various lengths of time, from 6 months to over 15 years. Each speaker's gender, and the number of months they have lived in the United States, are given in the bottom of the Figure. For example, Speaker "a" (a male having lived in the United States for 84 months) chose chip D-20 as the color he remembered the go-light back in Japan to be.

Even a cursory glance at Figure 11.7 suggests that there is a relationship between length of time spent in America and the hue of the selected chip. For instance, Speaker "u," a male professor who has resided in the United States for over fifteen years, picked chip H-29 as the color he remembered the stop light back in Japan to be. This is very close to the modal "best" *ao* (BLUE), as seen in Figure 11.1 (i.e., chip G-

30). Speakers who have resided longer in America generally tend to pick more bluish chips than do Japanese people who have resided in the United States for shorter periods of time.

It is possible, at least theoretically, to calculate a correlation coefficient between months of stay in the United States and the blueness of the selected chip. Ignoring level of brightness (that is, just looking at how far along a chip is on the horizontal dimension of hue), the r-correlation coefficient is .63, and is significant at the .01 level. That is, the longer a speaker stays in the United States, the more likely he or she will choose a more bluish chip. However, to be more mathematically precise, brightness and speakers' gender should also be factored into these calculations, as well as examining a larger sample. In any case, this correlation lends support to the intuitive response one gets from looking at Figure 11.7.[7]

What can account for this finding? It seems likely that Japanese people overseas, when asked to name the color of the stop light back in Japan, have no recourse except to turn to the linguistic code. In the absence of the stimulus itself (the "green" light), the linguistic label (*ao*, or BLUE) is the only clue they might have in making a selection. It appears that the longer people have been away, the more they trust the label: the light is named *ao*, therefore it probably *is* really BLUE-colored. This is all the more intriguing when it turns out that actually the stoplights all around them in America are not very different from those back in Japan.

To put the results of this experiment in terms of the Sapir–Whorf hypothesis, here is a situation where we find a cognitive effect – i.e., recollection of the color of the "green" light – due to the structural properties of a language – i.e., the encoding of certain greenish hues as BLUE for cultural and sociolinguistic reasons. This experiment suggests a Sapir–Whorf effect, then, but one of a rather reduced kind. Results such as these show that there can, indeed, actually be Sapir–Whorf incursions of linguistic categorization into areas of non-linguistic cognitive processes, even in psychophysiologically constrained realms such as perception (Kay and Kempton 1984: 77).

Loanwords, universals, and particulars

The stoplight data, and the English loanword evidence, show interesting universalist and particularist interactions when colors and cultures come into contact. General universalist properties – like the Berlin and Kay encoding sequence – are found for the Japanese data, but we also saw how specific social and linguistic situations – such as borrowing – modified them. That is, the universalist arguments of Berlin and Kay do not necessarily refute *all* Whorfian considerations under *all* conditions. Languages can certainly vary semantically, but obviously not without constraint; people cannot just call anything anything, after all. These constraints, however, are often a complex interface of both human cognitive universals, *and* the particulars of cultures and languages in contact. It is on this edge that much of the linguistic and social action takes place.[8]

Notes

1 As a notational convention, in the text (but not in the tables or figures) all Japanese terms are italicized, and glosses are enclosed in double quotes. English loanwords in Japanese are italicized throughout. Standard Berlin and Kay basic color categories are given in capitals. Japanese long vowels are indicated by repetition; otherwise, the Hepburn system of romanization is followed.

2 For more on colors in Japanese see the references in Kobayashi (1974) and Stanlaw (1987).

3 Berlin and Kay (1969: 5–7) define as "basic" those color terms fulfilling the following criteria (given here in somewhat modified form). (a) Basic color terms in a given language are monolexemic and unanalyzable. That is, a term's meaning is not predictable from the meaning of its parts (thus excluding words like *sunburst* or *olive green* as non-basic in English). (b) The focus of a basic color term should not be included within the boundary of any other color term. Thus, because *khaki* is "a kind of brown" it would not be an English basic color term. (c) The application of a basic color term must not be restricted to only a few referents, but should exist as an abstract label widely applicable to all objects. Using this criterion, *blond* would not be basic in English because it usually only refers to hair color. (d) Basic color terms must be psychologically salient, in terms either of frequency of usage or of extensive occurrence and acceptability in a speech community. Thus, *sepia* or *mauve* in English would not qualify as basic color terms as they are not well known to all speakers. (e) Basic color terms are consistently productive in their use of various morphemes in the language. Thus, *reddish* and *greenish* substantiate the status of *red* and *green* as basic color terms

in English, while the questionability of **chartreuse-ish* confirms that *chartreuse* is not a basic term. (f) Colors which name an object, and recent loanwords, are suspect. (g) Morphological complexity can be given some weight in determining a lexeme's status, especially in questionable instances.

4 As I have pointed out (Stanlaw 1987: 181), when doing color-term studies it is somewhat difficult to use sources like the Japanese National Language Research Institute samples, because they do not always make distinctions between spoken and written forms, nor do they always distinguish a head noun (say *cha* "tea") and a color (*cha-iro* "tea-colored", or BROWN).

5 The Japanese National Language Research Institute tabulations also seem to indicate that *kon* is actually more salient than many basic Japanese color terms. For more on the implications of this, see Stanlaw (1987). See Uchikawa and Boynton (1987), Boynton, MacLaury, and Uchikawa (1989), and Kobayashi (1990) for other Japanese color terms.

6 These associations are not atypical. Many basic Japanese color terms are closely connected to their referents (e.g. the BROWN term *cha-iro*, literally meaning "tea-colored"). However, there are often close emotional/connotative connections as well. For example, *murasaki* (PURPLE) – perhaps because of its origin as a name for a clothing dye – is still associated with kimonos, elegance, and traditional Japanese things.

7 One other caveat should be mentioned about making correlations between "selected hue" and "months in the United States." This has to do with the nature of the

Munsell color system, upon which the Berlin and Kay array is based. In theory, the scales of the Munsell chart are supposed to be perceptually equidistant in terms of JNDs (just noticeable differences). This would seem to imply that the dimension of hue could be classified as being at the statistical "interval" level, thus allowing for certain formal calculations – such as the r-correlation – involving hue distance to be made without violating standard statistical practices. However, the exact nature of the Munsell system has been the subject of much debate (e.g. Farmer, Taylor, and Belyavin 1980). Thus, I believe caution should be used when interpreting such correlations.

8 Indeed, a number of researchers in color theory have tried to incorporate a pragmatic or sociocultural perspective into a more general universalist theory of color nomenclature (cf. "vantage theory" [MacLaury 1992], "color image scales" [Kobayashi 1990], and "extended-feature models" [Stanlaw 1987]).

References

Berlin, B., and P. Kay 1969. *Basic Color Terms: Their Universality and Evolution*. Berkeley: University of California Press. 1st paperback edn. 1991, with a bibliography by Luisa Maffi.

Bolton, R. 1978. Black, white, and red all over: the riddle of color term salience. *Ethnology* 17: 287–311.

Bolton, R., A. Curtis, and L. Thomas 1980. Nepali color terms: salience on a listing task. *Journal of the Steward Anthropological Society* 12: 309–322.

Boynton, R. M., R. E. MacLaury, and K. Uchikawa 1989. Centroids of color categories compared by two methods. *Color Research and Application* 14: 6–15.

Carroll, J. B., P. Davies, and B. Richman 1971. *Word Frequency Book*. Boston: Houghton Mifflin/American Heritage.

Farmer, E. W., R. M. Taylor, and A. J. Belyavin 1980. Large color differences and the geometry of Munsell color space. *Journal of the Optical Society of America* 70: 243–245.

Francis, J., and F. Kucera 1982. *American Heritage Word Frequency Book*. New York: American Heritage.

Hays, D. G., E. Margolis, R. Naroll, and D. R. Perkins 1972. Color term salience. *American Anthropologist* 74: 1107–1121.

Kay, P., and W. Kempton 1984. What is the Sapir–Whorf hypothesis? *American Anthropologist* 86(1): 65–79.

Kay, P., and C. K. McDaniel 1978. The linguistic significance of the meanings of basic color terms. *Language* 54(3): 610–646.

Kay, P., B. Berlin, and W. R. Merrifield 1991. Biocultural implications of systems of color naming. *Journal of Linguistic Anthropology* 1(1): 12–25.

Kobayashi, S. 1974. *Nihon-jin no Kokoro to Iro* [The Japanese Heart and Color]. Tokyo: Kodansha.
      1990. *Color Image Scale*. Tokyo: Kodansha.

Kokuritsu Kokugo Kenkyuujo [Japanese National Language Research Institute] 1964. *Gendai Zasshi Kyuujusshu no Yooji Yoogo* [The Vocabulary and Chinese Characters of Ninety Magazines of Today]. Tokyo: Shuuei Shuppan.
      1971–1974. *Denki-keisanki ni yoru Shimbun no Goi Choosa* [Studies on the Vocabulary of Modern Newspapers]. Vols. I–IV. Tokyo: Shuuei Shuppan.

MacLaury, R. E. 1992. From brightness to hue: an explanatory model of color-category evolution. *Current Anthropology* 33: 137–186.

Stanlaw, J. 1987. Colors, culture, and contact: English loanwords and problems of color nomenclature in modern Japanese. Ph.D. dissertation, University of Illinois at Urbana-Champaign.
      1992a. "For beautiful human life": the use of English in Japan. In J. Tobin (ed.) *Re-made in Japan: Everyday Life and Consumer Taste in a Changing Society* (pp. 58–76). New Haven: Yale University Press.
      1992b. English in Japanese communicative strategies. In B. Kachru, (ed.) *The Other Tongue: English Across Cultures* (pp. 168–197). Urbana: University of Illinois Press.

Uchikawa, K., and R. M. Boynton 1987. Categorical color perception of Japanese observers: comparison with that of Americans. *Vision Research* 27(10): 1825–1833.

12 Skewing and darkening: dynamics of the cool category

Robert E. MacLaury

Introduction

How to demonstrate briefly my means of modeling color categorization? First, I review how category mapping procedures improve data. Next, I sketch a particular model and its rationale. Then, I display and discuss correspondences between different data, such as those between category mapping configurations and focus placements, that suggest how neurally grounded sensations and selective attention upon them may dynamically constitute a color category. Last, I appeal to this framework for an explanation of differences in the aggregate patterns of foci chosen for the so-called "cool" category by speakers of Mesoamerican languages versus speakers of languages elsewhere throughout the world. The cool category, which encompasses pure green and pure blue, is widespread among languages. Data derive from my Mesoamerican Color Survey (MCS) and the World Color Survey (WCS) of Kay, Berlin, and Merrifield (1991a, 1991b; Kay, Berlin, Maffi, and Merrifield this volume).[1]

Equipment for the MCS was generously supplied by Kay, Berlin, and Merrifield after they ended their WCS. It consists of 330 loose randomized chips plus a miniature version of them affixed to a flat, rectangular array with green near the center. This display orders chips by their positions within the spectrum, breaking its continuous band among reds at each end. I added a red-centered array so that the artificial break would not influence subject response involving reddish categories. Most elicitations took place in shade near sun, a few at night under a 100-watt incandescent bulb. Subjects were interviewed one at a time without help or interjection by onlookers. As was done in the WCS, I solicited a name for each loose chip one after another and, with an array, a focus for each name. Each volunteer understood that any name could designate many chips. As an improvement, I requested him or her to map the range of each name volunteered, saying "Put a grain of rice on every chip of this array that you can name X." When the individual stopped mapping, I would say "Put rice on those that you can still name X," and so on, often through several pauses and repeated requests, until the person could not justify including more colors in the range. I recorded this information step by step, then swept the array clean before asking for a mapping of another term. Three independently elicited sets of data resulted: (a) root names and, often added to them, their qualifiers; (b) foci, mostly one and rarely two or more per name; (c) mappings, sometimes completed in a single step but usually in two or more. I based my analyses of individual color category systems on relations between these kinds of data, never favoring one kind. I compared aggregates of data between populations, for example color category mappings by Tzeltal Mayan versus Tzotzil Mayan speakers (MacLaury 1991: 54–55), or the foci of continuously mapped cool categories versus those of disjunctively mapped categories (shown below). I attempted to model numerically significant patterns and differences between patterns.

How do mappings assist the interpretation of data?

Figure 12.1 displays naming ranges and foci elicited from an English speaker with the loose chips and the arrays.[2] The names are derandomized and diagrammed as hatchings in the format of the green-centered array. Each letter–number intersection of the display represents a separate color chip (see MacLaury 1987a, note 2, for a key relating these chips to their Munsell specifications). Foci are represented as ⊕. The categories of red, yellow, green, and blue include,

Figure 12.1 Naming ranges and foci in American English.

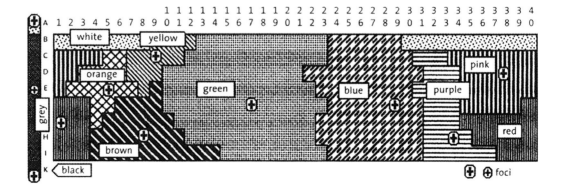

respectively, a unique hue that crosscuts them from light to dark in columns 1, 9, 17, and 29. Further, each of their four foci pinpoints a maximally vivid color in the unique-hue column, collectively called "elemental hues": G1, C9, F17, and F29.[3] Foci also fall on the lightest and darkest achromatic chips, Ao (unnumbered left column) and Ko, which I call "elemental white" and "elemental black." The foci of grey (Eo), orange (E5), brown (H8), purple (H34), and pink (D38) land on colors that show even mixtures of two or three of the six "elemental color points," hereby applying the word "color" to all hues, to white and black, and to combinations. This particular English speaker behaved deceptively "well," placing his foci on the perceptually salient colors. Most speakers, of either English or any other language, will not demonstrate such a tight fit between perception and focus choice. Thus, the elemental color points cannot be called "focal colors," as has been the practice (Heider 1971).[4]

Tzeltal naming ranges are shown in the upper halves of Figures 12.2–12.3, mappings in the lower. Mappings of black-focused *ʔihk'* and of blue- or green-focused *yaš* are depicted as bars that cross the cells representing every chip mapped for each term. Numbers that segment

Figure 12.2 Tzeltal, Tenejapa, Mexico, f. 60, 1980: (a) naming ranges and foci, (b) mappings.

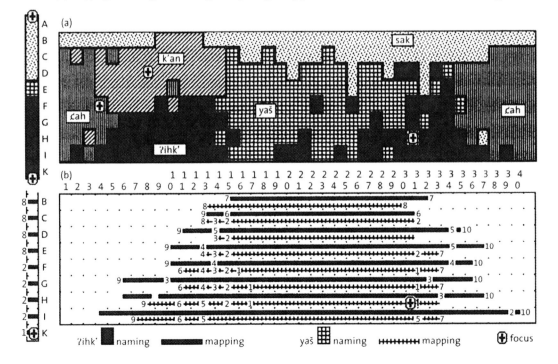

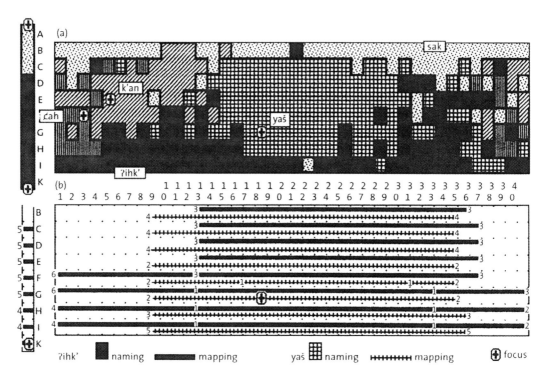

Figure 12.3 Tzeltal, Tenejapa, Mexico, m. 65, 1980: (a) naming ranges and foci, (b) mappings.

or frame the bars mark mapping steps. This bar display shows the overlap of ranges. Both Tzeltal speakers name as *?ihk'*chips near elemental green F17 and elemental blue F29 but not these hues themselves, which merely suggests that *?ihk'* names a dark–cool category (of black, green, and blue). The mappings support this hypothesis, however, by showing that the range of *?ihk'* encompasses all of black, green, and blue as well as the green and blue range of *yaš*, even though *yaš* is used abundantly. Six of the twelve Tzeltal interviewed mapped *?ihk'* in this way, which indicates the dark–cool category persists among them. It is worth noting that Tzeltal speaker 2 (i.e., of Figure 12.2) focused *yaš* at H30 in blue–purple and speaker 3 (of Figure 12.3) focused *yaš* at G18 in green. Chip H30 is the darker of the two and is on the outside of unique-blue column 29; G18 is the lighter and on the inside of unique-green column 17 – "inside" meaning between these two unique hues. This pattern within the cool category of a darker, polarized blue focus versus a lighter, more central green focus instantiates quantitative patterns analyzed below.[5]

A cognitive model

A particular model of categorization, "vantage theory," provides a hypothesis of how the "overt" organization of any color category results from a "covert" interplay of neurally grounded perception and a mode of cognition called "selective emphasis" (cf. MacLaury 1995, 1997). Certain perceptions are emphasized while others are ignored. The specific selections can differ from language to language. Whatever is selected may be emphasized to some flexible degree of strength. Overt organization consists of directly observable responses to the Munsell chips, such as the extent of a naming range, the position of its focus, or the characteristics of its mapping. Covert organization – its relations and dynamics – entails the surface behavior and, therefore, may be deduced from the surface and used to make further predictions about it, which, in turn, may falsify the projected scheme. However, the underlying relations and dynamics are never directly observable. The full deduction is my vantage model, which proposes that a category is covertly organized by analogy to a point of view in space and time.

Unlike other claims that linguistic categorization is based on spatial imagery (Lyons 1977: 18–24; Langacker 1987), vantage theory holds that the analogy between space–time and a category is conducted on the level of coordinates: the different selections that compose the category are analogies to the coordinates that constitute a physical point of view. In real terrain, people may reckon their own positions by taking into account multiple coordinates, but, probably, they concentrate on only two coordinates at a time. One of them will constitute a ground or stationary backdrop, a "fixed coordinate," while the other will be treated as a figure or highlighted item as though it were in motion – if, indeed, it is not actually moving – a "mobile coordinate." Moreover, the coordinate that is forefronted can subsequently be backgrounded or even pushed into the realm of presuppositions, whereas background and even presuppositions can be promoted to the position of a figure. To accommodate these likelihoods, I have arranged multiple coordinates hierarchically in my model of color categorization. As in space–time, people store multiple coordinates as presuppositions and access them directly by moving their attention up or down the hierarchy by processes that I call "zooming." People "zoom

in" by converting a mobile coordinate to a fixed status and by calling
to the fore a new mobile coordinate; they "zoom out" by reversing the
process. Presuppositions stand apart from a fixed-and-mobile coordinate pair in that they constitute the levels of the zooming hierarchy
that, at any given moment, are not concentrated upon, although these
roles will be shuffled when a person zooms in or out. To give a plain
example, "The newspaper is on the living room table" requires the pre-
supposition of a house design within which to locate the living room
that, in turn, acts as the fixed coordinate against which to locate the
table that, in turn and on the most concentrated level of zooming,
becomes the fixed coordinate in reference to which the newspaper
is spotted. At this final point, the living room too has faded back to
presuppositional status.

In an ordinary hue category, such as cool, the coordinates are (a)
the elemental color-points and (b) the reciprocally balanced emphases
on the similarity and the difference that pertain between the points.
The undeniable contribution to categorization made by attention to
similarity and attention to difference has been researched by Medin,
Goldstone, and Gentner (1990, 1993). However, they note a problem:
for such attentions to pertain within a category, some absolute frame
of reference is required in order to specify degrees of similarity and
difference, as these judgments are but relative points on a vast scale
that would range from unity to disparity (Goodman 1972). Further,
the judgments of similarity and difference are not opposites: subjects
look for relations when judging similarity whereas they seek attributes when assessing difference. Any model of categorization must
provide the frame and incorporate the asymmetries.

Judgments of similarity and difference are analogous to relative
velocities because both experiences occur on an axis between end-
points and both afford degrees, the former as increments of emphasis
and the latter as rates of speed whose zero-pole stands still. Inherently
fixed things, such as elemental color-points or physical landmarks,
likewise are comparable. It is of interest, then, how separate observers,
one on a moving train and one on the ground and standing, will
behold the trajectory of an object dropped from the train as straight
versus parabolic, respectively. Although the two observers share the
fixed reference of up–down, front–back, and right–left, their vantages
differ in accord with degree of motion. In the same way, a category

Figure 12.4 (a) The cool category constructed as inverse arrangements of coordinates by analogy to the method with which people construct vantages in space–time. (b) The basic green and basic blue categories constructed in reference to separate coordinate sets; attention to distinctiveness is strong and attention to similarity is weak, while a coordinate of darkness reinforces each set.

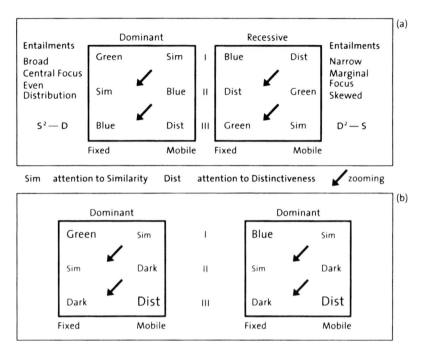

encompassing one definitive set of elemental color points will, nevertheless, assume a different size and shape when, on separate occasions, it is regarded in reference to perceptions of similarity and difference that are allotted distinct balances of attention.

Figure 12.4a models a cool category, such as that of Tzeltal, which may be focused in reference to either green or blue but with the green focus somewhat central and the blue focus polarized. Respectively, I call these views "dominant" and "recessive." Taking the dominant slant, elemental green is the "preferred" fixed point of reference; it is on the first and most preferred "level of concentration." Attention to similarity is coordinated with green, which entails a broad overt range when the attention is strong. On the second level of concentration, with attention to similarity established as background, elemental blue is coordinated with it. This entails that the range will overtly encompass blue rather than another elemental color, such as yellow; that is, the category will encompass cool colors rather than the ethnographically attested range of green-with-yellow (MacLaury 1987a: Figures. 1–3). On the third level, with blue established, attention to difference – or, as I shall refer to it, distinctiveness – is coordi-

nated with it. This entails that the overt range will be limited to green
and blue and will not extend further through the color space, as
indeed some categories do (MacLaury 1992: Figures. 14–17). A category,
then, consists of the manifest entailments of perceptual and cognitive
coordinates by which a mental point of view is constructed by analogy
to coordinates of a spatiotemporal point of view.

In this example, at least so far, the preferred fixed coordinate of
elemental green determines that the vantage point will be anchored
closer to green than to blue and membership values within the category will skew at least somewhat towards this point. Since attention
to similarity and attention to distinctiveness are both mobile coordinates on one or another level, the balance of the strength at which
they are emphasized can be shifted between them. Increased emphasis
on distinctiveness will contract the category range towards the vantage point until the range no longer encompasses blue. This will
divide the category. Division will advance gradually and will be
accompanied by progressively greater skewing towards green. The
organization of the category will always be determined by the tension
between coordinates, not exclusively by the location of elemental
hues. Thus, for example, the focus of the category may be placed
between green and blue – although closer to green – when attention
to similarity is emphasized most, or the focus may be placed between
green and the category margin when attention to distinctiveness
becomes very strong. This model offers an account of the skewing
and the dynamics of the cool category that have been observed in
many languages.

As shown in Figure 12.4[a], the recessive vantage is composed in
reference to the same coordinates of elemental green, elemental blue,
and attention to similarity and distinctiveness at reciprocal strengths.
But the coordinates are arranged in reverse order, with blue and distinctiveness at first preference. The opposite orders affect the shape
and size of the cool category. Whereas, from the dominant vantage,
similarity (S) is considered at two levels and distinctiveness (D) at one
level within the hierarchy of zooming, from the recessive vantage, distinctiveness is considered twice and similarity once. The doubling of
presuppositions may have a multiplicative effect on these inherently
quantitative coordinates, expressible as S^2-D for the dominant view
versus D^2-S for the recessive view. When regarded as S^2-D, the cool cat-

egory assumes a broader range and a more central focus, because reinforced attention to similarity induces the observer to represent all stimuli evenly and equally and to contract conceptual distance between them so as to fit more colors in the purview of the vantage. When regarded as $D^{2-}S$, the cool category assumes a narrower range and a more marginal focus, because bolstered attention to distinctiveness encourages the observer to protract distance between stimuli and, consequently, to polarize favored colors against the rest as well as to calibrate into scope fewer colors at a time.

Unlike attention to similarity or distinctiveness, coordinates of elemental green or blue harbor zero multiplicative powers because both of these hues reach an unsurpassable ceiling of perceived purity. For this reason they are inherently fixed coordinates; they are qualitative rather than quantitative, of limited leeway rather than points on a sweeping continuum. Notwithstanding, each steadfast hue can be treated as mobile by foregrounding it at the middle level of the zooming hierarchy; but double consideration of an elemental color on two levels of zooming cannot augment its vividness beyond its physiologically set maximum.

This model provides four benefits. First, it specifies how observers actively engage with the categories that they create, maintain, and modify. It stipulates that color categories are windows on a sensory realm that people construct by the same process by which they keep their bearings in physical terrain. It suggests that this analogy may have been a key ingredient in the primordial formulation of human-type categories that enabled hominids millions of years ago to develop rudimentary language and culture and, thereby, to take the first step on the path of evolution from which *Homo sapiens* eventually emerged. Second, the model provides the propellant of category change – as when covering a domain anew with more finely discriminating categories – which would occur when an individual emphasizes distinctiveness while deemphasizing similarity. Probably a person is impelled to actuate this shift by external events that call for increased analysis as a prevalent routine. Rapidly changing environs, social complications, persistent danger, or growing hardship may call for the mental change as a requirement of survival. Third, a vantage constructed as a system of coordinates provides the closed frame of reference within which judgments of similarity and distinctiveness can

balance against each other. A vantage is a small slice of worldly
possibilities that excludes all but selected points along a grand scale,
such as the continuum between unity and disparity in the case of
categorization, or between the speed of light and inertness in the case
of space–time. The vantage model addresses the cognitive psychological question of what frame of reference would justify including constrained judgments of similarity and difference in category theory, as
perforce must be the case. Fourth, dominant and recessive views constructed as S^2–D versus D^2–S foreordain that judgments of similarity
versus distinctiveness will be asymmetrically opposed and never perfect opposites, as Medin and his colleagues attest (1990). However, the
vantage hypothesis further stipulates that any such judgment must be
constructed as either S^2–D or D^2–S, never by equal measures of S and
D, because it is inescapably an act of categorization from a specific
point of view. Thus, perfect opposites are latently impossible in the
two kinds of comparison.

Strong numerical correlations have thwarted my attempts to falsify the vantage model of color categorization. I conducted the first
test against the coextensive naming ranges of warm (red-with-yellow)
categories from 6 Mayan languages (MacLaury 1987b). Semantic
coextension occurs when the dominant and recessive arrangements of
one set of coordinates are named separately. Each term is focused in
reference to an opposite elemental color point but its range encompasses the contrary color point. Their mappings progress step by step
in converse directions. Usually, the dominant range is named on more
chips, focused more centrally, and mapped over more chips with steps
of larger average size; the recessive range shows lower numbers on all
4 counts. In categories that have advanced in the division process, the
pattern begins to break down such that the correspondence may pertain in 3 of the 4 characteristics. A category proffering 2 such failures
does not show the dominant–recessive pattern and, thus, counts as 4
failures. Of the 20 coextensively named warm categories for which I
had collected full data, there were 80 characteristics of potential correspondence with a null hypothesis of 40 successes and 40 failures.
The data showed 65 successes ($p<.01$ chi square). The pattern was not
conditioned by perceptual neurology, as some dominant warm ranges
were focused in reference to red and others in reference to yellow.
Moreover, red- or yellow-dominance did not appear to have been

learned at the level of village society, as red-dominant and yellow-
dominant adults had grown up together and lived as neighbors. Next,
I tested the hypothesis of dominant–recessive patterning against all
coextensively named categories of the WCS (MacLaury 1996, forthcoming). As these data include only naming ranges and foci, I asked
whether the largest coextensive naming range between each pair
would have the most central focus, finding success-to-failure ratios
such as cool 154:107 (p<.01) and warm 31:12 (p<.01).[6] The WCS test
shows that the dominant–recessive pattern is found worldwide. It
seems to manifest an innate method by which people everywhere construct color categories; using the analogy of spatiotemporal coordinates may be an instinctive means of constituting categories. This
method may be employed within many domains, color categories
supplying only the original test.

Another line of evidence is the sequence of semantic relations
that transpires when a color category named with two terms divides:
near synonymy → dominant–recessive coextensivity → inclusion →
complementation (MacLaury 1992: 141–142). Always the recessive
range retracts to its focus before the dominant range does so, leaving
the latter to encompass the former. Finally the dominant range
retracts to become one in a pair of independent complementary
ranges that only overlap at their edges. Coextensive ranges seldom
pull apart symmetrically as, say, an amoeba would divide. Advanced
division of a color category with dual names exaggerates its dominant–recessive pattern, except that, during the phase of inclusion,
foci polarize randomly in response to the stronger overall emphasis
on distinctiveness that drives the separation (MacLaury 1992: Figures
3–4). Other evidence concerns the relationship between foci and
mapping configurations, some of which is exemplified below.

Comparing populations: correlation of foci
and mapping configurations

Like any model that does its job, vantage theory accounts for pat-
terned differences between ways in which independently elicited data
are related; such differences characterize separate populations. In the
two cases reviewed here, data consist of aggregated foci and configurations of mapping steps. The latter demonstrate further how mappings

contribute to building a model of categorization. Populations to be compared are (a) foci of cool categories showing distinct strategies of mapping, and (b) foci of nonbasic versus basic cool categories. Correlations imply specific processes of category change.

Foci and mappings

Figures 12.5 and 12.6 contrast continuous versus disjunctive mappings of the cool category. Figure 12.5 shows that a continuous mapping covers both unique hues and turquoise with its first step, while Figure 12.6 shows that a disjunctive mapping does not; another kind of disjunctive mapping covers both green and blue unequally with a first step that, nevertheless, excludes turquoise (Burgess, Kempton, and MacLaury 1983: Figure 7). Sample sizes of mappings are modest because some interviewers skipped this procedure.

Figure 12.7 represents distributions of Mesoamerican cool-category foci across Munsell columns, each of which provides a histogram cell. (For example, in Figure 12.7a, different individuals focused in total 15 chips in column 17, some choosing the same chip; each choice of a chip counts as one.) Focus-distribution (a) pertains to the cool categories mapped continuously, distribution (b) to cool

Figure 12.5 K'ekchi, Lanquín, Guatemala, m 30, 1980: (a) naming ranges and foci, (b) continuous mapping.

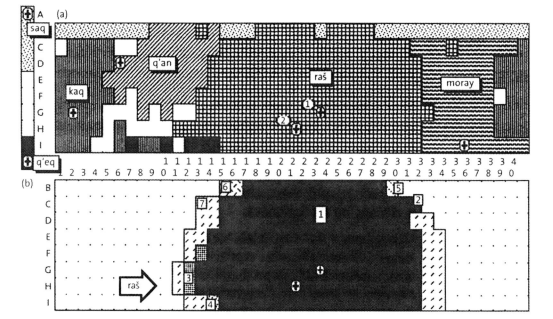

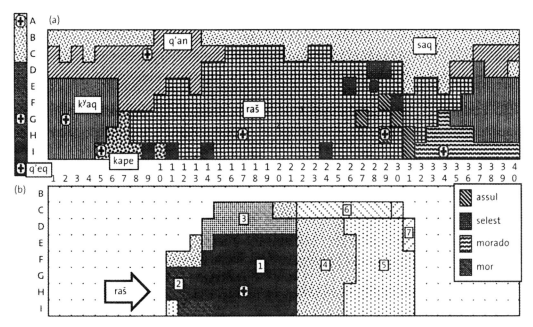

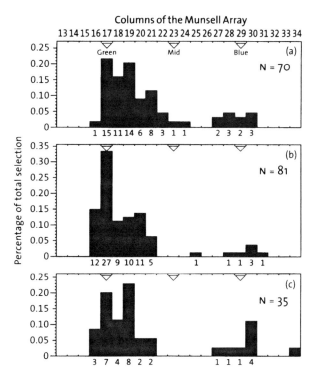

Figure 12.6 Quiché, Momostenango, Guatemala, m 29, 1980: (a) naming ranges and foci, (b) disjunctive mapping.

Figure 12.7 Frequency distributions of foci across hue (prismatic color) in Mesoamerican cool categories: (a) continuously mapped, (b) disjunctively mapped and basic, (c) continuously mapped and nonbasic.

categories mapped disjunctively. Distribution (a) is more centered while (b) is more skewed (p<.01 Pearson chi-square independence test). According to vantage theory, the correspondence between a continuous mapping and a central focus is produced by strong emphasis on similarity while the correspondence of a disjunctive mapping and a marginal focus occurs when the emphasis on distinctiveness is enhanced. Thus, choices of foci are not purely responses to perception of unique hues or elemental hues but are guided by a tension between hue perception and selective emphasis on similarity and distinctiveness. Vantage theory models this relation as one that pertains between coordinates of an analogous point of view, as in Figure 12.4a. Skewing progresses because a viewpoint is planted on one side of the category with one elemental color point as a preferred fixed coordinate. Increased emphasis on distinctiveness retracts the range of the category – the purview of the vantage – towards this viewpoint, until it no longer encompasses the opposite elemental color.

Foci of nonbasic versus basic categories

Figure 12.7c displays the distribution of foci for Mesoamerican nonbasic cool categories that were included in the range of a dark–cool category and mapped continuously, exemplified by Figures 12.2–12.3. This may be compared with the distribution of foci for cool categories mapped disjunctively, Figure 12.7b, all but two of which are basic.[7] If ever there was a difference between nonbasic and basic cool categories, these two extremes would reveal it. For example, do cool categories well-advanced in their division yield a greater proportion of foci in green than do cool categories whose division is incipient at best? Taking column 23 as the divide between green and blue (see Figure 12.7; cf. Kay and Kempton 1984: 68–69), nonbasic, continuously mapped, cool-category foci occur on either side of the divide at a ratio of 29 green to 9 blue, while basic disjunctively mapped categories show 74:7. The difference is weakly significant (p < .05 binomial proportion Z score: critical value 1.96; Z value 2.24476). The numbers suggest that greater emphasis on distinctiveness encourages placement of foci in green.

Why is green the preferred point of reference among most of the languages that name green and blue with one term? In Berlin and

Kay's (1969) universal order of color-term evolution, red is the first hue to be named as such; its name is added to terms for light and dark. David Miller (personal communication 1993) observes synchronic preferences for red over other colors among subjects of his experiments; for example, they usually guess reddish meanings for color terms unfamiliar to them. Green is the antagonist of red. This opposition is processed earlier in the post-retinal pathway than the contrast of yellow and blue (Albright 1991). Probably green presents a stronger point of opponency with neighboring red than does blue with red or blue with yellow; green most distinctively defines the cool category.[8] Perhaps this is the reason why – in languages that ambivalently focus the cool category or in languages that originally focus it in blue – speakers commonly shift the focus to the green side of the cool category as it approaches a full division; as distinctiveness is increasingly emphasized, the opposition of cool and red categories becomes more notable to the observer. This explanation requires a perceptual basis and a cognitive process. What an individual deems to be important about color stems from the relation between the two, which is subject to regular change. An alternative account is that Mesoamerican languages shift foci because widespread custom prescribes this maneuver at precisely the transition from nonbasic to basic, which, however, is not likely to be the kind of event that would be noticed, rewarded, and diffused.

Mesoamerican and worldwide focus aggregates

Figure 12.8 contrasts the aggregates of cool-category foci from (a) Mesoamerica and (d) the non-Mesoamerican WCS languages. The figure further contrasts the focus-aggregates of green categories and blue categories from (b) Mesoamerica and (c) WCS elsewhere. The MCS foci of (b) exclude those of blue or green categories attested to be included by a cool category and, thereby, to be nonbasic.[9] But basic versus nonbasic status is impossible to distinguish in certain cases. For example, two categories whose naming ranges appear entirely separate as chip-responses plotted on Munsell format may remain cognitively linked in the manner diagrammed in Figure 12.4a such that they retain a dominant–recessive focus contrast between them (MacLaury 1992: Figure 5, younger Sacapultec speaker). True basicness

276 Robert E. MacLaury

Figure 12.8 Focus aggregates of all Mesoamerican (a) cool categories and (b) basic green and basic blue categories, left and right respectively, and of all WCS non-Mesoamerican (c) cool categories and (d) green and blue categories, left and right respectively, whether basic or nonbasic.

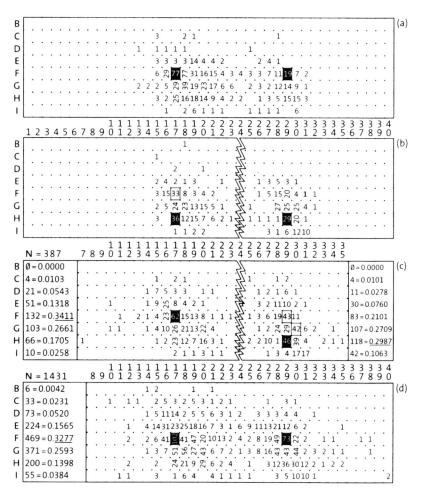

requires for each category a separate selection and autonomous arrangement of coordinates, as diagrammed in Figure 12.4b. So surely nonbasic categories are inadvertently represented in the aggregate of Figure 12.8b. Figure 12.8c includes the foci of all green and blue categories of the WCS regardless of status, since lack of mappings in the WCS further impedes differentiation of basic and nonbasic. In the figure, numbers indicate total selections of each chip as a focus; any selection covering more than two contiguous chips has been excluded. Open boxes frame high numbers while highest numbers are marked against dark background. Highest numbers within the cool category (a, d) occur on the elemental hue points, F17 and F29, while most of the highest numbers within green or blue categories (b–c) occur on a darker unique-hue value.

Figure 12.8 shows four patterns that call for an account. (i) Mesoamerican cool categories (a) show a significantly higher preference for a focus in green than do the cool categories of languages elsewhere (d): highest numbers contrast by ratios of (a) 77:19 versus (d) 102:73. (ii) Mesoamerican foci darken when green and blue are – so it seems – categorized separately (b), whereas (iii) foci from elsewhere darken in blue but not in green as part of their apparent separate categorization (c). (iv) Green foci are universally more resistant to darkening than are blue foci, as shown by (b) the high number of 33 at a middle-value green versus a highest number of 36 at a dark value in Mesoamerican languages, and as shown by (c) a singular highest number of 62 at middle-value green in languages elsewhere. The difference between (ii) and (iii) may have been enhanced by my (less than successful) effort to include foci from only basic categories in Figure 12.8b, although this does not discredit the cognitive validity of patterns. Whatever their circumstances, they would be induced by different attentions to similarity and distinctiveness.

The vantage model accounts for observations (i–iv) as follows:

(i) Perhaps speakers of Mesoamerican languages face faster culture change than do speakers of many other surveyed languages, which would enhance emphasis on distinctiveness in Mesoamerica and, thus, foster a tendency to favor green in keeping with the hypothesis of its maximal contrast with red (expressed above). "Tendency" allows that some languages will focus the cool category in blue regardless of concurrent processes, as in Figure 12.7b–c and in keeping with the attendant weak statistic. Every indigenous group of Mexico and Guatemala is now in the orbit of these nation states whereas in areas of Africa, South America, and Asia the assimilation of native people into national mainstreams may have progressed less.

(ii) The cells of Figure 12.9 are Munsell value rows; they depict distributions of foci from light to dark in (a) Mesoamerican cool categories (from Figure 12.8a) and (b) Mesoamerican basic green and basic blue categories combined (from Figure 12.8b). The foci of basic green and basic blue are darker than those of the cool category ($p = .00000$ Pearson chi-square independence test). Figure 12.4 depicts some of these dynamics, wherein (b) may be compared with (a). Foci darken as

Figure 12.9 Frequency distributions of foci across Value (light to dark) in Mesoamerican (a) cool categories and (b) basic green and basic blue categories combined (from data in Figure 12.8).

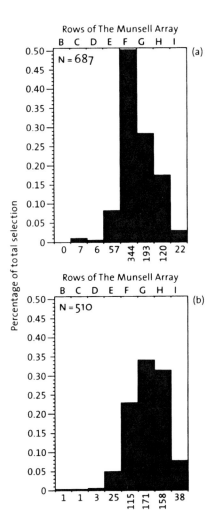

emphasis on distinctiveness increases to a strength that causes the cool category to divide into basic categories of green versus blue. Emphasis on similarity simultaneously and commensurably weakens. The weakening creates a felt need to reinforce the vantage by adding a coordinate of Darkness. Darkness is preferred over Lightness because – possibly – elemental green and elemental blue look more like black than like white.[10] Single systems exemplifying dark foci are seen in Uspantec Mayan and French (MacLaury 1992: Figure 5) and Tzeltal (MacLaury 1991: Figure 8).

    (iii) Outside Mesoamerica, foci darken more in blue than in green because elemental blue is most likely to be the preferred coordinate of the recessive vantage, as addressed by explanation (i). Two kinds of relation between coordinates could darken the blue focus while leaving the green focus at middle value. First, an individual may preserve the cool category from both green and blue viewpoints in spite of what his or her naming ranges seem to show on the surface. In this case, a pair of green and blue vantages remain covertly linked in the manner diagrammed in Figure 12.4a. As the recessive vantage is constructed as D^2–S, the weakening of attention to similarity will occur within the recessive vantage earliest, requiring reinforcement with a darkness coordinate only from that perspective. The blue focus will darken as S weakens and will polarize as D^2 gains strength. Or second, the cool category endures as long as colors are regarded from the dominant green vantage, although blue is constructed as a separate category when thought of from its own angle. The blue vantage does not (any longer) incorporate a green coordinate, taking the arrangement shown on the right in Figure 12.4b. The blue focus both will darken and will polarize in response to preponderant emphasis on unitary D. Both of these accounts accord with explanation (ii).

(iv) The dominant vantage is universally slow to develop a darkened focus because it will persist as a cool category after the recessive vantage has retracted to one elemental hue. Usually the preferred coordinate of the dominant vantage is elemental green, especially after category division has advanced substantially, as addressed under (i). At this time, the dominant naming range may not be evident among blue colors, even though this vantage covertly includes elemental blue. The dominant vantage will continue to be constituted as S^2–D and, thus, will be unlikely to require reinforcement as long as an increasing attention to difference (D) does not outweigh the multiplicative strength of attention to similarity (S^2). Although the latter may be on the wane, it must weaken beyond a critical threshold before a reinforcing coordinate of darkness may be wanted. If and when this happens, the green focus will darken, as is occurring among the Mesoamerican green-category foci in Figure 12.9b. The critical threshold may coincide with complete disappearance of the cool category whose retracting range will henceforth apply only to a basic category of green, overtly and covertly, as on the left in Figure 12.4b.

Summary

The objective here has been to demonstrate uses of a vantage theory in modeling color categorization. Implications of this model for cognitive science are developed elsewhere (MacLaury 1995, 1996). Among them are the active engagement of observers with their categories, the thrust behind category change, the frame of reference that would specify how attention to similarity and difference contribute to categorization, the reason for asymmetry judgments, and the dogged recurrence of spatial tropes in the language of category description. Suffice it to state for present purposes that vantage theory ties together observations of color categories into a coherent hypothesis when other theories of categorization, such as classical logic (Whitehead and Russell 1910–1913), fuzzy-set logic (Kay and McDaniel 1978), or the prototype concept (Rosch 1977), cannot do this.

Three general observations are sketched above. (a) A dominant–recessive pattern characterizes both coextensive naming of color categories and foci of the categories that include more than one elemental color point, even when the categories are named by a single term, as the Tzeltal designate the cool category. (b) Such singly named categories of two elemental colors skew when they divide; the focus moves to a margin while the range retracts towards it. (c) Upon this division, foci darken. Other events are peculiar to cool categories or to basic categories of blue vis à vis green, such as the incremental favoring of green as division progresses or the darkening of blue foci prior to green foci.

In overview, organization and process are inseparable within a category. Any worthy model of categorization must come to terms with the timing of events as part and parcel of the patterns that momentary experiments may record.

Notes

1 In a short chapter I can only highlight the model piecemeal while ignoring most of what it is and what it does. See MacLaury (1997) for book-length treatment.

2 The Munsell color solid consists of eleven levels of value or "rows," not ten as used here. Use of the ten in anthropology was established by Lenneberg and Roberts (1956), who eliminated Munsell Value 1/ or the second darkest row, the missing "J" between the rows that I label "I" and "K," probably because its chips were harder to distinguish than, say, those of its light counterpart, Munsell Value 9/ or "row B."

3 Collier *et al.* (1976), after leveling the Munsell array to

only Chroma /2, found that English speakers preferred to place foci at the same hue and value coordinates that, during Berlin and Kay's (1969: Fig. 5) experiment, speakers of twenty languages most often chose in response to uneven Chroma of the maximally saturated array. Thus, Chroma (or saturation) does not determine the location of elemental hues. The determinant has never been objectively expressed so as to improve upon my calling the hues "maximally vivid" and "perceptually salient."

4 "Elemental hues" follows Miller and Wooten (1990) for red, yellow, green, and blue, although "elemental color points" is my own. Johnson-Laird (1983: 344) calls these six points "the landmark colors." "Pure" or "primary colors" are alternatives. Lack of match between elemental color points and foci is exemplified by Figure 12.8a–d, although in (a), in the green half of (c), and in (d), the highest number of foci coincides with elemental green and blue. MCS and WCS foci also show such pluralities for G1 red, C9 yellow, Ao white, and Ko black (MacLaury forthcoming).

5 MacLaury (1986: Fig. 8.52a; 1997: Fig. 8.43a) demonstrates statistical significance for this pattern in Tzeltal.

6 Without mappings, many pairs of coextensive ranges in the WCS will remain unidentified, which is why the WCS yielded only 43 coextensively named warm categories while the much smaller MCS shows 20 among its full descriptions alone (MacLaury 1987b), 22 after hair-splitting scrutiny (MacLaury 1997, Table 6.1). As a case in point, MacLaury (1992: Figures 3–4) depicts ranges and mappings of four Tzeltal coextensively composed warm categories, whose coextension is affirmed by the eight mappings. But naming ranges prove coextension in none of them; the strictest proof would require each naming range to reach, if not surpass, both elemental red and elemental yellow at G1 and C9. For example, the present Figure 12.3 shows one of these four categories, named *çah* and *k'an*. By any criteria *k'an* manifests a warm range but *çah*, which names elemental red, does not name yellow beyond C8. (MacLaury [forthcoming] allows that an application of dual terms to or beyond both G2 and C8 will establish coextensivity among warm colors, because the second highest numbers of WCS warm-category foci occur at G2 and C8 while these numbers are almost twice as high as any that are lower and they are nearly as high as those of G1 and C9. By this looser valuation, *çah* and *k'an* of Tzeltal speaker 3 qualify as coextensive even without their mappings, whereas *çah* and *k'an* of Tzeltal 2 still do not.) The WCS ratio of 154:107 pertains to 227 coextensively named cool categories; as 34 are named with 3 terms, there are 261 coextensive relations. The ratio of 31:12 pertains to 41 warm categories, among

which one is named with triple coextension. Ratios enumerate whatever coextensive relations obtain rather than always one relation per category.

In the WCS, among both its Mesoamerican and non-Mesoamerican languages, there are 460 warm categories and 1,535 cool categories. Of the former, 41 (8.9%), and of the latter, 227 (14.8%) are named coextensively. Among equivalent data that I collected in Mesoamerica, the percentages are higher because mappings reveal more. Pooling all data from both my MCS and the WCS, there are 2,351 publicly accessible warm and cool categories elicited with the 330 Munsell chips, of which 337 (14.3%) are coextensively named or mapped or both (Kay, Berlin, and Merrifield 1991b; MacLaury 1997, forthcoming). Kay *et al.* (this volume) provide three examples of coextension in their Figure 2.1. Buglere speaker 5 names the warm category coextensively with (*) *moloin(re)* 84 times (+) *dabere* 39 times, focusing *moloinre* between the elemental hues (G1, C9) on E1-5 and *dabere* on elemental red G1-3, which presents a positive case of the more abundantly named range being focused more centrally, that is, the dominant–recessive pattern. Speaker 4 names the cool category coextensively with (@) *lerere* 87 times and (#) *leren* 88 times; as *lerere* is focused at F20 between elemental hues (F17, F29) while *leren* is focused marginally at G31, this case is negative. Speaker 5 also names the cool category coextensively, but with (o) *lejre* and (#) *leren*. The focus of *lejre* is not reported.

7 See MacLaury (1991: Figure 9d) for a rare disjunctive mapping of a non-basic cool category, which might be a recessive coextensive range and which, regardless, occurs under the extraordinary circumstance described therein.

8 I thank David Miller for this idea but alone take responsibility for it.

9 Figure 12.6 exemplifies two of the excluded non-basic blue categories, *asul* focused at H29 and *selest* E28 (whose lexical forms are of Spanish origin). As the cool category divides by retreating towards its focus, innovations such as these take over its forsaken half.

10 I asked participants at the Asilomar conference if middle-value green and blue (Munsell 5/ or my row F) look more like black than white. I asked why, among WCS data, dark–cool categories abound while light–cool categories never occur. No one answered either question. The OSA distances do not include poles of white or black (Boynton and Olson 1987: Figure 5). I suppose, if there were equal jnds (just noticeable differences) between a middle-value point and both white and black, large discriminations would be harder to make among dark colors. See note 4 regarding Lenneberg and Roberts.

References

Albright, T. D. 1991. Color and the integration of motion signals. *Trends in Neuroscience* 14: 266–269.

Berlin, B., and P. Kay 1969. *Basic Color Terms: Their Universality and Evolution*. Berkeley and Los Angeles: University of California Press. 1st paperback edn. 1991, with a bibliography by Luisa Maffi.

Boynton, R. M., and C. X. Olson 1987. Locating basic colors in the OSA space. *Color Research and Application* 12: 94–105.

Burgess, D., W. Kempton, and R. E. MacLaury 1983. Tarahumara color modifiers: category structure presaging evolutionary change. *American Ethnologist* 10: 133–149.

Collier, G. A., *et al.* 1976. Further evidence for universal color categories. *Language* 52: 884–890.

Goodman, N. 1972. Seven strictures on similarity. In N. Goodman (ed.) *Problems and Projects* (pp. 437–447). New York: Bobbs-Merill.

Heider, E. R. 1971. "Focal" color areas and the development of color names. *Developmental Psychology* 4: 447–455.

Johnson-Laird, P. N. 1983. *Mental Models: Towards a Cognitive Science of Language, Inference, and Consciousness*. Cambridge, MA: Harvard University Press.

Kay, P., and W. Kempton 1984. What is the Sapir–Whorf hypothesis? *American Anthropologist* 86(1): 65–79.

Kay, P., and C. McDaniel 1978. The linguistic significance of the meanings of basic color terms. *Language* 54(3): 610–646.

Kay, P., B. Berlin, and W. R. Merrifield 1991a. Biocultural implications of systems of color naming. *Journal of Linguistic Anthropology* 1: 12–25.

    1991b. The World Color Survey. Dallas: International Bookstore. Microfiche.

Langacker, R. W. 1987. *Foundations of Cognitive Grammar*. Vol. I, *Theoretical Prerequisites*. Stanford University Press.

Lenneberg, E. H., and J. M. Roberts 1956. *The Language of Experience: A Study in Methodology*. Indiana University Publications in Anthropology and Linguistics. Memoir 13: supplement to *International Journal of American Linguistics* 22(2). Baltimore: Waverly Press Inc.

Lyons, J. 1977. *Semantics*. 2 vols. Cambridge University Press.

MacLaury, R. E. 1986. Color in Mesoamerica. Vol. I, A theory of composite categorization. Doctoral dissertation. University of California at Berkeley. UMI 8718073.

    1987a. Color-category evolution and Shuswap yellow-with-green. *American Anthropologist* 89: 107–124.

    1987b. Coextensive semantic ranges: different names for distinct vantages of one category. In B Need, E. Schiller, and A Bosch (eds.) *Papers from the 23rd Annual Regional Meeting of the Chicago Linguistic Society*. Vol. I. (pp 268–282).

    1991. Social and cognitive motivations of change: measuring variability in color semantics. *Language* 67: 34–62.

    1992. From brightness to hue: an explanatory model of color-category evolution. *Current Anthropology* 33: 137–186.

    1995. Vantage theory. In J. R. Taylor and R. E. MacLaury (eds.), *Language and the Cognitive Construal of the World* (pp 231–276) Berlin and New York: Mouton de Gruyter.

    1997. *Color and Cognition in Mesoamerican: Constructing Categories as Vantages*. Austin: University of Texas Press.

    forthcoming. The universal pattern of coextensive color naming: categorizing by analogy to points of view in space. Under revision for *Behavioral and Brain Sciences*.

Medin, D., R. Goldstone, and D. Gentner 1990. Similarity involving attributes and relations: judgements of similarity and difference are not inverses. *Psychological Science* 1: 64–67.

    1993. Respects for Similarity. *Psychological Review* 100: 254–278.

Miller, D. L., and B. R. Wooten 1990. The elemental hues of spectral lights, and the occasionally anomalous nature of green. *Investigative Ophthalomology and Visual Science* 31(4): 262.

Rosch, E. 1977. Human categorization. In N. Warren (ed.), *Studies in Cross-Cultural Psychology*. Vol. I (pp.149). London: Academic Press.

Whitehead, A. N., and B. Russell 1910–1913. *Principia Mathematica*. Cambridge University Press.

13 Genes, opsins, neurons, and color categories: closing the gaps

Stephen L. Zegura

Evolution, in the broad sense, is the sequential transformation of a system through time. Any theory of evolution, whether in the physical, biological, or cultural realms, requires units that undergo change through time as well as forces that cause these transformations. Bill Durham, in his recent synthetic tome *Coevolution: Genes, Culture, and Human Diversity* (1991), has suggested that basic color terms represent the best available example of the interactive mode of coevolutionary relationship between genes and culture that he calls "genetic mediation." For Durham, "coevolution" describes the parallel action of cultural selection (i.e., preservation by preference advantage) and Darwinian natural selection (i.e., preservation by survival and reproductive advantage) in the evolution of human phenotypes. "Genetic mediation" is distinguished from four other modes of gene–culture coevolution, designated "cultural mediation," "enhancement," "neutrality," and "opposition," by its reliance on genetic differences as causal for the evolution of cultural differences.

According to Durham (1991), the relevant genotypes in the color term system are those responsible for the pigment-based system of light absorption in the eyes and for the neurophysiological processing of sensory input to the brain. The units of information or functional units of cultural transmission analogous to units of the genetic realm are the descriptive verbal labels for the experience of color. Differences in the cultural fitnesses within a set of color terms would, according to Durham's model, vary as a function of primary developmental values conditioned by genotype frequencies. Durham concludes that an underlying genetic similarity across human populations is responsible for the universal neural structures and functions involved in color vision (i.e., the trichromacy of retinal pigments and the spectral opponency of both retinal ganglion cells and the thalamic cells of the lateral geniculate nucleus). These biologically based pan-human similarities have supposedly acted as a species-wide primary or developmental value filter on the evolving pool of lexical variation in the color domain. The implication, therefore, is that genes are ultimately responsible for the cross-cultural similarity in the semantics of basic color terms uncovered by Berlin and Kay (1969).

Is there any truth to this set of nested conjectures? In fact, is there any evidence for Durham's coevolutionary scenario uniting the realms of genes, brain, and language? In broad terms it posits genes that are responsible for neurological processes which in turn affect the probability of color term usage via primary value cultural selection wherein decisions are governed mainly by developmental values, the representatives of the genes in matters of decision making. The only genetic system involving any of the neural correlates of color vision that we know something about at the molecular level entails the extraordinary work spearheaded by Jeremy Nathans on the retinal photopigment genes. It represents one of the truly noteworthy achievements spawned by the recent technological breakthroughs in molecular genetics, and the story it tells forms the backdrop for the rest of my analysis of Durham's rendering of the ultimate causation of the apparent universality of basic color terms.

In 1986 Nathans, then at Stanford, published two articles in the April 11 issue of *Science* reporting that he had isolated, cloned, and sequenced the genes for the so-called "blue," "green," and "red" photopigments which occur in the corresponding "blue," "green," and "red" cone cells of the retina (Nathans, Thomas, and Hogness 1986; Nathans, Piantanida, Eddy, Shows, and Hogness 1986). More accurately, these three apoproteins known as opsins should be labelled the short-wavelength-sensitive (SWS), middle-wavelength-sensitive (MWS), and long-wavelength-sensitive (LWS) opsins, since they do not really correspond to the sensations of "blue," "green," or "red" when stimulated individually. The actual function of the opsins is to fine-tune the associated chromophore (cis-retinal) to determine its light absorption properties. It is the cis-retinal that actually absorbs the photons, not the opsin component. All of the opsin genes are related to each other as members of a multigene family which includes rhodopsin, the photopigment found in the retinal rod cells. By comparing the amino acid and DNA base sequences of the various opsins it is possible to determine the evolutionary history of this multigene family. Both rhodopsin and the SWS opsin contain 5 exons, while the MWS and

LWS forms each contain 6 exons. It is exon #1 at the 5' end of the gene that has been added in both cases. All pairwise amino acid identity comparisons for the four opsins yield a value of 40–45% except the MWS versus LWS opsin comparison, which exhibits a 96% identity. This 96% identity in amino acid composition between the so-called "red" and "green" opsins is underscored by a 98% identity at the DNA level. Thus, although the four opsins are evolutionarily about equidistant from a presumed primordial opsin-like protein, the MWS and LWS proteins and their corresponding genes are much more closely related evolutionarily. In humans the gene for rhodopsin resides on chromosome #3 (3 q 21 → qter), the SWS opsin gene is on chromosome #7 (7 q 22 → qter), while the MWS and LWS opsin genes lie next to each other near the end of the long arm of the X-chromosome (X q 28).

The gene duplication event that produced the second visual pigment gene locus on the X-chromosome probably occurred sometime after the Platyrrhine–Catarrhine split (approximately 35 to 40 million years ago). All Platyrrhines so far tested have only 1 pigment gene on the X-chromosome, while all Catarrhines except a few dichromats have at least 2. The normal human condition requires 1 LWS opsin gene followed in the downstream or 3' direction by 1 to 3 copies of the MWS opsin gene (Vollrath, Nathans, and Davis 1988). Each of these genes is approximately 15 kilobases long with about 24 kilobases of intergenic DNA between the genes. Nathans has devised a model of unequal homologous crossing-over that accounts for the following phenomena: (a) the generation of the multiple copies of the MWS opsin gene; (b) the occasional loss of the MWS opsin gene resulting in deuteranopia, a "green-blind" dichromat; (c) the formation of hybrid opsin genes responsible for protanopia, a "red-blind" dichromat, and for both kinds of anomalous trichromats, protanomaly and deuteranomaly (Nathans, Piantanida, Eddy, Shows, and Hogness 1986; Nathans 1989). Nathans, Merbs, Sung, Weitz, and Wang (1992) subsequently tested his model on 93 human males who are "red–green" colorblind and his model was able to explain 91 of the cases. A point mutation explained the ninety-second case, and the final case resisted cloning, so that the number and structure of the MWS opsin genes are still unknown for this individual.

The importance of biological, and specifically genetic, evolution for the future color vision of our species was dramatically underscored by two papers that appeared in the April 2, 1992 issue of *Nature* (Merbs and Nathans 1992; Winderickx, Lindsey, Sanocki, Teller, Motulsky, and Deeb 1992). Building on the earlier work of Jay and Maureen Neitz (Neitz, Neitz, and Jacobs 1991), which identified a polymorphism at amino acid position #180 in the LWS photopigment gene of both New World monkeys and humans, these papers investigated the psycho-physical correlates of this genetic polymorphism. The Winderickx group studied 50 young Caucasian males and found that 62% had the hydroxyl-bearing amino acid, serine, at position #180, while the remaining 38% had alanine. This single amino acid difference was sufficient to explain the curious finding of two major groups in the distribution of color matching results among these 50 males, all of whom had normal color vision. Merbs and Nathans (1992) actually measured the absorption spectra of the human cone pigments corre-sponding to the same polymorphism at position #180 of the LWS opsin. They found that the serine 180 variant displayed an absorption maximum at 557 nm, while the alanine 180 variant had a maximum at 552 nm. This 5 nm difference corresponds closely to the 6 nm differ-ence for the same system found earlier in tamarin (New World) mon-keys by Neitz, Neitz, and Jacobs (1991). The direct evolutionary import of this genetic polymorphism on the X-chromosome becomes immedi-ately obvious: women have two X-chromosomes and can potentially be heterozygous for the genetic material in exon #3 coding for amino acid position #180. Thus, some females may be phenotypically serine 180/alanine 180. In female Platyrrhine monkeys, the two correspond-ing cone types are known to be able to sustain a color-opponent signal. Thus, it is certainly possible that human females heterozygous at this locus could be tetrachromic and thereby capable of experiencing an extra dimension of hue that can never be experienced by males who have only a single X-chromosome (Mollon 1992).

Recently, Neitz and Neitz (1995) have presented new data that call for a revision of the generally accepted model of "red" and "green" opsin gene organization. Their evidence suggests that human males with normal color vision can have as many as four "red" genes and as many as seven "green" genes. Thus, in some cases it is possible that at least two of the "red" genes present in normal-visioned males could both be functional, resulting in males with four functional cone pig-ment types.

The position #180 polymorphism is one of many newly discovered alternative amino acid constitutions in the LWS and MWS opsins. The SWS opsin system is less well characterized but should produce similar polymorphic variation, both within and between populations of various primate species, including *Homo sapiens*. It is important to underscore that the kinds of genetic variation uncovered by these recent studies pertain to *normal* phenotypic function. The serine/alanine 180 system does not produce color blindness; it involves what may be slightly different perceptual worlds for people with nominally "normal" color vision. The psychologist John Mollon, who commented on the two publications in *Nature* (Mollon 1992: 378), perhaps put it best when he said:

> The significance of these discoveries for psychologists cannot be overexaggerated. Here is a case where a difference of a single nucleotide places people in distinct phenomenal worlds and where we know almost all the steps in the causal chain from gene to molecule to neural signals; only the final steps from cortical activity to sensation elude us. It is the first such case in psychology. It cannot be the last.

Thus, it appears that the genetic apparatus underlying normal color vision is not truly universal. The universality assumption was used by Berlin and Kay (1969), MacLaury (1992a), and, indeed, by most linguists and cognitive anthropologists working on basic color terms and/or categories. This is also a major assumption behind Durham's (1991) treatment of basic color terms as an example of genetic mediation. The real situation promises to be even more interesting. For instance, could it be that normal genetic variation in the opsin system or in other genetic systems with neurological correlates might underlie behavioral differences at the linguistic level? Could the effects of genetic differences go beyond the perceptual realm to the realm of cognition? Could inter- and intrapopulation differences in basic and/or secondary color-term naming systems be genetically conditioned, and could Durham's genetic mediation be applied to account for occasional differences as well as general similarities?

It is the attendance to differences rather than similarity that is the cornerstone of MacLaury's vantage theory (1992a), a cognitively based model to explain the evolution of basic color terms from a simple two-term system to the full-blown eleven-term system of Kay,

Berlin, and Merrifield (1991). Interestingly, in the basic color term system, ontogeny does seem to recapitulate phylogeny as a series of category splits leads to the realization of a full set of basic color terms. The actual process of category division is reminiscent of a divisive routine for hierarchical clustering in multivariate statistics. This successive splitting algorithm also appears in the research of Ambrose-Ingerson, Granger, and Lynch (1990) on the olfactory bulb of the paleocortex, wherein processes analogous to hierarchical clustering and another multivariate statistical procedure, principal-components analysis, seem to organize olfactory input stimuli. Their paper concludes by raising the possibility that "this biologically generated mechanism for hierarchical clustering may be a routine part of perceptual recognition memory behavior in animals and humans" (Ambrose-Ingerson *et al.* 1990: 1347). Could, perhaps, a similar neural mechanism guide both the evolution and development of basic color-term vocabulary?

Since primate color vision is the neurologically filtered phenotypic manifestation of a multigene family, and since humans display ongoing evolution at the genetic level in the opsin system, Durham's genetic mediation model predicts the possibility of further evolution in the basic color term realm. MacLaury's (1992b) work on Karuk has provided a cultural evolutionary force to account for the Berlin and Kay sequence of basic color category decomposition: revision of the balance of attention to similarity and distinctiveness such that distinctiveness becomes emphasized, causing composite categories to decompose into more and more of the eleven separately labelled basic color categories. When the familiar list of eleven has been realized, a language is claimed to have a full and complete set of basic color terms. In their ground-breaking 1969 book, Berlin and Kay wrote: "There appears to be no evidence to indicate that differences in complexity of basic color lexicons between one language and another reflect perceptual differences between the speakers of these languages" (Berlin and Kay 1969: 5). Will this statement collapse as more is learned about the genetic variation at the opsin loci and when this variation is investigated within the framework of linguistic variation in basic color term usage? A resolution of the long-standing relativist/universalist debate about color naming will entail an explanation of general cross-cultural similarities in the meaning of these terms by identifying the specific genetic and phenotypic linkages posited by Durham's model. It will also require a demonstration that individual and population differences in color naming lexicons are correlated with genetic variation at the opsin loci. Methodologically we are on the verge of being able to test these conjectures.

Where might ongoing basic color term evolution be documented such that a twelfth and possibly subsequent terms might be caught in the process of addition? Boynton and Olson (1990) have put forward the color term *peach* as their candidate for the next emergent basic chromatic color term, primarily because it is used with high consensus over the range of lightnesses characteristic of basic chromatic color term usage. Other candidates for a twelfth basic color term include the postulated two primary red color terms in Hungarian and the two controversial primary blue terms found in languages as disparate as Russian, Japanese, Quechua, Pame, Southern Cakchiquel, and South American Spanish. Do these proposed extensions of the Berlin and Kay scheme represent cultural adaptations reflecting a more analytical viewpoint (MacLaury 1992a)? Are they, therefore, primarily cognitive phenomena or is there an underlying perceptual mediation channeling these linguistic changes?

Color vision is important for mating, food acquisition, recognition of dangerous predators and/or prey, communication, and extraction of various kinds of information about the environment in taxonomically diverse groups of organisms. Color vision is widely construed to be a biological adaptation for the members of these species. In what sense, then, does the analogy to the adaptiveness of basic color categories and terms inherent in Durham's model imply that basic color terms are both biological and cultural adaptations?

MacLaury (1992a) sees attention to distinctiveness as the prime mover behind cognitive change leading to the evolutionary development of basic human color terms. What in turn tips the scale in favor of attention to distinctiveness? Why are there "splitters" and "lumpers" in all cultures in a variety of cognitive settings? Why are there differences between linguistic groups in the amount of splitting and lumping done in a variety of cognitive domains, including color? Why do some groups choose to leave perceptual categories unnamed as Baines (1985) so eloquently demonstrated for ancient Egyptians? Why do individuals often become "conservative" as they age, attending to similarity and lumping where they once championed divisions? In chapter 2 of *On the Origin of Species*, Darwin (1859) discusses variation under nature and remarks that young, inexperienced naturalists often make many specific distinctions when first working on a group new to them. However, as their knowledge and taxonomic experience increase, this tendency towards splitting is replaced by the lumping of more variation into species-level taxa.

In biology, periods of splitting and lumping alternate with each other as different species concepts and taxonomic schools wax and wane and as new fossil and neontological specimens are discovered, analyzed, and classified. In the realm of basic color term evolution, directionality rather than cyclical change prevails. Composite categories divide and contain the potential to continue to do so as derived basic categories are formed from the six fundamental neural response categories by category intersection (Kay, Berlin, and Merrifield 1991). Color category relumping (or recombining) has never been attested to the satisfaction of Kay and Berlin. MacLaury's vantage theory generally predicts the appearance of a basic color term for the dominant range of a coextensively organized category as attention to distinctiveness overtakes attention to similarity. It is only the recessive range vantage category dynamic that can lead to increased attention to similarity as in the Darwin vignette. Unfortunately, recessive ranges usually do not lead to basic color terms. They can, however, account for the darkening of a recessive vantage such as a darker blue mapping range as grue divides, with the dominant vantage green category being named first. Are there psychological and/or neurophysiological correlates for the differential attention to similarity and distinctiveness that forms the key comparative axis in MacLaury's vantage theory? Might genetic systems be involved in individual tendencies towards splitting and lumping, just as they are responsible for the substantial heritability estimates of numerous other personality traits such as introversion/extroversion ($h^2 = .3 \rightarrow .5$), and neuroticism ($h^2 = .3 \rightarrow .5$) (Bouchard, Lykken, McGue, Segal, and Tellegen 1990; Plomin 1990).

Kay, Berlin, and Merrifield conclude their 1991 paper on the biocultural implications of systems of color naming with the following statement (Kay, Berlin, and Merrifield 1991: 24):

It is perhaps in showing a measure of detail regarding both the correspondence and the non-correspondence of cultural to biological variables that research on color semantics may throw light on broader issues regarding the relation between biology and culture. To the extent that we may judge from the present state of research on color term meanings and their biological basis, sweeping conclusions of any kind in the area of culture and biology appear unwarranted by currently available facts.

Today, color-vision research is poised to fill in the gaps in knowledge that separate the genetic, neurobiological, and cognitive structures and processes that interactively portray the world of color for *Homo sapiens*. One of the major potential fall-outs of the Human Genome Project may well be the falsification of Kay, Berlin, and Merrifield's (1991) pessimistic conclusion about the lack of concrete progress in understanding the biocultural bases of color term categorization and naming. The 1990s also promise to be *the* decade of neurobiology. As the twenty-first century approaches, so does the possibility of understanding both the perceptional aspects and the cognitive usages of human color vision at a fundamental and intellectually satisfying level (Fischbach 1992; Zeki 1992).

Acknowledgments   I would like to thank Rob MacLaury, Steve Baird, Larry Hardin, and all the participants in the National Science Foundation–sponsored Color Categories Conference (Asilomar, 1992) for introducing me to the manifold complexities of color-vision research.

References

Ambrose-Ingerson, J., R. Granger, and G. Lynch 1990. Simulation of paleocortex performs hierarchical clustering. *Science* 247: 1344–1348.

Baines, J. 1985. Color terminology and color classification: Ancient Egyptian color terminology and polychromy. *American Anthropologist* 87: 282–297.

Berlin, B., and P. Kay 1969. *Basic Color Terms: Their Universality and Evolution*. Berkeley: University of California Press. 1st paperback edn. 1991, with a bibliography by Luisa Maffi

Bouchard, T. J., Jr., D. T. Lykken, M. McGue, N. L. Segal, and A. Tellegen 1990. Sources of human psychological differences: the Minnesota study of twins reared apart. *Science* 250: 223–228.

Boynton, R. M., and C. X. Olson 1990. Salience of chromatic basic color terms confirmed by three measures. *Vision Research* 30(a): 1311–1317.

Darwin, C. 1859. *On the Origin of Species by Means of Natural Selection or the Preservation of Favored Races in the Struggle for Life*. London: John Murray.

Durham, W. H. 1991. *Coevolution: Genes, Culture, and Human Diversity*. Stanford University Press.

Fischbach, G. D. 1992. Mind and brain. *Scientific American* 267: 48–57.

Kay, P., B. Berlin, and W. R. Merrifield 1991. Biocultural implications of systems of color naming. *Journal of Linguistic Anthropology* 1: 12–25.

MacLaury, R. E. 1992a. From brightness to hue: an explanatory model of color-category evolution. *Current Anthropology* 33: 137–186.

    1992b. Karuk color: a close look at the yellow–green–blue category of northern California. Paper delivered at the 91st annual meeting of the American Anthropological Association, San Francisco.

Merbs, S. L., and J. Nathans 1992. Absorption spectra of human cone pigments. *Nature* 356: 433–435.

Mollon, J. 1992. Worlds of difference. *Nature* 356: 378–379.

Nathans, J. 1989. The genes for color vision. *Scientific American* 260: 42–49.

Nathans, J., D. Thomas, and D. S. Hogness 1986. Molecular genetics of human color vision: the genes encoding blue, green, and red pigments. *Science* 232: 193–202.

Nathans, J., S. L. Merbs, C. Sung, C. J. Weitz, and Y. Wang 1992. Molecular genetics of human visual pigments. *Annual Review of Genetics*, 26: 403–424.

Nathans, J., T. P. Piantanida, R. L. Eddy, T. B. Shows, and D. S. Hogness 1986. Molecular genetics of inherited variation in human color vision. *Science* 232: 203–210.

Neitz, M., and J. Neitz 1995. Numbers and ratios of visual pigment genes for normal red–green color vision. *Science* 267: 1013–1016.

Neitz, M., J. Neitz, and G. H. Jacobs 1991. Spectral tuning of pigments underlying red–green color vision. *Science* 252: 971–974.

Plomin, R. 1990. The role of inheritance in behavior. *Science* 248: 183–188.

Vollrath, D., J. Nathans, and R. W. Davis 1988. Tandem array of human visual pigment genes at Xq28. *Science* 240: 1669–1672.

Winderickx, J., D. T. Lindsey, E. Sanocki, D. Y. Teller, A. G. Motulsky, and S. S. Deeb 1992. Polymorphism in red photopigment underlies variation in color matching. *Nature* 356: 431–433.

Zeki, S. 1992. The visual image in mind and brain. *Scientific American* 267: 69–76.

IV DISSENTING VOICES

14 It's not really red, green, yellow, blue: an inquiry into perceptual color space

Kimberly Jameson and Roy G. D'Andrade

This chapter presents two arguments. The first argument is that, *contra* Hering, Hurvich and Jameson, De Valois, and others, the fundamental chromatic axes of the opponent processes are *not* red/green and yellow/blue. The second argument is that the results found by Berlin and Kay, Rosch, and others, which indicate that particular regions of the color space are selected as the natural locations for color terms, are not due to opponent processes, but to irregularities in perceptual color space. In general, we suggest that alternative theories should be sought as the bases for cognitive models of subjective color experience. To do this we present an overview of commonly used color spaces and scalings of these spaces; we discuss opponent-colors theory and related neurophysiology, and point to some problems with the theory; we examine some empirical phenomena (e.g. additive complements, negative afterimages, etc.) and the possible relation of these phenomena to the organization of color space; we consider unitary hues as relating to color space cardinal axes; and propose a plausible alternative model and discuss its relevance to research in anthropology and psychology.

In the literature addressing the psychological and physiological character of human color vision there is a general account that goes as follows.

(1) Color is organized perceptually in a three-dimensional space as presented in Figure 14.1 below, with red/green (R/G) and yellow/blue (Y/B) as cardinal axes of the space, plus light/dark (white/black for surface colors) as the third dimension. This is the standard diagram presented in numerous articles and texts.

(2) Further, the R/G axis and the Y/B axis of the color space are fixed by and correspond to the output of opponent-process cells measured in the lateral geniculate nucleus (LGN), which are the physiological basis of the subjective sense of purity or uniqueness of the colors red, green, yellow, and blue.

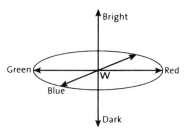

Figure 14.1 Perceptual color space illustrating the dimensions of hue, saturation and brightness, which describe color appearances of light sources. Hue varies around the perimeter of the color circle; saturation varies along the axis joining the central "white point" W to a pure color on the circumference, while brightness varies in the direction perpendicular to the color circle. The perceptual color space for surface color appearance is the same, although in this case one speaks of "lightness" rather than "brightness" (from Lennie and D'Zmura 1988).

(3) Finally, the underlying opponent-process mechanisms explain, at least in part, the evolutionary and developmental history of color terms, with the principal terms for red, green, blue, and yellow developing first in a child's lexicon or in the history of a language, while secondary colors, such as purple, pink, or brown develop later.

These three hypotheses are mutually supporting, and together are offered as a coherent account of a great range of phenomena. However, we think that this account is incorrect, and that the weight of the evidence supports a different set of hypotheses.

Color spaces

The color space illustrated in Figure 14.1 is just one of the many color spaces that have been constructed by vision scientists. The bases on which color spaces have been developed vary. For example, the CIE space locates colors within a tristimulus coordinate system. This space accurately predicts the effects of the color mixture of lights by the simple addition of vectors (Cornsweet 1970). There are varieties of this space, sometimes called tristimulus spaces (see, for example, Cornsweet 1970: 230, or MacLeod and Boynton 1979). From a psychological point of view, the CIE space has one major drawback: it does not correspond well to perceptual color differences. That is, the distance between different colors in CIE space does not correspond directly to human perceptual judgments of difference and similarity (Indow 1988).

Several other kinds of spaces have been developed. The Natural Color System (NCS) space, for example, was developed by using judgments of the *proportion* of specific color referents contained in color stimuli (Hård and Sivik 1981). The NCS space has the general shape of the space illustrated in Figure 14.1. The color referents – red, green, yellow, blue, black and white (labeled "dark" and "bright" in Figure 14.1) – are considered primary, and all other colors are treated as mixtures of these. Distance in the space from each of the primaries corresponds to the proportion of the primary present at that region of the space. Thus a "reddish orange" would be a color that the subject would judge to contain both red and yellow, but to have more red in it than yellow. However, the NCS space does not correspond to direct perceptual judgments of similarity and difference between colors, but rather to estimates of proportions of color subjectively analyzed.

A number of color spaces have been constructed with the goal of having distances between colors correspond directly to the perception of how similar the colors are. We will call these *perceptual spaces*. The Munsell system is one of the best known of these perceptual spaces. It was designed by Albert Munsell, a painter and art educator, to provide a scheme for comparison of colors. The system was first published in 1905, and a renotation of the system was constructed by the Optical Society of America in 1937. The basic idea is that adjacent color samples in each of the three dimensions of color (Hue, Value, and Chroma) should have a constant perceptual difference, so that the color chips are located at equal perceptual intervals along each dimension. However, no method is given for comparing distances along different dimensions. It is as if the distances between levels of lightness were in furlongs, the distance between levels of saturation in stadia, and the distance around the hue perimeter in paces, and no table of equivalences was provided. Illustrations of the Munsell space are presented in Figure 14.2.

Another perceptual color space, the OSA space, was developed by a special committee of the Optical Society of America. It contains a basic set of 424 color samples organized in 3 dimensions. The OSA color samples were constructed with the goal of forming an isotropic space; that is, a space in which perceptual distances between color samples along each dimension are equal. The space is organized in a grid fashion, with each level of lightness having a separate grid. Lightness levels are numbered from $+5$ to -7, and the grid at each level is defined by two coordinates, g and j (roughly, green and yellow).

Other kinds of spaces are also possible, such as spaces in which the judgments about colors are based on affective responses (Adams and Osgood 1973; D'Andrade and Egan 1974; Johnson, Johnson, and Bakash 1986), or based on judgments about the aesthetic quality of combinations of colors, or based on the semantic similarity of color terms (Shepard and Cooper 1992). However, in this chapter we are concerned

Figure 14.2 (a)
Diagrammatic
representation of the
Munsell color solid with
one quarter removed.
(b) Cylindrical
representation of the
Munsell notation
system. (c) The Munsell
Hue circle (from
D'Andrade and Egan
1974).

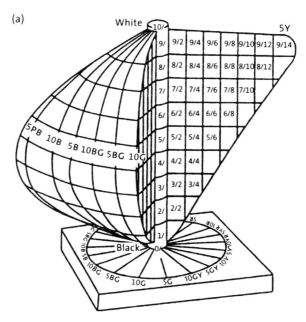

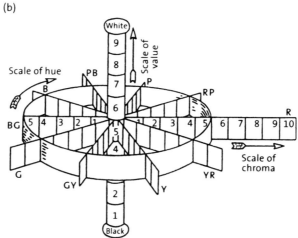

primarily with color spaces based on psychophysically determined
perceptual qualities.

The scaling of color spaces

Our first question concerns which of the color systems described above
best approximates an imagined perceptual color space in which dis-

(c)

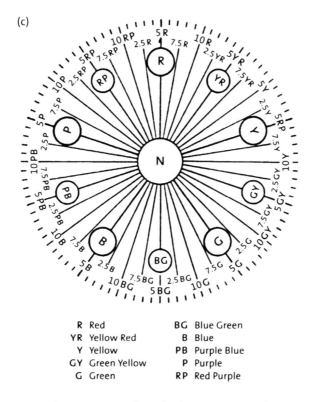

R	Red	BG	Blue Green
YR	Yellow Red	B	Blue
Y	Yellow	PB	Purple Blue
GY	Green Yellow	P	Purple
G	Green	RP	Red Purple

tances between samples of colors correspond accurately to subjective judgments of perceptual similarity. A great variety of methods for scaling perceptual judgments of similarity have been employed in color research, including Thurstonian scaling, ratio judgments, and interval judgments. Indow has summarized the results of nineteen different scaling studies, finding an overall pattern which clearly conforms to the Munsell type of organization (Indow and Aoki 1983; Indow 1988).

The major difference between the standard color space illustrated in Figure 14.1 and the Munsell-like space found in the scaling studies summarized by Indow involves the orientation of the axes. These scaling studies do not find an axis where green is opposite red; rather red is opposite to blue-green and green is opposite to red-purple. (Compare Figure 14.1 and Figure 14.2b.) Overall, the results show the color perimeter divided into roughly *five* equal sections, corresponding to red, yellow, green, blue, and purple. Empirical scaling of the OSA color samples also can be seen to support a five-hue organization with

Figure 14.3
Experimental results for naming OSA color samples. Octagons represent the 128 consensus colors, plotted in the chromatic (g vs. j) plane. Lightness values (L) are represented by the size of the octagons, with lightness increasing as octagons become larger. Shaded octagons represent the location of focal color samples. Smaller octagons within larger ones indicate that consensus colors with the same g- and j-values are to be found at different lightness levels. The squares show the locations in the chromatic plane only, of color centroids (adapted from Boynton and Olson 1987). See Boynton, this volume.

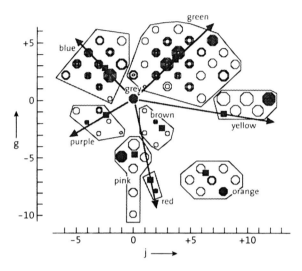

approximately equal sectors. Boynton and Olson (1987) in a study of consensus in color naming, obtained the English monolexemic names for 424 samples of the OSA set from 7 respondents. These results for the hue perimeter of the color space are presented in Figure 14.3.

The centroids in Figure 14.3 have been computed by averaging the values on each dimension for all color samples called by a particular name weighted by the number of times the sample was so named. Running radial lines from the grey center of the space through FIVE of the centroids (R, P, B, G, Y) gives the angular relations between the color terms, as indicated in Figure 14.3.[1]

About their general results, Boynton and Olson say:

> the locations of consensus colors based on this experiment do not agree fully with what seems to have been intended by the OSA committee. In her summary of their work, Nickerson (1981: 9) writes: "Fixing the position of one yellow hue on level L=0 establishes the position of all other hues in accord with the committee's uniform-spacing experimental results ... blues are thereby located along the negative *j* axis, green hues along the positive *g* axis, and red hues along the negative *g* axis." Our data show that color names cannot be used precisely to describe the chromatic axes ... Although the use of the symbol *j* from French *jaune* to identify the horizontal axis is apt for high lightness levels, it would not be appropriate to refer to a

yellow–blue axis, because no yellow is seen at low levels of lightness for positive values of *j*, and for negative values, although there is one consensus dark blue on it, the axis otherwise divides the blue and purple regions. Similarly, the label *g* (for green) poorly denotes the positive end of an axis that tends to divide the blue and green samples almost perfectly into two groups. And pink, not red, lies at the negative end of the *g* axis, along which there are not consensus colors at most lightness levels. (1987: 101)

It is significant that the OSA space can be shown to support the five-hue organization, since the position of the color samples was fixed solely by relative perceptual distances, without regard for how these samples might be named. If there was any expectation about the organization of the OSA space, it was that it would look like the four-hue space, as indicated by the Nickerson quote above.

These results do not *prove* that the cardinal axes of psychological color space are not R/G and Y/B, but they do suggest difficulties for such a position. Why, if pure red and pure green are assumed to be opposing colors in the opponent-process theory sense, are they not found to lie at opposite sides of an achromatic point in empirical scalings of perceptual space? Such a relation seems to be a natural consequence of the theory (see Abramov and Gordon 1994), and seems to be the way in which many color researchers understand both the theory and the relations in Figure 14.1. To explain this kind of discrepancy by postulating additional mechanisms external to a variant of opponent-process theory is reasonable; however, it undermines the usefulness of a strong opponent-colors model as a basis for understanding the cognitive organization of color perceptions.

Opponent processes

Hering's opponent-color theory hypothesizes two things: first, that the opponent pairs black/white, red/green, and yellow/blue are all that is needed to derive any other color that we can experience; and second, that there are neurophysiological opponent-process mechanisms in the visual system that produce the experience of these primary colors (Hurvich and Jameson 1957). Although modern physiological evidence was not available to Hering, current work

Figure 14.4 Chromatic
response functions for a
neutral state of
adaptation (from
Hurvich 1981).

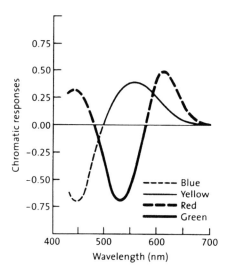

leaves no doubt that cells of the primate visual system do include
opponent-type responses to different wavelengths (De Valois 1960;
De Valois, Abramov, and Jacobs 1966; De Valois and Jacobs 1968).[2]

   A standard diagram to display the way the opponent process
might work is presented in Figure 14.4, taken from Hurvich (1981:
201). Basically, the model consists of two response output systems,
indicated by the two curves. Within this model, the point at which
each curve crosses zero defines a *unique hue*. Thus at about 580 nm the
R/G response function is at zero, which means that a normal observer
will see a "pure" yellow because the response has neither red nor
green in it. Similarly, at approximately 510 nm the Y/B response function is at zero, which means a pure green will be experienced, and at
approximately 475 nm the R/G response function is at zero, which
means a pure blue will be experienced. Notice that, according to the
diagram, there is no single wavelength at which a pure red can be perceived, since both red and yellow outputs occur from 600 nm to 700
nm (the color receptors are unresponsive to light of wavelengths
greater than 700 nm or less than 400 nm), and both red and blue outputs occur from 400 nm to 470 nm. This diagram provides an explanation of why pure red is extra-spectral; in order to see a pure red, the
yellow component of a 650 nm light must be canceled by the blue component of a 450 nm light so that only a red response occurs (also see
Dimmick and Hubbard 1939b).

De Valois and colleagues originally thought that the four types of opponent-process cells they identified in the macaque lateral geniculate nucleus had maximum response peaks and troughs at the wavelengths which people with normal color vision describe as *red, green, yellow,* and *blue* (De Valois and Jacobs 1968: 538). However, most of the peaks of the recorded opponent-process cells do not appear where one would expect from the theory. For example, according to the graphic figures presented in De Valois, Abramov, and Jacobs (1966), one of the sharpest peaks is displayed by the averaged yellow-plus cells at 600 nm, but this is typically seen as a reddish orange, not yellow. Similarly the peak for the averaged blue-plus cells is around 455 nm, which is a violet. For the green-plus cells the peak is around 540 nm, a yellowish green. Also, the cross-over points of individual opponent cells vary widely (Boynton 1979: 234–237).

These discrepancies undermine the argument that the subjective sense of uniqueness or purity of hues for highly specific wavelengths is determined by the LGN opponent-process cells. In a recent paper, De Valois and De Valois say:

> Although we, like others, were most strongly impressed with finding opponent cells, in accord with Hering's suggestions, when the Zeitgeist at the time was strongly opposed to the notion, the earliest recordings reveal a discrepancy between the Hering–Hurvich–Jameson opponent perceptual channels and the response characteristics of opponent cells in the macaque lateral geniculate nucleus (LGN) ... Later investigators also found the same discrepancy, with different stimulation techniques (Derrington, Krauskopf & Lennie 1984; Kaplan, Lee & Shapley 1990), and made the same point. Here we suggest (albeit somewhat belatedly) a third stage of color processing to reconcile this discrepancy. (1993: 1053–1054)[3]

(The third stage of processing proposed by De Valois and De Valois, which produces a set of response functions like those in Figure 14.4, is a hypothesis presented without direct physiological evidence.)

Abramov and Gordon also make the point that the recordings of opponent cells from the LGN do not support the R/G and Y/B hypothesis:

Universal color terms have been explicitly linked to spectrally opponent physiological mechanisms (Ratliff 1976). Specifically, the spectrally opponent and nonopponent cells in the LGN (De Valois et al. 1966) have been used to justify the grouping of white, black, R, Y, G, and B as fundamental terms (Kay & McDaniel 1978; Kay *et al.* [Berlin and Merrifield] 1991; MacLaury 1992). However, as we have pointed out, *these cells are not hue mechanisms and their detailed response properties should not be used to justify particular linguistic models of the development of color terms.* (1994: 468. Our italics.)

The subjective sense of purity and uniqueness for red, yellow, green, and blue might be determined by physiological events which occur after processing in the lateral geniculate nucleus. However, direct physiological recordings give no support to the hypothesis that red, green, yellow, and blue are the primary axes of the opponent cells. In fact, Abramov and Gordon state:

We now turn to the question of whether there is a necessary pair of perceptual axes that must be used to represent hue space. Stemming from Hering's original work, the accepted bipolar hue axes are RG and YB . . . But are these the necessary axes? . . . hue cancellation studies demonstrate that hue is organized in opponent fashion: any stimulus that elicits some sensation of G can be added to one eliciting R in order to cancel R . . . However, there is no obvious *a priori* justification for these precise axes; *the axes might be chartreuse–violet and teal–cherry, which are approximately the hues to which the LGN cardinal axes point.*[4] Introspectively, however, we find it virtually impossible to think of canceling or scaling all hues in these terms and ultimately this is the principal justification for using RG and YB as axes. (1994: 468. Our italics.)

Thus we find that the physiological recordings from opponent-processing cells in the LGN do not support the R/G and Y/B hypothesis; if anything, they support the hypothesis that the basic axes are the same as those given in Indow's scaling of the Munsell system, oriented roughly around – as Abramov and Gordon would say – cherry/teal and chartreuse/violet.

A serious problem with opponent-process theory assumptions: empirical results for additive complements and unique hues

To illustrate clearly one specific way opponent-colors theory conflicts with empirical data, we present three opponent-colors theory assumptions below which explicitly state the relationships between the theory, unique color appearances, and visual system neural responses.

Assumption 1: unique color appearance and visual channel response

There are two chromatic channels used in coding color appearance (hereafter "light"): the red–green and yellow–blue channels.

A light that has zero output on the red–green channel is blue, yellow, or white in appearance.

A light that has zero output on the yellow–blue channel is red, green, or white in appearance.

Each light produces either a positive, zero, or negative output on the red–green and yellow–blue channels. (Thus, a light that appears either bluish or yellowish has a non-zero output on the yellow–blue channel, and a light that appears either reddish or greenish has a non-zero output on the red–green channel.)

Definition 1: unique chromatic appearances

Unique red is a light that has zero output on the yellow–blue channel and is red in appearance.
Unique green is a light that has zero output on the yellow–blue channel and is green in appearance.
Unique yellow is a light that has zero output on the red–green channel and is yellow in appearance.
Unique blue is a light that has zero output on the red–green channel and is blue in appearance.
Unique white is a light that has zero output on *both* the red–green and the yellow–blue visual channels and is achromatic in appearance.

In the literature, Assumption 1 and Definition 1 are accepted as naturally stemming from Hering's notions of unitary and psychologically simple chromatic attributes, and it is also accepted that these attributes represent antagonistic or opponent pairs (Jameson and Hurvich 1955: 548; Krantz 1989: 279–80).

The color appearances described above can be combined in various ratios to produce different appearances. Below, Assumption 2 explicitly states some of the possible chromatic response relations for mixtures of unique appearances that are assumed by opponent-colors theory. (For brevity, below we consider only some of the cases for combining red and green stimuli at yellow–blue equilibrium.)

Assumption 2: additive mixtures of unique-appearance lights

Suppose L_1 and L_2 are two different lights that both have zero output on the yellow–blue channel. If L is the light that is produced by superimposing (hereafter *adding*) L_1 and L_2, then L must also have zero output on the yellow–blue channel.

Historically, this assumption of linear additivity, generally referred to as "linearity," has been an important property of the opponent-process model because it permits prediction of chromatic response functions from spectral light mixtures (see Judd 1951; Hurvich and Jameson 1957; Krantz 1989: 286).

For Assumption 2 to be deemed a reasonable assumption it must be validated through empirical tests of additive mixtures of L_1 and L_2, yellow–blue equilibrium lights. The underlying rationale is to have the opponent theory be a simple extension of Grassmann's laws (see Wyszecki and Stiles 1982: 118). If Assumption 2 were found to fail empirically then the relation between the standard model (i.e., the Grassmann structure underlying the CIE tristimulus space) for color mixtures of spectral lights and the opponent-process model becomes complicated and requires Assumption 2 to be modified to specify the exact form of the nonlinearity.[5]

Assumption 3: complementary additive light mixtures

If L_1 is a unique green light with zero output on the yellow–blue channel, then there exists a reddish light L_2 that has zero output on the yellow–blue channel such that when L_1 and L_2 are added to yield light L, then L has zero output on the red–green channel. (By Assumption 2 L has zero output on the yellow–blue channel also, thus L will appear white.) In this case, L_2 is called an *additive complement* of L_1.

Assumption 3 clearly follows from the theory formulated in the literature. For example, Jameson and Hurvich (1955: 548) state:

> The chromatic response of the visual system for a given hue is assumed to be proportional to the amount of the opponent cancellation stimulus necessary to extinguish that hue. To measure the amount, say, of yellow chromatic response evoked by a spectral test stimulus perceived as yellow, whether pure yellow, red-yellow, or green-yellow, the experimenter adds to the test stimulus a variable amount of blue stimulus (e.g. 467 nm) until the observer reports that the yellow hue of the test stimulus is exactly canceled. In other words, the observer's endpoint is a hue (or a neutral sensation) that is neither yellow nor blue.

An extension of this idea implies that a "neutral" sensation is tantamount to a phenomenological "white" experience. This idea was generalized and used to define "complementary" pairs of stimuli. As Hurvich (1981: 49) states, "pairs of wavelengths that generate a white experience when intermixed are known as complementary wavelengths."

Theorem 1

Assumptions 1, 2 and 3 imply that each additive complement of a unique green is a unique red.[6]

Theorem 1 is a special case of a point central to opponent-colors theory as stated by Hurvich: "Once we realize that the whiteness aspect is simply the uncanceled excitation produced by both stimuli of the complementary pair, we need only seek out two stimuli in the spectrum whose chromatic excitations are opposite and equal in order to find stimuli properly characterizable as complementary" (1981: 70).

However, when interpreted phenomenologically, the conclusion of Theorem 1 fails empirically. As early as 1907 Hering's student, A. von Tschermak, reported that "under usual conditions of observation, in order to produce a colorless appearing mixture [of lights] one needs for a unique (*urfarben*) red not a pure green but a somewhat bluish-green" (Tschermak 1907: 478). Others have subsequently also verified that unique red and unique green, when superimposed to produce a

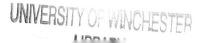

non-reddish and non-greenish color, always produce a yellowish appearance (e.g. Dimmick and Hubbard 1939a, 1939b; Judd 1951; Burns, Elsner, Porkorny, and Smith 1984).[7]

Thus, there is a defect in the theory and further postulating that a yellow appearance is an acceptable "neutral sensation" for red and green mixtures does not abrogate the problem because, by Theorem 1, at least one of the essential assumptions stated above remains incorrect.[8]

Although the above empirical results for mixtures of unique red and unique green are known by many color-vision experts, it is still often implied by theories presented in the current literature (e.g. De Valois and De Valois 1993) that the zero-output cross-over points in chromatic response functions correspond to unique hues that additively combine to yield *neutral* sensations. De Valois and De Valois (1993: 1060) say: "Unique blue and yellow occur at the cross-points of the red–green system, and unique green at the cross-point of the yellow–blue system . . . The fourth hue, red, is extraspectral, at a combination of short and long wavelengths which would just cancel the yellow–blue function." However, for the case of *unique* red and unique green this is empirically false.

The failure of Theorem 1 is a serious problem for opponent-process theory that can never be patched up as long as unique hues are maintained as unitary sensations *and* antagonistic channel zero-crossings. In light of these facts it seems wise to pursue alternate hue axes that model the empirical data more closely, and we suggest that one such model may be provided by a maximized interpoint-distance formulation in, for example, the Munsell color space, or in some other perceptual scaling space.

Additive complementary colors and afterimage complements

Given the above-mentioned conflict between observed empirical relations and opponent-colors theory, one question is naturally raised: how do the additive complements defined by light mixtures (as opposed to defined by a theory) relate to the Munsell or OSA surface spaces?[9] Nickerson prepared a series of charts which locate the Munsell system within the standard CIE diagram (Wyszecki and Stiles 1982, appendix 6.6.1). These charts indicate that the Munsell color perimeter (see Figure 14.2c) gives a reasonable approximation to the empirically observed structure of the additive complements in the sense that such complements are found at points diametrically opposite the achromatic center. (As defined by Schrödinger, "complementary colors . . . lie on a line on the chromaticity diagram that intersects the position assigned to white" [Niall 1988: 83]. Complements when mixed in suitable proportions yield a color match to some achromatic stimulus [Wyszecki and Stiles 1982: 176].) This approximation of the Munsell hue perimeter to the empirically observed relations of additive complementary hues is not discussed in the existing literature.

What does the correspondence between the Munsell space perimeter and the structure of the additive complements tell us? Given that the *true* axes representing actual opposing color-pair relations are aligned somewhere within the five-hue circle of the Munsell space (say, towards cherry/teal and chartreuse/violet), then one would expect hues on opposite sides of the circle to be additive complements, since they would, by definition, have "equal but opposite" response outputs.[10]

This line of argument is also supported by the structure of negative afterimage hues. Afterimage hues, produced by fixating one's gaze for several seconds on a color stimulus and then looking at a blank colorless surface, are a well-known and much-studied phenomenon. Negative afterimages correspond fairly closely to the empirical additive complements for all but yellow–blue pairings (Wilson and Brocklebank 1955; Bagley and Maxfield 1986). Thus the afterimage data accord with empirically observed complement relations, and both suggest a space with the Munsell-like axes we mentioned, rather than cardinal R/G and Y/B axes.

Moreover, using a paradigm that assessed thresholds for detecting changes in color stimuli, Krauskopf, Williams, and Heeley (1982) provide an interpretation of findings consistent with opponent-process theory axes, although they empirically found a tritanopic confusion line, and not the Y–B cardinal axis, as a direction in color space carrying signals along "separate, fatiguable, second stage pathways," making it distinct from other possible directions in the space, and suggesting an alternative cardinal direction. Although Krauskopf *et al.* do not suggest it, the results of this careful study seem to justify exploring and testing alternative color space models.

The basic hues

There is an experimental literature which shows that some hues are *elemental* – that is, they cannot be perceptually analyzed into more basic hues. In one kind of experiment, subjects are asked to give the percentage of some specific hue "directly experienced" when viewing a stimulus color. If there is a region of the hue perimeter which is described by the term for this hue, and no other hue terms are applicable to this region, the hue is elemental. For example, there exists a region of the hue perimeter which can only be described as *yellow*, and which is experienced as pure yellow in that it has no red or green in it. In various studies, red, yellow, green, and blue have been demonstrated to be elemental for at least some subjects (Sternheim and Boynton 1966; D. L. Miller and Wooten 1990). These "elemental" hues are usually taken to represent end-points of opposing pairs which define the relations among colors on the hue perimeter and the axes of color space.

The idea that the hue perimeter of color space is defined by the dimensions red–green and yellow–blue is relatively old. Waller in 1686, Hofler in 1886, Titchener in 1887, Ebbinghaus in 1902, Hering in 1911, Boring in 1929, and Plochere in 1948 all presented diagrams with red and green, yellow and blue as opposites (see Gerritsen 1975). For some reason, from Waller on, the hue perimeter was diagrammed not as a circle but as a square (except by Hering and Plochere). There was another tradition, starting with Goethe in 1793 and Herschel in 1817 in which the hues were arranged around six points, or three "complementary" pairs, with red opposite green, yellow opposite violet, and orange opposite blue.

The data collected by Sternheim and Boynton (1966) and D. L. Miller and Wooten (1990) support the intuition that red, green, yellow, and blue have a special "landmark" status as colors. This special status is hypothesized to result from R/G and Y/B opponent-process neurophysiology. However, we will argue below that this special status could be derived from irregularities in the perceptual color space. Some of the variability in findings concerning exactly which hues are opposite each other in the color space, reflected in the different color spaces proposed over 300 years, may also be due to limitations on judgments of similarity and difference for colors. It has been found that estimates of similarity between any 2 points in color space become indeterminate when the perceptual distances are large. Indow (1988: 461) says: "it is true that two colors such as [Munsell] 5R 4/14, 5G 5/8 [a focal red and a focal green] simply appear 'entirely different,' and the perceptual difference in these pairs is not intuitively palpable as in more moderate color differences. There seems to be a limit within which the impression of difference naturally takes place." Thus one cannot determine by direct perceptual comparisons whether green, blue-green, or blue is opposite, or "complementary," to red. The color scaling space is constructed by having a series of overlapping judgments, building up a global map from many local maps. The technology to accomplish this was not available to early color researchers.

In an analysis of psychologically basic hues in surface colors Indow (1987) compares a four-basic-hue model (i.e., R, G, Y, B) with a five-basic-hue model (i.e., R, G, Y, B, P) and finds that the fit of the five-hue model to the empirical data is better: "when P [purple] is not included, individual differences in R and B become much larger" (p. 255 and his Figure 2). Thus, "though P [purple] is not unique [by a non-reducibility criterion] it seems to help sharpen concepts of pure red and pure blue" in a vector representation of unique hues.

Indow's (1987) comparison of chromatic response curves illustrates that these can be represented equally well by either five hues or four. What is clear is that psychophysically there is no reason not to use five hues in representing data except that the criteria of "non-reducibility" is not upheld. The question raised is what are the compelling reasons for taking non-reducibility as *the* criterion for determining basic hue points? It seems that the need to link neural physiology with purity of primary color perceptions motivates the use of this criterion, but given the present inchoate state of color vision neurophysiology it seems that the main support for the four-basic-hue model is intuitive appeal and historical continuity.

The evolution of color terms and the irregularity of the perceptual color space

Berlin and Kay (1969) have presented much evidence suggesting color terms can be ordered in an evolutionary sequence. It has been hypothesized that opponent-process mechanisms play a role in bringing this about (Kay *et al.* 1991:14). If, however, the privileged position of red, green, yellow, and blue as opponent-process hues is denied, how can the evolution of color terms be understood?

One possible explanation is that the developmental order of color names is due to the irregular shape of the color space. The best way to illustrate the irregularity of the perceptual color space is to examine each of the hues as they are laid out on the pages of the *Munsell Book of Color*. This can also be seen in Figure 14.2a where the shape of the color solid deviates markedly from that of a sphere. Hue interacts with saturation and lightness to produce several large "bumps"; one large bump is at focal yellow, and another at focal red. The entire blue–green area is depressed (i.e., of low Chroma), as is the area below focal yellow. These "bumps" are not simply due to constraints imposed by restricted surface color-printing gamuts. Analogous color-space bumps are found when a light-mixture space is considered.

We assume that the names that get assigned to the color space at any one stage are likely to be those names which are most informative about color. If one has only two color terms, the most informative system is one that places the referents of the terms at the maximum distance from each other. A dark/cool versus light/warm division of the color space accomplishes exactly this. Once the light/warm versus dark/cool division has been made, the region of color space that is most distant from the regions specified by these two terms is red. After these three terms are in place, it becomes more difficult to determine which is the next most distant region because the differences in distances are smaller and depend in part on how the focal areas are determined. Based on the distances between centroids in the OSA space computed by Boynton and Olson (1987), one would expect either yellow or blue to be the next split, followed by green, purple, pink, orange, brown, and grey. This kind of interpoint distance model would generally predict the results found by the World Color Survey (see Maffi 1988).

This notion is also supported by recent empirical work (Smallman and Boynton 1990, 1993) which shows that performance in a visual search task is the same whether subjects employ individual sets of personal "nonbasic" colors or a standard set of similarly spaced "basic" colors for coding stimuli. The conclusion drawn, which questions the status of Berlin and Kay's eleven basic colors as neurologically based

perceptual fundamentals, is that "basic colors segregate well not because
they are universally named but because they are well separated in
color space" (1990: 1985). Whether additional criteria for determining
color codes (for example, an individual's *favorite* color set) might give
rise to performance improvements in a visual search task is an interesting question.

Thus, the general argument we are presenting is that the
irregularities of the perceptual color space give an informational
advantage to making the divisions so that category foci are maximally
different from each other. These irregularities also make certain
regions of the color space more perceptually salient than others, primarily because such regions achieve a great saturation. The yellow
and red peaks of the Munsell space, for example, are highly salient,
with extremely high saturation levels. Blue and green have less notable peaks, but are still distinctive. In our account, we consider it plausible that the large number of studies which show that categorization,
or memory, or focal naming are not random across color space suggest
that people are using the *perceptual* structure of the stimulus space
which is directly available to them.

A model for this general process can be found in an experiment by
James Boster (1986). Boster selected focal color chips for red, orange,
yellow, green, blue, black, and white. Subjects were asked to sort these
color chips into two groups on the basis of similarity: "Imagine you
speak a language which has two color words, how would you choose to
divide up the colors and which colors would you put together into
each group?" After the first sort, subjects were then asked to subdivide
each of the two groups they had created, and then to subdivide again
until all the chips were separated. The mean taxonomic tree for all
subjects is presented in Figure 14.5. The successive divisions of this
tree correspond closely to the Berlin and Kay evolutionary stages discussed above. The interpretation we offer is that the Berlin and Kay
evolution is obtained not because the first six elements represent
"fundamental neural response categories" (Kay *et al.* 1991) but because
successively these elements maximize the information in the perceptual color space.

Since we are using the irregularities of perceptual color space to
attempt to account for a variety of phenomena, it would be helpful if
there were some clear explanations for these irregularities. This, how-

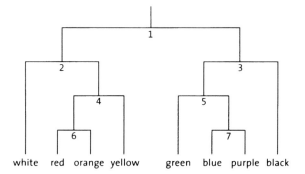

Figure 14.5 Taxonomic tree representing the overall group structure for successive divisions of color samples. Numbers indicate the average order in which clusters of samples were split (adapted from Boster 1986).

ever, is beyond our expertise – although one should note that not even in the world of feathers and flowers has anyone found a highly saturated dark yellow, or a blue-green that is as saturated as focal red. It would appear that the ratio of chromatic to achromatic responses, which varies by wavelength, plays a role in explaining the saturation differences across hues (Hurvich and Jameson 1957; Hardin 1988: 114–116).

Red, green, yellow, and blue in cognitive psychology research

It turns out that while psychophysicists have for a long time known about the many discrepancies between accepted opponent-colors theory and the empirical phenomena (e.g. Judd 1951), this has not reduced use of the model in cognitive psychology research. We have found that the cognitive psychology literature often invokes unproven assumptions about the relation between visual neurophysiology and subjective experience. Many examples of this can be found in psychology textbooks and scientific research articles. For example, investigations of the universality of color terminology and color memory have widely employed the opponent-hue neurophysiological model as a basis for predicting that the hues red, green, yellow, and blue should be empirically distinguished from other, less-fundamental, hues (e.g. Rosch 1972; Rosch 1973; Varela, Thompson, and Rosch 1991; Kay *et al.* 1991). Research in developmental psychology has also widely employed the four-opponent-hue model. Bornstein, Kessen, and Weiskopf (1976) tested whether at 4 months of age infants can discriminate and categorize color stimuli into "the four basic qualitative categories." In an extensive study of children's color naming, Cook (1931) tested over 100 2- and 6-year-olds in naming and matching red, yellow, green, and blue stimuli. In construction of intelligence tests Binet and Simon (1908/1916) required children to identify correctly all four "fundamental colors, red, blue, green, and yellow." Additional studies in which the standard opponent-colors model is employed as a rationale for hypothesis testing and stimulus selection are Johnson (1977) and G. A. Miller and Johnson-Laird (1976).

In addition to the examples cited here many other recent instances can be found in the cognitive psychology literature. In considering this literature we have found that the R/G and Y/B opponent-color model has been employed as a foundation for the construction of a color atlas; as an explanation for the subjective sensations of color experience; and as a rationale for cognitive model construction, stimulus selection, and the interpretation of results in investigations of the psychological color space. In view of the empirical evidence discussed above, we suggest that the use of the four-hue opponent-process model in these ways is unwarranted.

Moreover, we feel no strong test of the validity of the four-hue model as a basis for *cognitive* phenomena has been carried out in the existing research, and that most investigations have used the model, with all its assumptions, because it was a priori considered as a natural and valid basis for explaining higher-level cognitive phenomena. We have seen that often the psychological tests of opponent-process relations are conducted in such a way that the model is not really challenged.

Summary

The account we propose is as follows.

(1) Color is organized perceptually in a three-dimensional space which corresponds closely to the Munsell and OSA systems.
(2) This space is organized so that additive complementary hues are approximately opposite each other.
(3) Color matches to negative afterimages show a similar pattern, but there appear to be small anomalies in the Y/B region.
(4) These results are what one would expect if the opponent-processes

axes were cherry/teal and chartreuse/violet, or some simple rotation of these axes.

(5) The hypothesis that opponent-process neural mechanisms in the retina give rise to a perceptual space with R/G and Y/B axes is not empirically supported in that the unique hues cannot be both cross-over points and additive complements.

(6) The major support for the R/G and Y/B hypothesis is the subjective impression that these hues are "pure." The special salience of certain colors may be due to the irregular shape of perceptual color space.

(7) There is some support for the hypothesis that the evolution of color terms is based on a process whereby terms introduced into a language tend to be maximally distant in perceptual color space from already existing terms.

(8) The use of the R/G and Y/B opponent-process hypothesis as an explanation of various findings about the non-arbitrary nature of color memory, or color naming, or color categorization, is not warranted on the basis of present knowledge.

Notes

1 Running radial lines through the centroids of the five hues suggested, rather than all centroids presented in the data, gives an empirical space partitioned by roughly equal sectors, whereas subdividing the scaling using only the four standard hues (R, B, G, Y) leaves a large gap in the space between blue and red. Alternatively using six or seven centroids also yields sectors of unequal area (although the use of the orange centroid is possibly an acceptable division in this particular space). The point we emphasize is simply that there is a close structural correspondence between this perceptual scaling of the OSA stimuli and the structure of the Munsell color solid – they both present a considerable area devoted to blends of red and blue stimuli. The Munsell system's structure is given via five (R, P, B, G, Y) reference points rather than the opponent-colors theory standard four colors. It is interesting that the OSA system (constructed by researchers with opponent-colors theory in mind) when perceptually scaled does not yield orthogonal R/G, Y/B axes as opponent-colors theory might predict, but approximates a Munsell-like spatial organization. Convergent findings like these may suggest an alternative frame for thinking about models of color space and axes in that space.

2 Both non-human primates and humans have opponent-type visual neurophysiology. However, generalizing results from neurophysiological studies of other primates to humans is problematic for evaluating *phenomenological* experiences like the subjective color sensation of humans.

3 De Valois and De Valois acknowledge the work of G. E. Müller and D. B. Judd for first presenting the essential features of their proposed three-stage model.

4 The term "cherry" describes a bright red; "teal" is a greenish blue; "chartreuse" is a greenish yellow; and "violet" is a deep purple.

5 According to Krantz (1989), Hurvich and Jameson extended their theory to deal with problems of empirically observed non-linear relations (e.g. Bezold–Brücke phenomena). However, as Krantz notes, the nonlinearities suggested in the Hurvich and Jameson extended theory do not explain the nonlinearity of the yellow-ness/blueness equilibria (p. 289).

6 Proof: suppose G is a unique green light. Then G has zero output on the yellow–blue channel by Assumption 1

and Definition 1. By Assumption 3, let R be a reddish light with zero output on the yellow–blue channel such that the combination of G and R yields a light W that has zero output on the red–green channel. By Definition 1, R is unique red. By Assumption 2, W must also have zero output on the yellow–blue channel. Therefore, by Definition 1, W is unique white.

7 The Burns et al. (1984) study is careful and thorough in its test of opponent-process ideas and shows that an equiluminance mixture of unique green and unique red would appear yellowish for 2°40´ field sizes. They conclude: "our data rule out general linear models which have unique hues as balance points for either of the two opponent mechanisms" (p. 487).

8 Larimer, Krantz, and Cicerone (1975) have also empirically shown that increases in the luminance of an otherwise fixed red light which appears neither bluish nor yellowish produces "a striking increase in *apparent* yellowness" of the red light (p. 726). This can be viewed as a violation of Assumption 2 above.

9 An assumption inherent in this discussion is that color relations found in color cancellation studies (e.g. Hurvich and Jameson) should *agree*, to a large extent, with color relations found via perceptual scaling judgments (e.g. Indow or Boynton). By *agree* we mean that at the very least the relational structure of cancellation results should be structurally similar to the relational structure of perceptual scaling results. For example, if in a cancellation paradigm a monochromatic yellow light is found to exactly cancel a monochromatic blue light, then we would expect a similar structural relation for opposing colors to be approximated in the spatial organization of empirically determined perceptual distance judgments, in additive and complementary color relations, and perhaps in the organization of other cognitive color processing. We consider the existing cancellation results an important demonstration of underlying processes and thereby a limiting condition, or starting point, for models describing more complex color perception phenomena. Beyond "isomorphic" correspondence, it would be a happy coincidence if it is found that linear relations observed in cancellation data are also preserved in perceptually scaled colors connected by a straight line and which occur on opposing sides of a neutral achromatic point.

10 The CIE space was constructed to permit additive, or cancellation, pairs to be defined as corresponding points along a straight line through the achromatic "white" point. However, drawing a straight line through the white point of a perceptual space, like Munsell, to find

complementary pairs is somewhat different. That is, there is no a priori reason why surface "complements" should correspond to CIE cancellation complements. While the two spaces are topologically isomorphic, it is not logically necessary that their linear structures are isomorphic. To what extent then do the color-pair relations in the two kinds of spaces coincide? As mentioned earlier, Newhall, Nickerson, and Judd (1943) demonstrated that, when compared to an early version of CIE space, an adjusted Munsell space gives an approximation to the equispacing achieved in the CIE formulation. Indow (1987) points out that portions (i.e., the Y–B relation) of the Munsell scaling obtain opposing pairs of corresponding colors via a linear locus through the CIE white point. Deviations from strictly linear complement relations are attributed in part to Abney and Bezold–Brücke hue shifts (see Indow [1987] Figure 4, p. 258). Moreover, Indow (1987), citing Krantz (1975), states: "perceptual color differences and principal components, both obtained through subjective judgments, approximately behave as a linear system" (p. 259). This correspondence of CIE space with perceptual space needs further exploration to determine fully which metric relations, if any, are preserved in both spaces.

References

Abramov, I., and J. Gordon 1994. Color appearance: on seeing red – or yellow, or green, or blue. *Annual Review of Psychology* 45: 451–485.

Adams, F. M, and C. E. Osgood 1973. A cross-cultural study of the affective meaning of color. *Journal of Cross-cultural Psychology* 4: 2135–2156.

Bagley, M.-O., and M. S. Maxfield 1986. Afterimage color perception for designers. *Perceptual and Motor Skills* 63: 995–1007.

Berlin, B., and P. Kay 1969. *Basic Color Terms: Their Universality and Evolution*. Berkeley: University of California Press. 1st paprback edn. 1991, with bibliography by Luisa Maffi.

Binet, A., and T. H. Simon 1908/1916. The development of intelligence in the child. (E. S. Kiffe, trans.). In H. H. Goddard (ed.), *The Development of Intelligence in Children* (pp. 182–273). Baltimore: Williams & Wilkins.

Bornstein, M. H., W. Kessen, and S. Weiskopf 1976. Color vision and hue categorization in young human infants. *Journal of Experimental Psychology: Human Perception and Performance* 2: 115–129.

Boster, James S. 1986 Can individuals recapitulate

the evolutionary development of color lexicons? *Ethnology* 25(1): 61–74.

Boynton, R. M. 1979. *Human Color Vision*. New York: Holt, Rinehart, and Winston.

Boynton, R. M. and C. X. Olson 1987. Locating basic colors in the OSA space. *Color Research and Application* 12(2): 94–105.

Burns, S. A., A. E. Elsner, J. Pokorny, and V. C. Smith 1984. The Abney effect: chromaticity coordinates of unique and other constant hues. *Vision Research* 24(5): 479–489.

Cook, W. M. 1931. Ability of children in color discrimination. *Child Development* 2: 303–320.

Cornsweet, T. N. 1970. *Visual Perception*. New York: Academic Press.

D'Andrade, R. G., and M. J. Egan 1974. The color of emotion. *American Ethnologist* 1: 49–63.

Derrington, A. M., J. Krauskopf, and P. Lennie 1984. Chromatic mechanisms in lateral geniculate nucleus of macaque. *Journal of Physiology*, 357: 241–265.

De Valois, R. L. 1960. Color vision mechanisms in the monkey. *Journal of General Physiology*. 43: 115–128.

De Valois, R. L., and K. K. De Valois 1993. A multi-stage color model. *Vision Research* 33(8): 1053–1065.

De Valois, R. L., and G. H. Jacobs 1968. Primate color vision. *Science* 162: 533–540.

De Valois, R. L., I. Abramov, and G. H. Jacobs 1966. Analysis of response patterns of LGN cells. *Journal of the Optical Society of America* 56: 966–977.

Dimmick, F. L., and M. R. Hubbard 1939a. The spectral location of psychologically unique yellow, green, and blue. *American Journal of Psychology* 52: 242–254.

1939b. The spectral location of psychologically unique red. *American Journal of Psychology* 52: 348–353.

Gerritsen, F. 1975. *Theory and Practice of Color*. New York: Van Nostrand Reinhold.

Hård, A., and L. Sivik 1981. NCS – Natural Color System: a Swedish standard for color notation. *Color Research and Application* 6(3): 129–138.

Hardin, C. L. 1988. *Color for Philosophers: Unweaving the Rainbow*. Indianapolis, IN: Hackett Publishing Co.

Hurvich, L. M. 1981. *Color Vision*. Sunderland, MA: Sinauer Associates.

Hurvich, L. M., and D. Jameson 1957. An opponent-process theory of color vision. *Psychological Review* 64(6): 384–404.

Indow, T. 1987. Psychologically unique hues in aperture and surface colors. *Die Farbe* 34: 253–260.

1988. Multidimensional studies of Munsell solid. *Psychological Review* 95(4): 456–470.

Indow, T and N. Aoki 1983. Multidimensional mapping 178 Munsell colors. *Color Research and Application* 5(3): 145–152.

Jameson, D., and L. M. Hurvich 1955. Some quantitative aspects of an opponent-colors theory. I. Chromatic responses and spectral saturation. *Journal of the Optical Society of America* 45(7): 546–552.

Johnson, A., O. Johnson, and M. Bakash 1986. Cognitive and emotional aspects of Machiquenga color terms. *American Anthropologist* 88: 674–681.

Johnson, E. G. 1977. The development of color knowledge in preschool children. *Child Development* 48: 308–311.

Judd, D. B. 1951. Basic correlates of visual stimulus. In S. S. Stevens (ed.), *Handbook of Experimental Psychology* (pp. 811–867). New York: John Wiley & Sons, Inc.

Kaplan, E., B. B. Lee, and R. M. Shapley 1990. New views of primate retinal function. In N. N. Osborne and G. J. Chader (eds.), *Progress in Retinal Research*. Vol. IX (273–336). New York: Pergamon.

Kay, P., and C. K. McDaniel 1978. The linguistic significance of the meanings of basic color terms. *Language* 54(3): 610–646.

Kay, P., B. Berlin, and W. R. Merrifield 1991. Biocultural implications of systems of color naming. *Journal of Linguistic Anthropology* 1(1): 12–25.

Krantz, D. H. 1975. Color measurement and color theory II: opponent color theory. *Journal of Mathematical Psychology* 12: 304–327.

1989. Color and force measurement. In P. Suppes, D. M. Krantz, R. D. Luce, and A. Tversky (eds.), *Foundations of Measurement*. Vol. II, *Geometrical, Threshold, and Probabilistic Representations* (pp. 226–296). San Diego, CA: Academic Press.

Krauskopf, J., D. R. Williams, and D. R. Heeley 1982. Cardinal directions of color space. *Vision Research* 22: 1123–1131.

Larimer, J., D. H. Krantz, and C. M. Cicerone 1975. Opponent process additivity – II. Yellow/blue equilibria and nonlinear models. *Vision Research* 15: 723–731.

Lennie, P., and M. D'Zmura 1988. Mechanisms of color vision. *Critical Reviews in Neurobiology* 3(4): 333–400.

MacLaury, R. E. 1992. From brightness to hue: an explanatory model of color category evolution. *Current Anthropology* 33: 137–186.

MacLeod, D. I. A., and R. M. Boynton 1979. Chromaticity diagram showing cone excitation by stimuli of equal luminance. *Journal of the Optical Society of America* 69(8): 1183–1186.

Maffi, L. 1988. World Color Survey report. Unpublished ms., University of California, Berkeley.

Miller, D. L., and B. R. Wooten 1990. The elemental hues of spectral lights, and the occasionally anomalous nature of green. *Investigative Ophthalmology and Visual Science* 31(4): 262.

Miller, G. A., and P. N. Johnson-Laird 1976. *Language and Perception*. Cambridge, MA: Harvard University Press.

Munsell Book of Color 1929, 1976. Baltimore, MD: Munsell Color Company, Macbeth Division of Kollmorgen Corporation.

Newhall, S. M., D. Nickerson, and D. B. Judd 1943. Final report on the OSA subcommittee on the spacing of the Munsell colors. *Journal of the Optical Society of America* 33(7): 385–418.

Niall, K. K. 1988. On the trichromatic and opponent-process theories: an article by E. Schrödinger. A translation of E. Schrödinger's 1925 paper, "How to reconcile two theories of color." *Spatial Vision* 3(2): 79–95.

Nickerson, D. 1981. OSA color scale samples: a unique set. *Color Research and Application* 6: 7–33.

Ratliff, F. 1976. On the psychophysiological basis of universal color terms. *Proceedings of the American Philosophical Society* 120(5): 311–330.

Rosch, E. 1972. Universals in color naming and memory. *Journal of Experimental Psychology* 93(1): 10–20.

       1973. Natural categories. *Cognitive Psychology* 4: 328–350.

Shepard, R. N., and L. A. Cooper 1992. Representation of colors in the blind, color-blind, and normally sighted. *Psychological Science* 3(2): 97–104.

Smallman, H. S., and R. M. Boynton 1990. Segregation of ten basic colors in an information display. *Journal of the Optical Society of America A* 7(10): 1985–1994.

       1993. On the usefulness of basic colour coding in an information display. *Displays* 14(3): 158–165.

Sternheim, C. E., and R. M. Boynton 1966. Uniqueness of perceived hues investigated with a continuous judgmental technique. *Journal of Experimental Psychology* 72(5): 770–776.

Tschermak, A. von. 1907. Über das verhältnis von gegenfarbe, kompensationsfarbe und kontrastfarbe. *Pflüger Archiv für Physiologie* 129: 473–497.

Varela, F. J., E. Thompson, and E. Rosch 1991. *The Embodied Mind: Cognitive Science and Human Experience*. Cambridge, MA: MIT Press.

Wilson, M. H., and R. W. Brocklebank 1955. Complementary hues of after-images. *Journal of the Optical Society of America* 45(4): 293–299.

Wyszecki, G., and W. S. Stiles 1982. *Color Science*. 2nd edition. New York: Wiley.

15 The linguistics of "color"

John A. Lucy

Introduction

Returning home from a recent field trip in Mexico, some ten pieces of my luggage were lost by the airline. I was directed to a service desk where I was asked to describe my luggage to the clerk. I was given a large plastic sheet with an array of some eighty to ninety different bags pictured, grouped as to type and each marked with a code number. Apparently the folk vocabulary of most passengers is not adequate to the task of describing luggage accurately, and this chart with its numbered items had been invented to circumvent the indeterminacy of ordinary language and facilitate precise characterizations.

The clerk prompted my entry into this memory-based matching task by asking me whether the bags were latched or zippered, large or small, etc. Not all the selections were obvious: sometimes I wanted to change the code number when I encountered a better match for one of my bags or understood better what alternatives the various groups represented; and some matches were never very satisfactory: for example, my son's French horn had to be matched with the number for a flute case. After I selected a number for each item, I had to describe the color of the bag. Unfortunately, the clerk did not pull out a Munsell array for this part of the task,[1] so he had to settle for my folk descriptions in this respect – but of course, he might well have, since Munsell first designed his color chart at the turn of the twentieth century for just such purposes, for accurate communication, in this case among artists, about colors, where the everyday language seemed wanting, inadequate for precise reference. It is ironic that this specialized device, first developed to circumvent or augment the natural semantics of everyday language, has become a central tool in the investigation of how our semantic systems operate. It is more odd still that it has become the standard by which we evaluate the semantics of other languages. And it is slightly incredible that it has become the model for the general relationship between natural language and cognition.

Imagine someone trying to convince you that the chart of airline luggage types could profitably be used to study the semantics of nouns in English, even allowing us to find, for example, a set of "basic luggage terms," and could then be used to compare basic luggage terminologies across languages and establish the evolutionary emergence of "luggage terms," and, finally, that the patterns in such data could be explained by the physiological wiring for "luggage" perception characteristic of all humans, not to mention primates. Not to worry that some people do not even seem to have luggage terms at all, or that some systems seem to center on what the luggage is made of or how much it costs rather than on latches and zippers, or that luggage terms intermingle structurally with other terms for containers. The point is that these other people can somehow refer to the items we have pictured on our chart, and in so doing they have, *ipso facto*, "luggage terms" – although they may not all be "basic" ones to be sure, and some poor folks have clearly been struggling along for millennia with "flawed" or "defective" luggage nomenclature because they have not yet undergone sufficient "technological and cultural advancement."

But wait, you protest, color and luggage are entirely different orders of phenomena, one has to do with our physiology and the other with cultural implements. Well, I might agree, but I challenge you to defend that, or any other such contrast, from a *linguistic* point of view. In either case, you are not distinguishing on the basis of language form or function, but on the non-linguistic status of the domain of reference (whether biological or cultural). You are appealing to *the nature of the referents and not to language itself* for your diagnosis of difference. (This is analogous to confusing the physical nature of light with the psychophysiology of color perception.) It is not obvious that from a linguistic point of view the two domains – color and luggage – are different until you show this on linguistic grounds. Inversely, if color terms are in fact so different from other terms, then why should they be taken as a model either for linguistic semantics generally or for the general relations between language and thought?

All of which leads to the general topic I want to treat here, namely, that, in the study of so-called "color terms," serious linguistic analysis has been in short supply. Conceptual muddles abound with respect to how linguistic categories are *characterized*, how they are *compared*, and how they are *linked to cognition*. Let us examine each of these points in turn.

The characterization of linguistic categories

Berlin and Kay's *Basic Color Terms* (1969: 1) was intended, in the first instance, to be a contribution to linguistic semantics, so let us begin by discussing how to characterize the semantics of linguistic categories. By *semantics* is meant the meaning that a linguistic category contributes to acts of reference and predication across contexts, that is, partialling out the idiosyncrasies of individual uses. Two factors contribute to the semantic meaning value of most linguistic categories. The first is the category's *characteristic referential range*, that is, its routine use to pick out or differentially signal certain referents across a wide range of contexts.[2] Languages differ widely in the referents they merge together and in the number and types of contrasts they recognize. The second factor is the category's *formal distributional potential*, that is, its position within the available categories in the language with which it contrasts and combines. Languages differ widely, if systematically, in how a given referential content is treated; what is a verb in one language may be a noun in another, what is obligatory in one language may be optional in another, and so forth. Patterns of characteristic reference and of formal distribution work together to give a form its semantic value. Research on semantic universals necessarily takes both into consideration. Yet *both* dimensions are routinely ignored in research on color terms which focuses primarily on denotational overlap across languages without any consideration of the typical use of the terms or of their formal status.[3]

Berlin and Kay's initial theory, building on earlier work by Lenneberg and others (Lucy 1992b: ch. 5), tried to develop a semantics of lexical items primarily in terms of their capacity to label certain referents. For example, the meaning of the term *red* was taken to be the specific colors the term referred to, especially the color judged to be the best example of the term. The ordinary everyday referential use of such terms as *red* was apparently never actually assessed systematically, nor was any attention given to their grammatical status in the language. Instead, an artificial stimulus array was shown to informants and they were asked to label the items in it. This array consisted of a selection from a set of Munsell color samples which varied on hue, saturation, and brightness. As a representative of everyday contexts, the array was very restricted, both in its exclusive focus on color and in the kinds of colors presented (e.g. including no variation in luster, luminosity, or reflectance). In a sense, the stimulus array dictated in advance the possible meanings the terms could have since no other meanings were embodied in the samples. Although restricted in this way, the stimulus array was also very complex, and the labeling task performed with it forced informants to make referential microcomparisons and judgments of a sort rarely encountered in daily life. The task assumed that speech is about labeling accuracy rather than situational intelligibility – to use Havránek's (1964 [1932]) terms.

The particular semantic view that these terms primarily refer to color and the broader linguistic ideology that meaning is really about accurate denotation, both derive directly from the folk understandings of English speakers about how their language works. The hard lesson of linguistics, as with all other sciences, has been that folk views, however intuitively compelling, bear a very uncertain relationship to the full story. Yet nearly all subsequent research in this tradition preserves this restricted focus on the denotation of the three dimensions of color embodied in the Munsell array and of only those three dimensions.

Contrast this with Conklin's (1964 [1955]) approach in his well-known study of Hanunóo color categories. Let us look firstly at how he determined typical referential value. Conklin did use prepared artificial stimuli including painted cards and dyed fabrics; but he also recorded "the visual-quality attributes taken from descriptions of specific items of the natural and artificial surroundings" (1964 [1955]: 190). This made it possible for him to discover the typical referents of these terms without prejudging what they must mean. "This [procedure] resulted," he says, "in the collection of a profusion of attributive words of the nonformal . . . type" (ibid.), by which he means attributive words referring to all visual qualities other than the form or shape of the referent. The very profusion of terms as well as the inconsistencies and overlap in their use was daunting at first until he noticed that in certain

> *contrastive* situations this initial confusion and incongruity of
> informant's responses did not usually occur. In such situations, where
> the "nonformal" (i.e., not spatially organized) visible quality of one
> substance (plant part, dyed thread, or color card) was to be related to
> and contrasted with that of another, both of which were either at
> hand or well known, terminological agreement was reached with
> relative ease ... Such a defined situation seemed to provide the frame
> necessary for establishing a known level of specification. (ibid.;
> location of first closing parenthesis corrected)

In other words, once the terms were put into actual use in a task other
than that of labeling, their typical referential values became clear. We
sometimes forget that words exist not simply to provide a list of labels
for reality but rather to accomplish communicative work, in this case,
distinguishing objects or conditions. It is to such cases of use that we
must turn if we are to understand their semantics.

It was in this context that Conklin discovered that at the most
general level of contrast, there was an underlying four-way classification of such visual stimuli in Hanunóo. He first glosses these four
terms by their typical color reference as "black," "white," "red," and
"light green," along with his estimates of focus and range, as shown
in Table 15.1. Then he goes on to say, however: "this ... classification
appears to have certain correlates beyond what is usually considered
the range of chromatic differentiation, and which are associated with
nonlinguistic phenomena in the external environment" (1964 [1955]:
191). That is, the terms have other meaning values, meaning values
which are not, despite assertions by others to the contrary, merely
connotational colorings, but which have to do with other typical
referential values. Conklin lists three such additional dimensions of
meaning:

> First, there is the opposition between light and dark ... Second there
> is an opposition between dryness or desiccation and wetness or
> freshness (succulence) in visible components of the natural
> environment which are reflected in the terms *rára'* ["red"] and *latuy*
> ["green"] respectively. This distinction is of particular significance in
> terms of plant life ... A shiny, wet, brown-colored section of newly-cut
> bamboo is *malatuy* ["green"] (not *marara'* ["red"]). (ibid.)

Table 15.1   Conklin's (1964 [1955]) glosses of Hanunóo visual quality terms[a]

(ma) bi:ru

color reference: "relative darkness (of shade of color);
                  blackness" (black)

focal point: black

range: black, violet, indigo, blue, dark green, dark gray,
        and deep shades of other colors and mixtures

other reference: dark; deep, unfading, indelible

(ma)lagti'

color reference: "relative lightness (or tint of color);
                  whiteness" (white)

focal point: white

range: white and very light tints of others colors
        and mixtures

other reference: light; pale, weak, faded, or bleached

(ma)rara'

color reference: "relative presence of red; redness" (red)

focal point: orange-red

range: maroon, red, orange, yellow, and mixtures in which
        these qualities are seen to predominate

other reference: dryness or desiccation; desiccated; deep, unfading,
                  indelible

(ma)latuy

color reference: "relative presence of light greenness; greenness"
                  (green)

focal point: leaf-green

range: light green and mixtures of green, yellow, and light
        brown

other reference: wetness or freshness; raw; pale, weak, faded, or
                  bleached

---

[a]"The four ... terms occur as attributes [adjectives] with the prefix *ma-* 'exhibiting, having,' as
indicated in parentheses, or as free words (abstracts)" (Conklin 1964 [1955]: 190).

Notice that if we restrict ourselves to "color" we cannot explain this
pattern; and it is *not* a "mere" connotation of the term – it is direct
reference pure and simple: "A third opposition . . . is that of deep,
unfading, indelible, and hence often more desired material as against
pale, weak, faded, bleached, or 'colorless' substance, a distinction contrasting *mabi:ru* ["black"] and *marara'* ["red"] with *malagti'* ["white"] and
malatuy ["green"]" (ibid.). Conklin concludes by glossing the four terms
as "lightness, darkness, wetness, and dryness" and by noting that
"what appears to be color 'confusion' at first may result from an inadequate knowledge of the internal structure of a color system and from
a failure to distinguish sharply between sensory reception on the one
hand and perceptual categorization on the other" (1964 [1955]: 192).

What is crucial to recognize here is that an "adequate knowledge"
of the system would never have been produced *by restricting the stimuli
to color chips and the task to labeling.* Yet, to this day these remain the
two key methodological strategies within the tradition stimulated by
Berlin and Kay's work. Much has been made by those in this tradition
of the important similarities between the results of their approach
and those of Conklin: both reveal a small set of basic terms with colorific values. Yet, nowhere do they engage with the obvious fact that
these are not color terms at all in our sense, and that they conflate
non-colorific meanings as part of their core referential value.[4] When
we get into a position such that we have to say for the Hanunóo that
"light" really means "white," "wet" really means "green," and "dry"
really means "red," there is something terribly wrong from a linguistic point of view.[5]

Let us look secondly at how the issue of structural position, the
second contributor to the semantic value of each linguistic category,
might be handled. In the case of lexical items, we want to know what
constructions a term can enter into, since a part of its meaning lies in
the contribution it makes to an utterance as a whole; and we want to
know what other terms pattern in the same fashion, since the meaning of a term depends on what it is in contrast with. Berlin and Kay do
not analyze the syntactic status of these terms – there is no mention,
for example, of the fact that color terms tend to be included in one
type of adjective class in English along with certain other kinds of
adjectives, or that the various terms divide into subgroups as a function of their syntactic potential, or that they themselves can in turn

be modified in certain ways. Some of these issues do emerge in the criteria used for justifying the notion of basic term. Where the denotational net has caught too many fish, syntactic criteria such as morphological complexity, distributional potential, substitutability, and scope of modification are invoked to sort out the undesirables. That is, rather than being used as a discovery procedure for how the language works, formal analysis is employed only to justify what has, in the end, quite clearly been decided a priori on intuitive grounds.

Most subsequent work has followed the same general approach. However, in the Kay and McDaniel (1978) revision of the theory, the significance for the meaning of individual color terms of having different numbers of contrasting terms is discussed. Likewise, in MacLaury's (1992) proposed extensions of the theory, the significance of having different numbers and types of category alternates in a system is discussed. In both cases, however, morphosyntactic analysis plays virtually no substantive role in the discussion, the focus being entirely on the implications in the mapping task. Indeed, what little syntactic analysis there was in the Berlin and Kay approach has been even further reduced in subsequent work with some authors feeling substitutability relations of nonhyponymy suffice as a criterion of basicness, while others add unrestricted reference which is better cast as unrestricted combinatorial potential.[6] We do not see in this work an analysis of a language system, or even a formal subsystem within a language, in order to understand how that language structures reference in general, or the qualities of objects in particular, or even colorific information. Rather, we have the extraction of a set of individual lexical items from the grammar primarily on the basis of their capacity to refer to a fixed stimulus array, and then the reduction of that list in terms of the items' denotational potential and internal relations with one another.

Although Conklin, too, tends in this direction, focusing more on denotational value than on system value, he does at least begin by asking what the system-internal regularities are, and it is these regularities which define his set of four terms, not a set of criteria from outside the language. Further, in passing, he does tell us quite a bit about the terms, the kinds of modifiers they take, morphologically related forms, etc. He also discusses how secondary terms are created from the four basic terms which gives us insight into the native semantics. Here he stresses again the importance of non-colorific information: "Much attention is paid to the texture of the surface referred to, the resulting degree and type of reflection (iridescent, sparkling, dull), and to admixture of other nonformal [= nonspatial] qualities. Frequently these noncolorimetric aspects are considered of primary importance, the more spectrally-definable qualities serving only as secondary attributes. In either case polymorphemic descriptions are common" (1964 [1955]: 191). In short, even though primarily reference-based, Conklin is at least sensitive to the contours of the specific system he is dealing with.

It might be instructive in this regard to look at the distribution potential for a few English adjectives for visual qualities, as shown in Table 15.2. As is immediately evident, the terms having some reference to color are a heterogeneous lot, both in terms of their similarity to other adjectives and in terms of their own internal subgrouping. These differences in potential both contribute to and arise from the meanings of the terms. In particular, what accounts for the absence of the *-en* forms in E through I or for the absence of the *-ing* forms in F and G? There is clearly some difference in lexical meaning here which prompts the differential treatment. It is also reasonable to ask, on syntactic grounds, why terms in the B group are not considered "color terms" and what rules out some of the terms in E and F. The point is not that these questions cannot be answered – several of them can – but rather that the entire approach to color terms has lacked any serious comprehensive analysis of the grammatical dimension of these forms. Important aspects of the meanings of these forms are lost, the generalizability of these findings for other domains of grammar and to grammatical theory (e.g. marking theory) remains unclear, and, perhaps most importantly, one of the key methodological strategies for penetrating the semantics of other languages has been abandoned.[7]

I want to stress here that nothing especially remarkable is being called for – far from it. For over a hundred years now the centrality of distributional analysis in linguistics has been a hallmark of the discipline. It is detailed empirical and theoretical attention to such structural patterns which distinguishes linguistic science from folk understandings of language. To repeat, meaning is not reducible to denotation but is also a function of and a determinant of structural

Table 15.2   Distribution of some English adjectives for nonspatial visible qualities

A	hard		harden	hardening	
	rough		roughen	roughening	
	bright		brighten	brightening	
B	light	lightish	lighten	lightening	
	dark	darkish	darken	darkening	
C	black	blackish	blacken	blackening	dark black
	white	whitish	whiten	whitening	light white
D	red	reddish	redden	reddening	dark/light red
E	yellow	yellowish		yellowing	dark/light yellow
	brown	brownish		browning	dark/light brown
	tan	tannish		tanning	dark/light tan
	grey	greyish		greying	dark/light grey
	green	greenish		greening[a]	dark/light green
	blue	bluish		bluing[a]	dark/light blue
F	pink	pinkish			dark/light pink
	orange	orangish[b]			dark/light orange
	purple	purplish			dark/light purple
	blond	blondish			dark/light blond
G	maroon				dark/light maroon
	silver				dark/light silver
	beige				dark/light beige
	aqua				dark/light aqua
	crimson				dark/light crimson
	scarlet				dark/light scarlet
	violet				dark/light violet
H	dry			drying	
	clear			clearing	
	glossy			glossing	
	shiny			shining	
I	pale	palish			
J	vivid				
	brilliant				
	luminous				
	ruddy				

[a] Unlike other items in this group, *greening* and *bluing* cannot be used as predicate adjectives (is *greening* or is *bluing*) but can be used in certain fixed expressions (e.g. *the greening of America*, *a bluing agent*).
[b] Often *orangey* in British English (Crawford 1982: 341).

position. Yet in this attempt to probe the semantics of language, attention to linguistic structure is virtually lacking. Individual lexical items are culled from informants and their referential values established by a fixed denotational task. It really does not matter what language the terms come from. Articles surveying terms in a dozen or more languages never mention anything about those languages, or even about the structural value of the terms.[8] *You do not need to know anything about languages or linguistics at all to read this literature or even to conduct research within the tradition.* This should give us pause since the tradition claims to be contributing to our understanding of the semantics of natural languages. You cannot generate a typology of "color systems" across languages without establishing that such systems actually exist as identifiable "systems" in those languages. A content-based collection of lexical items does not constitute a linguistic system.[9]

The comparison of linguistic categories

All these difficulties come to a head in the second topic, namely, the analysis and comparison of different languages, for it is in the study of systems other than our own that intuition is especially suspect and reliance on formal methods absolutely essential, whether we are working with the referential or the distributional aspects of semantics. The key element of these methods is that they must be capable of revealing the diversity of language categories even as we seek to generalize across systems. It is here that the restriction of reference to the denotation of stimuli meeting our own conception of color and the neglect of systematic grammatical comparison limit our understanding.

What is it we want to know? Well, if we are studying semantic systems, looking in particular for semantic universals, then we want to know how the world's languages structure reference. It is worth mentioning at this point that color is not central to the semantic organization of any language that I know of. Unlike agency, time, number, or other such categories, it is never grammaticalized, and it is still not even clear that it forms a well-defined lexical set in distributional terms in very many languages. It is certainly not an obvious choice as a means to understanding the semantics of natural language.

Nonetheless, if we choose to focus on color, for whatever reason, then we want to know how the world's languages structure reference to color stimuli in their semantic systems – and the key words here are *structure* and *system*. We assume that all languages can refer to visual stimuli such as the Munsell array insofar as they are perceptible to most human beings and any language has the capacity to refer to such human experience in some way. So our problem is not simply to describe the capacity of a language to refer to this array, but rather to describe either the existence of a system of color categories, one or more structural units within the language that can be identified as having for their referential content what we call color, or the characteristic incorporation of colorific information into categories of other types. However, I would submit, neither of these goals is achievable without an analysis of the structure of the language. If you do not look at the grammar of the language, you cannot establish either that color terms form a unified syntactic set or that colorific information is incorporated into other morphosyntactic sets in a regular way.

You may ask, though, are there no other routes? Can we not simply use the Berlin and Kay procedure, that is, show our stimuli, extract a list of expressions, and then sort them out to establish the existence of a set of color words using criteria such as hyponymy and range? After all, systematic lexicalization of color reference across languages would constitute a systematic fact. Well, yes, you can do this, and many people have – but then I can do the same thing with reference to "luggage" or any other domain, eliciting responses and then sorting them according to my inclination – and, indeed, there have been many such efforts reported in the ethnoscience literature. Without serious attention to the structural side of the interaction, anything goes.

Or, you might ask, what about the success of the approach? After all, as apologists for this tradition often note, it works! These color systems are there! Surely that is an interesting and important fact in its own right. Well, I agree that something is there, but exactly what? I would argue that *what is there is a view of the world's languages through the lens of our own category,* namely, a systematic sorting of each language's vocabulary by reference to how, and how well, it matches our own. This approach might well be called the radical universalist position since it not only seeks universals, but sets up a procedure which guarantees both their discovery and their form.[10] To critique this radical universalism, one need not embrace relativism, but only draw the line between adequate and inadequate methodology, between projecting our assumptions and challenging them. I myself believe that there are universal patterns to the semantic treatment of the phenomena we call color perception, but I believe they bear a very indirect relationship to the findings of the basic color term tradition.

To see how the universal result is guaranteed, let us look at the procedure in its most usual form. We begin by having informants describe the color samples. This is not always easy. As Conklin notes, "Color, in a western technical sense, is not a universal concept and in many languages such as Hanunóo there is no unitary terminological equivalent" (1964 [1955]: 189). Without such a term, how can we attribute "color" as a concept to a language? Well, it is true that informants can have a concept in their language without a verbal label for it also being present in the language; but if there is to be a *linguistic* category, if we are to attribute the concept to the semantic system *of the language*, then there must be *some* mark in the language. Otherwise we have a perceptual or cognitive category, but not a linguistic one. Without either a lexical or other structural mark for the existence of "color" as a unified concept in a language, it should not be attributed to the semantics of the language.

Conklin then goes on to describe his difficulties in eliciting terms.[11] He was forced to ask questions such as "How is it to look at?" and then when his informants responded he asked them to stop providing the sorts of terms he did not want, such as shape terms. Use of the Munsell chips effectively solves this problem by eliminating virtually every other possible dimension of contrast aside from those we consider to be color. Any term applied to these chips and discriminating among them is by definition about color and, on the other hand, anything having to do with color ought to be elicitable using these chips. I am going to grant the second claim for the moment, namely, that this array represents color even though other visual qualities which one might arguably include in the domain of color – such as texture, reflectance, luster, luminosity, and so forth – are not systematically varied in the instrument. To go into this would deflect us from the argument at hand.

Consider now the first claim that any piece of language applied to these chips will be about color. Of course it may be a pretty complex piece of language and it might be about something else too, so we have to sift the terms by our criteria. That is, we have to decide which responses will count as basic color terms. What are the criteria? Well, we want forms like ours, lexemes which refer exclusively to color across many referents. If there is a complex construction referring to color and we recognize it as such, it is out. If there is a construction that also refers to something other than color and we recognize it as such, it is out. If there is a construction that refers to color only under some conditions and we recognize it as such, it is out. Granted, much of the time these criteria are grossly misapplied, but in aggregate, over many cases, they sharply delimit which of the speaker's responses count.

There are some sad ironies here. The actual grammar of the language being examined plays almost no role in the analysis, yet our own grammatical pattern is applied as the standard for identifying appropriate color forms.[12] The actual range of reference of the forms plays no role in the analysis, only its coverage of the denotational range characteristic of our forms. The local pattern of use of the forms is irrelevant, the only relevant usage being the application of the terms in the denotational naming task. Not surprisingly, this procedure cannot tell us how these other languages handle reference in general or even color reference in particular; it can only tell us how closely they approximate our own technique of color reference.

Wait, though, you say, look how few types of systems actually emerge out of the thousands of logical possibilities! There is structure in these data! Doesn't this show that something is really going on here? Well, to be sure there is some regularity here, but it is doubtful that it is simply due to the nature of color reference in language. The original calculations about logically possible systems were made at a point in the development of the theory when the focus was associated with specific chips; in this situation it made some sense to calculate the logical possibilities because one could know with some confidence when you had a system of a certain type: simply look at the focus. The fact is, however, that foci do not reliably align with unique chips or even with unique hues. Indeed, there are probably very few hues that have not been picked by informants in one language or another as the focus for some category (cf. charts in MacLaury 1992).

The category criteria now hinge on how the array is divided. So when a category is identified now, it is really the investigator who decides which "color" (or "composite color"[13]) it will count as. What are the odds that an investigator would ever report a system with terms corresponding to dark, white, purple, and brown? My suspicion is that it would be coded either as a two-term system of dark/cool versus light/warm with two other non-basic terms, or perhaps as a four-term system of black, white, red, and yellow. Either way, purple and brown simply will not emerge. Indeed, there is no objective way to prove that that is what they "really" are. (Notice that you cannot appeal to psychophysiology to assign these labels if you are trying to show, as a finding, that they match the psychophysiology.) So this "logical possibility" does not stand much of a chance; nor do most of the others. The point again is that what appears to be objective – in this case, a statement of statistical odds – is based on assumptions which are no longer tenable and is, as a consequence, vulnerable in application to a highly interpretive methodology readily skewed towards the theoretical expectations derived from our own language.[14]

No matter how much we pretend that this procedure is neutral or objective, it is not. The procedure strictly limits each speaker by rigidly defining what will be labeled, which labels will count, and how they will be interpreted. To use a political metaphor, it is as if one political party were entitled to dictate what you would vote on, to count the votes, and to report what the results meant. Is it any wonder that the party's candidate would win by a landslide validating a preset mandate? Is it any wonder, really, that all the world's languages look remarkably similar in their treatment of color and that our system represents the *telos* of evolution? What actually *is* astounding is that so much variability still shows up. Perhaps it is worth pointing out, finally, if it is not already obvious, that increased sample size will never address these methodological problems. The assertion that the procedure has worked for literally hundreds of languages counts for nothing if it is fundamentally flawed in the first place. The color chart may be a good tool for improving precision in communications in the worlds of art and commerce, but it is a poor tool for investigating natural language semantics.

Let us look at how a couple of examples would fare with this procedure. Suppose we applied it to Hanunóo speakers. Presumably, when

shown Munsell chips, Hanunóo speakers would use the terms presented in Table 15.1 because colorific information is part of their referential potential. I seriously doubt, however, that the other meanings
that Conklin first turned up in the course of analyzing descriptions
of plants would have ever been discovered. The system would be
characterized as a four-term system. If these other meanings did turn
up, by rights the system should be recast as a two-term system. Either
way, the interaction of "dryness" and "wetness" with color would
count for nothing. If this sort of pattern should be a fairly common
semantic pattern across languages – as it in fact is – you would never
discover it by this procedure.

The point here is not that Hanunóo is an exotic exception to the
basic color term thesis or that the peculiarities of this language are in
themselves important. Rather, the claim is that a whole level of analysis is missing from the basic color term tradition, namely, no attention whatsoever is paid to what the various terms actually mean in the
sense of what they typically refer to, their characteristic referential
range. Yet somehow a tradition that ignores these issues is supposed
to provide a way of discovering semantic universals.[15]

Let us take a second example. In an early study of color terms in the
Zuni language, Lenneberg and Roberts (1956: 24) claimed that Zuni
speakers do not differentiate the colors[16] "orange" and "yellow" but
define a common lexical category *lhupz/inna*[17] referring to the two. Let
us consider the Zuni case more closely. The Zuni terms used to refer to
colors seem to differ from ours more than in the ways just indicated,
that is, in their general cultural and linguistic-systemic values as well.
Linguist Stanley Newman (1954: 87–88) provided the following information concerning Zuni terms referring to the "color 'yellow'":

> Zuni has two lexemes expressing the literal notion of the color
> "yellow." Lexeme A would be used in contexts such as "yellow shirt,
> yellow paint." Lexeme B is employed in combinations such as "yellow
> skin, yellow leaves." The difference is not one of hue. Rather, lexeme A
> covers many shades of yellow characterizing an object, while lexeme B
> refers only to an object that has become yellow (or a related hue,
> which might be translated by English "pale" or "rusty") as a result of
> ripening or aging ... [S]uch a distinction ... suggest[s] that an
> investigation of color terms must recognize that such terms may

express discriminations other than those involved in the color spectrum.

The semantic range of lexeme B, in various morphological combinations, indicates the manner in which certain concepts are linked in terms of Zuni cultural associations. In its singular form lexeme B refers to any ripened or aged yellow object. In the plural it is specialized to refer to pollen or corn meal, a culturally important linkage for other related meanings of this lexeme. When it is preposed to an element meaning "stretching across," it forms the prayer term for "road" and, by extension, "the road of life." Reference here is to the ceremonial sprinkling of corn meal to form a path, symbolizing the sacred road.

In a comparison of the morphological status of the various Zuni terms referring to color, Hickerson (1975) reached a similar, although more general, conclusion about Zuni terminology, namely, that there were two basic kinds of terms with color reference, broad abstract terms deriving from verbs and specific terms deriving from substantives (nouns and particles). She says: "The verbs [referring to color] deal, ultimately, with processes of change or 'becoming'; most of the actual forms indicate an apprehended verbal state. Nouns and particles refer to intrinsic color, specific to a substance or object, and are unchanging. In other words, these two types of terms – verbals and substantives – seem to reflect two basically different types of experience" (Hickerson 1975: 328). Thus, the cultural and systemic meanings of the Zuni terms differ substantially from our own; to the denotational differences noted by Lenneberg and Roberts we must add other features such as a cultural concern with the origin of the color and various specific cultural associations. More generally, even where there is some denotational overlap with our own categories, it need not mean that the meaning value of the category in cultural and systemic terms is similar to our own or even that all the items grouped together as color terms are of the same grammatical type. Where we have adjectival primitives, the Zuni have derived verbal and nominal forms which overlap in denotation but not in overall sense. Where we have static qualities, the Zuni attend to the cause of the color. Focusing on the denotational overlap in the Munsell array misses this aspect of meaning altogether.

Again, the point here is not that the Zuni language is an exotic exception to the Berlin and Kay thesis[18] or that there are some interesting side details to be found in close case studies. Rather, the example reveals how a whole level of analysis is missing from the project, namely, attention to the structural or distributional place color terms occupy in a language. Dixon (1982) in a paper entitled "Where have all the adjectives gone?" surveys how the seven concepts encoded as adjectives in English (e.g. dimension, age, color) are treated in other languages. In the case of color concepts (in particular, black, white, and red), he found that they can be treated as verbs, as verbal classifiers, as nouns, as adjectives, as derived adjectives, as noun-specific adjunctives, or as free particles. Although color concepts tend to be treated as adjectives when a language has such a category, this is by no means universal either. Further, not all the relevant forms need fall within the same formal category within a language. As should be clear from the Zuni case, such grammatical properties have implications for the meanings of these terms. A serious attempt to extract semantic universals would begin with this array of language types and build on it, not ignore it.

If I may generalize here: what disturbs me the most is that nobody has been the least bit interested in all the data which have been discarded. What are the dimensions of visual experience that speakers of different languages tend to choose – and how do they relate to the overall organization of their grammar? What are the elements of meaning that are routinely bound with colorific meaning? What are the kinds of complex constructions that typically occur in reference to color? All of these constitute valid materials for constructing a view of the treatment of color in language. All of them should be of interest. The fact that they are not suggests that the investigators are not, in the last analysis, actually interested in the comparative semantics of languages and what generalities might be formed, but in something else.

The relation of language and thought

This brings us then to the third and final issue, the relation of language and thought. Since the very first, Berlin and Kay have connected their research with the Whorfian hypothesis, the proposal that the language we speak affects the way we think. Color was regarded by many as a perceptual continuum, and since the 1950s Eric Lenneberg, an American psycholinguist, had been using and promoting the color domain to test Whorf's thesis (Lucy 1992b: ch. 5). Berlin and Kay saw in the phenomenon of basic color terms counterevidence to Whorf's proposal and, indeed, evidence for the reverse, namely that the way we think (or at least perceive) affects, perhaps even determines, the form of our language. The desire to sustain this claim, rather than the impartial investigation of the semantics of natural languages, has been the driving force behind the research on color terms. Now there is nothing wrong in principle with trying to explore such a possibility; but I have argued elsewhere at great length (Lucy 1992b: ch. 5) that Lenneberg's whole approach was methodologically misguided from the outset and that it made something like the Berlin and Kay project and findings inevitable.[19] The universalist conclusions are built into the methodology and conceptualization of language employed in this research. Without repeating the details of the entire argument here, let me sketch the opposition at the heart of it.

If you begin convinced that you know what reality is and you go to see how languages "map" it, you will find, inevitably, that they map *the very same reality*. Why? Because the research procedure essentially *presupposes this common reality at every interpretive juncture*. This radical realism yields a *radical universalism*, because the universal finding is packed into the assumptions; it is definitional. This has really been the unifying theme of my criticism of the use of the Munsell array here. It does not really even matter whether the researchers involved are open-minded and consciously willing to recognize relativism as a possible outcome – because the universalist conclusion is guaranteed by their methodological assumptions. The languages being studied don't stand a chance.

On the other hand, if you begin convinced that you do not (or can not) know what reality is and you go to see how languages "construct" it, you will find, inevitably, that they construct *very different realities*. Why? Because the research procedure essentially *presupposes that every formal fact corresponds to a difference in reality*. Unrestrained, this radical formalism yields a *radical relativism*, because the relativity is packed into the assumptions; again, it is definitional. I happen not to believe that Whorf took this position, but that is immaterial to the present contrast because I know for certain that some of the critics of color tradition can rightly be called radical relativists. Again, their open-mindedness is of little consequence since their methodological assumptions will always preclude the essentialization necessary for comparison and generalization. One might say that, with them, reality does not stand a chance.[20]

The Asilomar conference was convened in the belief that we are close to a breakthrough in this impasse, that somehow research on color perception will show us a way out of this dilemma. What I want to emphasize in closing is that psychology and neuroscience really cannot resolve this opposition existing at the linguistic and cultural level. Our own culture's scientific goals of specifying what reality really is and what underlies our psychophysical experience of it are beside the point. The radical universalists might become more convinced that their reality is really real and writ into their physiology, but they never needed convincing in the first place; and knowing more about it will not in itself establish that the semantics of languages directly follow the same contours. Meanwhile, the radical relativists will continue to point to the facts of language difference as the irreducible primary fact (somehow more easily knowable than other forms of reality) and will, indeed, remain highly suspicious that the physical and psychophysical concern with color is, in the last analysis, itself an outgrowth of our own language.

I have spent the last ten years working out theory and methodology to address this opposition both conceptually and empirically.[21] I will not describe this research here except to say that it focuses on what I take to be the real linguistic relativity question, namely, whether the obvious differences we see across languages actually do affect thought; and it investigates the question empirically by examining the substantive domain of grammatical number which is of central structural importance in many languages. This is in contrast with the color-term tradition which focuses on whether visual neurophysiology has any effect on those lexical items referring to visual appearance, lexical items which are, in any event, of marginal structural significance everywhere.

I want to close by sketching a route out of this impasse – at least for the linguistic part of the analysis. Conceptually, we must avoid conflating cognitive and linguistic categories. It is misguided for the cognitive scientist to imagine that there is some innate physical or functional system for every lexical item in English. The fact that we have a word such as *color* or *brown* in English by no means establishes that it is a unified phenomenon at the biological level any more than it does for words such as *luggage* or *suitcase*. The lexicon of our language is not a sure guide to neurophysiology. The history of science has been marked by repeated efforts to evaluate critically rather than merely accept folk wisdom of just this sort. On the other hand, the fact that a physical, biological, or psychological "category" exists by no means implies that languages have to incorporate it into their *structures* either as a piece or, for that matter, at all. Language structures are built to serve human communicative needs and they will formally encode those aspects of experience which are maximally useful for communication and ignore those of little utility.

Methodologically, I recommend balancing the emphasis on form and substance (language and reality) in establishing the semantic system of a language. When working with a foreign language, we are better off first doing the formal analysis to as fine a level as is practical and then, and only then, applying the notional interpretations to those categories. These notional categories should be derived from a full investigation of the typical range of use (or functioning) of the forms. The formal–functional linkages emerging from this analysis (as well as characteristic arrangements of them) then provide the cases over which we form our generalizations. In this way we are forced to take account of both substantive usage and formal distributional facts when we make our comparisons and "translate." Although detailed studies of individual languages in their full complexity have value in their own right, this is not the particular point being advanced here; rather, what is being advocated is that the cases we use to form our generalizations about language universals be real cases with solid data on both characteristic referential range and structural distributional factors. Any approach which characterizes the domain in advance of analysis on the basis of the forms and referents from another language risks distorting the actual situation.

In the present case, based on what we already know, significant generalizations about the linguistics of "color" will be intimately tied up with such factors as whether or not a language has a formal class of adjectives; whether and how it encodes surface appearances; what animal, plant, or mineral[22] products are of local significance; the relative social importance of inferrable stages of ripeness, rawness, or decay; as well as various metaphoric regularities (e.g. Derrig 1978), etc. Within the context of such an analysis, one can then ask in light of wide-ranging exploration of actual usage whether any of the word classes seem to involve color meanings or whether such meanings distribute across classes or join with other concepts in regular ways. The results of such analyses form the basis for comparative generalizations across languages with regard to how colorific information is incorporated into linguistic systems in regular ways and, if we wish, to what extent "pure" systems of our type exist elsewhere. Such an approach should also provide an important counter-weight to premature judgments about "deficient" color systems, or evolutionarily "primitive" ones. If modern linguistics has shown anything, it is that apparent deficiency in one aspect of a referential system is reliably compensated for by relative elaboration somewhere else in the system. Figuring out these systematic interactions should be the real aim of research and theory and not some rank ordering by external criteria of individual subsystems in isolation.

To conclude, just as we now recognize that color is not "out there" in the light but in our perceptual interpretation of light, it is time to recognize that the communicatively relevant encodings of visual experience do not lie "in there" in the biology but out in socially anchored linguistic systems. It is time we reclaimed our lost linguistic luggage and started describing these linguistic systems in their full complexity. Then, and only then, can we actually address the issue of what regularities there are across languages and how they relate to thought.

Acknowledgments   This chapter was first presented as a paper at a conference on "Color Categories in Thought and Language" sponsored by the National Science Foundation and Syracuse University, held at the Asilomar Conference center, Pacific Grove, California, on October 27, 1992. Portions of the argument previously appeared in Lucy (1991). I thank all the conference participants for their comments.

Notes

1 I have since noticed that airport luggage charts usually do have a set of named color patches across the top.

2 Wierzbicka (1990) also criticizes equating the meaning of a color term with the perceptual qualities of a color chip. She proposes explaining cross-linguistic regularities in color term meaning by reference to the sequential encoding of widely recurrent salient experiences. Her approach, however, is intuitional and anecdotal: she provides no procedure for establishing the existence or specific meanings of color terms in a language.

3 The restricted focus on denotational overlap is not confined to the color research tradition. A companion paper (Lucy 1994) develops more fully the argument about the contribution of distributional potential to the meaning of forms by looking at research on the semantics of "space."

4 This criticism about other conceptual material being bound with color has been on the table for over two decades now (see Hickerson 1971, Conklin 1973) but has never been satisfactorily addressed. See also the discussion in Saunders (1992a: 52–53).

5 In a discussion of the "translation" of other languages by means of the Munsell array in the World Color Survey, Saunders points out similarly disconcerting equations: "when a Yupik (Alaska) speaker is claimed to use the black term for yellow, or a Yucuna (Peru) speaker focuses purple in green, or a Bhili (India) speaker focuses green on a pink chip called 'red', all connection between the utterance in the 'experiment' and the originating language is lost" (1992b: 21).

6 For critiques of the original criteria, see Crawford (1982), who calls for ignoring distributional potential, and Wescott (1970), who calls for a finer analysis of it. Of course, changing the criteria amounts to changing the definition of "basic color term." For related discussions concerned with how to reconcile varying kinds of "basic-ness" see Harkness (1973), Schaefer (1983), and Wierzbicka (1990). In a comparison of various measures for identifying and ranking basic color terms in several European languages, Corbett and Davies (this volume) examine derivational potential as one measure; but they assume basic color terms exist and are only interested in measures to sort them efficiently (into primary and secondary, basic and non-basic), not in whether the concept of "basicness" itself is coherent. They are not interested in the semantic implications of the derivational patterns themselves nor in the theoretical significance of using the various competing measures.

7 For an unusually thorough examination of the morpho-syntactic status of color terms see Schaefer (1983). The analysis recognizes and attempts to account for two distinct strata of color terms as well as some special anomalous forms. Kuschel and Monberg (1974: 217) likewise distinguish a stratum of "contextualised color terms, that is terms which are invariably linked to specific natural and cultural objects and which cannot be used in an indiscriminable [sic] or abstract way." Cf. note 6.

8 In discussion Paul Kay argued that some color researchers are knowledgeable about the languages they study. Some surely are. Many more, however, make use of the most naive of translation procedures without any systematic investigation of the language; and for those few who do undertake deeper investigation, such knowledge is rendered irrelevant by the method which makes the Munsell array the translation device. Cf. Quine (1990).

9 A number of discussers attempted to dismiss this critique as a call for case studies rather than "group study," but this misunderstands the point. The claim is that generalization must be across *actual* cases – real systems – not illusory ones generated by the research procedure. Generalization is the goal, but any generalization is only as good as the cases on which it is built.

10 Some discussants noted that the relativist climate within anthropology in the 1960s made the apparent discovery of a universal unexpected and impressive. In this sense, the universalist position was certainly not consciously "packed in." However, as the argument here indicates, the universalist conclusion is nonetheless built into the methodology and the conceptualization of language used in the research (Lucy 1992b: ch. 5). Moreover, the subsequent uncritical acceptance of this research stemmed in part from its "good fit" with the dominant universalist trend in linguistics during that same decade as signaled, for example, by the Jakobson and Halle (1956) statement of phonological universals, the ascendency of the Chomskian paradigm (Chomsky 1957, 1965) arguing for universal syntax, the emergence of Lenneberg's (1967) biologically based paradigm within psycholinguistics, and the publication of Greenberg's (1963) work on typological universals. Similar universalist trends prevailed in cognitive psychology. In this general universalist climate, devastating criticisms fell on deaf ears.

11 Kuschel and Monberg (1974) also describe in detail their difficulties with the general notion of color in

Bellona (Polynesia) and in getting informants to see any relationship between the small chips and colors in their natural environment. They suggest that the whole focus on "color" is ethnocentric. Saunders (1992a) makes much the same point about Kwakiutl.

12 Grammar enters into two of the main criteria: basic color terms must not be compounds (i.e., not morphologically complex) and their meaning must not be included within that of another (i.e., the distribution of one term must not be subsumed by another). These criteria, rather than local ones, become the filters through which the forms in other languages must pass. One of the subsidiary criteria also has to do with distributional features, but it is rarely ever invoked; see references in notes 6 and 7.

13 The more recent formulations of Kay and McDaniel (1978) and Kay, Berlin, and Merrifield (1991) concentrate their attention on how many of the sixty-three logical combinations of basic color categories have been empirically observed – especially in systems with fewer than six terms. The criticisms discussed in the text remain applicable although they are more difficult to illustrate because they are at a higher level of abstraction: they represent not the direct projection of our categories, but the projection of combinations of them. (Ironically, one critic of this approach, Wierzbicka [1990], makes use of the same sort of projection.) Composite categories joining yellow with blue, red with green, blue with black, etc., still seem difficult to reconcile with the supposed neurophysiological source of these categories (cf. McNeill 1972: 30–31; MacLaury 1991).

14 Note that this argument is quite independent of the facts that the total number of theoretically acceptable systems has grown quite large, that some researchers now recognize multiple systems within a single language, and that there are many data that do not fit well into any of the available models (see Kay, Berlin, and Merrifield 1991; MacLaury 1992; Saunders 1992a, 1992b).

15 We can encounter similar problems closer to home. In a detailed study of the terms *brun* "brown" and *marron* "brown" in Modern Standard French, Forbes (1979) argues that both terms meet the standard criteria of being monolexemic, not being hyponyms of the other, occurring early in elicited lists, and not being restricted to a narrow class of objects. They also share similar composite denotational ranges on the color chart with *marron*'s range encompassing *brun*'s. The focus for *marron* lies within the original Berlin and Kay cluster for BROWN whereas *brun* lies outside it – which might suggest that *marron* is the "more basic" term. On the other

hand, *marron* is about one tenth as frequent in text counts (contemporary oral use may be much higher; cf. discussion of Morgan's work in Corbett and Davies [this volume]), is different from other color terms in derivational and inflectional potential, and is still recognizably related to a fruit name. It is clearly the newcomer to the "basic" color lexicon of French. Although both terms have a wide referential range, Forbes finds that there is a preference for using *brun* to refer to physical types of person, to hair, and to skin, with *marron* relatively infrequent in such uses. This fact can arguably be considered part of the meaning of the term *brun*. This contrast is reminiscent of categories in many languages in which humans and other mammals (especially large ones) are singled out for distinctive linguistic treatment. (Compare, for example, English where there are color terms largely restricted to humans and large mammals [e.g. *blond*, *palomino*]. The same referents also take gender variants [e.g. *woman*, *bull*] and special collective terms [e.g. *people*, *cattle*] in English.) In short, while both French terms clearly meet the criteria of basic color terms and cover a similar range of color chips, they are different in their meanings when we consider their actual range of use. The color chart procedure does not, indeed cannot, capture such meaning differences because it rules them out of court as not relevant to how humans conceptualize color in language.

In the case of some African languages such as Mursi "there are no colour terms which are not also cattle-colour terms" (Turton 1980: 322), so that the entire labeling of an array of color samples is on analogy with these colors:

the fact that cattle-colour terms are exhaustive of the colour lexicon argues for a strong cultural influence on colour naming. On one of the rare occasions when an informant had difficulty deciding what colour term to apply to a particular stimulus card he muttered "There's no such beast"…That this informant chose this way to express his frustration is significant, for it shows that, in a sense, he was thinking of the cards not as representative examples of abstract colour categories, but as cattle, and he was thinking of them as cattle precisely because he was being asked to pay attention to them, and to classify them, solely in terms of colour. For the Mursi then, distinguishing between colours as such, any colours whatsoever, is analogous to distinguishing between the limited number of colours which naturally occur in their cattle. (ibid.)

Here is an efficient system for solving the referential problem of naming color samples, one long known to be characteristic of a range of African languages (Woodworth 1910: 329; Turton 1980: 333, 335 n. 3; Schaefer 1983: 174–175, 184 n. 6). Quite naturally, the system distinguishes with considerable delicacy in the red–brown–pink range of colors but more crudely in the green–blue range – not because of relative position in some evolutionary sequence but because of the very nature of the model on which the relevant terms are based. Such systems fusing reference to color sensation with socially significant objects are not confined to Hanunóo, or French, or English, or Mursi – they are a world-wide pattern which should figure centrally in any linguistically oriented description of color reference. Finally, even where a set of Western-style color terms are in use, we can expect there to be domain-specific variation in their salience in application (cf. Bolton 1978).

16 Hickerson (1975) reports that there appears to be no general term for "color" in Zuni. Lenneberg and Roberts give no indication of how the Zuni were asked to list their color terms and name the color samples.

17 Lenneberg and Roberts use a solidus (/) to indicate a glottal stop in Zuni.

18 Indeed the Zuni case is far from unusual. Kuschel and Monberg (1974: esp. 224–225, 230) report similar semantic linkages between a color and the factors precipitating that color. In the case of Samoan, Snow (1971) reports that there are two terms for green, one restricted to animate entities and the other to inanimate entities. This difference in meaning would be impossible to handle within the basic color term model and the term restricted to animates would not even be readily elicited using color chips. Notice that the problem in these cases is the inverse of the Mursi one discussed in note 15.

19 Not to mention that proposals of various sorts for the evolutionary development of color vocabularies have also long been part of the Western tradition (see Woodworth 1910).

20 Everybody seems to be against the simple relativist–universalist opposition these days – but not in quite the same ways. Kay, Berlin, and Merrifield (1991: 13) see biology providing the basic frame and culture accounting for the local, historical residual ("in particular times and places"). Sahlins (1976) forwards a variant of the same scheme in which he accepts the universality of color terms but regards them as input for a higher level of cultural symbolism – thus giving culture a greater, more autonomous role in manipulating the biological "givens." Turton (1980: 334) questions Sahlins's easy acceptance of the universality of terms, but himself accepts that the culturally anchored systems are used to "stand for the differences between universally recognized categories of colour and pattern." Wierzbicka (1990: 140–142) continues in this vein, but for her the universally recognized categories are cultural artefacts anchored in "universals of human experience" rather than direct products of neurophysiology. Finally, Saunders (1992a, 1992b) questions the universality of the human experience of "color" and sees the opposition between relativism and universalism as itself a product of shared underlying "empiricist" assumptions – especially those centering on a clear contrast of form and content (or scheme and reality) (cf. Lucy 1985). The argument presented here accepts many of these points but differs by proposing a procedure for analyzing and comparing systems by identifying formal–functional regularities across languages; that is, it makes identifying the actual range and degree of linguistic difference the first research problem within a concern for typology and explanation.

21 For the general position see Lucy (1992b, 1996); for empirical work on number, see Lucy (1992a); for work exploring whether color-term systems affect thought see Lucy and Shweder (1979) and Lucy (1981).

22 Navaho bases color reference on local minerals (McNeill 1972).

References

Berlin, B., and P. Kay 1969. *Basic Color Terms: Their Universality and Evolution*. Berkeley: University of California Press. 1st paperback edn. 1991, with bibliography by Luisa Maffi.

Bolton, R. 1978. Black, white, and red all over: the riddle of color term salience. *Ethnology* 17: 287–311.

Chomsky, N. 1957. *Syntactic Structures*. Janua Linguarum, Series Minor 4. The Hague: Mouton.

    1965. *Aspects of the Theory of Syntax*. Cambridge, MA: MIT Press.

Conklin, H. C. 1964 [1955]. Hanunóo color categories. In D. Hymes (ed.), *Language in Culture and Society: A Reader in Linguistics and Anthropology* (pp. 189–192). New York: Harper and Row. (From *Southwestern Journal of Anthropology* (1955) 11(4): 339–344.)

    1973. Color categorization: review of *Basic Color Terms*, by Brent Berlin and Paul Kay. *American Anthropologist* 75: 931–942.

Crawford, T. D. 1982. Defining "basic color term." *Anthropological Linguistics* 24(3): 338–343.

Derrig, S. 1978. Metaphor in the color lexicon. In D. Farkas, W. Jacobsen, and K. Todrys (eds.), *Papers from the Parasession on the Lexicon, Chicago Linguistic Society*. (pp. 85–96) Chicago Linguistic Society.

Dixon, R. 1982. Where have all the adjectives gone? In R. Dixon (ed.), *Where Have All the Adjectives Gone? and Other Essays in Semantics and Syntax* (pp. 1–62) Berlin: Mouton/Walter de Gruyter.

Forbes, I. 1979. The terms *brun* and *marron* in modern standard French. *Journal of Linguistics* 15: 203–395.

Greenberg, J. 1963. *Universals of Language*. Cambridge, MA: MIT Press.

Harkness, S. 1973. Universal aspects of learning color codes: a study in two cultures. *Ethos* 2: 175–200.

Havránek, B. 1964 [1932]. The functional differentiation of the standard language. In P. Garvin (ed.), *A Prague School Reader* (pp. 3–16). Washington, DC: Georgetown University Press.

Hickerson, N. 1971. Review of *Basic Color Terms: Their Universality and Evolution*, by B. Berlin and P. Kay. *International Journal of American Linguistics* 37: 257–270.

    1975. Two studies of color: implications for cross-cultural comparability of semantic categories. In M. Kinkade, K. Hale, and O. Werner (eds.), *Linguistics and Anthropology: In Honor of C. F. Voegelin* (pp. 317–330). Lisse: The Peter de Ridder Press.

Jakobson, R., and M. Halle 1956. *Fundamentals of Language*. The Hague: Mouton.

Kay, P., and C. McDaniel 1978. The linguistic significance of the meanings of basic color terms. *Language* 54(3): 610–646.

Kay, P., B. Berlin, and W. R. Merrifield 1991. Biocultural implications of systems of color naming. *Journal of Linguistic Anthropology* 1(1): 12–25.

Kuschel, R., and T. Monberg 1974. "We don't talk much about colour here": a study of colour semantics on Bellona Island. *Man* 9 (n.s.): 213–242.

Lenneberg, E. H. 1967. *Biological Foundations of Language*. New York: Wiley.

Lenneberg, E. H, and J. M. Roberts 1956. *The Language of Experience: A Study in Methodology*. Indiana University Publications in Anthropology and Linguistics. Memoir 13: supplement to *International Journal of American Linguistics* 22(2) Baltimore: Waverley Press Inc.

Lucy, J. 1981. Cultural factors in memory for color: the problem of language usage. Paper presented to the Annual Meeting of the American Anthropological Association.

    1985. The historical relativity of the linguistic relativity hypothesis. *Quarterly Newsletter of the Laboratory of Comparative Human Cognition* 7: 103–108.

    1991. How to wreak havoc with a category: the neglect of linguistic form in the analysis of categories. Paper presented to the Second Bi-Annual Meetings of the Society for Psychological Anthropology.

    1992a. *Grammatical Categories and Cognition: A Case Study of the Linguistic Relativity Hypothesis*. Cambridge University Press.

    1992b. *Language Diversity and Thought: A Reformulation of the Linguistic Relativity Hypothesis*. Cambridge University Press.

    1994. The role of semantic value in lexical comparison: motion and position roots in Yucatec Maya. *Linguistics* 32: 623–656.

    1996 The scope of linguistic relativity: an analysis and review of empirical research. In J. Gumperz and S. Levinson (eds.), *Rethinking Linguistic Relativity* (pp. 37–69). Cambridge University Press.

Lucy, J., and R. Shweder 1979. Whorf and his critics: linguistic and nonlinguistic influences on color memory. *American Anthropologist* 81: 581–615.

MacLaury, R. E. 1991. Exotic color categories: linguistic relativity to what extent? *Journal of Linguistic Anthropology* 1(1): 26–51.

    1992. From brightness to hue: an explanatory model of color-category evolution. *Current Anthropology* 33: 137–186.

McNeill, N. 1972. Colour and colour terminology. *Journal of Linguistics* 8: 21–33.

Newman, S. 1954. Semantic problems in grammatical systems and lexemes: a search for method. In H. Hoijer (ed.), *Language in Culture* (pp. 82–91). University of Chicago Press.

Quine, W. 1990. The phoneme's long shadow. In T. Headland, K. Pike, and M. Harris (eds.), *Emics and Etics: The Insider/Outsider Debate* (pp. 164–167). Newbury Park, CA: Sage.

Sahlins, M. 1976. Colors and cultures. *Semiotica* 16: 1–22.

Saunders, B. 1992a. The Invention of Basic Colour Terms. Doctoral thesis, Department of Anthropology, University of Utrecht, Netherlands. (Published copyright ISOR: Utrecht.)

    1992b. On translating the World Color Survey. Talk presented to the Max Planck Institute for Psycholinguistics, Nijmegen, Netherlands.

Schaefer, R. 1983. The synchronic behavior of Basic Color Terms in Tswana and its diachronic implications. *Studies in African Linguistics* 14: 159–194.

Snow, D. 1971. Samoan color terminology: a note on the universality and evolutionary ordering of color terms.

Anthropological Linguistics 13: 385–390.

Turton, D. 1980. There's no such beast: cattle and colour naming among the Mursi. *Man* 15 (n.s.): 320–328.

Wescott, R. W. 1970. Bini color terms. *Anthropological Linguistics* 13: 251–252.

Wierzbicka, A. 1990. The meaning of color terms: semantics, culture, and cognition. *Cognitive Linguistics* 1: 99–150.

Woodworth, R. S. 1910. The puzzle of color vocabularies. *Psychological Bulletin* 7(10): 325–334.

16 **Closing thoughts**

Luisa Maffi and C. L. Hardin

Over the years since the publication of Berlin and Kay's *Basic Color Terms* (Berlin and Kay 1969), an impressive amount of anthropological and linguistic research has been accumulating on the topic of color categorization and naming in different languages of the world (see Maffi 1991 for a bibliographic coverage of the period 1970–1990; many new titles should be added as of 1997). Linguistic ethnographers have probed the Berlin and Kay (henceforth B&K) universalist–evolutionary framework against the data from scores of different languages, and have brought confirmation to it in varying degrees, or questioned it on various grounds (see review of the literature in Maffi 1990a). A steady flow of research has come from B&K themselves and their collaborators (Berlin and Berlin 1975; Kay 1975; Kay and McDaniel 1978; Berlin, Kay, and Merrifield 1985; Maffi 1988a, 1988b; Kay, Berlin, and Merrifield 1991 [henceforth KB&M]; Kay, Berlin, Maffi, and Merrifield this volume [henceforth KBM&M]). As KBM&M indicate, this research and other findings and conceptual developments in the field have prompted modifications and refinements of the original B&K hypotheses on the universality and evolution of color-term systems. However, the basic tenets have stood the test of time. Alternative methodological approaches and theoretical accounts of the cross-linguistic findings on color terminology have also been proposed, still in a universalist–evolutionary framework (in particular, MacLaury's "vantage theory"; MacLaury 1986, 1987a, 1991a, 1991b, 1992, this volume). All along, more or less radical critiques, both theoretical and methodological, of that very framework have been put forth (from Hickerson 1971 to Wierzbicka 1990, Saunders 1992, Lucy this volume).

Although vision scientists and psychologists for a long time paid little attention to questions of color categorization, the technique of color naming, pioneered by Sternheim and Boynton (1966), has in recent years been used in a variety of settings to reveal much about the unitary–binary structure of perceived spectral colors in human adults (see Wooten and Miller this volume), as well as in infants and primates (see below). A series of studies of color categorization that sampled the whole of the OSA color space was undertaken by Boynton and his associates, beginning with the investigation by Boynton and Olson (1987). Overall, these confirmed the basic tenets of B&K for contemporary English and Japanese (Uchikawa and Boynton 1987; Boynton this volume). Employing the NCS color space, Sivik and his associates independently reached essentially the same results for a variety of European languages (Sivik this volume). Identification of the neural sites of chromatic perceptual structure has proved to be more difficult than the earlier electrophysiological studies of DeValois, Abramov, and Jacobs (1966) had suggested (Abramov this volume). On the other hand, some electrophysiological studies of color categorization have recently been undertaken (Yoshioka, Dow, and Vautin 1996), and neuropsychological data drawn from neural deficits and PET scans have given us some clues as to the localization of color categorization and language centers in the human brain (Davidoff this volume).

What can now be said about our present understanding of color categorization and naming? Which parts of the picture can we feel reasonably confident about, and which are still blurry? Where have we made progress, and where do major gaps remain? Can we benefit from the new approaches and the enduring critiques, and, if so, how? Most crucial to the topic of this volume, how does the emerging picture of color-term systems and their dynamics square with the current picture of the psychophysiology of color vision? Does one illuminate and corroborate the other? If so, how? Finally, where do we go from here?

To address these questions, let us consider in turn some of the main issues raised by this body of research. At the anthropological end, the whole enterprise, as conceived by B&K and pursued by them and others, rests on the notion of *basic* color terms: the idea that there will be an identifiable core of the color vocabulary in any language, formed by words that are general in reference, all-inclusive (i.e., not included in the meaning of another word), mostly monolexemic and morphologically simple, as well as psychologically salient. This notion has both come under intense criticism in some anthropological circles, and provided the basis for a linkage with findings in the psychophysiology of color vision. Let us then begin by examining what can now be said about the notion of basic color terms.

Basic color terms

It is worth pointing out that this notion was not created by B&K – something that has not been stressed enough in the literature. The concept was already present in the earlier work of Lenneberg and his associates, who operated in a language-relativist framework (cf. Lenneberg 1953; Brown and Lenneberg 1954; Lenneberg and Roberts 1956). A notion of basicness in color terminology was also explicitly present in Conklin's account of Hanunóo color categories (Conklin 1955), a work frequently mentioned as a prototype of culture-specific research in this domain. Conklin also provided basicness criteria that are virtually identical to those put forth by B&K. Overall, B&K noted that psychologists, linguists, and anthropologists had long operated with a concept of basic color word, which probably stemmed from centuries of philosophical, scientific, aesthetic, as well as common-sense thinking in the Old World. They found it in agreement with their own field experience with indigenous languages, and proposed to operationalize it in terms of a set of linguistic and psychological criteria, so that it could be used for systematic cross-linguistic research. (In the World Color Survey [henceforth WCS], a general definition of basic color terms has been added, as "the *smallest subset* of color terms such that any color can be named by one of them"; Kay, Berlin and Merrifield 1979: 3.)

In other words, B&K were not proposing to *demonstrate* the existence of basic color terms; they were assuming it, and they wanted to investigate some claims that had been made about them, such as that the linguistic segmenting of the color spectrum is totally arbitrary; (cf. Ray 1952). They were still operating in a relativistic framework, and did not expect the full-fledged universalistic clustering of color category foci that emerged from that research. They only doubted some of the most radical statements about the untranslatability of linguistic labels, and thought that, if any cross-linguistic regularities could be found at all, it would be in the realm of those general-reference color words that had come to be known as basic color terms. They also chose to concentrate on the denotational, decontextualized aspects of the meaning of color words, which were identified in terms of the hue and lightness dimensions of the color space, although they were not at all unaware of the cultural relevance of both non-basic terms and the connotational aspects of meaning (B&K 1969: 1).

Lucy (this volume) charges, as many others have, that thus restrict-ing the domain of investigation and the notion of meaning prede-termined the universalistic findings. However, as pointed out in Maffi (1990a), as well as by Kempton in discussion at the Asilomar confer-ence, even with these restrictions the outcome might well not have been universalistic at all: it might still have been possible to find that the basic color terms of a given language cut up the color spectrum in a way completely different from the next language, as Ray had claimed. Since this was not the outcome, one can conclude that the regularities that emerged from the B&K research represent a legiti-mate set of universals. It is also worth noting that such a restriction represents a perfectly legitimate, indeed typical, scientific procedure: as B&K (1969: 160, n. 2) themselves had indicated, the data may not be revealing *ethnographically*, but they are at other, equally meaningful, levels.

Other authors have addressed specific aspects of the basicness cri-teria put forth by B&K. Some have suggested their simplification, reducing them to inclusiveness, generality of reference, and salience (Crawford 1982), or even to just inclusiveness and generality (MacLaury 1982). Others (Wescott 1970) have objected to the B&K crite-ria by showing that, depending on their stricter or looser application, one could get several different pictures of the color-term system of a given language. Maffi (1990b) made a similar point about use of the criteria; however, she drew the conclusion that their stricter or looser application provides clues to the evolutionary history of a color-term system, and therefore called for a careful, case-by-case use of them all, something that B&K had stressed earlier. Bolton (1978) focused specifically on measures of salience, with results that show strong correlations with the B&K findings, although with explainable excep-tions. In this volume, Corbett and Davies assume the B&K criteria, pro-posing to test the validity of several behavioral and linguistic measures of basicness. Their finding that frequency and order of occurrence in elicited lists of color terms (a measure of psychological salience) does best at discriminating basic from non-basic terms sup-ports the use that has been made of the procedure in field research on color terminology, as well as the relevance of psychological salience as a criterion. As D'Andrade observed in discussion, this is crucial if one is interested in the connections between language and mind – in this case, in whether basicness of color categories may be both a linguistic and a psychological phenomenon. It is also of interest that a measure of linguistic use (frequency of occurrence in texts) is instead found by Corbett and Davies to work best in differentiating between primary basics (corresponding to the Hering elementals) and secondary basics (corresponding to the derived categories), and in bringing out regularities in the ordering of the basic terms of a given language. Both aspects point to the evolutionary underpinnings of a color system.

Debate on the notion of basicness and its defining criteria persists, particularly about whether a clear boundary can actually be drawn between basic and non-basic terms and categories. As Corbett and Davies have shown, how well the line can be drawn may depend on what measure is being used. More generally, one need not expect a sharp, rigid boundary under all circumstances. In discussion, Davies noted that this is not something special about the domain of color, but how the typology of language works as a whole. Typological features are not established in an absolute fashion, but in terms of a "sliding scale" of cases, from best cases satisfying all criteria, through cases satisfying only some, to a grey zone of unclear cases, to cases that do not satisfy any of the criteria. Given this, the point is for investigators to specify what their conditions are when it comes to the intermediate or unclear cases. Furthermore, as Corbett observed, it is in the nature of the dynamics of language, as a mutable system, for there to be grey zones, and for boundaries to be flexible. In the development of color-term systems, the non-basic terms of a language appear to form a pool out of which the names for new basic categories may be chosen. This is not the only possible factor of change in categorization and naming; language/culture contact is another major one, as Stanlaw shows in his contribution to this volume; see also Dougherty (1975); Berlin and Berlin (1975); Kay (1975). Non-basic categories themselves may be, so to speak, "upgraded" to basic category status. However, at a synchronic level, systematic data on color-term systems do allow for a reliable identification of established basic terms (on the basis of frequency and consensus in use), as well as of emerging ones (cf. KBM&M).

It should also be noted that even studies that have focused on the whole semantic domain of color – heeding the culture-specific and non-chromatic elements of meaning, without a priori restriction to basic terms, and employing open-ended procedures in data collection (see in particular Conklin 1955; Kuschel and Monberg 1974; Jernudd and White 1983) – reveal the emergence of a core of a given color system that is strikingly reminiscent of B&K's basic terms and categories. Conklin, as well as Kuschel and Monberg, actually suggest a taxonomic structure for the color systems under study, with the highly contextualized terms being subsumed under the basic ones. At Asilomar, Maffi also pointed to the case of Tzeltal Maya, a language with a variety of highly contextualized terms that are morphologically derived from the basic terms, and therefore logically presuppose them.

This is not to say that one can safely ignore the study of color domains in all of their complexity. Delimiting the domain of investigation to basic color terms has made possible the identification of the cross-linguistic regularities in color-term systems. However, even from a universalist–evolutionary point of view, and not only from that of ethnographic richness, the study of whole color-term systems has the potential to be very fruitful. Although in the literature there is no unquestionable evidence of languages without any basic color terms at all, the available data do include languages with just two or three basic terms and an independent set of secondary, context-bound words encoding chromatic along with non-chromatic information. One possible hypothesis from a cognitive and linguistic evolutionary perspective is that this state of affairs might point to the emergence of abstract conceptualization and naming of color out of a stage in which chromatic information is recognized as "object color" – that is, as an intrinsic property of objects, often not separate from other visual and non-visual properties (cf. Davidoff this volume). A process of restriction of contextualized "color" terms from multi-meaning to just color meaning was also suggested by Lucy in discussion; a loss of non-color meanings is documented by Casson, in this volume, in the evolution of English basic color terms. Again in language-evolutionary terms, the emergence of such abstract color words may signal historical changes within a community of speakers in which the need for decontextualized information becomes manifest, as the amount of shared, predictable knowledge diminishes (cf. Kay 1977). Incidentally, this does not prevent basic color words from maintaining connotations such as those described by Conklin (1955) – even in English, for example, the word *green* carries connotations of freshness, succulence, unripeness, etc., very similar to those of the corresponding word *malatuy* in Hanunóo. The basic term-derived secondary "color" words of Tzeltal Maya, mentioned above, are another indication of enduring contextualization processes.

Once named basic color categories emerge, however, it appears that they begin to take the lead, with respect both to salience and to further evolutionary developments. On the one hand, basic categories begin to function as readily available cognitive reference points, their foci being easily discriminated, while the domain of color as such itself begins progressively to acquire more salience, although perhaps relative to the contexts in which colors manifest themselves and are referred to. On the other hand, a taxonomic structure begins to develop. In some languages, context-bound secondary words may or may not be subsumed under the basic ones. As we have seen, in some languages this seems to be the case; in others, no relation of inclusion is found between basic and context-bound "color" terms. A development that does take place, though – especially once the domain has expanded further horizontally with the emergence of more basic terms – is the appearance of another kind of secondary terms: i.e., words that share with the basic ones in generality of reference, but are taxonomically included in them. As Casson (this volume) shows for English, this phenomenon may arise in response to specialized needs in certain domains (dyeing, weaving, etc.). It may also be interpreted in terms of changing communication needs. In time, these decontextualized secondary terms tend to multiply, while the set of context-bound ones tends to shrink, until only remnants are found, e.g. in terms for human and animal hair, skin, and the like.

This aspect of color categorization and naming has not often been given explicit attention in the literature, although it seems to be central to the evolution of the domain of color as a whole. It is even possible that numerous problems in the culturalist vs. universalist debate, as well as in discussion of specific aspects of the B&K theory, may be due to failure to recognize that not all secondary, or non-basic, color categories and terms are the same, and that this may have significant evolutionary implications (cf. Davidoff this volume). As Corbett noted in discussion, from a language-typological point of view it is common to see cycles of emergence, development, and loss of categories, as appears to be the case with the context-bound "color" words, but it is highly unusual to find a domain in which loss is not documented. One such domain seems to be basic color categories, counterexamples such as Kristol (1980) being arguably flawed. The only other instance of unidirectional development found by Corbett is that of numeral systems. The general trend with basic color categories appears to be towards growth up to a certain point, which perhaps may be beyond the eleven categories identified by B&K, but probably not much beyond that; discussion of this point will be taken up below. The decontextualized secondary color terms and categories seem to have the potential for unconstrained, if often idiosyncratic, development. This issue in and of itself seems worthy of further investigation.

Color and linguistic meaning

Another point concerning the study of whole color-term systems that warrants consideration is stressed by Lucy in this volume: the study of the grammatical (morphological, syntactic) context of color words. Although one of B&K's basicness criteria was distributional potential (frequency of occurrence of a color word in morphologically derived forms, modified phrases, compounds, etc.), this criterion has not been in the foreground in color classification studies. Lucy charges that, along with restriction of meaning to denotation, lack of attention to the formal characteristics of color terms even prevents determining whether color actually is a legitimate, well-defined, and salient semantic domain in a language. Only by finding out if words encoding chromatic information have structural and formal characteristics that make them stand out as a group, can one feel confident that a domain of color actually exists. Lucy's critique mostly focuses on B&K's original claim that their findings addressed issues of *semantic* universals, that is, that they had something to say about linguistic meaning. In his opinion, without taking into account contextual and connotational features, one cannot legitimately claim to be talking about linguistic meaning.

Issues of meaning in linguistic theory are too complex to be dealt with here. Suffice it to point out that linguistic meaning is found at different levels. The level of denotation and reference is one such level, and an important one. Lucy's call for greater attention to the formal characteristics of color words remains of relevance, though, not only from the point of view of ethnographic reliability, but also in a universalist–evolutionary perspective. One of the small number of studies that have considered the grammatical correlates of color words (Maffi 1990b) has shown that examination of morphological and syntactic features is revealing both of the status of a word as a basic or non-basic color term, and of the evolutionary ordering of terms. At Asilomar, Kempton also noted that collecting the kind of data advocated by Lucy should help identify the sources of "noise" (variance, anomaly, uncertainty) in cross-linguistic studies of color terminologies such as the WCS. (MacLaury's Mesoamerican Color Survey made greater programmatic allowance for modified or otherwise complex color words; see also Burgess, Kempton, and MacLaury 1983.) It is undoubtedly important, then, for more studies of this sort to be carried out as a complement to survey data.

Ultimately, the questions of interest to Lucy are ones of linguistic relativity – in his formulation, whether observable cross-linguistic differences affect how people think. Studies such as Kay and Kempton (1984) and Stanlaw (this volume) show that "Whorfian effects" may be identified in tasks involving judgments of similarity and difference, or memory and recall, without negative implications vis-à-vis B&K's universalistic findings. However, Lucy implies that the domain of color is actually not a good choice if one is interested in semantic principles and issues of universality vs. relativity, because the domain is not central to language (it does not have great relevance in communication within small-scale societies), and seems to have peculiar characteristics. Kempton observed that, while the semantics of color may be unusual in many ways, so that caution may be called for in drawing generalizations, it is also a domain that appears to be especially apt for productively connecting many different levels and fields of analysis: word meaning, language evolution, perception and cognition, the structure of the visual system, brain function. Color classification is obviously as much a matter of cognitive categories as it is of lexical ones. Although the two levels are distinct and not automatically linked, the greatest relevance of this field of research consists precisely in the effort to establish those links and the connections with the structures and processes underlying them.

Color categories and Hering's elemental colors

At the center of any account that can now be given of those underlying processes is the psychophysical opponent theory of color perception, first enunciated by Hering. As Wooten and Miller, as well as Abramov, point out in this volume, it is the psychophysics that must provide the constraints whereby the appropriate neural mechanisms can be identified. The mechanisms that have so far been isolated are consistent with opponent theory but, for reasons that Abramov sketches for us, the fundamental sites of unique hue perception cannot be said to have been identified as yet, contrary to many experimenters' expectations in the 1970s. For all of that, visual scientists generally find the psychophysical evidence for opponency persuasive. The evidence stems from the employment of two lines of experimental investigation: cancellation (see Wooten and Miller this volume) and color naming (see Wooten and Miller, Miller, and Boynton, this volume).

Jameson and D'Andrade's surprising though plausible challenge to the Hering theory provides a welcome opportunity to get clearer about the implications of the opponent theory generally, and the cancellation technique particularly. There are at least five distinct topics that Jameson and D'Andrade discuss, and tend to conflate: (a) the psychological primacy of Hering's elemental colors; (b) exclusion of one hue by another; (c) complementation relations; (d) perceptual distances between two colors; (e) what axes are selected as basic in the construction of a color-order scheme. We shall consider these points in turn.

(a) Hering's six colors are elementary in the sense that none of them contains any of the others as perceptual parts, whereas all of the other colors are experienced as blends of the six. Although they are salient, they are not under all circumstances and conditions necessarily more salient than non-elemental colors, such as orange or purple, and in that sense, may not be more basic (see both Boynton and Miller, this volume). It is clear that what is *basic* is to some extent task- and context-dependent, but what is *elemental* is not.

(b) No color is seen as reddish and greenish, nor as yellowish and bluish. A light that looks reddish may therefore be used to cancel the greenish appearance in another light (cf. Wooten and Miller this volume). It does not follow, however, that a light that looks red will, when canceling the greenishness in another light, yield a light that looks achromatic.

(c) A pair of lights that look to have colors A and B respectively, and are mixed so as to yield a light with an achromatic appearance, are *additive complements*. We would expect, say Jameson and D'Andrade, that since red and green exclude each other, a unique green light would be the complement of a unique red light *provided that the yellow–blue channel remains in equilibrium when the lights are mixed*, i.e., provided that the yellow–blue channel is linear. As Wooten and Miller (this volume) explain, however, the latter is not the case. Linearity of the opponent channels is a useful simplifying assumption, employed in the pioneering research of Hurvich and Jameson and now embalmed in the elementary textbooks, but it does not strictly hold, though it more nearly obtains for some subjects than for others. The red–green channel does seem to be nearly linear, so unique blue and unique yellow are in fact additive complements.

(d) The number of equal perceptual steps from one unique hue to the next is different for each pair of unique hues, and the stretch from red to blue is particularly large, as Jameson and D'Andrade tell us; but this is not inconsistent with any of the precepts of opponent-process theory, only with its simplified textbook presentations.

(e) If the objective is to order colors by selecting hue axes so that the perceptual-step distances from one to the next are approximately equal, introduce a purple "primary" *à la* Munsell. If the objective is to represent the degree of resemblance to the Hering elemental colors, choose the NCS system (see Sivik this volume). Each of the color-order systems has its advantages and disadvantages. None can lay claim to being *the* map of color space, since the relationships and salient features of that space are too rich to permit of any single geometric representation. Which of the color-order systems will prove to be the more revealing is certainly an open question, and here Jameson and D'Andrade offer some intriguing suggestions. Fortunately, it is possible to translate data from one system to another – although the Asilomar discussion brought out the need for more systematic work on the relative merits and demerits of different systems for different tasks, especially with a view to establishing better methodological and technical standards for field data collection.

As Wooten and Miller tell us in this volume, color-naming studies show that adult speakers of English find that four hue names – *red*, *yellow*, *green*, and *blue* – are necessary and sufficient to describe the colors of the spectrum. Furthermore, this verbal labeling of colors tracks opponent response. It thus appears that when names for the Hering elemental colors are available, their application is governed by perceptual saliences that depend upon innate biological organization. The argument that some color categories are more natural than others may be extended further by applying color-naming techniques to the study of color categorization in non-verbal and pre-verbal organisms. Here are two examples.

Four-month-old infants know precious little language, and they cannot describe what they see. Nevertheless, by watching their eye fixations one can tell whether they see two stimuli as similar or different. Infants will lose interest in a stimulus that looks similar to its predecessor (as judged by adults), but continue looking at a stimulus that they regard as different from what went before. This is the basis of a standard technique used to study categorization of various sorts among the very young. By exposing infants to sequences of colored lights whose dominant wavelengths are 20 nm apart, and recording their eye movements (the recorder did not look at the stimulus), Bornstein and his collaborators were able to map out their spectral color categories (Bornstein 1975; Bornstein, Kessen, and Weiskopf 1976). These proved to line up rather well with the spectral categories of adults that are mapped with color-naming procedures. In a similar fashion, a macaque was trained to respond differentially to spectral lights that human beings would see as good representatives of their categories, and then presented with randomized sequences of lights that did not match the training lights. These lights were categorized by the macaque in pretty much the same way as adult human English speakers would classify them (Sandell, Gross, and Bornstein 1979).

We should not of course suppose that color categories are consciously or explicitly borne in mind by monkeys or infants, but rather that their brains are so wired as to incline them to respond to certain classificatory demands in a characteristic fashion. This was strikingly demonstrated in a series of chimpanzee categorization experiments by Matsuzawa (1985). In these experiments, the chimp was trained on a set of 11 focal samples, learning to press the key that contained a contrived character for the appropriate basic color term. She was then presented with 215 of the Berlin and Kay chips that she had not seen. They were shown to her one at a time and in random order, and she was asked to name them. Following the sessions with the training chips, she did not receive reinforcement for her choices. The experimenter assigned a label to a chip when the chimpanzee gave it that label on at least 75% of the trials. The results were compared to those generated in a human color-naming experiment, again using the 75% consistency criterion. The outcomes were closely similar. The chimp had generalized from focal chips in essentially the same fashion as the human being. (It must be noted that, when more remote species such as pigeons are trained to "name" colors, their categories do not correspond so closely to those of the experimenters; see Jacobs 1981.)

These experiments provide a window on what Davidoff (this volume) calls "the internal color space," which is, he argues, required for the linguistic labeling of colors but does not in turn depend upon the possession of language. However, as the foundation for an account of color-concept and color-language acquisition such experiments must be approached with great caution. After all, as Davidoff points out, young children show surprising difficulty in correctly applying basic color names to objects (but see below on this point); and one certainly should not suppose that a trained chimpanzee possesses a more refined system of color categories than a monolingual speaker of Dani or Tzeltal Maya. It is clear that the categorical scheme that will be elicited on a given occasion will be highly, but by no means totally, task-dependent. The situation is roughly analogous to the knowledge of mathematics. A great body of mathematical knowledge is in some sense implicit in every normal human being, and the ability to categorize by number is to some extent present in a wide variety of animals, including birds and fish. However, it is obvious that its manifestation will depend heavily on circumstance, culture, and individual proclivities. The important issue is not whether mathematical practices are innate or individually variable or culture-bound; they are all of these. The important questions lie entirely in the details of the connections. In the case of color, how are primary, derived, and composite categories related to biological, cultural, and individual factors?

Primary categories

Wooten's and McDaniel's work showed that English-speaking subjects' focal choices of red, yellow, green, and blue Munsell color chips corresponded closely with their respective unique hue settings (cf. Wooten and Miller this volume). Kay and McDaniel (1978) suggested that the foci of primary categories correspond to Hering's six unique hue sensations, and focal choices of these colors in many field studies show a pronounced statistical tendency to cluster around average unique hues; but since many languages of the world do not have separate categories for all of the Hering elemental colors, it is unlikely for these sensations to be *directly* reflected in language (that is, without the mediation of cognitive mechanisms), as Kay and McDaniel proposed.

Indeed, given the psychophysiological bases of the Hering elementals, the relevant question here is why the six unique hue sensations are not encoded all at once in each language. Ratliff (1976) suggested that the B&K evolutionary ordering of color categories might be related to the Hering elemental colors by the relative salience of the perceptual contrasts involved. He considered the lightness dimension to be the most fundamental because it alone is common to both achromatic and chromatic vision; this, in his opinion, would justify the priority of recognition of white/black (or light/dark) contrasts. The primacy of the light/dark system is shown by the fact that most objects can be readily identified without the use of chromatic colors at all. This is indeed so strikingly true that it raises the question of just what biological function is performed by the chromatic system (Jacobs 1981; Hardin 1992; Thompson 1995). Ratliff also offered various physiological reasons why the red percept would appear the strongest and the blue one the weakest to the human eye. As Wooten and Miller (this volume) observe, these are not entirely persuasive, since the resulting differences in perceptual salience seem quite small. However, Humphrey (1976) offers a variety of reasons for supposing that red has special visual salience. Ratliff was less successful in finding plausible psychophysiological grounding for the relative ordering of yellow and green (cf. Wooten and Miller this volume).

Stephenson (1972) proposed that B&K's evolutionary ordering of basic color terms might to some extent reflect the order in which the ability to discriminate colors was acquired by primates. He suggested that, in the case of the chromatic elementary colors, the empirically observed ordering from red to yellow to green to blue according to wavelength may point to an evolutionary connection with the progressive adaptation of primate species to shorter wavelengths as they moved from nocturnal to diurnal environments. He cautioned, though, against any simplistic utilitarian argument in this connection. It is important as well to stress that caution is also in order in relating issues of the evolutionary emergence of primate color vision to issues of cognitive and linguistic evolution in modern humans.

The relative ordering of primary categories thus by and large remains to be accounted for. It may be useful to consider this point in light of the numerically prevalent order in which primary categories appear to emerge from composite categories, according to initial quantification of the WCS data (cf. Maffi 1988b; KBM&M): white first, then red, then yellow, followed closely by black (which can sometimes emerge before yellow, and in a few cases before both red and yellow), then green, and blue last. Overall, this clearly correlates with the proposal of KBM&M about the dissolution of the white/warm and black/cool "channels"; but why does the former begin prior to the latter, and what accounts for the specifics? We return to this question later.

Derived categories

As for derived categories (those, such as purple and brown, that are formed by the intersection of the primaries), psychophysicists have confirmed the non-elemental nature of the color sensations associated with them (see Wooten and Miller this volume). However, consensus has not yet been reached on the psychophysiological nature of these categories. Boynton (this volume) proposes the existence of eleven categorically separate varieties of activities, one for each of the primary and derived categories identified by B&K. In the Asilomar discussion, the other visual scientists were skeptical of this in the absence of corroborating evidence. There are many questions here that invite experimental investigation, already inaugurated by Miller (this volume). Why are orange and purple basic, while chartreuse and turquoise are not? Jameson and D'Andrade suggest a special role for purple, and indeed in the WCS the latter seems to be the derived category to emerge first in the largest number of languages. What about orange, the derived category that regularly emerges last, and is "well behaved," never mixing with the others, as purple, pink, brown, and grey often do, in various combinations with one another?

In the recent developments of B&K's work, cautionary notes have been sounded about the nature of derived vs. primary categories. A recognition that phenomena of a different order might be involved, and that the two types might have to be accounted for in different terms, may be found in KBM&M. There the notion of "basic stage" of a language is reconceptualized as the developmental status of that language vis-à-vis composite and/or primary categories; derived categories are no longer given a role in determining the basic stage, although their presence is noted.

Beyond eleven?

At Asilomar, Kay hypothesized that there may be a specific biological basis only for the primary categories, while in the case of derived categories, and perhaps also the composites, it may rather be a matter of color-specific hard-wired neural mechanisms interacting with some more general cognitive mechanisms that preside over category formation. If this were so, there would seem to be no logical barrier to prevent the continued recognition of intersections of primary categories (a point made by Kay and McDaniel 1978); and indeed other derived categories, such as turquoise, chartreuse, and peach have been variously proposed in the literature as possible candidates for acquiring basic status (see Boynton as well as Miller, this volume). However, no such case has so far been unquestionably established.

We should also keep in mind that another kind of expansion beyond eleven non-composites has been proposed: instances of languages naming the same color with two terms which are said to be complementary, that is, both basic. Such are the well-known cases of the two terms for blue in Russian (Corbett and Morgan 1988) and the two terms for red in Hungarian (Wierzbicka 1990). However, these cases are also controversial (see, e.g., discussion in Almási, Kövecses, and MacLaury 1994); furthermore, it should be noted that, even if confirmed, they would represent a phenomenon of a different nature from the recognition of derived categories: the splitting of primary ones.

There is evidence for an upper limit to the number of distinct basic color categories that could develop in a given language. In experiments with English speakers, Chapanis (1965) found that the most commonly used names for the color space amounted to a dozen, but calculated that the largest number of color names that a non-specialist could use to cover the whole color space without overlaps and confusions is about fifty. This study, conducted before the appearance of B&K (1969), does not mention different types of categories, although it does seem to imply a notion of basicness. It might be interesting to re-examine this issue in light of current knowledge of color categorization and its biological and cognitive correlates.

Composite categories

The third category type identified by Kay and McDaniel (1978), composite categories, has not so far received much attention in the psychophysical literature. This may be due in part to the fact that much of the experimental research that took the B&K framework into account referred to the 1969 version, in which this category type was not explicitly recognized. Furthermore, the principal research (see Boynton as well as Sivik, this volume) was conducted with speakers of languages that do not have composite categories. One related aspect that has been touched upon in that literature is the so-called "blue–green confusion," which had already attracted Rivers's attention at the beginning of this century (Rivers 1901) and was more recently reproposed by Bornstein (1973a, 1973b, 1978) in terms of racial differences in color vision. Given the prevailing consensus with regard to the essential sameness of the visual apparatus in *Homo sapiens* (but see Zegura this volume), this phenomenon, frequently found in languages all around the world, is instead generally discussed as a categorial and linguistic association between the green and blue percepts. The possible psychophysiological reasons (other than racial differences) for this association and its notable persistence even at advanced stages of color categorization (cf. KBM&M) are still being debated. It is worth considering that there is substantially more perceptual variation from one observer to another in the blue–green region than any other region of the spectrum (Pickford 1951). This would suggest that it would be correspondingly more difficult to secure consensus about how to categorize blue-green colors. The whole subject is in urgent need of further investigation.

Composite categories have been the object of greater attention by anthropologists and linguists than by psychologists, although the initial recognition of the two color categories of the Dani of Papua New Guinea as composite in their internal structure is due to a cognitive psychologist, Rosch (see Heider 1972a, 1972b). Contrary to what B&K originally thought, these early categories were shown to encode not only lightness, but also hue, thus covering the whole color space between the two of them. The structural features of composites, as emerging from the WCS, have been best formalized in KB&M. So-called white/warm composites include the white, yellow, and red elementals – yellow and white being found to have an especially close association (perhaps related to the fact that yellow is defined not only in terms of hue, but also as being a light color). Black/cool composites include black, blue, and green, with black and blue also showing a privileged mutual relationship – although no account is available from vision science in this case (but for a speculation, see below).

Less frequently, one also finds composite categories including yellow and green. These were discussed in Kay (1975) and first documented by MacLaury (1987b) in Northwest Coast Indian languages, but exist also in other genetically unrelated languages surveyed in the WCS. In some rare and not unquestionably documented cases, categories covering yellow and green extend into (light) blue. Such yellow/green/blue categories are problematic for the use of the Hering model in the B&K scheme, since they unexpectedly include two opponent responses, yellow and blue (cf. Wooten and Miller this volume). KB&M discuss these category types at length, but conclude that there is still a gap in how their model can account for them (cf. their treatment in KBM&M; see below for an alternative account by MacLaury).

KB&M also stress that what has not been found empirically, in any of the several hundred diverse languages studied so far, is any category extending all the way through yellow between the white/warm and the black/cool areas of the spectrum (such as a category encompassing red, yellow, and green, or white, yellow, and green). From this finding, they infer a pivotal role of yellow in early color categorization, while admitting to being unaware of results from vision science that would help explain it. Also not found are categories covering yellow, green, blue, and black, although theoretically admitted by this model. The hypothetical existence of such a category is of interest since it might represent the precursor of the attested yellow/green(/blue) categories. KB&M raise the question of whether there may be cognitive restrictions against having a category constituted by a four-way disjunction, or what other factors might account for this absence. These, then, are other areas open for further research.

In this context, basic stage evolution of color categorization systems is now conceptualized by KBM&M in terms of two distinct although interacting processes: the dissolution of the white/warm "channel" and that of the black/cool one – no technical notion being implied in the use of the word "channel." What is involved is the progressive dissolution of the white/warm and black/cool composite categories, until all six primaries have emerged (again, with the special problems posed by yellow/green[/blue] categories). The former process appears always to begin with the split of the white/warm category into a warm and a white/light category; it is often completed well before the other process is. The delay in the dissolution of the black/cool "channel" is due in part to the persistence of a green/blue (or cool) category, a product of the decomposition of the black/cool "channel," into late stages of categorization. Another persistent association in this latter "channel," not noted in the earlier B&K corpus, is that between black and blue in some languages, with green emerging as a separate category.

Warm and cool

This model clearly reflects striking empirical observations that call for explanation. What accounts for the specific associations found in the white/warm and black/cool composite categories and the other attested composites, including the problematic yellow/green(/blue) categories? In particular, what accounts for the cross-culturally robust association of longer-wavelength hues, conventionally identified by the label "warm," on the one hand, and that of the shorter-wavelength hues, identified as "cool," on the other (see Sivik this volume), as well as for their respective observed affinity for the light vs. the dark end of the lightness dimension? Is there a psychophysiological basis for these associations, or is it rather, as Kay suggested at Asilomar, a matter of cognitive processes of some sort? Katra and Wooten (1995) have been studying this question experimentally, arriving at a provocative conclusion:

> Higher ratings of warmth corresponded with levels of activation of the opponent channels in one direction, while cooler ratings corresponded with activation in the opposite direction. This suggests that a link to the activation level of the opponent channels, rather than the psychological quality of hue, drives the association of temperature with color, and that the association is more than simply a cognitive process.

Warmth and coolness mark an opponency in the temperature sense, so the pervasive cross-cultural tendency to bestow those labels on colors may therefore reflect an awareness of shared opponency rather than shared environmental associations with water, fire, and the like. The association between warmth and positive activation of opponent systems, and coolness with negative activation, would suggest a possible reason for the relationship of lightness with warm colors and darkness with cool ones in the WCS, but this issue has not received proper experimental investigation.

A brightness sequence?

Alternative interpretations of the evolution of color-term systems have recently been offered. It has been suggested that the recognition of brightness (construed to include both lightness and shininess) may be prior to that of hue (MacLaury 1992; Casson and Gardner 1992; Casson this volume). That this visual dimension should be particularly salient is, as we have noted above, plausible. It is the achromatic system that carries the lion's share of information about object shape and movement.

MacLaury (1992) has actually proposed two distinct but possibly merging category sequences: the first and prevailing one being represented by hue categories proper, as laid out by B&K; the second one being a sequence of brightness-to-hue (such as independently identified by Casson for English color terminology). According to

MacLaury, this hypothesis helps explain the existence of the yellow/green and yellow/green/blue category types. In MacLaury's opinion, the former type is a "leftover" of the latter, which he considers to be based not on hue, but on lightness or brightness. The idea is that, in the precursors of some of these systems, colors are first categorized as of high, middle, or low lightness, without primary hue distinctions, but the names for colors of middle lightness subsequently come to be given a predominantly hue sense, and differentiated into reds and non-reds. The suggested evolutionary priority of brightness categories and its possible implications vis-à-vis specific category types is clearly an important issue, requiring closer consideration and further investigation; other data corpuses such as that of the WCS might productively be checked against this hypothesis. On the other hand, it is relevant to note that Munsell chose as his fundamental green one that was "neither warm nor cool" (see Sivik this volume), and Katra and Wooten (1995) found that their subjects indeed rated a unique green as thermally neutral, so that yellowish greens (and not just yellows) were considered warm. Following this line of thought, we might view yellow/green categories as being predominantly warm rather than primarily light. Yellow/green/blue categories remain problematic under this interpretation.

Category change: MacLaury's account

In dealing with the nature of color categories, prototype theory (Rosch 1977, 1978) and fuzzy-set theory (Kay and McDaniel 1978) have been brought in – the former to account for the apparent organization of these categories in terms of foci and ranges, the latter as a formalism apt to represent graded category membership and to model the successive categorial divisions of the color space from composite to primary to derived categories (cf. KBM&M). Both prototypicality and fuzziness have generally been accepted as inherent characteristics of color categories. However, MacLaury (1986, 1987a) has pointed out that both theories are static and cannot account for the evolution of color categories, and has proposed his vantage theory as a dynamic theory of category formation, with categories organized by analogy to the construction of a physical point of view (cf. MacLaury this volume). As we have seen, the dynamic mechanism involved in this model is what

MacLaury calls "selective emphasis" on, or differential attendance to, similarity vs. difference. He interprets attendance to similarity as presiding over the formation of composite categories, and progressive attendance to difference as the motor of the development of primary and derived categories. Judgments of similarity and difference are of course largely recognized as the very basis of categorization; at the same time, in pointing to the role of "selective emphasis" on one or the other as an active principle, MacLaury has importantly addressed a key issue that had not been adequately tackled in earlier studies of color categorization: that of the processual aspects of categorization and the mechanisms of category change. This is clearly an area much in need of further investigation.

Some of the specific data interpretations proposed by MacLaury within this context have been questioned: in particular, his notions of coextensivity and inclusion of category ranges (MacLaury 1986, 1987a, 1991a, 1991b, this volume). These findings, commonly identified in data from older speakers, result from the addition, in MacLaury's Mesoamerican Color Survey, of a category range mapping task (asking speakers to map the range of a category, which generally happens in several steps, at the prompting of the investigator). Various alternatives were proposed at Asilomar to account for such data, mostly pointing to their possible task-dependence. Maffi suggested an effect analogous to the recapitulation of the evolutionary sequence of color lexicons identified by Boster (1986) in tasks involving the grouping of colors on the basis of similarity (see also Jameson and D'Andrade this volume). Zegura (this volume) mentioned the possible role of a cognitive tendency towards category lumping, particularly in older people. Abramov pointed to possible problems with the color vision of the interviewees due to ecological or nutritional factors, as well as to specific changes in the color vision of older people (with decreased sensitivity to the shorter wavelengths). The possible presence and effects of polysemy and connotative semantic features of the color terms involved were also brought up. However, MacLaury's notion of coextensivity and his vantage theory represent major new proposals concerning category formation and development, and as such they deserve careful evaluation, including replication of his data collection procedure.

The fate of ancient categories

According to both the KBM&M and the MacLaury model, the development of color categorization moves from stages characterized by broad composite categories, constructed on the basis of the recognition of gross similarities, to stages characterized by increasing attendance to difference, in particular along the hue dimension, until the perceptual differences between the Hering elementals are all encoded (and beyond). Here an intriguing question arises. When two separate named categories emerge from a composite category, what happens to that category? Is it lost, or is it retained in some form, perhaps as a cognitive, rather than a linguistic (named) category? If the latter were the case, this might help account for findings such as adults' recapitulation of the evolutionary sequence in Boster's (1986) experiments, although Boster himself has interpreted these results as task-dependent and cautioned against concluding that speakers carry proto-color categories in their minds. On the other hand, Mills (n.d.) has specifically made such a suggestion about English children's acquisition of color terms: their errors in the assignment of color labels to color percepts may not be random but systematic, stemming from children's cognitively functioning according to one or other early stage of categorization displaying composite categories. It is even possible that instances of polysemy and connotation of color words may be explainable in terms of the retention of composites at the cognitive level (so that in some circumstances *black* may stand for *dark*, or *red* for *warm*). These various orders of phenomena were earlier mentioned as possible alternative explanations for MacLaury's findings about coextensive categories. Therefore, the possible tacit psychological persistence of composite categories after they decompose bears looking into.

Searching for the salient

In these concluding pages, we have made an effort to highlight the main points of our current knowledge about the psychophysiological, cognitive, and linguistic aspects of color categorization and naming, as well as to indicate the connections that can plausibly be made at this time between the various levels. We have also pointed to some of the major gaps and open questions. These and many others cry out for further investigation. Here, we will stress one of the most important. The WCS data show that, without exception, light/warm categories break up before dark/cool ones do, and green/blue categories persist very far into the sequence. So why does the combination of light and warm seem to lend itself to earlier recognition of differences than the combination of dark and cool? It seems plausible that a difference in visual salience is involved here, but it is one that has never been investigated by visual psychologists. Although the opponent-process theory is important for many of the issues at the intersection of visual science and linguistic anthropology, its resources cannot be expected to answer all of the questions about color perception that we may legitimately ask. At the anthropological linguistic end, addressing issues related to such early composite categories and their evolution requires a continuing and urgent effort towards systematic documentation and archiving of data on color categorization and naming, as the indigenous groups of the world are facing massive and rapid language/culture change, often leading to outright language loss. Such processes are affecting these languages' color classification among other aspects, so that some of the earliest or rarer system types may be vanishing or have already vanished from the face of the earth. Our understanding of the cognitive and linguistic complexities of color categorization and naming will be all the poorer for that.

One thing is clear: the issues of color categories in thought and language, that so many people had supposed to have been laid to rest in the past, are still facing us in the future.

References

Almási, J., Z. Kövecses, and R. E. MacLaury 1994. Hungarian piros and vörös. Paper presented at the 93rd Annual Meeting of the American Anthropological Association.

Berlin, B., and E. A. Berlin 1975. Aguaruna color categories. *American Ethnologist* 2(1): 61–87.

Berlin, B., and P. Kay 1969. *Basic Color Terms: Their Universality and Evolution.* Berkeley: University of California Press. 1st paperback edn. 1991, with bibliography by Luisa Maffi.

Berlin, B., P. Kay, and W. R. Merrifield 1985. Color term evolution: recent evidence from the World Color Survey. Paper presented at the 84th Annual Meeting of the American Anthropological Association, Washington, DC.

Bolton, R. 1978. Black, white, and red all over: the riddle of color term salience. *Ethnology* 17(3): 287–311.

Bornstein, M. H. 1973a. The psychophysiological component of cultural difference in color naming and illusion susceptibility. *Behavioral Science Notes* 1: 41–101.

    1973b. Color vision and color naming: a

psychophysiological hypothesis of cultural difference. *Psychological Bulletin* 80(4): 257–285.

1975. Qualities of color vision in infancy. *Journal of Experimental Child Psychology* 19: 401–419.

1978. Considérations sur l'organisation des tonalités chromatiques. In S. Tornay (ed.), *Voir et nommer les couleurs* (pp. 71–82). Nanterre: Service de Publication du Laboratoire d'Ethnologie et de Sociologie Comparative de l'Université de Paris X.

Bornstein, M. H., W. Kessen, and S. Weiskopf 1976. The categories of hue in infancy. *Science* 191(4223): 201–202.

Boynton, R. M., and C. X. Olson 1987. Locating basic colors in the OSA space. *Color Research and Application* 12(2): 94–105.

Boster, J. S. 1986. Can individuals recapitulate the evolutionary development of color lexicons? *Ethnology* 25(1): 61–74.

Brown, R. W., and E. H. Lenneberg 1954. A study of language and cognition. *Journal of Abnormal and Social Psychology* 49: 454–462.

Burgess, D., W. Kempton, and R. E. MacLaury 1983. Tarahumara color modifiers: category structure presaging evolutionary change. *American Ethnologist* 10: 133–149.

Casson, R. W., and P. M. Gardner 1992. On brightness and color categories: additional data. *Current Anthropology* 33(4): 395–399.

Chapanis, A. 1965. Color names for color space. *American Scientist* 53: 327–346.

Conklin, H. C. 1955. Hanunóo color categories. *Southwestern Journal of Anthropology* 11(4): 339–344.

Corbett, G. G., and G. Morgan 1988. Colour terms in Russian: reflections of typological constraints in a single language. *Journal of Linguistics* 24: 31–64.

Crawford, T. D. 1982. Defining "basic color term." *Anthropological Linguistics* 24(3): 338–343.

De Valois, R. L., I. Abramov, and G. H. Jacobs 1966. Analysis of response patterns of LGN cells. *Journal of the Optical Society of America* 56: 966–977.

Dougherty, J. D.1975. A universalist analysis of variation and change in color semantics. Ph.D. dissertation, University of California, Berkeley.

Hardin, C. L. 1992. The virtues of illusion. *Philosophical Studies* 67: 153–166.

Heider, E. E. 1972a. Universals in color naming and memory. *Journal of Experimental Psychology* 93(1): 10–20.

1972b. Probabilities, sampling and the ethnographic method: the case of Dani colour names. *Man* 7(3): 448–466.

Hickerson, N. 1971. Review of *Basic Color Terms: Their Universality and Evolution*, by B. Berlin and P. Kay. *International Journal of American Linguistics* 37: 257–270.

Humphrey, N. K. 1976. The color currency of nature. In T. Porter and B. Mikellides, (eds.), *Color for Architects* (pp. 95–98). New York: Van Nostrand.

Jacobs, G. H. 1981. *Comparative Color Vision*. New York: Academic Press.

Jernudd, B. H., and G. M. White 1983. The concept of basic color terms: variability in For and Arabic. *Anthropological Linguistics* 25(1): 61–81.

Katra, E., and B. Wooten 1995. Perceived lightness/darkness and warmth/coolness in chromatic experience. Submitted to *Color Research and Application*.

Kay, P. 1975. Synchronic variability and diachronic change in basic color terms. *Language in Society* 4: 257–270.

1977. Language evolution and speech style. In B. G. Blount and M. Sanches (eds.), *Sociocultural Dimensions of Language Change* (pp. 21–33). New York: Academic Press.

Kay, P., and W. Kempton 1984. What is the Sapir–Whorf hypothesis? *American Anthropologist* 86(1): 65–79.

Kay, P., and C. K. McDaniel 1978. The linguistic significance of the meanings of basic color terms. *Language* 54(3): 610–646.

Kay, P., B. Berlin, and W. R. Merrifield 1979. Human color categorization: a survey of the world's unwritten languages. Research proposal submitted to the National Science Foundation.

1991. Biocultural implications of systems of color naming. *Journal of Linguistic Anthropology* 1(1): 12–25.

Kristol, A. M. 1980. Color systems in Southern Italy: a case of regression. *Language* 56(1): 137–145.

Kuschel, R., and T. Monberg 1974. "We don't talk much about colour here": a study of colour semantics on Bellona Island. *Man* 9(n.s.): 213–242.

Lenneberg, E. H. 1953. Cognition in ethnolinguistics. *Language* 29: 463–471.

Lenneberg, E. H., and J. M. Roberts 1956. *The Language of Experience: A Study in Methodology*. Indiana University Publications in Anthropology and Linguistics Memoir 13: supplement to *International Journal of American Linguistics* 22(2). Baltimore: Waverly Press Inc.

MacLaury, R. E. 1982. Prehistoric Mayan color categories. Unpublished ms. Language Behavior Research Laboratory, University of California, Berkeley.

1986. Color in Mesoamerica. Vol. I, A theory of composite categorization. Doctoral dissertation. University of California, Berkeley. UMI 8718073

1987a. Coextensive semantic ranges: different

names for distinct vantages of one category. In
B. Need, E. Schiller, and A. Bosch (eds.), *Papers from
the 23rd Annual Regional Meeting of the Chicago
Linguistic Society*. Vol. I (pp. 268–282).

  1987b. Color-category evolution and Shuswap
yellow-with-green. *American Anthropologist* 89:
107–124.

  1991a. Social and cognitive motivations of change:
measuring variability in color semantics. *Language*
67: 34–62.

  1991b. Exotic color categories: linguistic relativity
to what extent? *Journal of Linguistic Anthropology*
1(1): 26–51.

  1992. From brightness to hue: an explanatory
model of color-category evolution. *Current
Anthropology* 33: 137–186.

Maffi, L. 1988a. World Color Survey report. Unpublished
ms., University of California, Berkeley.

  1988b. World Color Survey typology. Unpublished
ms., University of California, Berkeley.

  1990a. Cognitive anthropology and human
categorization research: the case of color.
Unpublished ms., University of California, Berkeley.

  1990b. Somali color term evolution: grammatical
and semantic evidence. *Anthropological Linguistics* 32
(3–4): 316–334.

  1991. A bibliography of color categorization
research 1970–1990. In B. Berlin and P. Kay, *Basic Color
Terms: Their Universality and Evolution*, 1st paperback
edn. (pp. 173–189). Berkeley: University of California
Press.

Matsuzawa, T. 1985. Colour naming and classification in
a chimpanzee (*Pan troglodytes*). *Journal of Human
Evolution* 14: 283–291.

Mills, C. n.d. The acquisition of English color terms. Ms.
University of Cincinnati.

Pickford, R. W. 1951. *Individual differences in colour vision*.
London: Routledge and Kegan Paul.

Ratliff, F. 1976. On the psychophysiological basis of
universal color terms. *Proceedings of the American
Philosophical Society* 120(5): 311–330.

Ray, V. F. 1952. Techniques and problems in the study
of human color perception. *Southwestern Journal
of Anthropology* 8(3): 251–259.

Rivers, W. H. R. 1901. Primitive color vision. *Popular
Science Monthly* 59: 44–58.

Rosch, E. 1977. Human categorization. In N. Warren (ed.),
Studies in Cross-Cultural Psychology, Vol. I (pp. 1–49).
London: Academic Press.

  1978. Principles of categorization. In E. Rosch and
B. B. Lloyd (eds.), *Cognition and Categorization*
(pp. 27–48). Hillsdale: Laurence Erlbaum Associates.

Sandell, J. H., C. G. Gross, and M. H. Bornstein 1979. Color
categories in macaques. *Journal of Comparative and
Physiological Psychology* 93: 626–635.

Saunders, B. 1992. The invention of basic colour terms.
Doctoral thesis, Department of Anthropology,
University of Utrecht, Netherlands. (Published
copyright ISOR: Utrecht.)

Stephenson, P. H. 1972. The evolution of color vision in
the primates. *Journal of Human Evolution* 2: 379–386.

Sternheim, C. E., and R. M. Boynton 1966. Uniqueness of
perceived hues investigated with a continuous
judgmental technique. *Journal of Experimental
Psychology* 72(5): 770–776.

Thompson, E. 1995. *Colour Vision: A Study in Cognitive
Science and the Philosophy of Perception*. London
and New York: Routledge.

Uchikawa, K., and R. M. Boynton 1987. Categorical color
perception of Japanese observers: comparison with
that of Americans. *Vision Research* 27(10): 1825–1833.

Wescott, R. W. 1970. Bini color terms. *Anthropological
Linguistics* 13: 251–252.

Wierzbicka, A. 1990. The meaning of color terms:
semantics, culture, and cognition. *Cognitive
Linguistics* 1: 99–150.

Yoshioka, T., B. M. Dow, and R. G. Vautin 1996. Neuronal
mechanisms of color categorization in areas V_1, V_2,
and V_4 of Macaque monkey cortex. *Behavioural Brain
Research* 76: 51–70.

Subject index

Compiled by Hannah M. King

Page numbers in italic indicate a reference to a figure.

Author index

Printed in the United Kingdom by
Lightning Source UK Ltd., Milton Keynes
140252UK00001B/22/A